Take It Up

TAKE IT UP
One-Year Devotional

My **TAKE IT UP** *JOURNAL*
Companion Journal
also available

For more information,
visit **Words Unbound:**
www.words-unbound.blogspot.com

TAKE IT UP

ONE-YEAR DEVOTIONAL

CYNTHIA A.Y. RUPEL

WORDS
UNBOUND

© 2015 Cynthia A.Y. Rupel at Words Unbound
Published by Cynthia A.Y. Rupel
Printed by CreateSpace.com   3rd printing May 2016
ISBN-13: 978-1518645563

Copyrighted source materials:

Flickr photo credits used by permission under creative commons:

Other:

Any italics are the author's own and are added for emphasis.

Any abbreviations used by the author are defined on pages 9–10.

Contact information for the author can be found on page 382.

A PDF of *Take It Up* can be downloaded at **www.words-unbound.blogspot.com**.

Printed copies of *Take It Up* are available at **www.CreateSpace.com/5805535** and are made available only for the cost of printing and shipping. The author obtains no profit from the purchase of this book.

TABLE OF CONTENTS

ABBREVIATIONS

Old Testament Bible Books

Gen.	Genesis	Eccl.	Ecclesiastes
Exod.	Exodus	Song	Song of Solomon
Lev.	Leviticus	Isa.	Isaiah
Num.	Numbers	Jer.	Jeremiah
Deut.	Deuteronomy	Lam.	Lamentations
Josh.	Joshua	Ezek.	Ezekiel
Judg.	Judges	Dan.	Daniel
Ruth	Ruth	Hos.	Hosea
1 Sam.	1 Samuel	Joel	Joel
2 Sam.	2 Samuel	Amos	Amos
1 Kings	1 Kings	Obad.	Obadiah
2 Kings	2 Kings	Jon.	Jonah
1 Chron.	1 Chronicles	Mic.	Micah
2 Chron.	2 Chronicles	Nah.	Nahum
Ezra	Ezra	Hab.	Habakkuk
Neh.	Nehemiah	Zeph.	Zephaniah
Esth.	Esther	Hag.	Haggai
Job	Job	Zech.	Zechariah
Ps.	Psalms	Mal.	Malachi
Prov.	Proverbs		

New Testament Bible Books

Matt.	Matthew	1 Tim.	1 Timothy
Mark	Mark	2 Tim.	2 Timothy
Luke	Luke	Titus	Titus
John	John	Phil.	Philemon
Acts	Acts	Heb.	Hebrews
Rom.	Romans	James	James
1 Cor.	1 Corinthians	1 Pet.	1 Peter
2 Cor.	2 Corinthians	2 Pet.	2 Peter
Gal.	Galatians	1 John	1 John
Eph.	Ephesians	2 John	2 John
Phil.	Philippians	3 John	3 John
Col.	Colossians	Jude	Jude
1 Thes.	1 Thessalonians	Rev.	Revelation
2 Thes.	2 Thessalonians		

Versions of the Bible

AMP	Amplified Bible
KJV	King James Version
NASB	New American Standard Bible
NIV	New International Version
NKJV	New King James Version

Secondary Sources

Strongest	*The Strongest NIV Exhaustive Concordance*
Webster's	*Webster's New Collegiate Dictionary*, 8th edition

General Usage

Biblio.	Bibliography	Heb.	Hebrew
c.	circa, approximately	i.e.,	that is
ch.	chapter	NT	New Testament
chs.	chapters	OT	Old Testament
e.g.,	for example	p.	page
Eng.	English	pp.	pages
et al.	and others	trans.	translation
etc.,	and so on	v.	verse
Grk.	Greek	vv.	verses

ABOUT THIS BOOK

I'd had it in my mind to write a devotional. Giving Jesus Christ control of my life had changed me and given me so much peace, I wanted to share what I had learned with others. After all, I was a writer; I wanted to let God use my talent for a good purpose. I knew I could do this.

Except I couldn't. Whenever I tried to write, nothing would come. I was confused and halfway blamed God. This was a great idea! It was for His kingdom, so why wouldn't He help me? I had a lot to learn about God and the way He does things.

I'd thought it was *my* idea, and that I was offering it to God. But if it was just *my* idea, then it was just *my* ability, *my* strength, *my* glory. I would be in charge of the project, and not doing it carried no serious consequences. But no work for God will have any lasting impact for the kingdom unless it is done *by* God *through* us from beginning to end. "Apart from me you can do nothing" (John 15:5). He was not going to bless or work with me on my little project. He needed me to acknowledge Him as the author and finisher of everything in my life.

Once I realized that this was more than a talent I had, but a task I had been assigned—once I realized who was really in charge of it all—I was off and running. I wrote—and wrote—every day for a year, somehow fitting in several hours' worth of work while still doing all the things I'd filled up my day with before. That's how I knew it was God, especially when I'd written day 366. I'd never stuck to a major project all the way to completion. I was an accomplished beginner; follow-through was another matter!

I'd thought that writing day 366 meant that I was done. Oh, I knew there was still proofreading and editing work to do, but I naïvely thought the hard part was over. I had no idea that the hard part was just beginning.

As it turned out, fixing the typos and fine tuning the phrases was not the kind of editing work God had in mind. Jesus didn't so much want *me* to edit the *book* as much as He wanted the *book* to edit *me*. It wasn't the information in the writing He was after. These truths are already out there. It wasn't supposed to be written from my head, but straight from my heart. Each page is supposed to be *my* experience, *my* story. He was looking for a witness. He wanted me to learn to walk out into my own life what He was having me write. That is a process I know will be ongoing for the rest of my life!

Becoming a witness for God does not require eloquence or talent. It takes trusting submission . . . obedience. His searching Spirit is peeling me like an onion: layer after layer of pride, selfishness, anger, laziness . . . And yes, it has made the tears flow, but they are cleansing, healing tears. Growing in Christ is always a process of breaking down and building up. There is still so much to be done.

As I wrote, I wondered how in the world I was going to get it published. I was in prison; who was going to type up the manuscript? How was I going to find a publisher? But God has a plan for every part of His plan. He knew all of this before He ever assigned the task. He put people in my life who could do the parts I could not. Prison walls are no obstacle to fulfilling God's purpose for me. His words are *truly* unbound!

To be sure they were His words and not mine, I had to learn to seek God's will for this book more and more deeply, to get still and quiet before God so He could speak His truth into me.

There was so much I thought I knew that I needed to unlearn. There were other things He'd been showing me since the day I'd said yes to Jesus that I'd been too timid to put forth, because it wasn't what so many were teaching. I needed to see that what was traditional and what was popular were not necessarily what was true. As Christ followers, we cannot afford to believe or do something just because it has long been that way, or because it is what we want to hear.

This finished result is very different than the book I began to write before God began using it to edit me. I could have published the first version a long time ago. I'd have had a book credit to my name, and maybe I'd have gone on to write another one. But it would not have been the truth. It would not have pointed to the *true* way of Jesus Christ. It would have been worthless, because it would not have been a work of God. God wanted me to learn to walk out in my life what He was having me write. I have attempted to do this on a deeper and deeper level as time goes on. We are accountable for every word we write and speak in the Name of Jesus into the lives of others. Now this is not simply "a book I wrote," but a compilation of things God spoke to me and taught me as I sought Him through this process.

He has taught me that the way of the cross is the way of surrender and sacrifice. Not to earn His favor and love, but because He is worth it. No matter what our path may lead us to, lead us through, He is worth it all.

Take it up!

BEFORE YOU READ FURTHER

*T*his book is written for those who are already believers in Jesus Christ, for those whose desire is to follow Him, to serve Him, to become like Him. If you have never met the One called Jesus, or have yet to make up your mind about Him, I invite you to ponder my experience, my encounter with what happened nearly 2,000 years ago on that hill outside Jerusalem. I didn't want to write *about* this encounter; I wanted to *write the encounter*, its pulse and its pain, its horror and its hope. I ask you to see it, hear it, feel it–and honestly consider the impact of all that is claimed about Calvary and the Jesus who chose to endure it. For me, it started with a question . . .

What does it really mean that Jesus died for me?

I don't know the theology of it. All I know is that one day, in the hidden pain of my heart, I came to that hill outside Jerusalem–Calvary, the Place of the Skull. There, on the big screen of my heart, I watched Him crucified. I saw His suffering–suffering for everything I did. Like some strange double vision, I saw Jesus, and I saw me. They drove the nails through His hands, through my hands. And then it was my hand on the hammer–pounding, pounding. With each blow, I saw my crime. It was horrible. But through my tears, I felt God say, "Killing was not the worst thing you ever did."

Not the worst? What have I done that was worse than murder?

"Turning your back on Me. Now–look at Him."

I looked. Pain, agony, despair, darkness. I felt the ice as the Father turned His back on His own Son. I struggled to breathe as Jesus breathed His last. This is the only place truly Godforsaken.

It was me: my sin, my self-sufficiency that dared to live without acknowledging God. It was me! Not Him . . . not Jesus; He is innocent! I wanted to beg for mercy for Him–but I didn't dare. Because then I would have no hope. Then it would be *me* . . . *my* flesh shredded, *my* body skewered, *my* breath choking in my throat, *my* blood. It was supposed to be *me* feeling all that pain, feeling the burning holiness of God destroying every sin-soaked cell of my soul. Because there is an absolute truth, inseparable from the God who defines it: turning my back on the One who gives life only means death. It was supposed to be *me*.

But it is *not* me. Because of Jesus, I will never have to face that holy fire, to suffer as He did. I will not burn because of what happened on that cross, because He was willing to take my place.

Accepting Christ's sacrifice meant accepting the truth of that. It meant acknowledging that God is right, and I am wrong, and that I am helpless to save myself. It meant saying thank you with a changed life, with humility and obedience to His truth and His will.

Is it worth it? *You* tell *me*! God Himself volunteered to take that bullet for me, because He loves me. How could I not love Him back?

Deciding to stop fighting, to just say *yes* to God isn't as complicated as all the rituals and religious traditions have made it out to be. It's not a 1-2-3-step thing with its own prearranged script. It's just getting to know God through the only lifeline He gave us: His Son Jesus. When we come to God only on the basis of Jesus Christ and what He did for us, God opens Himself to us. We get to know Him like we get to know anybody: talking with Him. Asking Him questions, paying attention for His answers. Learning to recognize Him. What we learn, we do . . . and we become.

That is what *yes* to God looks like.

JANUARY 1

Come, see a man . . .
John 4:29

*T*he day came when I asked myself, "Do I really want a dynamic, living faith–a relationship with the Living God that would grow and change and expand every day?"[1] I knew I could only go so far on the witness of another.[2] I could grow only so much on the testimony of someone else.[3] Eventually, I had to "come, see a man . . ." for myself.

I considered the townspeople of Sychar, the village of the first real missionary of the New Testament: the woman at the well. This woman, unnamed, yet intimately known by God, on a hot, dusty day in the loneliness of her shame, met Jesus. It changed her life forever.

With no more thought for her water jar or her reputation, she ran straight to those who had shunned her, spited her, talked about her[4]–she didn't care any more about that. All she cared about was Jesus, the Christ, the Messiah. "Come see a man!"

The townspeople believed her. Her change was dramatic, her story of her experience powerful, her delivery honest. Many of the Samaritans from that town believed in him because of the woman's testimony.[5]

How many of us today come only this far! We hear the woman's testimony and say we believe. We attend all her meetings, listen to all her tapes, soak up her experience. We lean on her every word, eager and excited.[6] *This Christ is powerful! Look what He's done in her life!*

And all the while, Jesus is just outside of town, waiting at the well.

Sychar did not just listen to the woman, though. They came and saw–and invited Him into their lives. They did not merely come to know about Jesus vicariously, though another's experience. They chose to experience Him for themselves.[7] I, too, must do the same.

Another's testimony isn't given for entertainment. Their experience is an invitation for me to experience Christ–for me to come–and see the Man for myself.

Another's testimony isn't given for entertainment.
Their experience is an invitation
for me to experience Christ.

---

[1] 1 Pet. 2:2   [2] Acts 17:11   [3] Matt. 16:13–16   [4] Luke 6:27–28   [5] John 4:39   [6] Ezek. 33:30–32   [7] John 4:42

JANUARY 2

. . . Look to the rock from which you were cut . . .
Isaiah 51:1

*J*esus constantly warned us to beware of false teachings, false prophets.[1] It's not really a new threat, either. False ideas insinuated themselves in the Garden of Eden, when the enemy *explained* what God meant when He said that the day they ate of the fruit they would surely die.[2] What if Eve, instead of following the serpent's logic, had gone back to God for clarification?

Time and distance are often the enemies of truth. The farther you get from the standard, the more inaccuracies creep in. That's why God told us over and over again to be sure we always used a perfect and just measure.[3] With God, there is only one perfect measure: Jesus Christ. Nobody else comes close,[4] nobody else knows the heart and mind of God—or lived the heart and mind of God[5]—like Jesus Christ, The Rock of our salvation.

"Look to the rock from which you were cut . . ." the only way to recognize the false is to know the true.[6] To judge the false—to evaluate any idea, teaching, or example—hold it up to the true standard. Is this what Jesus taught? Is this how Jesus did things? Where does this lead me, what does it produce—good fruit or thorns?[7]

Expertise intimidates me. I find it hard to challenge those I consider more knowledgeable than I am. It helps me when I realize, however, that even the disciples didn't always get it right,[8] either, when they tried to figure out on their own what Jesus meant. They had to ask Jesus Himself to explain it.[9] So do I.

No one is my teacher but Jesus Christ.[10] Everyone, everything else must be measured against and compared to the plumb line of Jesus Christ. No one else is so exalted that they cannot ever be mistaken, misleading, or just plain wrong. I must learn to filter all instruction through the words and life of Jesus, asking the Holy Spirit to guide me into all truth.[11]

Everyone, everything else must be measured against
and compared to the plumb line of Jesus Christ.

---

[1]Matt. 7:15–20 [2]Gen. 3:1–5 [3]Deut. 25:15 [KJV] [4]Eccl. 7:20 [5]John 14:9 [6]John 1:8–9
[7]James 3:17 [8]Mark 9:32 [9]Matt. 13:36 [10]Matt. 23:10 [11]John 16:13

JANUARY 3

. . . Where you go I will go . . .
Ruth 1:16

*W*here am I going today? Where are my feet taking me? Are my steps ordered by the Lord,[1] or am I just wandering wherever I will, giving no thought to my steps,[2] following no prodding, plan, or purpose of the Lord? Jesus said, "Whoever serves me must follow me; and where I am, my servant will also be."[3]

God's work is not waiting for me. His work has been going on from the beginning,[4] and He will carry it through[5] with or without me. My purpose is not to do a great work *for* God. My purpose is to find my pre-ordained place in the ongoing work *of* God.[6] My ordered steps will carry me down the path of His choosing.[7]

"Where You go I will go . . ." Where is God going? Where is He moving in and around me? Where do I see His Spirit working—wooing, comforting, convicting, and drawing souls to the Savior? Have I learned how to discern not only the moving of the Holy Spirit, but His leading *in me*? He is gentle, subtle, like the blowing of the wind.[8] If I look for the hard ground of hearts being broken up by the disappointments, dissatisfactions, discouragements, and frustrations of life, I will hear when He tells me what to do. When the promises of the world come up empty—again—He is there. There is an answer, a solution far more satisfying than any fix the world can offer. There is a Savior.

"Where you go I will go . . ." Where is He going? He is going wherever there is an open door. He is seeking the seekers. If I want to go with Him and join Him in His work, I must not go where I *think* He is; I may miss Him. I must listen for His Spirit, His instructions on *how* to be His feet, His hands, His voice to this world.[9] I must no longer wander through my days as though *I* am my only concern. I need to look around me with the eyes of the Spirit. When I am alert and actively seeking His open doors, there are no chance encounters. There is only the work of God.

I must not go where I think He is; I may miss Him.
I must listen for His Spirit . . .

---

[1]Prov. 20:24 [2]Prov. 14:15 [3]John 12:26 [4]John 5:17 [5]Isa. 46:10 [6]John 3:27–29 [7]Ps. 25:12
[8]John 3:8 [9]Mark 16:15–18

JANUARY 4

. . . and where you stay I will stay. . . .
Ruth 1:16

God is all-seeing, all-knowing. There is no fact, no situation, no circumstance that escapes His notice. I know this–*don't I*? It's easier to believe and trust when things are happening and I can measure progress. But my faith in God's compassionate *knowing* is tested not so much in the *going* as in the *staying*–in waiting on the Lord. I am discovering that waiting is the most difficult task God will ever assign me.

Think about it: Saul grew desperate waiting for Samuel and lost his kingdom.[1] Even Abraham, the father of the faithful, grew impatient waiting on God, and we still suffer from the jealousy and rivalry begun in Ishmael.[2] David, however, trusted in God and waited for his crown, in spite of many temptations to take matters into his own hands.[3] It is never wise to attempt to bring about God's promise through man's means.[4]

Walking in the light of the Spirit[5] means not only moving with the Spirit, but stopping and standing still with the Spirit. Every soldier understands the command, "Halt!" Ecclesiastes reminds me that there is a time and a season to every purpose under heaven.[6] Waiting on God is naturally easier when I know the what and when of God's plan. But God rarely reveals such things in their entirety. Instead, my season of waiting often feels frighteningly like abandonment–God simply seems to stop moving. I am left in the dark and the silence, wondering if God has forgotten me, or if He has suddenly changed His mind.[7] Or I am tempted to doubt *myself: Did I miss something? Aren't I supposed to be doing something?*

Yes, I am. Like a soldier awaiting orders, I am to stay fit (study), see to my gear (stay ready),[8] and keep the lines of communication open (watch and pray). This is what it means to be ready at an hour we do not expect.[9] Above all, I must not run ahead of God.[10] "Wait for the Lord; be strong and take heart and wait for the Lord."[11] I will trust in the name of the Lord and rely on my God,[12] and declare, "Where You stay I will stay."

Walking in the light of the Spirit means not only moving with, but also standing still with the Spirit.

---

[1]1 Sam. 10:8; 13:7–14 [2]Gen. 16 [3]1 Sam. 24:3–7; 26:9–11 [4]Prov. 3:5 [5]John 12:35 [6]Eccl. 3:1
[7]Num. 23:19 [8]Prov. 21:31 [9]Matt. 24:44 [10]2 John 1:9 [11]Ps. 27:14 [12]Isa. 50:10

JANUARY 5

. . . Your people will be my people . . .
Ruth 1:16

*R*uth was at the crossroads. Her husband was dead, and her mother-in-law, Naomi, was going back to Israel. Three times Naomi, in her despair, told Ruth to go back to her people, her gods, her old way of life. Her sister protested—weakly—but chose her familiar (from the same word as *family*) pagan past.[1] But something in Ruth knew that her future was wherever God took Naomi. In one cataclysmic decision, Ruth chose to adopt a whole new people, instead of all she knew and had.

It's that *instead of* choice that we struggle with. We begin to follow Jesus, *in addition to* what we're used to: *in addition to* our family, friends and associates. As Jesus leads us down the path of obedience, we keep running back, trying to assimilate the old into the new, to keep both.[2] The farther we go with Jesus, though, the greater the gap between the places, people, and traditions we've always known, until the inconsistencies become too much to maintain. Then comes our crossroads, when God calls us to the wilderness,[3] to "come out . . . my people,"[4] to be where Jesus is[5] and to let the dead bury the dead.[6] It is an alone experience that opens our eyes to *truly* see, and our ears to *really* hear what God is saying to us. It's not an unusual call; Abraham, Moses, David, and John the Baptist, (among others), all had to leave home and family and spend time in the wilderness in preparation for their purpose.[7]

I went through many years before I realized I needed this alone-ness,[8] before I understood how much I needed to unlearn in order to learn how to hear God more clearly. Only then could I have the confidence to stand firm, even against the tide.[9] Like Ruth, I had to leave everything and everyone from my past to pursue God's plan for my life.[10] I had to choose a whole new identity.

Like Elijah, we may sometimes feel like we're the only ones, but the people of God are always out there. Those who hear the will of God and do it are the true brothers and sisters of Jesus.[11]

Those who hear the will of God and do it are the true brothers and sisters of Jesus.

---

[1]Ruth 1:14   [2]Matt. 9:17   [3]Mark 1:12–13   [4]Rev. 18:4   [5]John 12:26   [6]Matt. 8:22   [7]Matt. 19:29
[8]Lam. 3:28   [9]Matt. 7:13–14   [10]Matt. 10:35–39   [11]Luke 8:21

JANUARY 6

. . . and your God [will be] my God.
Ruth 1:16

o I really know the One I worship?[1] Everybody has their own ideas of what and who God is. *I* thought *I* understood: *God wouldn't let that happen*, or *God wouldn't say* that, or *God wouldn't do that.* I, with a brain that weighs less than a gallon of water, boxed up the Infinite in a rigid set of expectations and called *that* knowing God. How my world is rocked when God, being God, utterly shatters my little box, breaking out in unexpected, shocking ways!

Look at the Jews, the only nation on earth with a direct revelation of God. They were confident of what they expected in the Messiah, sure they *knew* what God would do when He showed up and showed out—and they relished the revenge they envisioned for the Romans. Their expectations were shattered from the moment Gabriel greeted the young fiancée of a poor carpenter from a despised town in a heathenized part of the country.

Look at the disciples—the ones closest to Jesus, who sat at His feet, who followed His path, who saw things of God no one else saw. They didn't understand a single thing about Jesus: not His calm,[2] not His anger,[3] not His sorrow,[4] not His joy.[5] They didn't understand His message,[6] His divinity[7], His humanity.[8] They certainly didn't understand His mission,[9] yet they followed, because deep down, they knew one undeniable fact: He was their only hope. "Lord to whom shall we go? You have the words of eternal life. We believe and know that you are the Holy One of God."[10] They had decided that above all else, God was God, and that He could be trusted.

Only when I, too, lay down my own cherished, limited *idea* of God and reach out for the hand of the infinite, shocking, totally trustworthy One, will I begin to worship in spirit and in truth.[11] Only then will I be worshipping my Father and your Father, . . . my God and your God.[12]

---

*How our worlds are rocked when God,
being God, utterly shatters the box,
breaking out in unexpected, shocking ways!*

---

[1]John 4:22 [2]Luke 8:22–25 [3]Matt. 16:21–23 [4]Matt. 26:38–40 [5]John 4:27–34 [6]John 14:8–9 [7]Luke 9:28–36 [8]Mark 10:38 [9]Luke 9:44–45 [10]John 6:68–69 [11]John 4:24 [12]John 20:17

JANUARY 7

. . . May the LORD *deal with me . . .*
if anything but death separates you and me.
Ruth 1:17

I love the unconditional love of God for me.[1] I need His love to be unconditional, because I am not perfect. I *love* that He loves me in spite of me.[2] Unfortunately, *my* love tends to be *very* conditional. I struggle to overcome my tendency to write off those who do not respect or return my love, who don't perform.[3] Who am I to demand perfection of others?

Loving someone through thick and thin, through failures and disappointments, challenges our expectation of what love entails. It's so easy to throw in the towel when we are not appreciated, when our efforts are taken for granted or rejected outright.[4] Wounded pride draws back and throws up walls. Who wants to be hurt over and over again? When is enough enough? When is it okay to cross someone off my concern list?

Maybe *that* is why my love is conditional. I am too busy thinking about me: *my* hurts, *my* needs. Maybe the question in my heart, instead, should be, "What is the value of a soul?" I accept as truth that if it were only one who needed Him, Jesus would still have died for just that one.[5] No rejection, insult, pain, or sorrow was too much to ask of Jesus to redeem even one soul.[6] Why do I think *my* hurt is worth more than His?

All this would be easier to bear if I saw quick results; short term is easy. But feeding into another's life for a lifetime quickly loses its shine. Again I start asking, "What about me? Is all this struggle worth it?[7] It's not working."

"A friend loves at all times."[8] We are called to love and serve others as Jesus does.[9] Though it may cost us a lifetime of heartache, one soul is worth my persisting, worth the long haul. That one soul was worth the life and death of the Son of God.[10] One soul cannot mean less to us.

What is the value of a soul?

[1] John 4:10   [2] Hos. 3:1   [3] Prov. 20:6   [4] Matt. 5:46   [5] Luke 15:7   [6] Heb. 12:2–3   [7] Matt. 24:12–13
[8] Prov. 17:17   [9] John 15:12   [10] Ps. 49:8–9

JANUARY 8

I will listen to what God the LORD will say . . .
Psalm 85:8

*M*y life in Jesus has been a journey of longing, an ache to hear the voice of God. From my earliest days, I knew somehow that it was not just a privilege; it was my most desperate need to hear His voice, to be taught by God.[1] I was not content to have others interpret my Father's message, to speak for God to me.[2]

That burning desire is the first ingredient; if that was all it took, I'd have aced the test! But Jesus has spent *years* teaching me how to hear His voice, refining my understanding. One of the most crucial lessons, surprisingly, was that I had to believe He not only *would* speak to me, but that He already *was*.[3] When my faith grasped that, I stopped chasing after everyone who seemed to have a prophetic gift, stopped looking to others to give me a "word from God." I learned to ask *Jesus* my questions, and wait expectantly for His answers.[4]

Then came the hard part–recognizing His answer. From the Bible stories, I had the impression that God's voice would echo in a deep baritone from the upper corner of my room. He would speak clearly, in complete sentences, like an audible vision. Although He has done this on occasion with others,[5] it is not the method he usually uses with me.

No, I quickly recognized that God speaks through *His* Spirit to my spirit.[6] I "hear" His thoughts in my own voice–which is why we often struggle with, "Was that God, or was it me?" The bulk of my experience has been learning to discern that difference. He's teaching me how to ask the right questions, to make myself available for His answers: to get quiet before Him, shut out distractions, and give Him a chance to get a word in edgewise![7] I'm learning that there are some things I'm not meant to know, and to focus on what I *can* know:[8] the step-by-step versus the panoramic Big Picture.[9]

Most of all, the more I understand God's ways–the more I actually do what He says[10]–the more clearly I discern His voice. *This* is relationship.

God speaks through His Spirit to my spirit.

---

[1]Isa. 54:13 [2]Deut. 5:27 [3]Ps. 81:13 [4]Ps. 5:3 [5]John 12:28–30 [6]John 14:16–17 [7]Ps. 46:10 [8]Deut. 29:29 [9]Prov. 20:24 [10]Ezek. 33:31–32

JANUARY 9

Then Moses said, "Now show me your glory."
Exodus 33:18

*H*ow hungry am I? I have tasted and seen that the Lord is good[1]— but has that small glimpse been enough to satisfy me? Like the Israelites in the desert who saw the awesome magnificence of the presence of God, veiled and hidden as it was in the darkness of the cloud, His voice alone was more than I thought I could handle.[2] I remained at a distance and asked others to speak to God *for* me, and *for* God *to* me.

But then, like Moses, I was no longer content with a distant relationship. My hunger for more urged me—and urges me still—to approach the thick darkness where God is.[3] I press in, trembling, yet suspecting that somehow God is not offended. I feel it in my bones—God is delighted with such audacity.

There was never anyone like Moses, whom God knew face to face.[4] How that must break the heart of our Father God! Can you not feel the pain of rejection in our Abba's cry, "What fault did your fathers find in me, that they strayed so far from me?"[5] Jesus echoed this ache as He wept over Jerusalem. "How often I have longed to gather your children together as a hen gathers her chicks under her wings, but you were not willing."[6]

Perhaps we have hesitated, remembering the consuming fire.[7] We know His eyes are too pure to look on evil,[8] and we have too long made light of the evil in our hearts. We have cherished our sin,[9] and we fear His glory! The glory of God is not His wrath and judgment. When Moses dared ask to see the glory of the Eternal I Am, what did God parade before his eyes? All His goodness, mercy, and compassion! And right there, awash in the awesome radiance of the manifest glory of God Almighty, Moses dared ask for (and received!) forgiveness.[10]

Come boldly to the throne of grace to ask for mercy.[11] Ask the Lord God Jehovah, "Show me Your glory."

You will touch the heart of God as only a true lover can.

Come boldly to the throne of grace to ask for mercy.

---

[1]Ps. 34:8 [2]Exod. 20:18–19 [3]Exod. 20:21 [4]Deut. 34:10 [5]Jer. 2:5 [6]Matt. 23:37 [7]Deut. 4:24 [8]Hab. 1:13 [9]Ps. 66:18 [10]Exod. 34:6–9 [11]Heb. 4:16

JANUARY 10

When the disciples saw him walking on the lake, they were terrified.
"It's a ghost," they said, and cried out in fear.
Matthew 14:26

*F*ear. Paralyzing, draining, mind-numbing fear. Have you ever felt it? One moment, everything is fine. The lake is smooth, the air calm, the night balmy. You and your faith are safe in the hands of God. Then the wind shifts—and in the darkest hour of the night, you suddenly find yourself battling for your life in the midst of a storm that literally sprang out of nowhere.[1] You do everything you know to do—strike the sail, throw out the anchor, and bail for all you're worth—but the fury of this maelstrom is more than you can handle. It roars back at you as if it's *personal*. In the desperation of the moment, fear takes over.

The first thing fear does is make us nearsighted; we cannot see beyond our immediate circumstances. Fear *sees* the flood, and forgets that the Lord sits enthroned over the flood.[2] Fear *feels* the power of the waves and fails to remember that God commands, "Here is where your proud waves halt."[3] Fear *hears* the roar of the thunder and does not consider that God can speak to us out of the storm.[4]

Fear paralyzes. It saps our strength[5] and short-circuits our brain. Fear shuts us down; we can't think, we can't choose, and we can't act. It distorts reality. When we're in the grip of fear, *everything* takes on an ominous shape. When we are possessed by fear, we risk not recognizing our own deliverance! It is panic that makes a drowning man drown his rescuer. The disciples succumbed. In the clutches of terror, they mistook Jesus Himself for a ghost! Yes, he was walking on water, but they had just seen Him feed over 5,000 people with a little boy's lunch.[6] He'd turned water into wine, healed the sick, raised the dead, and commanded the demons of hell.

Fear makes us forget what we need most to remember: our God is the God who does the impossible, and He is in control![7] *Do not fear!*[8]

Fear makes us forget what we need most to remember:
our God is the God who does the impossible,
and He is in control!

---

[1]Mark 6:47–48 [2]Ps. 29:10 [3]Job 38:11 [4]Job 38:1 [5]Isa. 40:29–31 [6]Matt. 14:15–21 [7]Ps. 47:7–8
[8]Zeph. 3:16

JANUARY 11

. . . I am the only one left . . .
1 Kings 19:10

*J*esus warned us that the way to life is narrow and so is the gate; only a few find it.[1] Crowds and mobs are hardly ever associated with doing good and making right choices.[2] Mob mentality is not a positive thing! When you determine to take up your cross and follow Jesus, do not be surprised if you don't find a lot of company going your way. In fact, He warned us that even our family[3] and closest friends[4] would be the ones to turn on us.

It is easy, then, to feel completely alone in our walk with the Lord. The temptation is to despair. "Give up," the enemy sneers. "Nobody cares. Everyone else is gone. You're not going to make it either." Elijah felt this way, too. He had just stood up to all the combined forces of evil and had even seen God Himself confirm his call to repentance with fire from heaven[5] —and it didn't seem to do a bit of good. Ahab was still Ahab, Jezebel was still threatening, and the people were as idolatrous as ever. He ran away, threw himself down, and begged God to kill him before his enemies could![6]

The other temptation is to doubt yourself. "Am I missing it? How can I be the only one who thinks this way?" Although pausing to evaluate yourself[7] and judge your fruit is a good thing,[8] remember Jesus' warning: the road *is* lonely, and not many will find it. God even said that man would become more rare than the purest gold.[9]

Take comfort, however. In spite of all appearances, you are *not* alone! God has always reserved a remnant to Himself,[10] the faithful few whose knees have not bowed down to Baal. In the midst of lukewarmness, hypocrisy, and apostasy, there are always those who are the True Church of the Firstborn,[11] the pure and spotless Bride of Christ. Best of all, your Bridegroom has promised, "I am with you always."[12] You are *not* alone!

---

*When you determine to take up your cross
and follow Jesus, do not be surprised
if you don't find a lot of company going your way.*

---

[1]Matt. 7:14 [2]Exod. 23:2 [3]Matt. 10:35–36 [4]Ps. 55:12–14 [5]1 Kings 18:19–38 [6]1 Kings 19:1–4 [7]Prov. 14:8 [8]Matt. 7:17 [9]Isa. 13:12 [10]Isa. 37:31–32 [11]Heb. 12:23 [12]Matt. 28:20

JANUARY 12

. . . this matter cannot be taken care of in a day or two,
because we have sinned greatly in this thing.
Ezra 10:13

*G*od is in the restoration business.[1] There is tremendous brokenness in our lives that He desires to restore, and our sins have wreaked much havoc not only in our own lives, but in the lives of others we have touched.[2] Although He created us for His glory[3] and ordained our lives to be useful,[4] a thing of beauty, He had to reclaim us from the junk heaps and yard sales of the world. Our fearfully and wonderfully made craftmanship[5] was stained with sin, our finish marred, cracked, gouged and scarred. Lovingly, He strips us down with forgiveness until all that ugly, old stain is gone. His forgiveness is complete. We stand before Him clean and bare of any trace of our sin and mess.[6] Oh, see the shine in His eyes as He envisions our coming beauty! He's the Master Carpenter, and He knows best how to bring forth the glory of our fine grain and intricate details.

But forgiveness, the stripping off of the old, is only the beginning. To fully restore us to our intended purpose and glory, there is still much to be done. It is a matter that cannot be taken care of in a day or two, and unfortunately, it is a matter often neglected. We are too content to stop at the reclamation and stripping. We think forgiveness is all that is necessary.[7] But for all the dents and dings, gouges and wounds–the effects of our sin–He desires to fill us in, sand us down, and rub us deeply with oil to restore us.[8]

When we have "sinned greatly in this thing," our healing may require that we deal with the specifics of what we've done to others. Confessing to those we've hurt[9] and making restitution[10] may be just what the doctor ordered. It can be the difference between being healed and being made whole. It is humbling,[11] but we must not give up. We have all sinned greatly, but Jesus is patiently restoring us to our full, intended glory.

God had to reclaim us from the junk heaps
and yard sales of the world.

---

[1] 1 Pet. 5:10 [2] Josh. 22:20 [3] Isa. 43:7 [4] John 15:16 [5] Ps. 139:14 [6] Isa. 1:18 [7] 1 John 1:9
[8] Heb. 1:9 [9] James 5:16 [10] Luke 19:8–9 [11] Isa. 66:2

JANUARY 13

*. . . Which one do you want me to release to you:
Barabbas, or Jesus who is called Christ?*
Matthew 27:17

A fascinating exercise I found in a certain do-it-yourself drawing course produced amazing results. I had to turn an artist's line drawing upside-down, then draw what I saw. When turned right-side up, even my rank beginner's reproduction was astonishingly accurate. It worked, because reversing the orientation confused my brain just enough to force me to draw what I really saw, not what I thought I should see. Expectation is everything; if I think I know what something is, I stop seeing it and see only my *idea* or image of it. Anything that does not match that image is rejected or ignored—not seen at all.[1]

What has that got to do with Barabbas? Have you ever considered how the Jews could choose a notorious murderer[2] over Jesus? It had everything to do with their expectations of the Messiah. They looked for a deliverer—not from sin, but from the Romans. They sought a conquering king, not a suffering servant. Barabbas was not just a murderer; he was a revolutionary, a member of an uprising against Rome[3]—a hero to the Jews. In standing the two side by side, God was giving His people one last chance to choose: Will you have merely an external, temporal deliverance (at the edge of the sword), or true freedom and peace (by a new birth)? Which do you want: Barabbas, meaning "son of *a* father,"[4] or Jesus—Son of *the* Father? Will it be your messiah, or mine?

I may have to break down my expectations; set aside my *idea*—my image—of who Jesus the Messiah is. I need to turn the image of the promise upside-down, and then I will begin to see Him *as He is*. In doing this, I should be forewarned: He may overturn a few tables in my temple,[5] and He may strip down to wash my feet.[6] He may disrupt some funeral processions in my life,[7] and speak kindly to some of my enemies.[8] He may ask me to do the same.[9]

He asks you today: Which one will *you* have—Jesus or Barabbas?

---

*Will you have merely an external,
temporal deliverance (at the edge of the sword) . . .
or true freedom and peace (by a new birth)?*

---

[1]John 9:39–41 [2]Acts 3:14 [3]Mark 15:7 [4]*Strongest:* p. 1,535 [5]Mark 11:15 [6]John 13:4–5
[7]Luke 7:11–15 [8]John 4:27 [9]Luke 10:37

JANUARY 14

But may all who seek you rejoice and be glad in you . . .
Psalm 70:4

So many people put off salvation because they say they want to have fun first. What is wrong with this picture? To a lot of people, salvation means religion—all those *shalts* and *shalt nots* (mostly *nots*). All they can imagine is having to give up everything they enjoy and becoming one of those scowling, sour-face pew-sitters. Hardly attractive! And Hollywood's slow-motion, mortician-solemn version of Jesus hasn't helped.

Yes, Jesus was a man of sorrows and familiar with suffering.[1] There was a lot of grief in Jesus' life: disciples who didn't understand Him,[2] family that thought He was nuts,[3] no place to really call home,[4] constant rejection and scorn by the leaders.[5] Pervading it all was the anticipation of the agony to come, for Jesus not only knew He was born to die, but He knew exactly *how* and *when* it would happen,[6] including being betrayed by one of His own men.[7] Such pressure, such extreme circumstances, can easily rob anyone of peace.

But somehow, through it all, Jesus found contentment, He found joy. He radiated so much peace and joy that people wanted to be with Him; they crowded and pressed in on Him. He hung out with prostitutes and sinners—the Pharisees accused Him of being a drunkard and a glutton![8] Definitely not a wet blanket.

Yes, Jesus got angry, and He got sad. He cried in agony over His mission. But these emotions did not define His temperament. He knew how to be strong in spirit: through joy.[9] Instead of dwelling on His sorrow, His burden, He chose to find beauty, peace, and hope in knowing His Father. He chose to live each day abundantly so He would be able to give it all to us.[10] What could life more abundantly possibly be, but one so overflowing with joy, it warms everyone it touches?

Throughout my prison journey, Jesus has shown me that I can experience joy, regardless of the razor wire and bars. Joy is not dependent on circumstances, but upon knowing the unfailing love of God.[11] When times are tough, or people are cruel, or problems pile up, relying on God's love[12] keeps me from being overwhelmed. He has promised to help me.[13] The cross proves Him true. That is good news . . . the Gospel! And it gives me joy enough to face life and trials.

Jesus knew how to be strong in spirit: through joy.

---

[1]Isa. 53:3 [2]John 16:18 [3]Mark 3:21 [4]Matt. 8:20 [5]Luke 16:14 [6]Luke 18:31–33 [7]John 6:64
[8]Matt. 11:19 [9]Neh. 8:10 [10]John 10:10 [KJV] [11]Ps. 13:4–6 [12]1 John 4:16 [13]Isa. 41:10

JANUARY 15

Jesus said to them, "I tell you the truth,
unless you eat the flesh of the Son of Man and drink his blood,
you have no life in you."
John 6:53

*P*hew! If you think this is a tough saying, you are not alone. Most of Jesus' followers couldn't handle such a statement. They stumbled on that stone and fell; they gave up and went back to their miserable little lives in their miserable little towns, all because they could not understand that Jesus was not talking about becoming vampire-cannibals.

But what *was* He talking about? Jesus explained, "The Spirit gives life; the flesh counts for nothing. The *words I have spoken to you* are spirit and they are life."[1] Spiritual things are taught by the Spirit.[2] The Spirit reminds us that "Man does not live on bread alone, but on every *word* that comes from the mouth of God."[3] Jesus is the Word made flesh,[4] He is the Bread of Life.[5] To "eat the flesh of the Son of Man" is to live by every word in the Word of God. It is to read it, eat it, devour it, until God's words to us fill every fiber of our being; until our thoughts are His words, our words are His words, and our actions are His words. "If you remain in me and *my words* remain in you . . ."[6]

Followers of Christ know about the blood of Jesus.[7] We know that "drinking His blood" is receiving His sacrifice in our stead.[8] Drinking His blood is salvation, eternal life—it is remembered in the communion cup.[9] But Jesus said that we must not only drink of His saving blood, we must also eat His flesh—or we *have no life in us*. The communion bread, His body.[10] The Bread of Life, His flesh. Food *and* drink.

Physical bodies need them both—and so do our spiritual bodies. "When your words came, I ate them . . ."[11]

Let us come and drink deeply from the wells of salvation,[12] while we also nourish and strengthen our spirit by *feeding* on the Scriptures, the words of God.

"Man does not live on bread alone, but on every word
that comes from the mouth of God."

---

[1]John 6:63 [2]John 16:12–15 [3]Matt. 4:4 [4]John 1:14 [5]John 6:48 [6]John 15:7 [7]Heb. 9:19–22 [8]Heb. 9:12, 14 [9]Matt. 26:27–28 [10]Matt. 26:26 [11]Jer. 15:16 [12]Isa. 12:3

JANUARY 16

How shall we escape, if we neglect so great salvation . . . ?
Hebrews 2:3 [KJV]

Although flagrant sin may gratify the devil's twisted sensibilities, even he knows he can destroy more souls by tempting us to carelessly neglect our salvation. It's those constantly pressing cares of the world[1] that draw us away. These are the urgent, but not important[2] things that rob us of our purpose and keep us from fulfilling God's will in our lives. We get so busy living from day to day that we forget to live our *lives*.[3]

Neglect creeps up on us quietly. Not everyone always *decides* to neglect their relationship with the Lord; it just—happens. Routine contributes to neglect. Whenever I fall into a pattern, my brain goes on autopilot, and my sense of awe and discovery dries up. Conversations with God become one sided, and I don't always notice. Busy-ness is another thief[4]—and who isn't busy nowadays? The demands of life[5] not only eat up my time,[6] they eat up my energy. And though nurturing my relationship with God does take time, time by itself is not the measure nor the cure. It's not a matter of praying longer or reading more chapters. A neglected relationship is one taken for granted. I assume much of God, and no longer intentionally seek Him out to discover Him in each situation.

The good news is that no matter how wilted our relationship with God has become, it can be revived.[7] Intention is key: when we take action to intentionally and purposefully seek out God's desires and will for the situations in our lives,[8] when we stop going along on autopilot assumptions, instead honestly seeking to please Him[9]—joy, passion, and worship are ignited.

Jesus gave everything to make salvation available; I want to show Him how precious He is to me. I will not neglect our relationship, but nurture it with attention and loving care. He is worth it![10]

When we honestly seek to please God—
joy, passion, and worship are ignited.

[1]Luke 8:14   [2]Eccl. 3:1   [3]Luke 10:40–41   [4]Luke 14:16–20   [5]Hag. 1:9   [6]John 7:33–34   [7]Isa. 57:15
[8]2 Chron. 18:4   [9]Matt. 6:33   [10]Rev. 5:9

JANUARY 17

A man of knowledge uses words with restraint . . .
Proverbs 17:27

The wisdom of God has much to say about not saying much! It tells us that even a fool can fool us if he just keeps his mouth shut.[1] My trouble is, I love to inflate the value of my own two cents' worth. I have been too eager to speak, to offer my opinion, to jump in and try to answer someone else's problem. My own life's story ought to convince me of the danger of an undisciplined tongue. It is the only muscle we have that actually benefits from a *lack* of exercise! God is showing me, however, that true teaching is more *listening* and *being,* and not just speaking.[2] He reminds me, "When words are many, sin is not absent."[3]

There is a well-known children's rhyme that makes light of the power of words: "Sticks and stones may break our bones, but words will never harm us." But God knows better. He said, "The tongue has the power of life and death, and those who love it will eat its fruit."[4] Words are so powerful that when God came to earth, He came as His own Word made flesh. Jesus is the Word of God wrapped in a physical body, speaking only the words of God.[5] Jesus so understood the power and importance of words that He told His listeners, "I do nothing on my own but speak just what the Father has taught me."[6] What a contrast to my own words, which are usually just that: my *own* words! God's Spirit stays busy in me, constantly calling attention to my conversation: "*Why* do you want to say that?" My words reveal my heart, and my motives need to be purified and love driven. He often reminds me that I will one day have to give an account of every careless word I speak, and that it is "by your words you will be acquitted, and by your words you will be condemned."[7] I must pay attention to what I am sowing with my lips, for I will surely have to eat its fruit—and so will others!

He reminds me, though, "No man can tame the tongue."[8] Only the Holy Spirit can give me the words I should say.[9] When I do speak, I should do it as one speaking the very words of God[10]—not from some know-it-all pedestal, but from the vulnerability of sharing my heart, the path I have truly walked.

*True teaching is more listening and being,
and not just speaking.*

[1]Prov. 17:28 [2]James 1:19 [3]Prov. 10:19 [4]Prov. 18:21 [5]John 3:34 [6]John 8:28 [7]Matt. 12:36–37 [8]James 3:8 [9]Matt. 10:19 [10]1 Pet. 4:11

JANUARY 18

. . . If you, even you, had only known on this day
what would bring you peace . . .
Luke 19:42

From the Crusades to the "Final Solution;" from the Hundred Years' War to the Thirty Years' War to the Six Day War, to the War to End all Wars (Parts I and II); from murder at the very gates of Eden[1] to Armageddon's final assault,[2] we have not figured out what would bring us peace.

From the back of a cloak-draped donkey, before a rocky, robe-strewn path, surrounded by a cheering, palm-waving, Hosanna-shouting crowd of momentarily enthusiastic supporters, Jesus stopped the whole parade to cry out His frustration:[3] "My people, my people—you just don't get it!"

Do I? Do I know what would bring me peace? *If only my (spouse, parents, children, boss . . .) would understand me. If only I had more (money, time, friends . . .), if only I were (taller, shorter, thinner, prettier, smarter . . .), if only I hadn't been (abused, sick, crippled, poor . . .), then I would be at peace.*

No, I would not. Man's sin means that we live on a rebellious planet among rebellious people. We think rebellious thoughts, cherish rebellious attitudes, and do rebellious things against the Prince of Peace Himself.[4] "'There is no peace,' says the LORD, 'for the wicked.'"[5]

You see, He Himself *is* my peace.[6] The things that belong to my peace are all found in Him—as He is, not as I wish Him to be. "Be still, and know that I am God."[7] Be still. I must cease my endless wishing and sighing and pushing and struggling to change everything outside of myself. Peace is not in the external.

Peace is not a state of circumstance, but a state of being. I can be in chaos and confusion in the midst of silence, even as I can have serene peace in the midst of chaos. Peace is peace internally, or it is not peace at all.

When I stop depending on my circumstances and allow Jesus to work within me, then I will be able to shout Him into Jerusalem on Sunday, and still say, "Hosanna!" on Friday, when everything around me is going to Hades in a handbasket. I will know what brings me peace.

Peace is peace internally, or it is not peace at all.

---

[1]Gen. 4:8   [2]Rev. 20:7–9   [3]Luke 19:35–41   [4]Isa. 9:6   [5]Isa. 48:22   [6]John 16:33   [7]Ps. 46:10

JANUARY 19

but my dove, my perfect one, is unique . . .
Song of Solomon 6:9

*H*ave you ever considered the wonder of snow? God holds in the heavens vast storehouses of the snow,[1] and each flake is completely unique, unmatched, unduplicated. Why so much trouble for mere snow? Our God is so great that such a thing is not only no trouble, but it is infinitely satisfying and worthwhile to Him to make each snowflake a marvelously unique creation. Am I not much more valuable than they?[2]

God is not a cookie-cutter God; He did not make me identical to any other creature. I am His dove, His unique creation. He took His time with me, fashioning my individual form and envisioning my individual future.[3] Even identical twins are not carbon copies of each other; their fingerprints and personalities are as unique as any two snowflakes.

Yet for all this wondrous variety, God has no favorites.[4] He loves us all the same—exactly as He loves Jesus.[5] God is absolutely just,[6] and also deals with every one of us in fairness. But *fair* does not mean *the same*. To mistake the two is to open wide the door to envy, jealousy, and discontent. I want the same gifts as this person, the same blessings as that person, the same answers to prayers, given in the same manner. God in His infinite wisdom does not do this. With His all-knowing love, He custom designs everything in my life to match my unique personality, understanding, abilities, and needs. He has not called me to the same purpose as anyone else,[7] so why would He give me the same gifts?[8]

It is common knowledge that no one parenting method or technique works for every child. We are too unique. God understands this, too, in the way He is raising me. His discipline is not one size fits all.[9] I should not compare myself to others.[10] Instead, I should trust my heavenly Father, and let Him work in my life uniquely and individually—exactly as I am treasured.

God is not a cookie-cutter God;
He did not make me identical to any other creature . . .
I am His unique creation.

---

[1]Job 38:22 [2]Matt. 6:26 [3]Ps. 139:13–16 [4]Acts 10:34 [5]John 17:23 [6]2 Chron. 12:6
[7]John 21:21–22 [8]Heb. 2:4 [9]Heb. 12:10 [10]Matt. 20:14–15

JANUARY 20

. . . forgive men their trespasses . . .
Matthew 6:14 [KJV]

Consider the word *trespasses*. How appropriate an expression to describe sin! To trespass is to violate a boundary; to cross a line that was never meant to be crossed.[1] I step out of my allotted, safe territory. I not only believe that the grass is greener on the other side,[2] but like a cow greedily thrusting its neck through the fence, I devour the other side's portion. *Webster's*, in its efforts to define the term, uses such aggressive words as *encroach, infringe*, and even *invade*.[3]

Now consider this: when I trespass, no matter whom I sin against, I sin against God.[4] I violate His boundaries; I cross that line that should never be crossed. I encroach on His prerogatives, I infringe upon His authority—I invade His rulership. I become just like Satan: "I will ascend to heaven; I will raise *my* throne above the stars of God . . . I will make *myself* like the Most High."[5] It is a violent act: "And there was war in heaven."[6]

I must not try to fool myself—my sin affects more than me alone.[7] Sin is completely egocentric; it is all about the capital I. *I* want, *I* think, *I* will. Selfishness is inherently degrading. My capital I sets my throne above the stars of God, a position for which I am woefully inadequate. The damage I do trying to be God with my limited knowledge and puny power only proves that God is good, right, just, fair and loving to lay down His law and forbid me that throne.

When I sin, I *trespass* on God's side of the line. I violate Him and all that He is. To sin is to declare that Satan is right, and God is a liar. Is God true? Can He be trusted? Am I willing to acknowledge that He alone is God, the Creator, the only One with the right to declare what is right and wrong? When I find myself toe to toe with His line in the sand, will I trespass on His glory,[8] or will I show Him the love and respect He deserves as my God and Father?

God alone is God, the Creator, the only One
with the right to declare what is right and what is wrong.

---

[1]Gen. 31:52   [2]Eccl. 4:8   [3]*Webster's:* "trespass"   [4]Ps. 51:4   [5]Isa. 14:13–14   [6]Rev. 12:7
[7]Josh. 22:20   [8]Isa. 42:8

JANUARY 21

My command is this: Love each other as I have loved you.
John 15:12

The call of Christ is a call to love,[1] to soak in and be defined by the all-consuming, unconditional love of God. This is not a natural love, not the kind of love we understand or can work up in our own hearts.[2] No, *this* love—this living, breathing, alternate-universe kind of love—is a supernatural invasion of God Himself, seeking to conquer men's hearts and souls.[3] Its seed is the cross of Christ.

The seed of the cross, planted in me, roots itself in my salvation. As I water it by my growing discipleship,[4] its vibrancy begins to unfurl in me. A seedling, however, does not usually resemble the full-grown plant. Even so, the beginning of God's love in me does not resemble the mature fruit of God's love *through* me.

The seed-leaf of love develops as I sincerely pray for others.[5] In prayer, God softens my heart, often allowing me a glimpse behind the mask they project to the pain they protect. I am moved to pity, realizing how used and abused, blinded and bullied they are by the enemy.[6] It hasn't been long since I suffered under that hand, too. But pity is not love; it is merely a step *toward* love.

Pity must put forth leaves of compassion: acts of generous mercy.[7] It is still possible, however, to do generous and charitable things without real love. At this stage, I often find myself trying to love others from a distance, because I've been burned by ingratitude, selfishness, and outright greed. My wounded self immediately retreats, putting up walls of protection around my heart and only measuring out of my love to those who *appreciate* it, who *deserve* it. This is loving in theory, but not in full practice. I am not to stay stunted at this conditional level of love. God would have me learn wisdom,[8] without withdrawing from those around me.

Jesus said, "Love as *I* have loved *you.*" God does not love us from a distance. God loves us up close and personal, actively pursuing us with His love. He loves us when we are unlovely, ungodly, and ungrateful. I cannot love like this by myself. I am not asked to. God has poured *His* love into me so I could allow Him to overflow and pour Himself out to others *through* me.[9] He is only awaiting my submission. This is what it means to love others. I cannot settle for a lesser, immature—and therefore unfruitful—expression of God's love.

God loves us up close and personal . . .

[1] John 4:11 [2] Prov. 20:6 [3] Jer. 31:3 [4] Luke 8:15 [5] Matt. 5:44 [6] Matt. 9:36 [7] James 2:15–17 [8] Matt. 10:16 [9] 1 John 4:19

JANUARY 22

. . .The LORD said to him, "Who gave man his mouth? . . ."
Exodus 4:11

*W*hat does it take to fulfill the call of God? There is such a tendency when God taps us on the shoulder and tells us to step up to the plate to say, "Who—*me*?!" We feel so inadequate.

But when we read about those heroes of the faith whose weakness was turned to strength,[1] we realize it isn't about our outstanding abilities or winsome personalities.

Essentially, God chooses us because we *can't* do the job! Natural ability gets in the way of depending on the Spirit, and we can only do *His* work through the Spirit.[2] Let's stop listing all the reasons why we can't do the job, as if they were factors that God had somehow overlooked or failed to take into account.

Willingness makes our offering acceptable.[3] What offering? Our availability. We don't need special skills. After all, God has used a donkey to deliver His message,[4] and He'll use a rock if we refuse to cooperate![5] All God needs is a submitted soul, willing to obey. You see, this is the God who knows the end from the beginning,[6] our before-they-call God.[7] He has already figured out how the task is to be accomplished and has plans in place to provide everything it will require.

Just think of the Israelites, a nation of poverty-stricken slaves with extensive experience in making mud bricks, suddenly set free and commanded to construct a sumptuous, elaborate tabernacle in the middle of a barren wasteland. And what? They found they had everything they needed: fine thread in gorgeous colors, tons of gold, silver, and bronze. They obtained waterproof animal skins, incense spices, precious stones, acacia wood—because God had already taken care of these details![8] And the skills? He simply downloaded all the knowledge and artistry, including the ability to teach others, into two men of His choosing.[9]

As for that call of God, we can trust in the Lord without wavering.[10] Let's step forward, knowing it is the Father in us doing the work.[11] We can do anything He asks us to do!

God doesn't need our abilities;
He needs our availability.

---

[1]Heb. 11:34   [2]Zech. 4:6   [3]Isa. 1:19   [4]Num. 22:28–30   [5]Luke 19:40   [6]Isa. 46:10   [7]Isa. 65:24
[8]Exod. 12:35–36   [9]Exod. 35:30–35   [10]Ps. 26:1   [11]John 14:10

JANUARY 23

Who among you fears the LORD and obeys the word of his servant?
Let him who walks in the dark, who has no light,
trust in the name of the LORD and rely on his God.

Isaiah 50:10

What is the foundation, the anchor, of my faith? Upon what have I built my hopes and dreams, my confession and profession, my whole relationship with Christ? Whatsoever my faith is built upon *will be tested*.[1] What will carry me through the fire?

There have come times in my life when everything I have ever believed was turned upside-down,[2] when all that I hoped for seemed lost, and all that I thought I knew no longer seemed certain.[3] The devastation seemed to mock every promise I had ever claimed,[4] and God was suddenly, painfully silent.[5] I desperately threw my prayers at the ceiling at night, but in the morning the suffering was still there.[6]

I have learned that when everything I have ever leaned on, every crutch, is knocked out from under me, I can let everything go but this: God can be trusted.[7] I do not need to understand, to know the reasons why, to see the purpose in anything of what has happened to me. I need only to know that *He* knows. I have cried out from the depths of my ravaged soul, "God, I don't understand this at all! But *I know that You know what You are doing . . .*" It is a great statement of faith.

Jesus said, "He who sent me is reliable."[8] God is God. That will never change—whether He does what I want Him to do or not. He said He loves me; He sent Jesus to prove it. Will I take Him at His word?[9] I can let God be God and do what He alone, in His all-knowing love, knows is necessary. And in my time of darkness, I will trust in the name of the Lord, and rely on my God.

Whatsoever my faith is built upon will be tested.
What will carry me through the fire?

---

[1] Job 23:10 [2] Isa. 45:7 [3] Job 42:3–5 [4] Job 3:25–26 [5] Ps. 13:1 [6] Ps. 22:1–2 [7] Ps. 56:3
[8] John 8:26 [9] John 4:50

JANUARY 24

They dress the wound of my people as though it were not serious.
"Peace, peace," they say, when there is no peace.
Jeremiah 8:11

Feeling bad is not always a bad thing. Negative emotions of guilt, shame, or fear are signs that God is dealing with sin in my life that I have been hiding in my heart. Those uncomfortable itches in my conscience force me to face my issues and get right with God. It is in these times especially that I truly value an honest friend, one who is willing to stare me down and tell me the bald truth about myself. What I don't need is someone's soothing sympathy, or to have someone pat me on the back and tell me, "Don't worry . . . it'll be alright." I don't need someone to cover over my sin, saying, "Peace," when there is no peace. And I don't dare to do it to someone else, either.

After all, no one comes to Jesus on his own; no one can decide to be saved unless God makes it possible.[1] To confess that Jesus died for your sins, you first have to understand that you have sinned. That is the work of the Holy Spirit only.[2] All my eloquence, all my persuasiveness, is powerless[3] to convince a single person that he is a sinner[4] and is going to die, unless he repents.

God's gentle whisper is so easy to resist,[5] and life's worries, riches, and pleasures[6] choke its power. How hard God tries to get his message through! But even God knows that continual resistance eventually hardens a soul beyond His reach.[7]

How dangerous, then, to shrug off those nudges from God, to go on doing what He has been dealing with me about, as though it were no big deal. As if His voice, His patience, will never fade to where I no longer hear Him. I can say, "Peace, peace," to myself, and God will let me do what I have determined to do[8]—and I will not even notice when that nagging little voice goes quiet in me.[9] When it is time to pay the consequences, wisdom will laugh at my calamity.[10]

I need a genuine horror of sin—and that comes from a genuine love and reverence for God.[11] When the Holy Spirit convicts of sin, I will not downplay it—not for me, not for anybody. I will not say, "Peace;"[11] I will turn them to Jesus.

To confess that Jesus died for your sins,
you first have to understand that you have sinned.

---

[1]John 6:65 [2]John 16:8 [3]Luke 12:15 [4]John 12:32 [5]1 Kings 19:12 [6]Luke 8:14 [7]Gen. 6:3
[8]Jer. 44:24–26 [9]Judg. 16:20 [10]Prov. 1:25–26 [11]James 5:20

JANUARY 25

*Oh my dove, in the clefts of the rock, in the secret place
of the steep pathway, let me see your form, let me hear your voice . . .*
Song of Solomon 2:14 [NASB]

*Y*ou have undoubtedly discovered by now that walking with Jesus is an adventure–and adventurous journeys are fraught with risk, danger, and difficulties. Often the path, which at the beginning was smooth and clear, suddenly narrows, twists, and seemingly disappears altogether.[1] Obstacles block my way, sheer drops threaten my steps, fog steals in and obscures my vision. The sunshine of His presence is hidden behind clouds, and the air around me, once warm with His touch, grows chill with doubt and confusion. When I started out, the way was clearly marked and choices were easy. But now many tempting paths branch off, and the signposts are not always easy to read. The answers are not so obvious. How do I keep from growing discouraged? How do I find the strength to persevere?

I have to find the secret place of the steep pathway. This secret place, the cleft, the sheltered niche, is not so much a place as it is a time. It is a moment to stop and draw breath and call on the Holy Spirit in the midst of my steep pathway, my trials. It is taking the time to come into His presence ("Let me see your form"), and to commune with Him ("Let me hear your voice").

I must not be so caught up in the situation that I forget He is with me always, to the very end of the age.[2] This secret place of comfort, strength, and revelation–answers–is found only on the *steep pathway,* only by those who have been willing to leave the elementary things behind and go on to maturity,[3] by those who have gladly taken up their crosses and followed Him.[4] Those who prefer the wide path–the broad, easy, unchallenging way[5]–will never find this sweet fellowship.[6]

I have no doubt that He will meet me in the secret place, for it is Jesus Himself who calls to His dove in the clefts of the rock. This is not the cry of the saint to his beloved; it is the call of Jesus, the Lover, to His dove! He is longing for my presence; He is aching for *me* to reveal my heart: "Let me see your form, let me hear your voice!"

Slip away into the secret place–right there on the steep pathway–to meet with Him, and you will find strength to continue your climb.

*The secret place of comfort and strength
is found only on the steep pathway.*

[1]Matt. 7:14 [2]Matt. 28:20 [3]Heb. 6:1 [4]Luke 14:27 [5]Matt. 7:13 [6]1 John 1:3

JANUARY 26

One thing I ask of the LORD . . .
Psalm 27:4

*I*f I could ask only one thing of God, what would it be? I should not be too quick to answer![1] If I have a lot of chances, I might waste a few on insignificant matters—but *one* chance, *one* shot to receive whatever I ask? Surely it must be reserved for only my deepest heart's desire.[2] Herein is my soul revealed.[3] My "one thing" is my treasure, and Jesus said, ". . . where your treasure is, there your heart will be also."[4] Where is my heart? What do I treasure?

Am I still seeking only the things of God, and not the God of the things? Do I want God, or just what God can do for me? There is actually a religious group that believes in several levels of heaven, including one that is bright, peaceful, and full of good things but still separated from the actual, immediate presence of God. Could such a contradictory thing as that even be attractive to me? But is that what I'm seeking if all I do is ask God to help me/give me/bless me, but spend no time simply worshipping in the splendor of His holiness?[5] There are many names and titles for God given in Scripture: *Jehovah-jireh* (provider)[6], *Jehovah-rapha* (healer)[7], *Jehovah-nissi* (victory)[8], *Jehovah-shalom* (peace)[9], *Jehovah-tsidkenu* (righteousness).[10] Who is God to me?

To Moses, God's face-to-face friend, for whose pleasure alone He paraded the greatest display of His fiery, eternal, all-consuming glory, He was simply *Jehovah*: I AM.[11] Moses needed nothing else, desired nothing less. So, too, for the psalmist David. Of all the things he could ask for as a son, a brother, a husband, a father—of all he needed as a soldier, a general, and a king, he had but one desire: "that I may dwell in the house of the LORD all the days of my life, to gaze upon the beauty of the LORD and to seek Him in His temple."[12]

What is my one thing? I realize now that if it is anything less than God Himself, I am cheating myself. And I am cheating God.

---

*Are you still seeking the things of God
and not the God of the things?*

---

[1]Eccl. 5:2 [2]2 Sam. 23:5 [3]Heb. 12:4 [4]Matt. 6:21 [5]1 Chron. 16:29 [6]Gen. 22:14 [7]Exod. 15:26
[8]Exod. 17:15 [9]Judg. 6:24 [10]Jer. 23:6 [11]Exod. 3:14 [12]Ps. 27:4

JANUARY 27

*. . . Go . . . and tell them how much the Lord has done for you,
and how he has had mercy on you.*
Mark 5:19

he world is big on qualifications. It molds us into believing that we need academic training (preferably with certified documents) before we're ready to go out and share this Jesus we've met, before God will call us to serve Him. But really, all we need to know is how much the Lord has done for us, how much mercy He has had on us. It was all the demon-possessed man in Gadara needed. When Jesus cast out a legion of demons from him, the man begged to go away with Him. But instead, Jesus sent him home to his family (one of the most difficult mission fields of all[1]) with the story of all that the Lord had done for him.

This was a man with no theological training, no seminary degree. He hadn't sat in on a single Bible class, lecture, or sermon. This man had spent his years scrabbling naked and bleeding among pigs in a graveyard![2] How effective could he possibly be? Yet only two chapters later, the very people who had urged Jesus to leave their region now crowded hungrily around Him, devouring His message, because this man began to tell the Decapolis how much Jesus had done for him.[3]

This man's calling was to share Jesus with his family, friends and neighbors. He didn't need to be taught a three-point approach, a five-step plan, or how to close the deal.[4] He just needed a passionate, grateful awareness of what Jesus had done for him[5]—and what Jesus now required of him.

It is no different with us. Walking in our callings is not a matter of training; God teaches us as we move in obedience, step by step.[6] We don't have to know everything before we obey. The more we walk with God, the more He opens our eyes, and we begin to really understand just how much He has done—and is still doing—for us.[7]

Yes—the Lord has done great things for us, and we are filled with joy.[8]

---

*Walking in our callings is not a matter of training;
God teaches us as we move in obedience.*

---

[1]Matt. 10:35–36 [2]Mark 5:3–5 [3]Mark 5:20; Mark 7:31–37 [4]Mark 13:9–11 [5]1 Sam. 12:24
[6]John 12:49–50 [7]John 16:12–15 [8]Ps. 126:3

JANUARY 28

. . . we shall be like him . . .
1 John 3:2

*W*hat is God's purpose in me? I have realized that all of God's purposes *for* me will be achieved through the accomplishment of His one purpose *in* me: that I become like Him. God is love,[1] and because He is love, He is relentless in the pursuit of this one overarching goal: to see Christ in me.[2] God is not random; He has a specific goal in mind. Everything in my life—every blessing and every trial, every circumstance and event, every *yes, no,* and *wait* answer to prayer, *everything*—has been lovingly designed or allowed in order to reveal Christ in me.

True beauty is always born of pain. Sculptors chisel and scrape, potters throw and fire the clay, smiths hammer and pound, athletes press and sweat. They endure because their goal is ever in mind. *I* can endure the same way, by keeping the purpose, the goal, always before me: to reveal Christ in me.

When I face troubles, heartaches, and trials, I shouldn't be surprised.[3] "Do two walk together unless they have agreed to do so?"[4] I can walk together with God and cooperate with His purpose, or I can resist and rebel[5] and prolong my trials. I can crumple up and complain, "Why me, God?" or I can rise to the challenge and ask God to work in me to do His work.[6] I have definitely learned that if I pray away the situation without experiencing a greater manifestation of Christ in me, I have merely postponed the test. It will return, because my loving Father knows it is necessary to conform me to the likeness of His Son. He would hardly cheat me of my chance to grow. To accept the challenge, to cooperate with God's purpose, I can ask, "What would Jesus do?"—and do it.

That is how I shall be like Him.

If I pray away the situation without experiencing
a greater manifestation of Christ in me,
I have merely postponed the test.

---

[1]1 John 4:8   [2]John 17:22–23   [3]1 Pet. 1:6–7, 4:12   [4]Amos 3:3   [5]Isa. 1:20   [6]John 14:10

JANUARY 29

*But I tell you who hear me: Love your enemies,
do good to those who hate you, bless those who curse you,
pray for those who mistreat you.*

Luke 6:27–28

I write these thoughts on the heels of a deep betrayal—not the hurt of a momentary carelessness, but the raw wound of a considered, deliberate deception and manipulation of my trust and friendship. Pain, rage, and bitterness, along with thoughts of cold revenge, flood my soul. It goes against my every instinct, my very nature, to love this one—to do good to her, to bless her, to pray for her.

That's the point.

Walking in obedience to Jesus is not natural; it rubs us the wrong way. The flesh bridles against it. *This* mandate, above all, is the acid test of faith, the thing that separates fair-weather followers from true disciples. A hypocrite can do many astonishing acts of religious piety,[1] and cry, "Lord, Lord!"[2] Jesus said even an outright pagan can love those who love them.[3] But he cannot do *this*.

Neither can I. In this, as in all He asks of us, God asks the impossible. Impossible love, impossible forgiveness, impossible mercy, impossible grace. Following Jesus is an impossible calling, but He is *God*: The Omnipotent, Omniscient, Almighty, Eternal God of Infinite Impossibilities Made Possible.[4] He demands and deserves perfection,[5] but He never says for me to do it by myself. No, it is God Himself who has put His Spirit in me so I can walk in His ways.[6]

I can do this; I can forgive her, bless her, love her. I can be patient and kind, not rude or offended. I can keep no record of this wrong.[7] All I have to do is set aside—surrender—*my* will for His, and move forward in it. I can pray the prayer of Gethsemane[8]—the sum of all that Christ is—and His grace, His impossible grace, makes even this possible for me. With Jesus, I can do even this.

---

*Walking in obedience to Jesus is not natural;
it rubs us the wrong way.*

---

[1]Matt. 23:27–28 [2]Luke 6:46 [3]Luke 6:32 [4]Luke 18:27 [5]Matt. 5:48 [6]Ezek. 36:27 [7]Ps. 130:3
[8]Matt. 26:39–42

JANUARY 30

Then I will teach transgressors your ways,
and sinners will turn back to you.

Psalm 51:13

I am on a dangerous journey[1] through rough and treacherous terrain. It is unfamiliar territory, filled with tricks and traps[2] set by an enemy who is tracking my every move[3] in the hope that he can ambush me, steal my blessings, and leave me for dead.[4] Who would I pay more attention to as a guide—the rookie tenderfoot city slicker who's never been this way before, or the seasoned veteran who's been there, who has seen the enemy in action, and who is familiar—even painfully so—of the pitfalls I will face?[5]

No contest, right? Why then do we buy into the enemy's lie that because I've been there, because I've stumbled, fallen—*sinned*—I cannot tell someone else, "Wrong way! Don't go there! Go the other way!"? Parents think that because they've made dumb mistakes, they can't effectively teach their children the right way. Former addicts think they can't tell someone to "just say no!" Yet who better to tell you how bad fire is than one who's been burned?

If anyone could've felt this way, it was David—guilty of adultery and murder, and not even repenting until his sin found him out.[6] But David knew the power of a personal testimony. He'd used it before to convince King Saul to allow him to fight Goliath.[7] In his heart-rending prayer of repentance to God, David acknowledged the power of a forgiven sinner to teach others the right way.

Have you fallen? Have you messed up, sinned, and received the mercy of God to rise again?[8] *You* have a testimony that others need to hear—others who will avoid the same mistakes *because* of what you have to say.[9] That's why the devil is trying to discourage you with condemnation[10]—to silence your warning voice! Grab hold of the revelation David had—God's grace toward you gives you the authority to teach transgressors His ways!

Have you fallen? Have you messed up . . . ?
You have a testimony that others need to hear . . .

---

[1] 1 Kings 19:7 [2] Job 18:8–12 [3] Lam. 4:18–19 [4] John 10:10 [5] Matt. 15:14 [6] Num. 32:23
[7] 1 Sam. 17:34–37 [8] Mic. 7:8 [9] Rev. 12:11 [10] Ps. 34:22

JANUARY 31

From that time on Jesus began to preach,
"Repent, for the kingdom of heaven is near."
Matthew 4:17

*W*hat is the kingdom of heaven? Do I know? Jesus spent His whole earthly ministry bringing us the kingdom of heaven. It was His life's work and His death's purpose—to make the kingdom of heaven available to all.[1] Everything He taught was designed to explain the kingdom of heaven, and everything He did was a demonstration of life in the kingdom.

First of all, the kingdom of heaven requires repentance. In order to receive it and participate in it, I have to change my whole way of thinking and doing. No ordinary kingdom is like that. Jesus said that the kingdom does not come with our careful observation.[2] Not only is it not a physical thing I can see, it is also not a bunch of rules that I can carefully observe to qualify.[3] It is not outward at all. "The kingdom of God is within you."[4]

The curious streamed to Jesus to hear more, and Jesus began to paint them a picture of the kingdom of heaven. We call it the Beatitudes.[5] He opened with the qualification for kingdom people—to be poor in spirit—then listed the attitudes of the heart[6] that are the ways of the kingdom. He closed with the blessing that those who do things this way (God's way) would be so fundamentally different from the world, that the world would do what the world always does with anything different—hate them and persecute them. And in the kingdom—God's way of doing, thinking and being—that *is* a blessing.

The Sermon on the Mount explains these kingdom ways as they're lived out in the nitty-gritty. Radical, upside-down, about-face. Can I do it?[7] The poor in spirit can, because they rely on God's power. And the kingdom of God is not a place—it's power.[8] It's the power to do things God's way and have comfort, inherit the earth, be filled to satisfaction, find mercy, see God face to face, and be called by His own name. It is worth everything I have,[9] because God's ways always work. Repent—the kingdom of heaven is at hand!

The kingdom of heaven requires repentance.

In order to receive it and participate in it,

I have to change my whole way of thinking and doing.

---

[1]Rev. 11:15 [2]Luke 17:20 [3]Matt. 15:9 [4]Luke 17:21 [5]Matt. 5:1–12 [6]Prov. 21:2 [7]Jude 1:24
[8]Mark 9:1 [9]Matt. 13:44–46

FEBRUARY 1

The older brother became angry and refused to go in.
So his father went out and pleaded with him.
Luke 15:28

his father had two children: the reckless, foolish younger one and the responsible, reliable older one. I have been both in my life. For many years, I squandered my wealth in wild living.[1] I did what *I* wanted and didn't care about what my Father wanted. I came home only after I'd completely wasted and ruined my life, after I had no other option but to come crawling for mercy from the very Father I had turned my back on—the same Father who came running and celebrated my return with great joy.[2]

It's surprising (and embarrassing) that I could ever consider myself like the older son, the "good son"—upset and jealous when some outrageously profligate *sinner* seems to get off scot-free, no consequences for their defiance or disobedience.[3] So quick to forget my own prodigal years, I can only think of my life since—how I struggle to obey, and how all that sacrifice and suffering doesn't seem to merit much from God[4]—especially compared to the huge party of blessings showered on these newcomers.[5]

I've read this parable many times, and I'd never before identified with the older brother. But that it's-not-fair thinking *is* in me sometimes—and I doubt I'm the only one. How many more have thought, "I deserve better than this. Why do the selfish, rude, and inconsiderate ones get all the breaks?[6] When do they get their comeuppance?" Like the workers hired at the beginning of the day, I expect to get more than those just barely making it in at the last hour.[7]

Why? Why do I feel like I deserve more, especially in *this* life? How can I forget the mercy I need myself?[8] What makes me think I deserve *anything* for doing what I ought to have been doing all along?[9] I can break out of my pity party, though, when I remember that my Father is more than *fair*—He is generous;[10] kind, not blind—or forgetful.[11] And that when the ashes settle, there will be a distinction between those who serve God and those who don't.[12] I will be satisfied.[13]

When the ashes settle, there will be a distinction
between those who serve God and those who don't.

---

[1]Luke 15:13   [2]Luke 15:20–24   [3]Ps. 73:2–12   [4]Mal. 3:13–15; Ps. 73:13–14   [5]Luke 15:7
[6]Job 21:7–15   [7]Matt. 20:9–12   [8]Matt. 18:32–33   [9]Luke 17:7–10   [10]Matt. 20:15   [11]Heb. 6:10
[12]Mal. 3:17–18   [13]Isa. 53:11

FEBRUARY 2

The servant's master took pity on him,
canceled the debt and let him go.
Matthew 18:27

It is hard for everyone to identify with the servant in Jesus' parable who, though forgiven a vast debt of several million dollars' worth, cruelly and harshly refused to forgive a fellow servant's debt of only a few dollars.[1] Jesus spoke this parable to illustrate the huge gulf of difference between what we owe God and what our fellow man owes us. Forgiveness should not be so difficult when viewed in the light of such a comparison.

I have known many who have suffered greatly at the hands of another. Lies, abuse, physical and sexual assaults . . . The life stories of people I have met are enough to etch an ache permanently deep in my heart. Victims of domestic abuse and violent crime have suffered tremendous pain and heart-rending loss. It is hard for some to consider such a wrong as a debt of only a few dollars.

Perhaps it is not the few dollars that is causing us to stumble and quail at the thought of forgiving. Perhaps it is that matter of several million of which Jesus spoke—the debt we owe the King.[2] Maybe it's our accounting, but all the wrongs we've done don't seem to add up to so high a figure. Yes, we have sinned—we understand that. But several million dollars' worth?[3]

We can only view our debt this way when we fail to consider our *real* sin. Not our *sins*, as in the numerous misdeeds committed against our fellow man, but our one sin—the sin that David acknowledged: "Against you, you only, have I sinned."[4] All sins are one: rebellion against the One who gives us our very life.[5] We are guilty of the brazen torture,[6] humiliation,[7] and cold-blooded murder[8] of the only Son of the Eternal God, who did nothing but love us, help us, heal us and redeem us. Several million dollars? Not nearly enough. The cost of His forgiveness is utterly *priceless*.[9] And what we have received, we can give.[10]

All sins are one:
rebellion against the One who gives us our very life.

---

[1]Matt. 18:21–35   [2]Luke 7:40–43   [3]Luke 18:9–14   [4]Ps. 51:4   [5]Ps. 78:56   [6]John 19:1–3
[7]Mark 15:16–20   [8]Luke 23:26–47   [9]Ps. 49:7–9   [10]Matt. 10:8

FEBRUARY 3

Listen and hear my voice; pay attention and hear what I say.
When a farmer plows for planting, does he plow continually? . . .
Isaiah 28:23–24

"*There* is a time for everything, and a season for every activity under heaven."[1] Sometimes the only comfort I can hold onto in the dark times is the understanding that this, too, shall pass. I know I am not the only one who, after days of dark valleys,[2] has longed for more of those bright mountaintop hours.[3] I have found myself dragging through dry spells. I can't help but wonder, *What am I doing wrong? Where did it all go?*

Jesus described God as a husbandman—a farmer[4]—and in Isaiah, God spoke about what all farmers know: there is a time and a season for everything. God reassured Israel, who was about to go through a serious dry spell, that it was not doom, but discipline,[5] and that it would not last forever. "When a farmer plows for planting, does he plow continually? . . . When he has leveled the surface, does he not sow . . . ?" God was breaking up Israel's unplowed ground.[6] Being plowed is painful. Have you ever been through a harrowing experience? A harrow is a farm implement used for leveling and smoothing plowed ground in preparation for sowing seed.[7]

In my walk with God, I will go through seasons, too. God has a purpose for me, and He expects me to bear much fruit.[8] To guarantee a good harvest, He is faithful to ensure I am properly plowed, harrowed, planted, reaped, and threshed. Trying to rush the process, skip steps, or remain too long in the wrong season is counterproductive. Everything is in His hands: the timing, the process, and even the place. He is expecting specific fruit, and He plants me in the midst of situations and circumstances designed to produce it. "Does he not plant wheat in its place, barley in its plot, and spelt in its field?"[9]

Have you ever watched a farmer reap and thresh his grain? It looks horribly violent—so much chopping, beating and tossing about! Threshing season looks and feels like punishment. But threshing is the most celebrated season of all—it is what is needed to harvest mature fruit.

Threshing is the most celebrated season of all—
it is what is needed to harvest mature fruit.

---

[1]Eccl. 3:1 [2]Ps. 23:4 [3]Mark 9:2–8 [4]John 15:1 [5]Heb. 12:5–6 [6]Jer. 4:3 [7]*Webster's:* "harrow"
[8]John 15:5 [9]Isa. 28:25

FEBRUARY 4

The LORD will write in the register of the peoples:
"This one was born in Zion."
Psalm 87:6

*W*here were you born? If you belong to the Lord, your birth-place is Zion, your citizenship is in heaven, and you're only a resident alien here.[1] Your native language is Spiritual, and your accent is praise. Others have a hard time understanding you.[2] There are certain words and expressions that do not translate clearly from Spiritual to Natural; their meaning must be demonstrated. Phrases like, "I love you," and "I forgive you," can only be fully expressed in actions. Words like *mercy* and *freedom* and *truth* have meanings utterly different than those spoken in Natural.

Although our language and customs are foreign and incomprehensible to the natives of the world, it is not so in reverse. We understand the ways of the world all too well, for every one of us had originally been born a Natural citizen.[3] "We all, like sheep, have gone astray."[4] What they do, we also did. The way they speak, we spoke. Their whole mindset, thoughts, and attitudes were ours. Their chains were our chains, too.

There is no dual citizenship.[5] When we choose Jesus, we are born again—in Zion. Our names are written in the register of the peoples—*The Lamb's Book of Life.*[6] Everything else dies. We no longer belong to the natural, to the world. We are agents for the King—but not secret agents. We should stand out, be different, radically opposite. The way we live should confuse people who are not born in Zion.

We must be careful! This is not the case of "When in Rome, do as the Romans do."[7] If we are no different from anyone else, we have gone native! We need to remember the height from which we have fallen.[8] We have been born in Zion, and Zion's King has sent us forth as His representatives.[9] Others might want to change their citizenship, too.

There is no dual citizenship. When you chose Jesus,
you were born again . . . everything else died.

---

[1]Heb. 11:13–16   [2]John 8:43   [3]John 3:6   [4]Isa. 53:6   [5]James 4:4   [6]Rev. 21:27   [7]Lev. 18:2–3
[8]Rev. 2:5   [9]John 20:21

FEBRUARY 5

*Yet when he heard that Lazarus was sick,
he stayed where he was two more days.*

John 11:6

Two more days. Have you ever heard the saying, "He's an on-time God"? I put myself in Martha and Mary's shoes: their brother Lazarus lies desperately sick. There is no 9-1-1, no ambulance, no emergency room. All their natural remedies have failed, and the only sure hope they have—their friend Jesus, who often stayed at their house—is far away, by the Jordan. A messenger has been sent, but Lazarus is fading fast; he cannot last much longer.

The messenger, breathless from his headlong journey, gasps out the urgent summons, "Lord, the one you love is sick."[1]

If I were Mary or Martha, what would I expect? This is the same Jesus who rose immediately at the request of a Roman soldier—the enemy—to go and heal his servant.[2] This is the Jesus who went to heal Jairus' dying daughter, who didn't turn back even when word came that the child had died.[3] This is Jesus, who the Bible says especially loved Lazarus and his sisters.[4]

This Jesus deliberately waited two more days, in their darkest hour.

Have you been there? Have you been desperate, with time running out, waiting on a God that doesn't show up when you expect, when you look for Him?

"Lord, the one you love is sick."

Can you identify with the accusation of Martha and Mary: "Lord . . . if you had been here, my brother would not have died."[5]

Jesus was late. Too late to heal their brother. Too late even to attend the funeral. Four days too late.

But He was right on time.

Because Jesus *is* the resurrection and the life.[6] Because nothing is impossible with God.[7] Because, "Before they call, I will answer."[8] Because if you believe, you will see the glory of God.[9] Judge nothing before the end of the story, because God's time is always on time.

---

*Have you been desperate, with time running out, waiting
on a God that doesn't show up when you expect . . . ?*

---

[1]John 11:3 [2]Matt. 8:5–7 [3]Mark 5:21–27, 35–42 [4]John 11:5 [5]John 11:21 [6]John 11:25
[7]Luke 1:37 [8]Isa. 65:24 [9]John 11:40

FEBRUARY 6

*Jesus replied, "You are in error because you do not know
the Scriptures or the power of God."*
Matthew 22:29

*B*eing teachable is noble; being a sponge is foolish. In the book of Acts, the Bereans were teachable[1]—eager, open-minded learners—but they were definitely not sponges. They tempered their zeal for learning with the wisdom to filter everything they were told through the holy Scriptures. Oh, how many of us would be spared the tricks and traps of the enemy, if only we would do this diligently! Jesus warned us: "Beware of false prophets."[2] Peter plainly said, "There will be false teachers among you."[3] John, too, warned us that many false prophets have gone out into the world.[4] And that doesn't include all the warnings from the Old Testament!

With so much at stake and so many to lead us astray, only a fool would simply accept what someone else says without asking God about it. We *must* remember: Jesus is our Teacher through the Holy Spirit.[5] "As for you, the anointing you received from Him remains in you, and you do not need anyone to teach you. But as his anointing teaches you all things,"[6] *use* that anointing to guide you into all truth.[7] That means we are supposed to take every sermon, every Bible study, every teaching and ask the Holy Spirit to confirm its meaning to us. We must remember—Jesus *is* the Word. His life is the best illustration of the meaning of His words. He is the lens through which we see and understand the ways of God. All teachings are to be compared to and filtered through Jesus Christ, not the other way around. The Spirit in us will warn us when a Scripture is being pulled out of context, misquoted, or twisted, *if* we pay attention to His voice in us. For this, we must be intimately familiar with the Scriptures *for ourselves*. There are numerous Bible references on every one of these pages. Have you looked them up for yourself to confirm what I have written?

With this anointing, we are responsible for what we are taught. We have been commanded: "Test the spirits."[8] We must be teachable without being a sponge.

---

*Jesus is our Teacher
through the Holy Spirit.*

---

[1]Acts 17:11   [2]Matt. 7:15 [KJV]   [3]2 Pet. 2:1   [4]1 John 4:1   [5]Matt. 23:10   [6]1 John 2:27   [7]John 16:13   [8]1 John 4:1

FEBRUARY 7

I will come to your temple with burnt offerings and fulfill my vows to you—
vows my lips promised and my mouth spoke when I was in trouble.
Psalm 66:13–14

*M*any are the promises we make when we are in trouble. Turning to God in times of trouble is almost universal. God knows that, sadly, trouble is what it often takes to get our attention. Unfortunately, once God has gotten our attention, we tend to negotiate with Him instead of surrendering to Him. We attempt to buy His help while limiting the deal; we don't offer Him everything. But we need *God*, not just what He can do. He says to us, "Call upon me in the day of trouble; I will deliver you, and you will honor me."[1] The cliché of making vows is that once the trouble is forgotten, so is the vow—and so is the Lord. Calling on God—total surrender—continues beyond the rescue.

But what about my vows, my declarations of faith when all is well?[2] It is easy for me to say, "The Lord will provide," when there is plenty of bread on the table, or to agree that "God is good," when I've been blessed with health, a good job, a safe journey. I can easily say, "God is good *all the time*," when times are good. I can promise even to lay down my life for the Lord, especially when the chance of facing a deny-God-or-die choice is remote.[3]

So, should I not make promises in the day that are meant for the night? Ecclesiastes warns, "Do not be quick with your mouth, do not be hasty in your heart to utter anything before God"[4] and goes on to talk about rash vows.[5] Jesus Himself urged us to count the cost.[6]

I need to remember that my declarations, my faith, will be tested to the uttermost. It does help to make that deliberate, determined decision before trouble comes.[7] The difference between fair-weather friendship and true faithfulness to God, however, lies in whose strength I am trusting in to make it happen.[8] If I declare, "I will," I have also learned to trust only in His grace—not my own strength—to carry me through the fire. I will not vow or bargain with God, but I will choose this day whom I will serve;[9] He will not let me be put to shame.[10]

My faith will be tested to the uttermost.

---

[1]Ps. 50:15 [2]Prov. 20:25 [3]Luke 22:33 [4]Eccl. 5:2 [5]Eccl. 5:4–6 [6]Luke 14:28 [7]Ps. 119:30–31 [8]Prov. 21:31 [9]Josh. 24:15 [10]Ps. 71:1

FEBRUARY 8

If only you had paid attention to my commands,
your peace would have been like a river,
your righteousness like the waves of the sea.

Isaiah 48:18

*W*hat kind of person do you most admire? What qualities draw your spirit? People everywhere, regardless of how they live their lives personally, have universally admired certain traits like honesty, kindness, courage, mercy, wisdom, etc. When asked to define the perfect friend, people usually describe someone who accepts them for who they are, who loves them enough to tell them the truth—even if it hurts—and who will stick by them no matter what. Givers and helpers are high on everyone's respect list.

After listing all these wonderful traits of an ideal friend, do you realize you have just described Jesus? He is the friend that sticks closer than a brother.[1] Christ has accepted you,[2] and He will never leave you nor forsake you.[3] He not only tells you the truth, He *is* the truth.[4] Christ is everything you admire.

What does all this have to do with Isaiah 48:18?

One of the greatest ills of our time is our inability to see ourselves through God's eyes. Mankind was created to be honorable,[5] and sin wounds our spirit. We are left only able to admire from afar an ideal, an honor we can't seem to attain. We have no peace.

God knows that the way to true peace and happiness is to walk in honor and integrity. It is His way, and He wants us to be like Him,[6] because *being like God in character is our highest joy.*[7] He gives us His commands, not because He's a tyrannical taskmaster, a drill sergeant who loves to bark orders and make people jump. He gives us His commands because when we follow them, we become like Him. We become the kind of person we ourselves admire!

Peace comes through honor and integrity, and honor comes from walking in God's ways.[8] And you will have Jesus as your perfect Friend.

Peace comes through honor and integrity,
and honor comes from walking in God's ways.

[1]Prov. 18:24 [2]John 6:37 [3]Heb. 13:5 [4]John 14:6 [5]Eccl. 7:29 [6]1 John 4:17 [7]Matt. 10:25
[8]John 12:26

FEBRUARY 9

As for me, far be it from me that I should sin
against the LORD *by failing to pray for you. . . .*
1 Samuel 12:23

To be able to live out Jesus' command to love others, I absolutely need to pray.[1] I need this not only for the sake of others, but for my own sake as well.[2] You see, I don't use the term *unlovable*, because God loves everybody. But some people are definitely difficult for me to love, especially in that up-close-and-personal way that Jesus loves me. That is how He commands us to love,[3] and why He also told us to pray for our enemies, the difficult to love.[4] Prayer changes people—and I am the one most in need of change! When I really pray for someone, my feelings and attitudes toward them change, and I can begin to honestly love them.

Honest love requires involvement. There is no way around it; sometimes the need is very great, inconvenient, complicated, and long term. Sometimes the answer requires more than a hug, or a casserole, or a check. These are all helpful, but sometimes loving others in their need means to stick by them—with them—until the need is met.[5] How far am I willing to go? How long am I willing to *keep* doing and going?

What does God ask of me? That is the question that only honest prayer can answer. His wisdom directs me in the who, what, and how to help and not harm.[6] God desires to answer prayers and fill needs,[7] and He asks people all the time—prompting us—nudging us—to step in and do for others what they are unable to do for themselves.[8] Too many needs go unmet because we ignored, put off, or reasoned away those nudges.[9]

Loving others can be messy business. It demands sacrifices—time, energy, attention, money, things.[10] But there is no other way to genuinely love my neighbor but to help him get his needs met. That requires deep, seeking prayer—and the gift of myself.

Honest love requires involvement.

---

[1] 1 Pet. 4:7–8   [2] Jude 1:20   [3] John 15:12   [4] Luke 6:27, 28   [5] 1 John 3:16–18   [6] Matt. 10:16
[7] Matt. 6:25–33   [8] 1 Pet. 4:9–10   [9] Isa. 50:2   [10] Luke 10:30–37

FEBRUARY 10

*The L*ORD *continued to appear at Shiloh,*
and there he revealed himself to Samuel through his word.
1 Samuel 3:21

*G*od speaks to us. I used to think I could learn all there was to know about God—all He would let me know of Him[1]—from reading and studying deeply the Bible. I was greatly encouraged in this quest by Samuel's experience—that God revealed Himself to him through His Word. I wanted Him to reveal Himself to me, too. So I read the Bible, and pored over it, and pondered what I'd read. My reading raised questions, and my questions drove me deeper into the Scriptures. And I learned a lot about God (relatively speaking).[2]

Yet I knew God wanted more.[3] He wanted a relationship with me—a relationship like He had with Adam and Eve in the garden;[4] with Abraham, Isaac, and Jacob;[5] with His prophets. He wanted to be as personal in my life as He was with Mary, with His disciples, with the woman at the well. I wanted it, too.

God speaks to us![6] I suddenly realized that the Bible I've been studying is really a record of God speaking to all these different people—and their reaction to it, to Him. Samuel's revelation of God came through His Word: *dabar* in the Hebrew, meaning speech—the spoken word.[7] Samuel's relationship with God grew day by day as God spoke to him.

Why wouldn't He speak to me as He spoke to Samuel? I wanted it; I wanted Him. The Bible says that in those days the word of the Lord was rare.[8] Was it rare because He wasn't speaking? Or was He speaking and *nobody was listening*? When Samuel responded, "Speak, for your servant is listening,"[9] God poured out revelation. Everything He told him revealed more and more of Himself.

God speaks to us. He has been speaking all along. When I learned to ask Him my questions directly, He answered me—sometimes from the Bible, sometimes through situations, and sometimes He simply touches my understanding, and I *know*. Every word He gives me—instruction,[10] direction,[11] warning[12]—is a revelation of Himself. Not just knowledge, but an experience of Him, a relationship.

What is God speaking to you?

God speaks to us.
He has been speaking all along.

---

[1]Ps. 131:1–2 [2]John 5:39–40 [3]Hos. 6:6 [4]Gen. 1:26–31 [5]Luke 20:37–38 [6]Matt. 22:31
[7]*Strongest:* p. 1,388 [8]1 Sam. 3:1 [9]1 Sam. 3:10 [10]Ps. 25:12, 14 [11]Ps. 32:8 [12]Isa. 30:21

FEBRUARY 11

*Blessed is the man who listens to me,
watching daily at my doors, waiting at my doorway.*
Proverbs 8:34

Eagerness. Fire. Passion.[1] God says to seek Him with *all* my heart and soul. Only then will I find Him.[2] He is not for the casual, wishful-thinking fence-sitter. The identifying mark of a Christ follower is love,[3] and love is persistent, love is unfailing.[4]

How much do I really want God? To know for sure, I must look at my everyday life and let it speak to me. How eager am I to meet with Him? How often do my thoughts turn to Him?[5] A lover in love finds it hard to do anything else. In the midst of business, his mind is seeing the face of his beloved.[6] In her innermost spirit, she is hearing the music of her lover's voice.[7] They hurry though their day to rush back into each other's presence.

Jesus, our Beloved, eagerly desires our company. He has wisdom from the throne room of heaven to help us navigate the tricks and pitfalls of this life.[8] He has loving insight and attention to heal all the empty and broken places in ourselves—in our lives, in our bodies, in our minds, all the way into our hearts and souls.[9] Everything He has to tell us is good and right and true, and full of the life that flows forth from the very center of creation's well.

"Do you want it? Do you want to hear what I can tell you? Would you like answers? Solutions? Love that will never leave you, never forsake you?[10] How much of Me do you want?

"Many only know that I exist—they know nothing of Me. I want to open My heart to you and share My intimate thoughts. I can teach you things you would never know otherwise.[11] Such knowledge is so wonderful,[12] only those who *hunger and thirst* for Me will find it. Only the driven, only those who want it enough to pursue it, who will wait at My door in eager expectation every day will hear My voice, and find Me."

---

*The identifying mark of a Christ follower is love,
and love is persistent, love is unfailing.*

---

[1]Ps. 63:1 [2]Jer. 29:13 [3]John 13:35 [4]Ps. 136:1–26 [5]Ps. 63:6 [6]Heb. 3:1 [7]Song 2:14
[8]Ps. 81:13–14 [9]Matt. 13:15 [10]Heb. 13:5 [11]Jer. 33:3 [12]Ps. 139:6

FEBRUARY 12

. . . God has made me fruitful in the land of my suffering.
Genesis 41:52

A man named Tertullian said that the blood of the martyrs is the seed of the church.* It is true. Others want what I have if what I have is so precious to me that I would rather die than surrender it. Pain makes things valuable. Anything I have sweated and bled for means a lot more to me—and to others. What I have to say about it carries more weight.[1]

Suffering is the universal condition of man.[2] Although there are those who would teach that God's children are supposed to be blessed with health, wealth, and total prosperity, the truth is that believers suffer the ills and evils of this world like anybody else.[3] It is not what happens to us that proves whether or not our relationship with Christ is real; it is what we do with it.[4] The shocking truth is that it is sometimes *God's will* that we suffer[5]—and not always because we've messed up. Sometimes, God needs to get a message across to someone else, someone whose life is touched by our pain. Sometimes, our suffering is so that the work of God may be displayed in our lives.[6] God used Job's extreme suffering not only to prove to the heavens that his faithfulness was genuine, but to erase the false belief of his friends that righteous people do not suffer.

Jesus, who suffered more than any human can,[7] still calls us to a life of sacred, submitted suffering.[8] He calls us the light of the world[9]—a candle in the dark. Candles burn and spend themselves to give their light. This is productive pain; this is being fruitful in the land of my suffering. Suffering is a crucible: I am revealed and refined in the struggles He sends me.[10] Suffering is also an opportunity: Jesus uses the fragrance of my faithfulness, my trust in Him in the midst of my pain, to shake up and wake up people around me. How I deal with my trials can say there is hope, there is a God, there is grace and strength, and purpose—there can be a beautiful ending.[11] Quietness and trust[12] will make me fruitful in the land of my suffering.

It is not what happens to us that proves whether or not our relationship with Christ is real; it is what we do with it.

---

[1]Heb. 2:17–18 [2]Job 5:7 [3]Luke 13:2–5 [4]1 Pet. 1:6–7 [5]1 Pet. 4:19 [6]John 9:3
[7]Isa. 52:14, 55:3–11 [8]1 Pet. 2:21 [9]Matt. 5:14 [10]Isa. 38:17 [11]Luke 24:46–48 [12]Isa. 30:15
*Biblio. p. 385

FEBRUARY 13

To him who is able to keep you from falling and to present you
before his glorious presence without fault and with great joy . . .
Jude 1:24

*Y*es, He is able—and yet I still fall. For years I have struggled, insisted, pleaded, and despaired over this verse. He *is* able to keep me from falling, because He is my amazing God for whom nothing is impossible.[1] If it were up to Him alone, no one would ever fall again.[2] I believed with all my naïve heart that I could go five minutes without sinning, if I could just keep focused, keep my thought from wandering[3] . . . and if five minutes, why not ten? Why not an hour? Why not a day, a year, or more? But this world and my old nature steal my focus all too easily, and again I fall.[4]

In this adamant belief, I was full of pride. I realize now how much I trusted in my own strength,[5] my own ability to rein in my old ways, my ingrained thoughts and attitudes.[6] God had to teach me a hard lesson, to show me how my confidence was sorely misplaced. He sent me a word, and admonished me, "Do not disobey Me again—not even once!" It struck terror to my heart! For all my belief in the possibility of living in this life without falling, I knew I couldn't do it. I fell to my knees and cried.

His grace met me there. Yes, He is able. *He* is able; I am not. John understood this deeply—but he was more gracious to himself (and others). In his letter, he wrote, "I write this to you so that you will not sin. But if anybody does sin, we have one who speaks to the Father in our defense—Jesus Christ . . ."[7] All of my standing, my faith, my acceptability, is in Jesus Christ alone. By myself I can do nothing.[8]

"Do not gloat over me, my enemy! Though I have fallen, I will rise . . . the LORD will be my light."[9] I cannot write about not falling. I can only write what I've walked myself,[10] and my experience is that Jesus Christ is able to keep me from falling, but He forgives me when I do.[11] And He alone will be the one to present me faultless before His glorious presence—not me.

He is able to keep me from falling, because
He is my amazing God for whom nothing is impossible.

---

[1]Luke 1:37   [2]2 Pet. 3:9   [3]Ps. 94:11   [4]Matt. 26:41   [5]Ps. 49:13–14   [6]Heb. 4:12   [7]1 John 2:1
[8]John 15:5   [9]Mic. 7:8   [10]1 John 1:1   [11]1 John 1:9

FEBRUARY 14

The one who sent me is with me; he has not left me,
for I always do what pleases him.

John 8:29

*D*oing what pleases another.[1] I spent much of my life trying to please another.[2] At first it was easy,[3] the desire to spend myself pursuing another's interests. Because back then, I was in love. Living for the joy of pleasing another is easy when you're in love. But I was disappointed because he didn't treasure the gift, didn't give himself in return. It wasn't real love.

Real love changes everything. For so long, I thought God was like *him* and needless to say, I dragged my feet over all those *shalts* and *shalt nots*. Until I met the real Jesus. Until I felt His love[4]—and felt love well up in me in return.[5] Doing what pleases Him leaped off my old, dead checklist and became a genuine adventure in loving Him who loved me so much. And the more I learn about Him, the easier it is to love Him more; He shows Himself worthy to be loved.[6]

It isn't crazy to actually try to do what Jesus said, to try to live as Jesus did. Love changes everything. Love moves me from "I've *got* to do this," to "I *get* to do this." I *get* to follow in His steps; I *get* to become like Him.[7] I *get* to rise above the petty, selfish, self-absorbed ways of this world and become someone courageous, noble, admirable. To go beyond the checklist makes no sense, unless you *love God.*

That's how John (the "beloved disciple") could easily say of Jesus, "His commands are not burdensome"[8]—even when suffering exile to the island of Patmos for the testimony of Jesus.[9] This is how the heroes of faith in Hebrews 11 could endure torture, jeers, flogging, prison, and even stoning—counting it all worth gaining a better resurrection.[10] The power of true love is that it sets you free from the tyranny of yourself and makes pleasing God your highest joy. His love will never disappoint you.[11]

The power of true love is
that it sets you free from the tyranny of yourself
and makes pleasing God your highest joy.

---

[1] John 3:22 [2] Song 1:6 [3] Jer. 2:2 [4] Jer. 31:3 [5] 1 John 4:19 [6] Rev. 5:12 [7] Matt. 10:25 [8] 1 John 5:3 [9] Rev. 1:9 [10] Heb. 11:35–38 [11] Ps. 91:14–16

FEBRUARY 15

". . . Is that not what it means to know me?"
declares the LORD.
Jeremiah 22:16

*W*hat does it mean to know the Lord? God is infinite; how can any mere mortal know Him? We don't know our own hearts.[1] How can we know His? It is not by His miracles, His great and mighty acts. By these we can only know that He *is* God—the same way Pharaoh knew that the Lord is God: as he stood in the ruin of his country and buried all the firstborn of Egypt.[2] It isn't enough to know that He *is* God—take warning from Pharaoh. Belief in the reality and power of the Eternal One will not save you—take warning from Lucifer. What he knows about God is enough to make him tremble in terror![3]

If anyone could have been said to know God, it would have been Moses. Called upon from a burning bush; anointed and ordained by direct command of the great I AM, (the first one ever to hear the name of God [4]), Moses was the very voice and hand of God to two nations. No one aside from Jesus Himself did more or mightier miracles than Moses, to whom God spoke face to face, as to a friend.[5] He even spent eighty whole days (and nights!)[6] on Mt. Sinai in the fiery presence of God Almighty, hearing Him pronounce the law and watching His finger write it in stone.[7]

It was this, more than anything else, that made Moses realize that in spite of the bush and the miracles, and even the face-to-face conversations, he really didn't know God. It was this concentrated, intense revelation of the law of God, the expression—in human terms—of His perfection, His character. *After* all of those awesome experiences of God—*after* all that—Moses suddenly makes this astonishing request: "Teach me your ways so I may know you."[8] The Israelites knew *about* God through His miracles, His *deeds*. Moses wanted more. He learned God's *ways*[9]—the whens, hows, and most importantly, the *whys*. Time spent in the fire of His presence made him hungry, and God said, "Blessed are those who hunger . . . for they will be filled."[10]

Get hungry. Get in His presence, learn His ways and walk in them. Is that not what it means to know Him?

God is infinite; how can any mere mortal know Him?

---

[1]Jer. 17:9 [2]Exod. 12:29–32 [3]James 2:19 [4]Exod. 6:3 [5]Exod. 33:11 [6]Exod. 24:15–18; Exod. 34:1, 28 [7]Exod. 32:15–16 [8]Exod. 33:13 [9]Ps. 103:7 [10]Matt. 5:6

FEBRUARY 16

I have set the LORD always before me.
Because he is at my right hand, I will not be shaken.

Psalm 16:8

One of the hardest things to do is to stay focused. Even now as I write these thoughts about paying attention, my mind is wandering! There is a saying you may have heard, "The devil is in the details." That may be so, but I find that more commonly, the devil is in the *distraction*. Have you ever found yourself startled by something you *suddenly realized* you had just done or said, or shaken yourself with a jolt out of a train of thought that was heading off the godly track? That sudden realization–that jolt–is like waking up, as though you were on autopilot for a moment.

Though dangerous, this is nothing new. The writer of Hebrews sternly warned us that we must pay more careful attention, therefore, to what we have heard so that we do not drift away.[1] *Drift* away. A gentle, almost unnoticeable, floating off course, caused by inattention.

The natural mind–the flesh–is extremely weak,[2] and maintaining focus even in the face of obvious need is hard. Peter, James, and John couldn't pay attention long enough to stay awake and pray for their beloved Master, even when Jesus had specifically asked them to, saying He was overwhelmed with sorrow to the point of death![3]

What can we do? We are told to not only fix our *eyes* on Jesus,[4] but to also fix our *thoughts* on Jesus.[5] The responsibility is ours. The Holy Spirit is our Helper, but He will not do it *for* us. The decision to think about what you are thinking about is yours–as is the choice to reject the wrong and choose the right.[6] Let's keep the Lord always before us and not let inattention cause us to drift into sin.[7]

The natural mind—the flesh—is extremely weak,
and maintaining focus even in the face
of obvious need is hard.

---

[1]Heb. 2:1   [2]Ps.103:14   [3]Mark 14:34–38   [4]Heb. 12:2   [5]Heb. 3:1   [6]Isa. 7:16   [7]Prov. 4:20–27

FEBRUARY 17

. . . leaving you an example
that you should follow in his steps.
1 Peter 2:21

Flattery is praise with a bad reputation; her honor and intentions are questionable. She does have something in common with her pure sister Praise, however: imitation is truly her sincerest form. Unfortunately, much of what is supposed to be praise among believers is really just flattery. For those who hear and do not do,[1] God is nothing more than one who sings love songs with a beautiful voice and plays an instrument well. They hear His words but do not put them into practice.[2] The Bible condemns flattery[3] and warns us to beware of its deceitful ways.[4]

But praise is commended and commanded over and over again. If I truly want to praise God, I will follow Him, do what He does, speak what He speaks. I will imitate God, just like kids imitate their parents. Have you ever seen a toddler as he watches his father shave? He tries to stand the same way and make the same moves, even imitating the same stretched-out facial expressions his father makes. Why? Because he loves and admires his daddy and wants to be just like him.

Jesus modeled this for us, too. When He disturbed the Pharisees' idea of religion by healing a man on the Sabbath, He replied, "The Son can do nothing by himself; he can do only what he sees his Father doing, because whatever the Father does the Son also does."[5]

There is no greater way of honoring God than by doing what God does.[6] True praise is action—love is only true love when it is demonstrated.[7] Jesus cleared up any doubts about what God does, any confusion about what God is like. "Anyone who has seen me has seen the Father."[8] If I want to imitate God, I must imitate Jesus. "What would Jesus do?" is another way of saying, "How can I truly praise You, Father?"

Hallelujah is not the highest praise. Imitating God is.

If you truly want to praise God, follow Him.
Do what He does. Speak what He speaks. Imitate God!

---

[1]James 1:22 [2]Ezek. 33:31–32 [3]Job 32:22 [4]Prov. 29:5 [5]John 5:19 [6]John 14:12 [7]1 John 3:18
[8]John 14:9

FEBRUARY 18

When they saw the courage of Peter and John and realized that they were unschooled, ordinary men, they were astonished and they took note that these men had been with Jesus.

Acts 4:13

Crowds, multitudes and throngs of people had been with Jesus. Everywhere He went, people went with Him.[1] There were so many people with Jesus, as a matter of fact, that He could hardly even eat a meal for ministering to them all.[2] That is not what the Sanhedrin saw.

Peter and John's three-and-a-half years of being with the Lord was not what they saw, either. For years, I had been with the Lord that way, too–following Him, sitting in a pew, listening to His words–but I was no different for the encounter. I came away still thinking, speaking, and doing the same as I always had.[3] Like Peter,[4] that kind of being with the Lord cannot keep me from denying Him.[5]

No, Peter and John had had an encounter with the unveiled Jesus,[6] an encounter after which they could never be the same again. From cowardly to courageous; from ignorant and unlearned to bold preachers of the truth; from selfish glory seekers[7] to vessels of His love and compassion[8]–they had been with Jesus in a way that everybody who saw them could see.

Without this encounter, the three-and-a-half years of being with Jesus would've counted for nothing. The seeds Jesus had sown in them would've withered and died in this first, fiery blast of persecution, having no root.[9] The root *is* this encounter. It changed me from the inside out.

When people look at me, can they see what the Sanhedrin saw in Peter and John? Can the world *see* that I have been with Jesus? When someone has been with Jesus, they are deeply, fundamentally changed. And it shows.

When someone has been with Jesus,
they are deeply, fundamentally changed. And it shows.

---

[1]Luke 8:40–45   [2]Mark 3:20   [3]James 1:23–24   [4]Luke 22:54–60   [5]2 Pet. 2:1   [6]2 Pet. 1:16–18   [7]Mark 9:33–34   [8]Acts 5:12–16   [9]Luke 8:13

FEBRUARY 19

He asked this only to test him,
for he already had in mind what he was going to do.

John 6:6

inally, I have figured out that when God asks a question, it is not because He needs to know something. God asks questions because *I* need to know something. You see, my problem is not what I don't know. The problem is what I think I *do* know. Socrates said it somewhat like this: "True knowledge is knowing that you know nothing."*

As a supervisor, I learned quickly that the hardest people to train were those with experience. They thought they knew everything already! They would actually get insulted if I tried to teach them something.[1] How much more did I prefer to work with someone who knew they didn't know! They had a teachable spirit.

None of us, however, is a blank slate. We all know things; we all have some kind of experience. Yet how much of what we know is true? How can we tell? Jeremiah asked, "The heart is deceitful above all things . . . who can understand it?"[2] David felt it, too. "Who can discern his errors? Forgive my hidden faults."[3] Can I trust my own heart? Does a quiet conscience necessarily mean I am completely on track?[4]

Where does that leave us? Are we doomed to ignorance? Can we never know as we ought to know? Of course not. God does not want His people destroyed from lack of knowledge.[5] He wants what I had wanted—people with a teachable spirit. You have a teachable spirit if you can admit your ignorance, question your knowledge, and listen to your Teacher.[6] If you have ears to hear, consider carefully *how* you listen.[7] When God asks you questions, be teachable![8]

You have a teachable spirit if you can admit
your ignorance, question your knowledge,
and listen to your Teacher.

---

[1]Heb. 5:11   [2]Jer. 17:9   [3]Ps. 19:12   [4]Gen. 20:1–7   [5]Hos. 4:6   [6]John 14:26   [7]Luke 8:18
[8]John 6:45   *Biblio. p. 385

FEBRUARY 20

*Be self-controlled and alert. Your enemy the devil prowls around
like a roaring lion looking for someone to devour.
Resist him, standing firm in the faith . . .*
1 Peter 5:8–9

The devil is looking for someone to devour. How does he find them?
He prowls around like a roaring lion. A lion roars to intimidate its
prey. Intimidation is fear, and fear is not faith. That's why one of
the most-repeated commands in the Bible is "Do not fear . . . "[1] And that's
why the way we resist the devil is by standing firm in the faith. The devil has
our faith in his cross-hairs. His strategy is understandable, when we consider
all that faith does:

- We are justified by faith (Hab. 2:4).
- We are protected and shielded by faith (1 Pet. 1:5).
- We overcome by faith (1 John 5:4).
- We please God by faith (Heb. 11:6).
- We are healed by faith (Luke 17:19, et al.).
- We receive by faith (Mark 11:22–24).
- We inherit the promises by faith (Heb. 6:12).

If we live by faith, we die by doubt.[2] *That* should get our attention! The
devil has a poison with my name on it—a poison called doubt. Would I take it
if he offered it to me? That is what is meant by "the testing of my faith."[3] My
faith is tested by the temptation to doubt. God says, "I love you.[4] Trust Me."[5]
Doubt says that God can't be trusted—that He did not mean what He said,
that He will not do as He promised, that I will lose if I believe.[6]

Faith says God is good, God is love, and He can be trusted no matter what.
I cannot have half-way faith; you cannot believe God in some things but not in
others. It is all or nothing. I can believe God, or believe the devil. One wants
to bless, the other seeks to devour. I will stand firm in the faith.

If we live by faith, we die by doubt.

---

[1] Isa. 43:1, 5 [2] John 20:27 [3] James 1:3 [4] Isa. 43:4 [5] John 14:1 [6] Gen. 3:1–5

FEBRUARY 21

Blessed are the merciful,
for they will be shown mercy.
Matthew 5:7

I don't know about you, but I need a lot of mercy. Like the man in Jesus' parable, I need more than a few dollars' worth.[1] I owe so much, I need a *miraculous* amount of mercy. The miracle is, that kind of mercy is available! Jesus said, "With the measure you use, it will be measured to you."[2] This is not just a warning against judgment; it is a remarkable promise. I can *sow* mercy to others, and God says He'll *show* mercy to me.

Many of us have lived our lives in worlds unknown to mercy. We have no idea what mercy looks like, so God painted us a picture. He colored our world with mercy in the shades of Jesus. *Jesus* is what mercy looks like. Think about it: He treated everyone as important and valuable. He touched lepers, ate with tax collectors and prostitutes, and healed everyone from rulers to foreigners to street beggars. Mercy honors the image of God in everyone with attention and respect.

Jesus did not hold people's sins against them. He didn't stone the woman caught in adultery. He didn't call down fire on the Samaritan town that would not welcome Him, and He even healed the wound of the man who was arresting Him.[3] Mercy is forgiveness; it is treating people better than they deserve.[4]

Jesus' mercy considered our needs above His comfort, above His desires, above His very life. He ministered in His weariness and exhaustion, and performed miracles just to provide lunch—or wine at a wedding. He went to the cross, even though every ounce of His humanity shrank from the prospect[5]—all because we needed it. He remembered we are dust,[6] and He prayed to forgive us, saying, "They do not know what they are doing."[7] Mercy is real love in action.

Jesus lived the mercy you and I need. He said, "Be merciful, just as your Father is merciful.[8] I have set you an example that you should do as I have done for you.[9] Mercy triumphs over judgment."[10]

Mercy honors the image of God
in everyone with attention and respect.

---

[1]Matt. 18:21–35   [2]Luke 6:38   [3]Luke 22:50–51   [4]Ps. 103:10   [5]Mark 14:32–36   [6]Ps. 103:14
[7]Luke 23:34   [8]Luke 6:36   [9]John 13:15   [10]James 2:13

FEBRUARY 22

. . . without holiness no one will see the Lord.
Hebrews 12:14

Throughout the Bible, holiness and power are inseparably linked.[1] I cannot walk in the power of God apart from holiness, and holiness opens the floodgates for His power to operate in and through me. "Without holiness no one will see the Lord." No wonder the enemy constantly seeks to undermine holiness, especially our understanding of what it is.

Holiness is a separateness, yes—but not simply in fashion or hairstyles. I am not separating myself *from* others so much as I am setting myself apart *for* God. To be holy (Hebrew: *qodes*, Greek: *hagios*) means to be dedicated to the sole purpose of serving God, set apart for His use only.[2]

A radio frequency that is open to anyone is easily overwhelmed by useless chatter. When it is dedicated, all of its power is given to one purpose; its communications are clear and strong. Jesus' power came from His complete surrender and dedication to the plan and purposes of His Father[3]—He was the Holy One of God, and no demon could withstand His authority and power.[4]

The more I dedicate the frequencies of my life to serve God, the more His power can flow through me to accomplish His purpose. There are many frequencies: my time, talents, energy, resources, attitudes, amusements, etc.[5] Fleshly, worldly living comes from choosing to hold back, to use any of these frequencies for my own purposes instead.[6] That's when I'm most vulnerable to temptation, to stumbling—to sin. That's when I feel the power drain in my life, when it's a struggle to live pleasing to God.[7] When I give myself to God without reservation or distraction, His power makes all things possible[8]—even holiness.

Without holiness no one will see the Lord. No one will see the Lord's power, no one will see the Lord moving in their life. Only those who want Him with everything they are and everything they have will see the Lord.[9]

The more I dedicate the frequencies of my life to serve God, the more His power can flow through me to accomplish His purpose.

---

[1]Ps. 99:1–3   [2]*Strongest:* pp. 1,482; 1,523   [3]John 5:19   [4]Luke 4:34–36   [5]Mark 12:30
[6]Luke 12:16–21   [7]Matt. 6:24   [8]Mark 10:27   [9]Jer. 29:12

FEBRUARY 23

Do not touch my anointed ones; do my prophets no harm.
Psalm 105:15

*T*here are certain things of God you should not touch. Do not touch God's glory: King Herod died horribly when he claimed it for his own.[1] Do not touch God's holiness: Uzzah fell instantly when he put his hand on the holy ark of the covenant.[2] And do not touch God's anointed servants.

Anointed is over-used and often misunderstood nowadays, stuffed with pomp and incense. It simply means "someone or something set apart and empowered by God to perform an act or service." Recognizing the anointing of men is easy: in olden days, oil was rubbed on the forehead; in modern times, degrees and titles are conferred. Recognizing the anointing of God is harder. I must listen to the Spirit of God in me. Failing to recognize the anointing of God is disastrous. The religious leaders in Jesus' time refused to see it. They were more concerned with defending their rejection of Him than in admitting the hand of God was at work.[3] In their stubbornness, they found themselves fighting against God,[4] and Jesus warned them against committing the unpardonable sin.[5]

With so many people and ministries and messages being declared *anointed*, I dare not let someone else decide this for me. I must learn to recognize when something is truly from God or is just emotionally moving.[6] Miracles are not the acid test, either, for the enemy can do many signs and wonders, too.[7]

The Holy Spirit *is* the anointing of God,[8] and His purpose is to bring conviction of what is sinful, what is righteous, and of the consequences (judgment) to come.[9] When it is truly a message or move of God, it will bring conviction, repentance, and changed lives.[10] God is not limited to using man-ordained ministers; sometimes He speaks through unlikely mouths.[11] More than anything, though, is having a heart that honestly wants to hear what God has to say in order to please Him by obeying.[12] With such a heart, I will not reject the anointing of God.

---

*I dare not let someone else decide . . . I must learn
to recognize when something is truly from God
or is just emotionally moving.*

---

[1]Acts 12:19–23 [2]2 Sam. 6:6–7 [3]Luke 20:1–8 [4]Acts 5:39 [5]Mark 3:22–30 [6]James 3:15–18 [7]Mark 13:22 [8]1 John 2:27 [9]John 16:8 [10]Matt. 7:15–20 [11]Num. 22:28 [12]John 7:17

FEBRUARY 24

*Perseverance must finish its work so that you may be mature
and complete, not lacking anything.*

James 1:4

*E*very baker knows that once you have put the bread into the oven, you cannot take it out until it is done. Up to that point, you can interrupt the process, wrap up your dough and refrigerate or freeze it until later, but once you have set the pan into the heat, you're committed. To turn off the heat and take the bread out of the oven before it is ready ruins it completely.

Before telling us about perseverance finishing its work, James had just said to "consider it pure joy . . . whenever you face trials of many kinds."[1] No, he was not a masochist, and neither was he crazy. He simply understood the goal.[2] You see, God does *nothing* without purpose.[3]

Isn't it mercifully wonderful that God is not surprised or disappointed when we are not immediately and instantly perfect from the moment of our new birth? Our *spirit* is newborn, clean, partaking of the divine nature.[4] Our soul—the mind, will and emotions—is not, and neither is our body. That's what the writer of Hebrews meant when he said that by one sacrifice he has made perfect forever those who are being made holy.[5] The spirit was made perfect forever; it's the soul that is still in the process. Among the tools of that process are trials.

The quickest way to get through a trial, then, is to learn the lesson it is intended to teach.[6] That's why James tells us to look at trials with joy. Have you ever tried to teach someone who bucked you at every turn? A complaining and impatient mind simply cannot be taught! Instead of asking God to deliver us from the trial, we should get excited about the new level of relationship He is growing us into.[7] We shouldn't beg to come out of the oven too soon. Instead, we can say, "Mmmm—fresh bread comin' up!"

---

*God is not surprised or disappointed
when we are not immediately and instantly perfect
from the moment of our new birth.*

---

[1]James 1:2 [2]1 Pet. 1:7 [KJV] [3]Acts 2:23 [4]2 Pet. 1:4 [5]Heb. 10:14 [6]Heb. 12:5–6 [7]Heb. 12:7–11

FEBRUARY 25

When Jesus saw their faith, He said to the paralytic,
"Son, your sins are forgiven."

Mark 2:5

*W*hat does faith look like? What did Jesus see? How can a concept have a look? Well, why not? We speak of the look of love, the evidence of mercy, and the face of fear. It's the expression that reveals all; the doing that bears witness to the *being*. To borrow from Forrest Gump, *faith* is as *faith* does.*

What was their faith doing? Overcoming every obstacle, no matter how radical or shocking the means, to get their needy friend into the presence of the One who answers every need. Like the woman with the bleeding problem,[1] no amount of potential embarrassment or social convention was going to stop them from doing whatever it took to get the job done.[2]

What Jesus saw was *action* . . . action based on an unshakable belief in the power and goodness of Jesus. They knew He not only *could* heal, but that He absolutely *would* heal. That kind of faith moved Jesus. That kind of faith got results.

What is *my* faith doing? I can sit and believe until the cows come home, but only when I *do something* with my belief will I see results. I can believe in my car all I want, but unless I get in, turn it on and put it in gear, it'll never take me anywhere.[3]

If your faith is not visible, if it doesn't drive you into action,[4] it is because you do not have a revelation of: a) your need,[5] b) His power,[6] or c) His goodness.[7] I don't know *anyone* without a need. I can understand His power, by considering the Creation—a world made from less than scratch—or by some of the happenings in Exodus. A God like that can be *my* commander any day!

I can believe His goodness by considering the cross and the twelve legions of angels He *didn't* call to stop it.[8] For me—and for you.

How is *my* faith showing?

If you don't believe God's goodness,
consider the cross and the twelve legions of angels
He didn't call to stop it.

---

[1]Luke 8:43–48   [2]Luke 7:36–39   [3]James 2:17–19   [4]1 John 3:18   [5]Matt. 9:12   [6]Gen. 18:14
[7]Isa. 30:18   [8]Matt. 26:53   *Biblio. p. 385

FEBRUARY 26

. . . I am willing . . .
Luke 5:13

*I*f He was willing *then*, why doesn't He do it for me *now*? This is the most agonizing puzzle of faith. Whatever *it* may be—healing, provision, protection—the *no* or *not now* answer of God, His heavy silence, challenges everything I believe about Him. Epicurus said of God, "Is he willing to prevent evil, but not able? Then he is impotent. Is he able but not willing? Then he is malevolent . . ."*

I know my God is neither impotent nor malevolent. Even in my personal, unanswered pain, I choose to trust Him.[1] I have learned that God is not reducible to a formula;[2] His will is not an always/never proposition. What I have experienced is the same as the earliest of believers experienced before me: sometimes He heals, sets free, defends against injustice, provides—and sometimes He does not.[3] Peter was set free, but James was beheaded.[4] He allowed all of His disciples to be martyred except John—who was exiled. God's people do not always automatically get a *yes* answer to desperate prayer.

There are some who teach that it is always God's will to heal, bless, and deliver, and that if believers do not receive these, it is because either they are ignorant of His will or they are not "applying their faith." What a load of guilt and grief this has piled upon the suffering! If God's will were so obvious all the time, then why is He called a "God who hides himself"?[5] Why is He found only by those who seek Him with everything in their being?[6]

I know my God is able and willing. I know He loves me and will never allow anything to harm my soul.[7] But I also know this world is full of suffering, and no one is exempt.[8] I can accept His bruising *no*, because I also believe that He has a greater purpose He is working out.[9] When His purpose calls for healing, I will bless His name. If His message is to rely on His grace to endure instead,[10] I will still bless His name.[11] I will not be disappointed by what He does with my pain.[12]

Sometimes He heals, sets free, defends against injustice,
provides—and sometimes He does not.

---

[1]Job 13:15   [2]Matt. 15:8–9   [3]Heb. 11:32–38   [4]Acts 12:1–19   [5]Isa. 45:15   [6]Jer. 29:13
[7]John 10:28–29   [8]John 16:33   [9]Heb. 11:40   [10]1 Pet. 5:10   [11]Job 1:21   [12]Rev. 21:4
*Biblio. p. 385

FEBRUARY 27

. . . My Father will honor the one who serves me.
John 12:26

*L*ove gives. It can do no less. Love showers its beloved with gifts, delights to satisfy every need, every desire. But what can I give to the One who has everything?[1] What needs does the Almighty have?[2] How fortunate were the disciples to have Jesus physically in their midst! They could wash the dust of the road from His feet when He was tired, offer Him a cup of cool water,[3] or throw an extra cloak over Him when He shivered in His sleep. But what about us? How can I shower my love on Jesus? Words can only go so far. Like any true lover, I want not only to *say*, "I love you," but I want to *show* it.[4]

Jesus knew we would face this dilemma. Loving God with all our heart, all our mind, and all our soul is something we can grasp, but loving God with all our strength[5] means physically doing something to express our worship and adoration for our Beloved. To satisfy this holy urge, Jesus gave us each other.

Whatever we do to each other, we do to Christ.[6] The way we treat people is the way we treat Christ. The words we speak, we speak to Christ. For the purposes of love, my boss is Christ, your next-door neighbor is Christ, the cashier at the grocery store is Christ. For the purposes of love, everyone is Christ. Each other. "I am with you always, even to the end of the age."[7]

How much more fortunate and blessed are we than the disciples! How many more ways and opportunities we have to serve Christ. One man can receive only so much; there are only so many cups of water one man can drink. But there are several billion "each others" we can serve to serve Christ. If we do it consciously, intentionally, and excellently for the purposes of love,[8] we give Christ the most precious gift of all. It is Jesus Himself we are serving.

---

*There are several billion "each others"
we can serve to serve Christ.*

---

[1]Exod. 19:5   [2]Ps. 50:10–12   [3]Matt. 10:42   [4]1 John 3:18   [5]Luke 10:27   [6]Matt. 25:40   [7]Matt. 28:20
[8]John 14:23

FEBRUARY 28

*. . . I will put my law in their minds
and write it on their hearts. . . .*

Jeremiah 31:33

*J*esus said, "Anyone who has faith in me will do what I have been doing."[1] The first thing I thought of when I read this was *miracles*: healing with a touch, casting out demons, raising the dead, walking on water . . . Wow. Those are some pretty big sandals to fill! I haven't performed any miracles, though. I thought I wasn't trying hard enough, that there was something wrong with my faith. I felt like I was a big disappointment.

But I don't think Jesus was talking about miracles. After all, He rebuked the Jews for demanding miracles and signs. No—what Jesus did was only what the Father did.[2] He went where the Father told Him to go, spoke only what the Father told Him to speak.[3] He lived in such close communion with His Father that He could say, "I and the Father are one."[4] Jesus prayed that we would be able to say this, too.[5]

My life in Christ has been a constant stretching toward this union. What is my struggle? Attention is one thing. Too many times I find myself living on autopilot—the habits, thoughts, and attitudes of a lifetime.[6] When God wrote His law—His royal law of love[7]—on my heart and mind, He did not override my will. In every situation I encounter, I hear His voice[8]—and the voice of my old self, my old ways. I get to choose. It's like I am a car fitted with two tanks—gasoline and propane: I must decide which fuel to use.

His law is written on my heart as well as my mind. The old me wants to be selfish, but choosing to love is what my new spirit wants to do. When I agree and do it, it turns out to be not as hard as that old voice feared. The more I pay attention and continue to choose love, the more I can walk as Jesus walked[9] and do what He did[10]—loving others, showing compassion, listening to the Father, and fulfilling my purpose.[11]

. . . what Jesus did was only what the Father did.

---

[1]John 14:12 [2]John 5:19 [3]John 8:28 [4]John 10:30 [5]John 17:11, 21 [6]Heb. 2:1 [7]James 2:8
[8]Isa. 30:21 [9]1 John 2:6 [10]Acts 10:38 [11]John 17:4

FEBRUARY 29

. . . Whoever lives in love lives in God, and God in him.
1 John 4:16

Once when I was very young, my uncle took me fishing out on the Atlantic Ocean. My line pulled and jerked with every roll of the boat, and I was convinced each tug was a fish on my line. "Nope," my uncle said. "When it's the real thing, you'll know it." I was mystified, and unconvinced . . . until I finally hooked one. He was right. When it's the real thing, you know it.

It's no different spiritually. How does anyone know I am a follower of Christ? It is not my words; any actor can learn the right lines.[1] It is not my church attendance; too many churches are like seafood factories (full of cold, dead fish). It is not my songs, my prayers, or even my praise—outright pagans can be equally enthusiastic. It is definitely not my bumper sticker!

No. Jesus said, "By this all men will know that you are my disciples, if you love one another."[2] *Love!* Love is the defining element, the dividing line between truth and error, real and fake. To a world glutted with hypocrisy and lukewarm shadows without substance,[3] "correctness" without compassion,[4] one genuine[5] living, breathing, loving soul surrendered to the Lordship of Jesus Christ is like an electric shock to the system. They instantly know it's the real thing.[6]

When I am struggling in my walk with Jesus, and I hunger for a closer relationship with Him, I know I need to start loving other people[7]—not in the grand gesture, but in the myriad kindnesses and dignities I can offer as I rub elbows with others. Patience can cool hot heads,[8] and mercy gives others the benefit of the doubt.[9] I can learn to be considerate of others without worrying so much about I, me, and mine,[10] to learn to be gentle with their feelings and happy for their blessings.[11] Seeking to fill their honest needs lifts me out of my own selfishness.[12]

Love people. Trust that God is in control. Hope always for the good, and stick with it for the long haul, because love endures to the end.[13]

Love is the defining element, the dividing line between truth and error, real and fake.

---

[1]1 John 3:18 [2]John 13:35 [3]Jude 1:12–13 [4]Matt. 23:23–28 [5]1 Pet. 1:7 [6]Prov. 12:17
[7]1 John 3:23–24 [8]Prov. 19:11 [9]James 2:13 [10]Heb. 13:16 [11]Prov. 14:30 [12]1 John 3:17–18
[13]Mark 13:13

MARCH 1

. . . Remember the LORD in a distant land,
and think on Jerusalem.
Jeremiah 51:50

*W*here is the distant land spoken of in this verse? I remember traveling to several distant lands. As I think on it, they all had two things in common; they took a long time to get to because they were far away, and their customs and language were different than mine. Everywhere I turned, I was constantly reminded that I was not at home. If I stayed there long enough, eventually the strangeness wore off, and I'd begin to feel comfortable.[1] Yet always, something undeniably foreign would suddenly jolt me out of my delusion and remind me that I was an alien and a stranger there.[2]

Spiritually speaking, this distant land is no different.[3] When I became a child of God, I was called out of darkness to live in His kingdom of light.[4] My home is the kingdom of heaven, and I must remember that the kingdom of heaven is not a *place* but a *way of being*, an attitude of the heart. "The kingdom of heaven is within you."[5] To end up in a distant land is to get off track, off the beaten path; to journey step by step, decision by decision, until I find myself in an attitude of the heart[6] far from where I started. I am then surrounded by people whose customs are not the love-driven practices of the kingdom. Their language is not in the accents of life and has none of the God-honoring words of truth I speak.[7] If I stay long enough, however, I'll learn their language and I'll begin to blend in with the natives.[8]

God will not leave me to lose my way in a foreign kingdom, however. His Spirit will always strive to jolt me out of my growing complacency and remind me how foreign–dark–that kingdom really is.

Are you in a distant land? Have you ventured off the narrow way?[9] It is never too late to remember the Lord. Your Father is holding a ticket for you on the next flight home!

The kingdom of heaven is not a place
but a way of being, an attitude of the heart.

---

[1]Lev. 18:3 [2]Heb. 11:13 [3]Luke 15:13 [4]1 Pet. 2:9 [5]Luke 17:21 [6]Heb. 4:12 [7]1 Pet. 4:11
[8]Ezek. 25:8 [9]Matt. 7:14

MARCH 2

. . . I am ready; let him do to me
whatever seems good to him.
2 Samuel 15:26

*H*as God conquered me yet?[1] Have I laid down my weapons and surrendered to Him? Or am I still skirmishing in the valleys, running an insurgent campaign against His rule over me,[2] hoping to retain some say in my affairs? True surrender is unconditional. I must acknowledge that God is God, and I am subject to Him. I must give up the fight. Much of our struggle lies in giving up our right to ourselves. The mark of conditional surrender is the word *but*.

- "I know God says to turn the other cheek, *but . . .*"[3]
- "I know God wants me to bless those who curse me, *but . . .*"[4]
- "I know I should do this, *but . . .*"[5]

But automatically cancels my surrender. *But* is not obedience; *but* is not trust, nor faith. *But* says that God doesn't know what He is talking about, that He doesn't understand.[6] *But* says there are some factors that He has failed to consider[7]—*my* case is special.

When I break it down, *but* actually means, "No, God." That is not surrender; that is fooling myself. Unconditional surrender means God can do whatever He pleases with me, whatever seems good to Him, no *ifs*, no *buts*—and whatever He does (or does not do) will not change my surrender, my submission to His will. It is the *nevertheless* of Gethsemane.[8] It is the stand of the three Hebrews, facing the fire of Nebuchadnezzar. "The God we serve is able to save us . . . But even if He does not, we want you to know, O king, that we will not serve your gods."[9] *That* is faith. *That* is what it means to surrender to God.

I am ready . . .

True surrender is unconditional. You acknowledge
that God is God, and you are subject to Him.

---

[1]Rev. 6:2 [2]2 Chron. 13:12 [3]Matt. 5:39 [4]Luke 6:28 [5]James 4:17 [6]John 6:7–9 [7]Acts 9:13–14
[8]Luke 22:42 [9]Dan. 3:17–18

MARCH 3

Though he slay me,
yet will I trust in him . . .
Job 13:15 [KJV]

*S*ervant is a poor word choice to translate the Greek *doulos*. *Servant* implies employee status. An employee has some say in his work, and reasonable expectations of pay and working conditions. If these conditions are not met, he will quit and find work elsewhere. But *doulos* does not mean "servant"; it means "slave."[1]

Job's story is one of a man who went from servant to slave in the fires of tragedy, when all of his expectations and assumptions of God were shattered in a single, horrifying day.[2] His transformation was not easy. Job cried out to God for twenty-nine chapters before God finally answered him out of the storm.[3] This answer alone drove Job from frustrated servant to utterly submitted slave: *God is God, and He owes me nothing.* What Job got was not an explanation, but a revelation of God: His wisdom, power, and sovereignty over His creation. It was all Job needed to despise himself and repent in dust and ashes.[4]

Satan accused Job of serving God for mercenary reasons—for the blessings. He says the same thing about us. If the enemy of my soul were given free rein to test my devotion,[5] if everything I expected and thought I knew about God were suddenly turned inside-out and upside-down, would God still be *my* God? Can God truly and absolutely do anything He desires with my life? Would I still stand up with Job and say, "Though He slay me, yet will I trust in Him . . ."?

Only a slave so willing becomes great in the kingdom of Heaven.[6]

If everything I expected and thought I knew about God
were suddenly turned inside-out and upside-down,
would God still be my God?

---

[1]*Strongest:* p. 1,542 [2]Job 1:13–19 [3]Job 38:1 [4]Job 42:6 [5]1 Pet. 5:8 [6]Mark 10:43–44

MARCH 4

*. . . May they also be in us so that the world may believe
that you have sent me.*
John 17:21

*W*hat makes the gospel believable? It is not my words alone. Jesus reserved His harshest criticism for those who do not practice what they preach.[1] He spared no feelings; He minced no words. He called them snakes, unmarked graves,[2] whitewashed tombs, hypocrites—even sons of hell![3] In the Greek, a hypocrite was a stage actor—someone who wore a mask, playing a part.[4] It meant someone who pretended to be something or someone they were not. Hypocrisy is a deadly disease. One of its debilitating side-effects is blindness. First among all those fooled by a hypocrite is himself.

The one thing the world actually understands about spiritual things is that you can know the real thing by its fruit.[5] The world has had enough talk. The noise of insincerity, falsehood, failure, and outright foolishness is deafening. They don't want to hear the gospel, they want to see it! People are hungry for one soul truly transformed by the Spirit; one soul full of the sweet, juicy everlasting fruit of lovingkindness.[6] There is no more powerful attraction to the gospel of God's grace than one such soul.[7] Being one with Jesus means being one with His ways and His purpose. Can you imagine the impact of a whole army of souls whose only mission is to share God's love and kindness to anybody and everybody, no matter who they are?

The gospel is believable when I walk in love; when, in the midst of chaos and confusion, I am at peace. It is credible when I am kind to others, even to those who are not kind. People believe that I have been with Jesus[8] when I treat them with gentleness and faithfulness, as Jesus would. The gospel becomes real to them when they see its power in my life; power to change, to be different, to overcome. As a man named Francis of Assisi reportedly said, "Preach Christ, and—if you must—use words."*

The world doesn't want to hear the gospel,

they want to see it.

---

[1]Matt. 23:3   [2]Luke 11:44   [3]Matt. 23:13–33   [4]*Strongest:* p. 1,599   [5]Matt. 7:15–20   [6]John 15:16
[7]John 12:32   [8]Acts 4:13   *Biblio. p. 385

MARCH 5

*Whoever can be trusted with very little can also be trusted with much,
and whoever is dishonest with very little will also be dishonest with much.*

Luke 16:10

If you think a little thing doesn't matter very much, consider the O-ring. One of millions on an assembly line, how important could one tiny, rubber O-ring be? Ask the crew of Apollo 13: because of the failure of a single O-ring, their space capsule very nearly became their tomb! You can't ask the crew of the space shuttle Challenger, though, because the failure of that tiny O-ring destroyed the ship, killing all seven people in it.

Life and death are in the little things.[1] Sin is the microscopic extra chromosome, the subatomic extra electron—two awfully little things that create hugely horrible results: Down's Syndrome, and a cancer-causing free radical. Sin is the deadliest substance, the most fatal "little thing" ever known, with a 100% kill rate.[2] Even the Son of God Himself, by choosing to take our sin upon Himself, suffered and died for it.[3]

The problem is that sin is not actually a substance, but a decision, and life is nothing if not a whole series of decisions.[4] Little things matter because each "little thing" is a revelation of my heart. Unfaithfulness is dishonesty, and is rooted in selfishness. It is a decision to not value truth, to not honor God, to not do things His way. I can only make such a decision when my heart does not value Him above all. It makes no difference if it is in a little thing or a big thing. The heart is *everything*.

Faithfulness loves God supremely and thoroughly. The faithful lover of God holds nothing back, keeps no corner of his heart reserved for self. The faithful lover loves at all times,[5] in the very little as well as the much. It is his deepest pleasure.

---

*Sin is the deadliest substance, the most fatal "little thing"
ever known, with a 100% kill rate.*

---

[1]James 3:3–6   [2]Ezek. 18:4   [3]Isa. 53:4–12   [4]Deut. 30:19   [5]Prov. 17:17

MARCH 6

Let those who love the LORD hate evil . . .
Psalm 97:10

*B*eware of the seemingly obvious. That which goes without saying may need to be said. God felt that way here, with this urgent admonition. His Spirit drove the psalmist to include it, though you would think it is like telling us to remember to breathe. We love the Lord. We hate evil. Don't we?

No, we don't, or we wouldn't, by conscious, selective choice, parade it continually before our eyes.[1] We wouldn't pay to watch it, read it, and listen to it. We do not hate evil; we find it immensely entertaining! If I consider–even for a moment–the things I willingly set before my eyes,[2] I could ask myself, "What captures my interest on television?[3] With what books and magazines am I abundantly filling my heart (out of which my mouth is speaking)?[4] What music am I pouring into the worship center between my ears?[5] Would I share my earphones with Jesus? Would He be as absorbed with what absorbs me?"[6]

It's not that Jesus hasn't seen it all; He has. Up close and very personal. Rape, murder, child abuse, hatred, mob lynchings, cannibalism, torture, race riots, Hitler, human sacrifice, lies, treachery and betrayals, home invasions, gang initiations, slavery, branding, perversions, manslaughter . . . He's seen it. He felt every blow. All that blood dripped down from His cross. It nailed Him there.[7]

Every wound wounds Him. Every perversion rapes His purity; every killing murders Him. His flesh was shredded for that sin. The world's entertainment tortured Him, bloodied Him beyond recognition[8] and drained the lifeblood from Him. And for us–for our sake–He didn't call twelve legions of angels to avoid it.[9]

Hate evil. Let those who love the Lord hate evil. Thoroughly.

Would you share your earphones with Jesus?
Would He be as absorbed with what absorbs you?

---

[1]Isa. 66:3–4 [2]Ps. 101:3–4 [3]Isa. 33:15 [4]Matt. 12:34 [5]Job 15:21 [6]Gen. 6:5–6 [7]Isa. 53:5–6
[8]Isa. 52:14 [9]Matt. 26:53

MARCH 7

That which . . . we have heard, which we have seen with our eyes,
which we have looked at and our hands have touched—this we proclaim . . .

1 John 1:1

*M*adison Avenue understands the amazing allure of the anecdote. Having a satisfied customer stand and say, "I know this works, because it has worked for me," is far more convincing than reams and reams of dry facts and pie charts. Personal experience sells!

The Gospel is no different. It is not an academic, historical thesis; it is the story of the God-Man, told by the very ones whose lives He touched.[1] They saw Him, ate with Him, walked dusty roads with Him. They knew the color of His eyes, how He looked in the morning, the way He gestured when He was trying to make a point, how He held the bread when He blessed it.[2] They'd watched Him walk across the surface of the sea,[3] reach out and touch lepers,[4] stop funerals, and literally raise the dead—who would open their eyes and breathe and talk and laugh again at the sound of His voice.[5] They even knew the taste of His cooking![6] Their memories of the events were so clear and compelling, they found themselves reverting to Jesus' original Aramaic when writing them years later.[7] That's the power of eyewitness testimony! Personal experience—you can't argue with it.

The authenticity of the disciples' eyewitness experience is a powerful draw to the Gospel, but that's as far as it goes. That's as far as it can go. Their story is not my story. I have to experience it for myself. Only then can I share what I have heard and seen and touched with my own hands. Only then will my testimony have that same, unmistakable stamp of authority, as Peter's—an eyewitness of His majesty.[8] I cannot tell another's story; I can only tell my own. What have *I* witnessed Jesus do? If He is my personal Savior, then I must have personal experiences of which to testify![9] You do, too. There are souls dying to hear what we have to say.

I cannot tell another's story, I can only tell my own.
What have I witnessed Jesus do?

---

[1]John 1:7, 14   [2]Luke 24:30–31   [3]Matt. 14:25   [4]Matt. 8:1–3   [5]Luke 7:14–15   [6]John 21:9–12
[7]Mark 5:41; 7:34   [8]2 Pet. 1:16–18   [9]Rev. 12:11

MARCH 8

. . . but the Lord looks at the heart.
1 Samuel 16:7

*A*h, the double-edged sword of the Word of God! It cuts both ways. I cannot righteously wield it against error and falsehood *without*, unless I have first wielded it *within*, letting its piercing judgment discern the very thoughts and attitudes of my heart.[1] The heart is everything. What I have poured in, what I have fed and nurtured and believed and cherished is all held within my heart. It is the seat of my soul, the throne of all that is my "self."[2] It is the heart that prompts every action. Jesus said that out of the abundance of the heart, the mouth speaks.[3] What the mouth speaks, the hands perform. Attitudes prompt words, and words prompt actions.

We think we know ourselves, yet Scripture warns us, "The heart is deceitful above all things . . . who can know it?"[4] God knows exactly how we think. In Proverbs, He admonishes, "All a man's ways seem innocent to him."[5] We are truly the ultimate spin masters; we are all PR pros for the self. Oh, the slack we cut ourselves–the wideness of the mercy we willingly grant for our own failures! If we were half as merciful to others as we are to ourselves, this world would overflow with forgiveness.[6]

"But all is well," we tell ourselves, "for the Lord knows my heart."

Yes, He does–truly–with no rose-colored excuses to paint a prettier picture than the reality of our rebellious selves. He looks at every act and judges not just the act, but the motives behind it.[7] What does He see? When He examines my intentions, what does He notice? Wholehearted devotion to truth? A love of doing right for right's sake alone? A willingness to die rather than betray Him?[8] Crucified flesh? Eagerness and diligence to search out the things of the Spirit?[9] Does He see Himself on the throne of my heart?

May it be so! May He never see laziness, carelessness, hesitation, lukewarmness, or divided loyalty. May He never find that usurper called *self* on His throne. I will take a hard, cold, Holy Spirit-guided inventory of my heart and stage a coup, if I must, to dethrone myself![10]

May God, who truly knows the heart, smile when He sees ours.

Attitudes prompt words, and words prompt actions.

---

[1]Heb. 4:12   [2]Prov. 4:23   [3]Matt. 12:34   [4]Jer. 17:9 [KJV]   [5]Prov. 16:2   [6]Luke 6:36   [7]1 Chron. 28:9   [8]Dan. 3:16–18   [9]1 Pet. 1:10–12   [10]James 4:8

MARCH 9

Thou shalt not take the name of the LORD thy God in vain . . .
Exodus 20:7 [KJV]

*J*esus' Sermon on the Mount packs a hard punch. Consider what He did with each "You have heard it said . . . but I tell you . . ." statement: He fulfilled the law. You see, Jesus did not come to abolish the law . . . but to fulfill it[1]—not as an obligation is fulfilled (and therefore no longer an obligation), but as a deeply satisfying task is fulfilling: it completes you in a way you want to continue!

In His sermon, Jesus took all of the *thou shalt nots* of the law and expanded them beyond the *nots*, showing that to obey the law truly, we must do more than merely refrain from harm. He showed us what it really means to "take the name of the LORD thy God," explaining what that would look like. He didn't mean speaking it. He meant *bear* the name;[2] *carry* the name.[3] Like a bride takes her husband's name, so we, the Bride of Christ,[4] take His name as our own.

To profane that name with my lips is one thing, but to profane that name with my life is far worse! Think about it: *Webster's* defines vain as: "to no end; without success or result." It lists as synonyms words like *idle, worthless, useless, futile,* and *ineffective.* It goes on to say that something that is *vain* is "devoid of worth or significance."[5] To take the name of the Lord in vain is to bear it, to carry it idly, uselessly, to no end, without success or result. It means "to fail to achieve the goal."[6] It is to rob that name of all its worth and significance. By extension, since I bear that name, I have robbed myself, and made myself worthless and insignificant!

Obeying the letter of the law is not fulfilling the law.[7] The only way to fulfill the law is to love[8] as a way of life. This is what Jesus was showing us in His sermon: failing to love is what it really means to take the name of the Lord in vain.

We have been entrusted with the most powerful name ever named.[9] We must not take it in vain!

---

*Failing to love is what it really means
to take the name of the Lord in vain.*

---

[1]Matt. 5:17   [2]Dan. 9:19   [3]1 Pet. 4:16   [4]Rev. 19:7   [5]*Webster's:* "vain"   [6]Heb. 6:4–8
[7]Matt. 19:16–21   [8]James 2:8   [9]Ps. 138:2

MARCH 10

*So you also, when you have done everything you were told to do,
should say, "We are unworthy servants;
we have only done our duty."*
Luke 17:10

*I*n a spirit of overwhelming worship and devotion, I once told God, "If you were to do nothing more for me for the rest of this life, You have truly done enough!" I was meditating on Calvary, on the price paid for my salvation,[1] and love for Jesus was simply washing over me. Later, I cried— because I realized that it wasn't true. I still need Him to do so much for me. Without Him, I could never make it through this life at all![2]

But I wasn't talking about His sustaining and overcoming power;[3] I was talking about all those "bless me" prayers—all the things I wanted Him to do for me, to give me—to make my life easier, more comfortable, more to my liking. I had finally realized that being comfortable was not the goal. Serving God is.[4] The only "give us" part of the prayer Jesus taught is for our daily bread.[5] That's a way of saying, "Lord, you know me. You love me. I trust You. Give me only what I need day by day. I leave it up to You."[6] And that comes *after* praying His name be upheld as holy and His will be done.[7] For that, I should be asking *Him*, "What can I do for You?"[8]

Obeying God, doing His will with a life that is surrendered to His control and command, is the *minimum* service—it is simply what I am supposed to do. To truly love God with all that is in me[9] demands that I seek Him, get to know Him and His ways.[10] To do His will, I must discover what His will for me is—and I must eliminate anything that hinders me from doing that.[11] Instead of always asking for more, perhaps I should ask Him to take away anything that is holding me back. If I simplified my life, perhaps I could see more clearly, and focus less on trying to be happy and more on becoming holy.[12]

After all He has done for me, it is the very least I can do for Him.

Being comfortable is not the goal. Serving God is.

---

[1] 1 Pet. 1:18–19   [2] John 15:5   [3] 2 Pet. 1:3   [4] Heb. 9:14   [5] Matt. 6:11   [6] Prov. 30:8–9   [7] Matt. 6:9–10
[8] Ps. 40:8   [9] Mark 12:30   [10] Isa. 55:8–9   [11] Heb. 12:1   [12] 1 Pet. 1:15–16

MARCH 11

Is anything too hard for the LORD? . . .
Genesis 18:14

*I*s there anything God cannot do? Is there anything Jesus cannot do *in me*?

- Nothing is impossible for God (Luke 1:37).
- All things are possible for him who believes (Mark 9:23).
- Nothing will be impossible for you. (Matt. 17:20).

When I chew on these Scriptures, I feel hope and confidence rising up in me—confidence in God to bring me through.

This is God—the Lord God Almighty, who created everything from nothing by a word; who split the sea and poured water out of a solid rock. This is God, who—even in frail human flesh—walked on water, commanded the weather, and changed water to wine without even touching it. The devil didn't frighten Him at all, not in the slightest. In fact, demons begged *Him* for mercy,[1] then fled screaming from His presence. This is God, the author of life, so overflowing with power[2] that nothing unclean or diseased could infect Him.[3] So much pure *life* flowed from Him, from His touch, that diseases instantly reversed themselves.[4] Nothing—not even death[5]—could hold onto its victims when Jesus commanded otherwise.[6]

This is the God that lives *in me,*[7] who commands me, "Be holy, because I am holy."[8] who says to me, "Go, and sin no more."[9] He died for me to make it possible; He lives in me now to make it possible.

What do I do with this? If I love Him truly, sin cuts me to the heart; it is not something I want to continue in.[10] Do I love Him enough to stop making excuses? Will I let the Mighty One who lives in me cleanse me?[11]

Nothing—not even death—could hold onto its victims when Jesus commanded otherwise.

---

[1]Mark 5:10–12   [2]Luke 6:19   [3]Matt. 8:3   [4]Mark 8:25   [5]John 10:18   [6]John 5:25   [7]1 John 4:4   [8]1 Pet. 1:16   [9]John 8:11 [KJV]   [10]1 John 3:6   [11]1 John 1:7

MARCH 12

*Then Noah built an altar to the LORD and, taking some of
all the clean animals and clean birds, he sacrificed burnt offerings on it.*

Genesis 8:20

Of all the thousands upon thousands of sacrifices offered to God in the Bible, three above all stun and amaze me. The foremost by far, of course, is Jesus Christ on Calvary's cross. The second is Abraham and Isaac on Mt. Moriah. And the third? This offering of Noah.

This sacrifice, so casually mentioned as to be barely a footnote to the drama of the Flood, is a sacrifice few would be willing to make. To grasp the significance of Noah's act, consider the whole picture: he had spent every day of one hundred and twenty years[1] looking at everything for the last time. He had worked carefully and diligently to do everything exactly as God had instructed,[2] knowing that only *this boat and whatever it carried* would survive the most horrifying and devastating supernatural disaster inconceivable to the mind of man: the end of the world.[3]

Imagine it! This was no mere thunderstorm; this was every earthquake, tsunami, typhoon, and hurricane in all of history rolled into one earth-exploding, continent-busting, forty-day-and-night maelstrom.[4] This was Hiroshima and Nagasaki times ten thousand thousand. And for a year and ten days, the only living things to survive it huddled together in a fragile, hand-built, wooden boat.

Now, on the twenty-seventh day of the second month of Noah's six hundred and first year,[5] he is once again—finally—standing on dry land. And staring at a world so empty, it took weeks just to find one olive leaf![6] From the ark behind him comes forth the tiny remnant of all life—the seed of the future.

What does he do? Noah takes some of the only surviving clean animals and birds in all the earth and sacrifices them as a burnt offering to God. This is not just a thank You to God for protecting them; this is absolute faith in God's ability to provide—to supply every need, if He has to do it from next to nothing at all. And God blessed him.[7]

I need not ever hesitate to give to God my first, my best—and my very last.[8]

---

*Never hesitate to give God your first,
your best, and your very last.*

---

[1]Gen. 6:3   [2]Gen. 7:5   [3]Gen. 6:13–21   [4]Gen. 7:11–12   [5]Gen. 8:13–14   [6]Gen. 8:10–11   [7]Gen. 9:1
[8]1 Kings 17:7–16

MARCH 13

Jesus answered, "I am the way and the truth and the life.
No one comes to the Father except through me."
John 14:6

The gospel is a paradox, at the same time both absolutely inclusive and radically exclusive. "God so loved *the world* . . ."[1] The whole population, every single person since Adam and Eve to the last baby crying out his birth pains, is desperately loved by God, and the gospel–the good news–is that every single one of their sins has been paid for. Jesus is the Lamb of God who takes away the sin of *the world.*[2] Jesus said, "When I am lifted up . . . I will draw *all* men to myself."[3] This is grace. This is mercy. This is that good and perfect gift of God.[4]

But the gospel is also radically, extremely, uncompromisingly exclusive. There is a great danger today of ignoring the exclusivity of the good news of Jesus Christ–that it is the gospel *of Jesus Christ.* "There is no other name under heaven given to men by which we must be saved."[5] Jesus Himself excluded all other paths to God: "No one comes to the Father except through me." Even the all-inclusive *whosoever* of John 3:16 is exclusive: it excludes any who will not believe in Him.

In our eagerness to appear tolerant and not judgmental, we have played down the absolute necessity of forsaking sin.[6] Repentance is rarely mentioned except in general. Even gross sin *among believers* is ignored or glossed over– sometimes even brazenly embraced. Make no mistake: the gospel is exclusive. To avail yourself of it, you must repent–turn away from your sins.[7] You must take up your cross (a cross is for dying) and follow Jesus Christ.[8] If you will not do this–daily[9]–you are excluded from the gospel. Of your own free will.

How sad that for a freely offered, all-inclusive gospel, few will find it.[10] Are you one of those few?

Jesus Himself excluded all other paths to God:
"No one comes to the Father except through me."

---

[1]John 3:16   [2]John 1:29   [3]John 12:32   [4]James 1:17   [5]Acts 4:12   [6]1 John 3:4–10   [7]Acts 2:38
[8]Matt. 16:24   [9]Luke 9:23   [10]Matt. 7:14

MARCH 14

I will lead the blind by ways they have not known,
along unfamiliar paths I will guide them . . .
Isaiah 42:16

*H*ow different has my life been since I met Jesus? Since I came face to face with Him, have I seen new directions? Being a follower of Jesus moves me out of my comfort zone, as well it should, considering that my old self was very comfortable in sin! We need to wake up and open our eyes to see and our ears to hear, because God is about to take us to a place we've never been (the kingdom of God[1]) by a way we've never walked (the Way of Holiness[2]). We cannot find this path by ourselves, but God has promised He would show us every step of the way[3] and even whisper the directions into our ears.[4]

If I have truly met Jesus and embraced Him in my heart, I will never again long for my old ways. If I have fallen in love with the spotless Lamb of God,[5] sin should become utterly ugly, hateful, and disgusting to me. Who, becoming rich, ever longed for their days of poverty? Or who, being healed and made whole, ever craved their pain again?[6]

God did not save me to leave me wallowing in misery, aching within and lashing out at others.[7] Jesus did not take all my sin upon Himself so I could continue in its bondage.[8] Yet in order to take hold of everything Jesus bought and paid for with His blood—peace and joy, holiness and purity, freedom and absolute love—I have to let Him lead me, blind, by ways I have not known, and I must begin to step down unfamiliar paths. Why do you think God always has to encourage His people to "be strong and courageous" and "do not be afraid"?[9] God's ways are not man's ways, and He tells us to forsake our ways.[10] Over and over again, He promises, "I will hold you with My right hand."[11] So I will get bold! I will step out in a new direction, into a new life—a life of right-being and right-doing. God Himself will be my guide.

If I have fallen in love with the spotless Lamb of God,
sin should become utterly ugly,
hateful, and disgusting to me.

---

[1]Luke 17:21 [2]Isa. 35:8 [3]Isa. 58:11 [4]Isa. 30:21 [5]John 1:29 [6]Eccl. 7:10 [7]Prov. 19:3
[8]John 8:34–36 [9]Josh. 1:9 [10]Isa. 55:7–8 [11]Isa. 41:10

MARCH 15

So be very careful to love the LORD your God.
Joshua 23:11

Nostalgia buffs will remember a time when T-shirts, buttons, and bumper stickers proclaimed the slogan of the day: "Love is a warm puppy." As simple and cutesy as that sounds, it *is* a workable analogy. Puppies require lots of attention. Ask any mother left with the task after her once-eager child has given up! Puppies must be fed—regularly.[1] They must be taken outside—often.[2] They must be cleaned up after—frequently.[3] They must be trained—diligently.[4] They need things: a bed, a leash, a collar, tags, shots, parasite protections, and . . . baths.[5] If I neglect or ignore any of these *musts*, I will quickly regret it.[6]

Unlike a puppy, however, love does not give reminders to pay attention to it. Love doesn't whine at the back door, bring me its food bowl, or get tangled up underfoot begging for a belly rub.

It's not that I don't *intend* to do all those things. I mean to; I remember to—late at night as I'm slipping under the covers and turning out the light. And I put it down as one of the first things on tomorrow's to-do list: 1) Do something purely for the love of Jesus.

But tomorrow is just as busy as today. There's so much to do just to keep on living—so many bills, so many distractions.[7] So "think about the things He's done for me,"[8] gets relegated to the bottom of the list. "Spend time telling Him how wonderful He is"[9] gets forwarded to another day. "Love the Jesus in another person"[10] gets shuffled to sometime next week, and before I know it, my sword[11] is rusty, my prayer journal dusty, and my relationship with God has been choked cold by inattention, neglect, and carelessness.[12]

Love is a warm puppy. If I pay deliberate, diligent attention to it, it will be my best friend forever.

Pay deliberate, diligent attention to love,
and it will be your best friend forever.

---

[1]John 6:53–55 [2]Heb. 13:12–13 [3]Ezek. 22:15 [4]Heb. 5:14 [5]Matt. 6:33 [6]Ps. 119:16 [7]Luke 8:14 [8]Ps. 77:12 [9]Ps. 9:1 [10]Matt. 25:40 [11]Heb. 4:12 [12]Song 5:2–8

MARCH 16

. . . The man took Jesus at His word and departed.
John 4:50

*H*ow simple this statement, yet how astounding its dimensions! And how much it must have blessed the heart of Jesus just to be believed. No doubts, no questions, no assurances required, no signs demanded, no controversies stirred—just belief. He took Jesus at his word and departed. He didn't have to see it happen before he believed.[1] He departed, and while he was still on the way,[2] he was told of the miracle. Because he believed Jesus, his child lived.

So—what has Jesus said to me? When I read the Bible, I need to remember; everything is written for me.[3] What He said, He said *to me.* Jesus wasn't just talking to a bunch of folks who lived 2,000 years ago. What if I listened to everything He said as if He were speaking directly to me[4] and meant for me to take action on it?

How different would my life be if for everything Jesus said, I simply took Him at His word *and did it*? That's the *and departed* part of this decision. The man immediately acted on what he believed: that Jesus had told him the truth, for real, straight up, and not spiritualized away into meaninglessness. It must have stopped Jesus in His tracks for the joy of it!

Don't we all need changes? Aren't we hungry for some victory, instead of the same old try-fail-repent cycle? Let's try taking Jesus at His Word. Let's get radical. Let's stop putting qualifications, explanations, and situational exceptions to His commands—effectively making them null and void. Let's stop sputtering, "But-but," and *do it*. It's amazing to discover that God actually does back up His Word.[5] Someone who says something he does not mean is a liar. God is not a liar.[6] He says what He means and He means what He says.

Do I want to truly bless the Lord?[7] No amount of hallelujahs will do it, if I do not believe Him.[8] I want to be a true disciple. I am going to get radical, get changed. I am going to take Him at His Word and depart.

How different would your life be if for everything Jesus said, you simply took Him at His word and did it?

---

[1]Gen. 15:6   [2]John 4:51   [3]John 20:31   [4]Matt. 22:31   [5]Jer. 1:12   [6]Num. 23:19   [7]Ps. 103:1   [8]Heb. 11:6

MARCH 17

. . . the devil . . . was a murderer from the beginning . . .
John 8:44

The solemn faces of the police added to the seriousness of the news: "We have information that you have been targeted by a serial killer. He is very cunning and sickly cruel; he likes to torment and torture his victims before he kills them. He's been operating for many years, and no one has ever been able to capture him. We can't even show you what he looks like, because he's a master of disguise. All we can tell you is that he's not the strong-arm type; he likes to worm his way into your confidence with his charm and the promise of a good time—all lies, of course. We do know that he is relentless, extremely clever, and carefully studies his victims. He stalks his prey, and knows more about you than you can imagine. He finds your weaknesses and exploits them. He's killed so many people, it's impossible to count, and you are definitely on his hit list."

If this were me, what would I do? Install an alarm system? Hire a bodyguard? I'd at least avoid dark places, blind dates, and probably would think twice about where I hung out and who I invited in! I'd definitely be alert to everything around me, and locking my door's a given.

The bad news is: this scenario is not hypothetical, it's for real, and I have already been his victim. Satan is the most successful serial killer of all time;[1] no one has been untouched by his cruelty. Hollywood and all its gore is his brainchild.

The good news is: I do not have to remain his victim. After all Jesus has done, I now have a choice. The enemy cannot "make me do it." I can repent; I can choose to cut sin out of my life.[2] It's a serious choice: if I keep flip-flopping in and out of my old sinful ways, I can end up seven times worse than before.[3] But Jesus' love in me is strong enough to slam the door in the enemy's face.

What doors? Bitterness[4] and unforgiveness.[5] Compromise[6] and neglect.[7] Not walking in love.[8] Every sin tolerated is an open door to the devil, a foothold. It is my authorization to Satan to come in and take me down.[9] I've got to shut the door! I will root out sin and not allow it to flourish. My enemy is on the hunt;[10] I refuse to give him the gun!

My enemy is on the hunt. I refuse to give him the gun!

---

[1]John 10:10   [2]Mark 9:43–47   [3]Matt. 12:43–45   [4]Amos 6:12   [5]Matt. 6:14–15   [6]James 4:4
[7]Heb. 2:1   [8]John 15:9–10   [9]1 John 3:6   [10]1 Pet. 5:8

MARCH 18

*Ten days later the word of the L*ORD *came to Jeremiah.*
Jeremiah 42:7

*T*he problem with reading about something in the Bible is time compression. All the in-between waiting is omitted, and it looks like God said it, and bingo! It happened. But Noah waited 120 years after God announced the flood before a single raindrop fell.[1] Abraham waited twenty-five years after God promised to make him a great nation before he held Isaac in his arms.[2] Adam and Eve died still waiting to see her seed crush Satan's head. God waited thirteen years to answer Solomon's prayer of dedication for the temple.[3] Elijah prayed seven times before a rain cloud appeared.[4] Jeremiah waited ten days, and Daniel fasted three weeks before each received his answer.[5] The disciples spent ten earnest days (Pentecost being ten days after Jesus' ascension)[6] in the upper room, waiting to be clothed with power from on high.[7]

Waiting is truly the hardest work you'll ever perform. "Ask," Jesus said, "and it will be given to you; seek and you will find; knock and the door will be opened to you."[8] What the English doesn't explain is that the Greek verb structure literally means, "Ask (and keep on asking) . . . seek (and keep on seeking) . . . knock (and keep on knocking) . . ." Persistence. Staying power. Don't give up until you hold your answer in your hands.

"But they that wait upon the LORD shall renew their strength."[9] Notice it doesn't say "they that *work for* the LORD shall renew their strength." It says, "wait." It takes strength to hold back the flesh, which feels like it must be doing something, which thinks that if the answer doesn't come instantly, it isn't coming at all. It takes strength to stay calm, to hold onto expectancy, to not throw away your confidence.[10] The anchor for that strength is the unshakable conviction that God is faithful who promised.[11] Faith honors God: "therefore strong peoples will honor you."[12]

Do not give up.[13] "Wait for the LORD; be strong and take heart and wait for the LORD."[14]

Waiting is truly the hardest work you will ever perform.

---

[1]Gen. 6:3 [2]Gen. 12:1–4; 21:5 [3]1 Kings 6:38–7:1; 9:1–2 [4]1 Kings 18:42–44 [5]Dan. 10:2–3, 12–14
[6]Acts 2:1–4 [7]Luke 24:49 [8]Matt. 7:7 [9]Isa. 40:31 [KJV] [10]Heb. 10:35 [11]Heb. 10:23 [12]Isa. 25:3
[13]Luke 18:1 [14]Ps. 27:14

MARCH 19

God said to Moses, "I Am . . ."
Exodus 3:14

If you were to introduce yourself, and you stopped at "I am," the sentence would be incomplete. Others would be confused, expecting something to follow—a name, an occupation, a relationship—*something*. "Hello. I am Jane. I teach at the school. I'm Tommy's mother." Folks want an explanation, a description, a definition—something that tells them a bit about who you are so they will know how to relate to you.

Why didn't God do this? I AM WHO I AM. What kind of a name is that? What does it mean?

How can you express all that God is in a single, pronounceable name? He is the Infinite, Eternally Existent, Three–In–One Source and Focus of All Life, Creator-Sustainer-Redeemer, Mighty-Yet-Gentle, All-Knowing, All-Powerful, Everywhere Present, Perfectly Just-Yet-Merciful, Hearing, Seeing, Being . . . All of heaven and earth cannot contain God.[1] How can you cram Him into the limited confines of a name? Whatever name you choose would necessarily exclude something or someone. Just think how many are offended that the Bible refers to God as *Him*!

I AM. Present tense. Because God is never too early or too late. He is an ever-present help in trouble.[2] Now—when I need Him—He is.

I AM. Everything I need. Fill in the blank—I will find it in God. All the hyphenated Names of God found in the Bible—*Jehovah-jireh* (Provider),[3] *Jehovah-rapha* (Healer),[4] *Jehovah-nissi* (Victory),[5] *Jehovah-shalom* (Peace),[6] etc.,—are summed up in I AM. He is sufficient.[7]

I AM. I need search no further. I can rest in the fullness, completeness, and absoluteness of the Great I AM.

Rest in the fullness, completeness,
and absoluteness of God: the Great I AM.

[1] 1 Kings 8:27 [2] Ps. 46:1 [3] Gen. 22:13–14 [4] Exod. 15:26 [5] Exod. 17:15 [6] Judg. 6:24 [7] 2 Pet. 1:3

MARCH 20

. . . Your name will no longer be Jacob, but Israel,
because you have struggled with God and with men and have overcome.
Genesis 32:28

*W*hat really happened that strange night at the fords of the Jabbok so many thousands of years ago? What was this struggle that so changed a man that God Himself renamed him? And not just any name! Consider: Abraham was the father of the faithful,[1] the one to whom the promises were given and with whom the covenant was made. Yet the people of God are not called Abrahamites. Isaac, his son, was the miracle child *through* whom the promises and the covenant were to come,[2] yet we are not named after Isaac.

It is Jacob, the *deceiver*, the *supplanter*, grasping and grabbing even from birth–the quiet, clean-faced, mama's boy who extracted his brother's birthright by extortion[3] and his blessing by a lie.[4] God had spoken a future over his unborn body[5] as He has spoken over us,[6] yet Jacob had not the spirit to wait and trust the Lord to make it happen; he had to con and manipulate, trying to bring about God's promise by man's means. The bitterness and hatred he sowed drove him away from all he knew and loved[7] and left him subject to a liar and a cheat for twenty years.[8] Does this sowing and reaping sound even slightly familiar yet?

And here he is, homeward bound, face to face with his past. His sins rise up to accuse him, to challenge his right to a relationship with God.[9] In wrestling with God, Jacob really wrestled against himself: all that he was versus all God had promised. He overcame–not God, because who can overcome God?–but himself. His past, his nature, his name. He refused to let God go, except He bless him.[10] God changed his name. And for the first time, God became Jacob's God: *El Elohe Israel*–God, the God of Israel.[11]

Jacob's story is our story. We, too, are like Israel. We struggle with God. We struggle against our past, our nature, ourselves. We overcome when we decide to hold onto God and not let go, except He bless us. He has promised to change our names, too.[12]

We overcome when we decide to hold onto God
and not let go, except He bless us.

[1]Heb. 11:11–12 [2]Gen. 17:21 [3]Gen. 25:26–34 [4]Gen. 27:1–40 [5]Gen. 25:23 [6]Jer. 29:11 [7]Gen. 27:41–45 [8]Gen. 31:38–42 [9]Gen. 32:7–12 [10]Gen. 32:26 [11]Gen. 33:20 [12]Rev. 2:17

MARCH 21

But he wanted to justify himself . . .
Luke 10:29

*W*hy would you ask a question to which you already know the answer? Consider the man, this lawyer, who asked Jesus, "What must I do to inherit eternal life?"[1] It was a loaded question; he already knew the answer. Pride made him speak it, but pride also made him hope it wasn't so. He wanted to justify himself.

"What must I do to inherit eternal life?"

"You know the answer; you are a lawyer. What does it say?"

"Love the Lord your God with everything in you, and love your neighbor as yourself."

"You have answered correctly . . . do this and you will live."[2]

We may shake our heads at the lawyer, but we are just as desperate for loopholes today. The way is simple, but narrow.[3] The answer hasn't changed, but our guilty hearts still grasp for an excuse—any excuse—to keep on doing as we always have. The lawyer hoped his loophole lay in the definition of *neighbor.*[4] If not everyone is my neighbor, then it is okay to go on hating or ignoring certain people. Our loopholes are not so different:

"Turn the other cheek."[5]

But God doesn't want me to be a doormat.

"Give to everyone who asks."[6]

But God doesn't want me to be used.

"Bless those who curse you,"[7]

But God knows I'm only human.

Pride wants to be right, and that zing of Holy Spirit conviction hurts,[8] so we ask questions loaded with reluctance, dissembling, and fear—fear that there is no loophole, that God actually meant what He said. And to our loaded questions, Jesus says, "What do the Scriptures say?"

I need to stop trying to justify myself, stop seeking a loophole, and instead seek to do the will of God with all my heart and with all my soul and with all my mind and with all my strength.

---

*I need to stop trying to justify myself,
stop seeking a loophole . . .*

---

[1]Luke 10:25 [2]Luke 10:26–29 [3]Matt. 7:14 [4]Luke 10:29 [5]Matt. 5:39 [6]Luke 6:30 [7]Luke 6:28
[8]John 16:8

MARCH 22

. . . break up your unplowed ground; for it is time to seek the LORD . . .
Hosea 10:12

*W*hen I was a child, our family farm had several fields that were fallow—unplowed, unplanted, unused. Weeds grew tall there, and a distinct air of wildness hung over them. One year, my father decided to plant potatoes in one of them. It was a lot of work just getting the field ready! The weeds had to be chopped down, and the ground itself—as hard-packed as stone—had to be plowed and broken up. This was an awful process, and the earth resisted vigorously. The field lay beside the woods, and thick roots reached deep and far beyond the edge of the trees out into the field. Over and over again, the plow hit unseen roots and buried boulders, and my father had to stop and deal with each one, digging it out of the way. The freshly turned earth steamed in the morning sun as hidden heat was suddenly released. We, too, steamed, because the turning had revealed more rocks. Rocks that had to be removed before the field could be planted.

What has all this got to do with following Jesus? God tells us to break up our unplowed ground, that it is time to seek the Lord. It is time. He is ready for us, calling for us to seek His face.[1] And we have been seeking Him[2]—calling to Him to speak to us more clearly,[3] to reveal Himself more deeply,[4] and to manifest in our lives more powerfully[5] than ever before.

But He tells us, "Break up your unplowed ground." There are areas of our lives untouched by Him, held back from His presence, from His hand. These are fields kept fallow—unplowed, unplanted, unused. They are covered with weeds,[6] hard and unbroken, hiding long roots of sin and bitterness,[7] our rocks and boulders of pain and hurt[8]—unproductive.[9]

Jesus says, "Let Me in. I can soften your hard ground. My love can remove those rocks and roots, and weed out your sin. I can plant seeds of healing and love, if you will let Me." It is time to seek the Lord. I don't have to be afraid to let Him into every part of my life.

Break up *your* unplowed ground.

God tells us to break up our unplowed ground,

that it is time to seek the Lord.

---

[1]Ps. 27:8   [2]Ps. 63:1   [3]1 Sam. 3:10   [4]John 14:8   [5]John 14:12   [6]Prov. 24:31   [7]Heb. 12:15
[8]Ezek. 36:26   [9]2 Pet. 1:8

MARCH 23

Then those who feared the Lord talked with each other, and the Lord listened and heard. A scroll of remembrance was written in his presence concerning those who feared the Lord and honored his name.

Malachi 3:16

It's hard to imagine God like a teenager, but I can't dismiss the imagery of this verse: a love-struck teenage girl keeping a diary, noting every wonderful word and look from the object of her desire! "Today he said I was his strong fortress . . ." "Oh, diary! She said my words in her heart were her songs in the night!"[1] "Thursday, 3:25 P.M. . . . Did you see the sparkle in their eyes when they lifted their hands to me?"

Think about it. God sees all, knows all, hears all. Every cry of pain and suffering. Each sigh of sorrow. Hot words of rage and anger, ugly words of hatred, chilling cries of fear. Bitter words of unforgiveness. Desperate pleas for help, for healing, for miracles. Requests and petitions; rote nursery-rhyme grace and bedtime bless me's, genuine needs and greedy gimmes. Love songs and lust moans. Shouts of praise drowned by screams of sex, drugs and rock 'n' roll.

And He remembers it all.[2] Jesus said that one day men will have to give an account for every careless word they have spoken.[3]

Yet the Scripture says that in the midst of all this cacophony, over all the noise of this sin-filled world, all heaven stops and God bends close to listen to the sound of His children speaking to each other words that honor Him. It says this blesses Him so much to hear us speaking wonderful things about Him that He instantly commands an angel to record it in His presence.

Did you not know that God can hurt? Genesis tells us that our constant sinfulness fills His heart with pain.[4] Anger, hatred, cruelty, carelessness, and indifference grieve Him.[5] Our words of love and honor cut through the harsh clamor of sin—and their sound is music to His ears and a balm of joy to His great heart of love. You and I can bless the Lord.[6] Let us do it! Let us speak often to each other of His goodness, to honor Him. He is listening.

Jesus said that one day men will have to give an account for every careless word they have spoken.

---

[1] Ps. 63:6–7   [2] Jude 1:15   [3] Matt. 12:36   [4] Gen. 6:6   [5] Isa. 63:10   [6] Ps. 34:1

MARCH 24

Above all else, guard your heart . . .
Proverbs 4:23

bove all else . . . above all desires, regrets, and fears; above all on which I spend my intentions and my energy. When life's worries, riches, pleasures, and disappointments[1] threaten to derail every spiritual good intention I have, I must above all else guard my heart. Unless I diligently guard it, my heart easily becomes hard, cold, insensitive, and cynical.[2] The unreliability, greed, and outright cruelty of people around me constantly wear down my capacity for mercy and compassion. My own acts of selfishness only feed the cycle, ripping at my attempts to grow childlike faith and hope.[3] The heat of my trials constantly threatens to set my heart like cement, and I have to consciously, earnestly overcome my natural self-preserving instincts[4] in order to love others as Jesus loves me.

Reminding myself of Jesus' constant, unconditional, sacrificial love for all of these obnoxious, inconsiderate, and selfish folks (myself included) is my first line of defense in guarding my heart.[5] Loving God above all else involves keeping the ugliness He hates out of my heart—not feeding on the tempting excitement of all that sensual, dog-eat-dog violence of the world (real *or* make believe). I have a lifetime of sinful input to counteract; I need massive doses of godly thoughts and visions of kindness, compassion, generosity, and humility[6] to soften my heart. After all, what goes in, comes out![7]

Having a heart melted with love for God makes it easier to have a soft heart toward others.[8] I must beware my old desire to close off my heart to the needs of the people God puts in my path.[9] Guarding my heart against hardness involves taking up the challenge to reach out, to be vulnerable, to sacrifice for the good of someone else[10]—in whatever way (big or small) and for however long it takes. And to trust God to heal the inevitable bruises and breaks that come with loving fallible people. After all, Jesus commanded me: "Love one another as I have loved you."[11]

Having a heart melted with love for God
makes it easier to have a soft heart toward others.

---

[1]Luke 8:14 [2]Zech. 7:8–12 [3]Matt. 18:4 [4]Luke 9:24–25 [5]Prov. 28:14 [6]James 3:17–18
[7]Matt. 12:34–35 [8]Mark 12:29–31 [9]Ps. 95:7–8 [10]Heb. 13:16 [11]John 15:12

MARCH 25

What should we do then? . . .
Luke 3:10

*W*hat do you think of when you think of doing the work of God? When John the Baptist's Spirit-fired calls to repentance drove the crowd to ask this question, he didn't tell anyone to quit his job and go preach. He told them to live their ordinary lives the way God intended—honestly, caringly, diligently. What John understood is that the work of God is not *doing*, it is *believing*.[1] *Being a believer* should be reflected in everything I do.[2]

It is a common misconception that secular work is not God's work. It is a trap of the enemy, compartmentalizing my life—separating what we deem to be religious activities from regular, everyday work and play, *God's* time from *my* time. It is Satan's sly way of keeping self on the throne. He would have me conveniently forget that I am part of a chosen people . . . people belonging to God . . .[3] It is *all* God's time. This is what the psalmist means by "the day is yours, and yours also the night."[4] To a person consistently conscious of God, everything becomes an act of worship. God's presence sanctifies it, making it holy. God prophesied that one day, "HOLY TO THE LORD" will be inscribed on such ordinary, everyday objects as horses' bells and cooking pots.[5] He will have a people so filled with His Spirit, so completely given over to Him that whatever they did would glorify Him.[6] We want to serve Him by preaching, teaching, or healing. But He may be calling us to serve Him instead by doing the dirty, everyday, thankless jobs that nobody else wants to do.[7]

What should we do then? My daily life, my everyday things,[8] my ordinary work done with consecration and praise to His glory and honor *is* the work of God.

Go and do likewise.[9]

To a person consistently conscious of God,
everything becomes an act of worship.

---

[1]John 6:29 [2]James 2:14–17 [3]1 Pet. 2:9 [4]Ps. 74:16 [5]Zech. 14:20 [6]John 15:8 [7]John 13:3–5 [8]Prov. 8:34 [9]Luke 10:37

MARCH 26

*. . . unless a kernel of wheat falls to the ground and dies,
it remains only a single seed. But if it dies, it produces many seeds.*
John 12:24

*J*esus was speaking of His glorification—of that magnificent, horrendous hour of being lifted up from the earth and drawing all men to Himself.[1] That is not what I usually think of when I think of glory. I've always thought of glory as being more, well—comfortable. Light and airy. I don't know why; Jesus said He'd brought glory to His Father by completing the work He'd been sent to do.[2] That work involved a lot of agony, humiliation, rejection, and scorn—blood, sweat, and tears. His manner of glorifying God included being lied about, betrayed, and arrested. He was spit upon and beaten. His own glorification was a torturous, shameful death. He was that kernel of wheat, falling and dying—and producing many seeds.

We are those seeds. We are the ones created for His glory.[3] He gave Peter a glimpse of the kind of *death* (not life) by which he would glorify God.[4] Although music and meditation and prayers are means of giving glory to God, the kind of glorifying that makes the world sit up and take notice is more often the kind that comes through intense and horrendous suffering.

Everyone suffers; this world is full of pain. But the kind of suffering Jesus meant is that *purposeful* suffering of taking up my cross, submitting to His re-creating process in my life,[5] and following Him. I can choose to accept my suffering as suffering *for* Him, *with* Him.[6] It is in the struggle that I get to know Jesus more deeply,[7] and to show Jesus to others.

For years, I had been taught that God intends His children to be blessed, to prosper in every aspect of their lives. I even heard one preacher say that wealth brought God more glory than poverty—as if my being poor was bad advertising for God. But I am one of those many seeds,[8] and I want to glorify God with every part of my life. I am willing to let my life fall to the ground and die in order to do it.

---

*The kind of suffering Jesus meant
is that purposeful suffering of taking up my cross . . .*

---

[1]John 12:32   [2]John 17:4   [3]Isa. 43:7   [4]John 21:19   [5]Matt. 12:33   [6]Heb. 13:12–13   [7]Jer. 9:24
[8]John 17:20

MARCH 27

*. . . I was neither a prophet nor a prophet's son,
but I was a shepherd, and I also took care of sycamore-fig trees.*

Amos 7:14

The catch-22 of job hunting is that experience requirement: you have to get it in order to have it, and you can't get it unless you have it. Not so with God! He chooses those who are poor in the eyes of the world . . . to inherit the kingdom.[1] He isn't looking for impressive résumés, star quality, or Olympic ability. In fact, extraordinary qualifications often get in the way of usability.

If it's not experience or ability that God desires, then what *is* He looking for? He certainly doesn't consider what we consider. Israel loved Saul because he was tall and handsome;[2] they rejected Jesus because He had no beauty or majesty to attract us to him.[3] We already know that God doesn't care a fig about the outward appearance, but that He looks at the heart.[4] We *know* this, and yet we continue to discredit and discount our usefulness to God because we, like Amos, are not seminary graduates; we get tongue-tied talking to a grocery clerk, and we have a family history more like a rogue's gallery than a Who's Who Roster of Righteousness. We think God can't possibly use us.

There are only two abilities necessary to the call of God: availability and teachability—or as He says, "If you are willing and obedient . . ."[5] After all, *He* is the One who will be doing the work,[6] speaking the words,[7] touching the heart.[8] He alone has the power to convict and to convert;[9] I am merely the vessel.[10] I am His skin and bones. All He needs is someone so in love with Him that they have stopped fighting Him. They go where He says to go, they do what He says to do, and they speak what He tells them to speak.

Do you love the Lord? Are you available? Are you teachable? God can take you from tending the flock.[11] He can use you.

---

*There are only two abilities necessary to the call of God:
availability and teachability.*

---

[1]James 2:5 [2]1 Sam. 9:2 [3]Isa. 53:2 [4]1 Sam. 16:7 [5]Isa. 1:19 [6]John 14:10 [7]Luke 21:15
[8]John 12:32 [9]John 16:8 [10]Jer. 18:6 [11]Amos 7:15

MARCH 28

. . . the God we serve is able to save us . . .
But even if He does not . . . we will not serve your gods . . .
Daniel 3:17–18

Is my faith an *even if* faith? The barometer of spiritual surrender is in the *even if* responses of God.[1] I should examine the desires of my heart: what if God were to refuse this, that—even each cherished hope I hold? Is there a desire, a fervent prayer deep in the center of my being for which I would not accept a *no* answer from God?

God is both omniscient and omnipotent. If God were not also love, this would be frightening! But Calvary proves that God is, indeed, love.[2] The question is, how much do I *believe* His love? Faith in God is the absolute conviction that He does what He does because He loves me and truly knows what is best. Faith is not just knowing that God is love; faith is *relying* on the love of God.[3] It is this conviction that says yes to God *even if* He says *no* to me.

God does not negotiate, bargain for, nor buy our worship. Those who come to Him on a quid-pro-quo, tit-for-tat, you-scratch-my-back-and-I'll-worship-You basis[4] have completely misjudged their condition. Without the mercy of God, I am dead; decayed dust; no brain, no breath, no bargaining power. What I was offering Him He calls filthy rags.[5] He is my Presiding Judge, with a *legal mandate* to order the death penalty[6] for my fully guilty soul.[7] He holds all the cards, and I stand speechless, with blood on my hands, the blood of His own Son.

Instead of banging down the gavel, though, He looks me straight in the eye and offers me mercy:[8] a full pardon and a welcome into His very own family![9]

A God like that can do anything He wants with me, *even if.*

Faith is relying on the love of God. It is this conviction
that says yes to God, even if He says no to me.

---

[1]Job 1:21 [2]1 John 4:8 [3]1 John 4:16 [4]Mic. 6:6–7 [5]Isa. 64:6 [6]John 8:24 [7]1 Kings 8:46
[8]James 2:13 [9]1 John 3:1

MARCH 29

Why were you searching for me? . . .
Luke 2:49

*M*ary and Joseph had been called for one of the most awesome tasks ever given to a human: raising God's own Son, the Savior of the world. Among the several reasons God chose them was their faith, and their willingness to do God's will in spite of the consequences.[1] For twelve years they had done so, through taxing journeys, a stable, being hunted by a king, fleeing to Egypt, and returning to Nazareth in the face of their neighbors' gossip. Every year, they dutifully and carefully obeyed God to pilgrimage to Jerusalem for the Passover.[2] Though they were poor, it was vital that Jesus walk in the faith of the fathers.

Twelve years—and still they lost sight of Jesus.

The daily struggles, obstacles, and endurance involved in walking in our callings and pressing through our purpose sometimes numbs our awareness of God's presence—or His absence.[3] Jesus can be accomplishing His promises and purposes all around us, in the midst of our lives, but routine can blind us so we don't recognize it.[4] We get so used to doing and doing, we sometimes forget why He called us to do it in the first place.[5] As the saying goes, we get so caught up beating off the alligators, we forget that we came to drain the swamp!

Like Mary and Joseph, too, the way we've always done things can make us deaf to a change of season. Jesus was twelve; it was time for Him to be about His Father's business. Our seasons change, too. God does not continually plow us. There comes a time of planting, then a season of watering and waiting before the harvest is ready to then be reaped.[6] Different seasons call for different things to be done in different ways,[7] and if we continue as we always have,[8] losing sight of Jesus, we may actually end up getting in the way, interfering with what He is trying to accomplish—even negating it.

"Why were you searching for me?" Seeking God is a constant process in our lives. I need to beware of assuming that *what* and *how* God did things in the past is what and how He will keep on doing. I must pay careful attention so I don't drift off in the wrong direction.[9]

Why am I not conscious of His presence—or His absence?

[1]Matt. 1:18–25 [2]Luke 2:41–42 [3]Judg. 16:20 [4]Matt. 13:15 [5]Isa. 42:6 [6]Isa. 28:24–29 [7]Isa. 43:18–19 [8]2 John 1:9 [9]Heb. 2:1

MARCH 30

for he breaks down gates of bronze and cuts through bars of iron.
Psalm 107:16

*I*t took a few readings of this passage before the sweetness of its promise hit me. This is protection, rescue, and deliverance aimed at—not the righteous, not the pure and holy, not the "deserving," but the rebellious, those suffering the consequences of their own foolish choices! This was a place in Scripture where I could put my own name and not feel like a fraud. This was me! God had not been my hope, nor my confidence since my youth.[1] He had certainly not been my God from my mother's womb.[2] No—I had rebelled against the words of God; I had despised the counsel of the Most High.[3] These were people like me—not the persecuted saints who suffer for the name of Christ; My heart broke when I read that "If you suffer, it should not be as a murderer or thief or any other kind of criminal, or even as a meddler."[4] I felt rejected, crossed off the list of those to whom God would show mercy, because I was certainly suffering for my own sins, my own rebellion against God. How dare I ask for deliverance? "Serves you right!" is what I expected.

But then I found Psalm 107. What an awesome song of God's mercy and grace! See if you can see yourself in its verses. They speak of rebellious, disobedient, despising, wicked fools. It says they are suffering for their own sinful ways. Not a pretty picture, but accurate.

And rather than glorying in the punishment God could justly dish out to those foolish sinners—to us—the psalmist sings of God's mercy: He hears our cries of repentance and charges to the rescue! He bursts on the scene, smashes down those impenetrable bronze gates, and utterly shatters our iron chains! He soothes our distress,[5] heals our afflictions,[6] and sets the prisoners free.[7] He even rides in on a white stallion to do it.[8]

How eager is our God to hear one honest cry of repentance! How quick He is to deliver! This is our God—this is *my* God, for that foolish rebel was me. We were all foolish rebels, so this is for you, too.

God is eager to hear our honest cry of repentance
and He is quick to deliver!

---

[1]Ps. 71:5   [2]Ps. 22:10   [3]Ps. 107:11   [4]1 Pet. 4:15   [5]Ps. 107:13   [6]Ps. 107:20   [7]Ps. 146:7   [8]Rev. 19:11

MARCH 31

They overcame him by the blood of the Lamb
and by the word of their testimony . . .
Revelation 12:11

*O*vercame whom? The accuser, who accuses us day and night.[1] We have but one enemy, though he speaks through many voices. I hear his accusations in the voice of my past. He has a photographic memory, and he loves to replay my every unholy act, telling me I have gone too far to be rescued or used by God. When he sees me struggling, he accuses me for still having ungodly thoughts and desires. He speaks through the scorn of people around me, who doubt my faith and mock every effort to live holy.[2] I hear him in the voice of my circumstances, telling me God can't be trusted, that I've been abandoned.[3] He piles on guilt and discouragement. His goal? To get me to quit. Give up. Turn back.[4]

Jesus never said it would be easy. He told us it would require sacrifice.[5] He said we'd be betrayed, imprisoned, hated, even killed.[6] He said to count the cost, because abandoning my purpose half-way through would leave me with nothing but mockery.[7] Only those who endure *to the end* will be saved.[8] In all the letters in Revelation, there are no prizes for those who do not finish, only for those who *overcome*. Overcoming means sticking with it and not shrinking back;[9] not giving up, enduring to the end—no matter how much (or how much *more*) God asks of us.[10]

This overcoming in the face of insurmountable odds *is* the word of our testimony. *Testimony* comes from the Greek *martyria*, also meaning "evidence" and "good reputation."[11] This means my testimony is the evidence of the whole trend of my life in Christ, not just a moment of preaching. Giving up is not overcoming.

And overcoming is done only by the blood of the Lamb. It is the only way to overcome from the inside out: not just a whitewashed job, but a true new birth.[12] *Jesus* is the one who has overcome the world.[13] He is the only one who can do it in me, if I rely only on the power of His blood, not my own cleverness or self-discipline. Only on the precious blood of the Lamb!

Only those who endure to the end will be saved.

---

[1]Rev. 12:10 [2]Matt. 5:11 [3]Job 19:7–10 [4]Job 2:9 [5]Luke 14:33 [6]Luke 21:12–17 [7]Luke 14:28–30
[8]Mark 13:13 [9]Heb. 10:38 [10]Luke 12:48 [11]*Strongest:* p. 1,569 [12]Matt. 23:27 [13]John 16:33

APRIL 1

*Jesus answered him, "I tell you the truth,
today you will be with me in paradise."*
Luke 23:43

The thief on the cross: the epitome of last-minute, deathbed confessions. Except as an inspiration to say, "It's never too late,"[1] I'd never really credited much to him as a shining example . . . until it hit me what he really did.

Picture the scene: Jesus, betrayed by a friend,[2] rejected by His own people,[3] handed over to the enemy Romans—mocked, beaten, crucified.[4] All but a few of His followers have abandoned Him;[5] those who remain stay at a distance, silent. Everyone else is heaping insults and abuse on Him, even one of the criminals suffering the same punishment.[6]

In everyone's eyes, it is over. There is no glory, no Messiah, no Savior, no hope.[7] All His teaching, all of the healings, every miracle—all for nothing. Jesus is dying, and death is the end of everything. (Sure, Jesus raised people from the dead, but if *Jesus* is dead, who can raise *Him*?[8])

Yet in the face of this apparently total defeat, against all of the evidence bleeding and suffocating to death beside him, this one man—not even one of the disciples—proclaims the victorious Messiahship of the Son of God: "Jesus, remember me when you come into your kingdom."

What a confession! When it looked like there was *no way* it could ever happen, when the very idea seemed completely impossible, this one man alone declared his faith in Jesus and in the absolute reality of His kingdom! *He alone* believed that death itself would not stop Jesus[9] from being all He said He was, and from doing all He said He would do. And he wasn't ashamed to say so.

Is that the kind of faith I have? What obstacles loom between me and what Jesus has promised me?[10] Does it seem impossible?[11] Have I lost hope? Or—when I look to Jesus, do I see what the dying thief saw, and *believe*?

---

*Death itself will not stop Jesus from being all He said
He was, and from doing all He said He would do.*

---

[1]Heb. 4:7 [2]Mark 14:17–20 [3]John 1:11 [4]Matt. 27:26–31 [5]Matt. 26:56 [6]Luke 23:39
[7]Luke 24:20–21 [8]John 10:17–18 [9]John 11:25–26 [10]Heb. 10:23 [11]Luke 1:37

APRIL 2

*After this I looked, and there before me was a door
standing open in heaven. And the voice I had first heard . . . said,
"Come up here, and I will show you . . ."*
Revelation 4:1

erspective is everything. What is high—or low? What is long? What is short? What is a lot, or a little? How much is too much? It all depends on your perspective. Is God's way hard?[1] Yes, but the question really is, "Is it worth it?" Many worshippers of God have lived lives of privation and persecution. They have been tortured, chained, stoned and destitute.[2] Believers throughout the ages have always been handed over to be persecuted and put to death.[3] How could they continue in such a life? Not only the heroes of the faith listed in *Foxe's Book of Martyrs*, but everyday people all over the world today suffer beatings with whips and rods, imprisonment and torture, community expulsion, extreme hardship and poverty, even execution. Not many unbelievers would consider it worth all that, but servants of God endure it to follow in Jesus' steps.[4] How is it possible? Perspective. This life is only flesh, and the flesh counts for nothing.[5] I am not looking at this life. When I come up to heaven's door, nothing in this life looks the same. It is the perspective of eternity.

That's how Abraham could wander through Canaan as a stranger and a pilgrim and be content.[6] That's how Job could say, "Though he slay me, yet will I trust in him."[7] Because he could also say, "I know that my Redeemer lives . . . in my flesh I will see God."[8] That's how Jesus endured the cross, scorning its shame—because He kept His eyes on the joy set before Him.[9]

When I start to feel overwhelmed and overpowered, I come up to heaven's door and fortify my spirit with the joy set before me: an eternity of peace, joy, and holiness in the beautiful presence of our loving God and Father.[10] Oh, yes, it is worth it!

Perspective is everything.

---

*Nothing in this life looks the same
once you have the perspective of eternity.*

---

[1]Mark 10:24   [2]Heb.11:35–38   [3]Matt. 24:9   [4]1 Pet. 2:20–21   [5]John 6:63   [6]Heb. 11:13–16
[7]Job 13:15 [KJV]   [8]Job 19:25–26   [9]Heb. 12:2   [10]Rev. 21–22

APRIL 3

. . . for my house will be called a house of prayer for all nations.
Isaiah 56:7

I have read this verse many times, and each time, my understanding zeroed in on the "for all nations" part: no one is excluded, no matter your nationality. This is not incorrect, either, because it is part of a larger prophecy about foreigners who bind themselves to the Lord to serve him.[1]

Yet when Jesus quoted this verse in the gospels, He was not talking about the international aspects of the temple. Jesus instead focused on the fact that His Father's house is a *house of prayer*.

A house of prayer. Consider the significance of that! Of all the ways and words God could've used to describe His temple, He chose prayer. Not healing, not salvation, not preaching nor teaching, nor even praise and worship! Why is that? Isn't a temple a place of worship? Are we not told to enter His courts with praise? *We* call churches houses of worship—why doesn't God? Could it be that prayer is not a part of worship, but that worship is a part of prayer? The gift of salvation is a gift of restored relationship with God, and prayer is the essence and manifestation of relationship: communication. Remember Jesus' warning? "Apart from me you can do nothing."[2]

Beyond that, however, is the realization that God chose "house of prayer" to describe His dwelling place because it is fellowship with Him.[3] Prayer is the intimate communion of our spirit with His—the fellowship and relationship lost in Eden because of sin.[4] Do we not yet realize how achingly God has longed to fellowship with us?[5] How much delight He takes in sharing our heart and His thoughts—how long He has waited to have a conversation with us?[6] We have been estranged for too long, and now His family is back![7]

There is no temple. The dwelling place of God is now in our hearts.[8] We carry this house of prayer with us wherever we go. Our prayers are unbound! Let's talk with our Father.

Prayer: the intimate communion of our spirit with God's—
the fellowship and relationship lost in Eden
because of sin.

---

[1]Isa. 56:6 [2]John 15:5 [3]1 John 1:3 [4]Gen. 3:9 [5]Isa. 30:18 [6]Zeph. 3:17 [7]Rev. 21:3–4
[8]John 14:17

APRIL 4

The twelve gates were twelve pearls,
each gate made of a single pearl. . . .
Revelation 21:21

e already know that we enter his gates with thanksgiving,[1] but have you ever given thought to the gates themselves? As we approach the rainbow-jeweled, breathtaking beauty of the holy city,[2] our eyes are drawn to the magnificence of these gates. Glitteringly iridescent, it is stunning to realize that each gate is made of a *single pearl*. One. One precious jewel immense enough to be a gate through a wall that measures nearly 200 feet thick![3] How is it even possible? And what can it mean?

Consider how pearls are formed: an irritant—a grain of sand, perhaps—works its way into the tender parts of a shellfish and becomes lodged like a splinter. Wrongly dealt with, the constant friction and aggravation would wear a hole right through the mollusk's shell. To prevent such a gaping wound, the shellfish responds to the irritation by putting forth nacre—the gracefully beautiful mother-of-pearl that covers over the irritant, transforming it into a valuable gem.[4]

And *graceful* is exactly the word to describe nacre. It is divinely beautiful, and it is so much more than that splinter deserves. It is grace-full; and it is only by the all-sufficient grace of God that we can overcome every irritating, aggravating, thorny source of friction in our lives.[5] The world pokes, jabs, rubs us the wrong way, offends and irritates.[6] When we, in response, exude God's grace, a marvelous transformation occurs: that which was harsh and ugly becomes a thing of beauty, precious and infinitely valuable.[7]

By the experience, we enter into the presence of God, into the place where purity, holiness and righteousness dwell.[8] Ultimately, the sum of all our trials and tribulations, suffered with grace, are honored by God and made beautiful—made into the very gates of glory.

When we exude God's grace,
a marvelous transformation occurs: that which was
harsh and ugly becomes a thing of beauty.

---

[1]Ps. 100:4   [2]Rev. 21:11   [3]Rev. 21:17   [4]James 5:20   [5]James 4:6–7   [6]Prov. 19:11   [7]Isa. 61:3–4
[8]Heb. 12:10–11

APRIL 5

Then the LORD said to Moses, "Why are you crying out to me?
Tell the Israelites to move on."
Exodus 14:15

God never does anything halfway. When He delivers, He delivers completely. He saves you completely.[1] When you cooperate with God, not one shred, no shadow, no skeleton from your past can come and snatch you back into slavery.

Consider the Israelites, marching out boldly from a broken Egypt.[2] Their deliverance was not their doing; it was so obviously the power of God that His terrifying miracles were still being talked about by Israel's enemies centuries later![3] When Pharaoh's army came riding out after them (the slavery of their past trying to drag them back), God was not surprised nor caught off-guard—and neither should the Israelites have been. God had already told them Pharaoh would do this.[4] God had specifically and deliberately led them to this particular spot, told them what was coming—and reassured them that He was in control and the glory would be great. Their fear and panic is like mine—forgetting how God has already delivered, suddenly doubting (again) His love.

I shouldn't shake my head at Israel if I have ever panicked at the threat of disaster. This message is for me, too. I know the devil does not let his slaves go easily. But he is nothing more than Pharaoh with his army, about to drown in their own insolence. "The Egyptians you see today, you will never see again."[5]

When I'm between a rock and a hard place—between the devil and the deep Red Sea—I can't forget all that my mighty God has already done for me.[6] Why should I cry out in terror, as if God has changed His mind about delivering me? What He says, He will accomplish.[7] I will look to Him in anticipation and awe, ready to glorify Him for His certain rescue. And I will move forward.

When you are between a rock and a hard place
don't forget all that your mighty God
has already done for you.

---

[1]Heb. 7:25 [2]Exod. 14:8 [3]1 Sam. 4:8 [4]Exod. 14:4 [5]Exod. 14:13 [6]Ps. 105:5 [7]Isa. 55:11

APRIL 6

But as for me, I am filled with power,
with the Spirit of the Lord . . .
Micah 3:8

O
h, to be a Micah among the people of God today! Oh, to be so drenched with power from on high,[1] saturated with such a Spirit of holy boldness that nothing intimidates me from my victory! I'm not talking about self-confidence. We know we can place no confidence in the flesh.[2] But some of us have been so schooled in the attitude of weakness, we've forgotten the promise of God: "He gives strength to the weary and increases the power of the weak."[3]

I have no business being defeated, because nothing can defeat the power of God. Jesus never flinched in the face of Satan. He was never out of control or lost command of a situation. Demons could shout, scream, and foam at the mouth all they wanted at Him, and Jesus would simply tell them to shut up and leave. And they'd obey, usually testifying to His power and authority as they fled in terror.

"But, that was Jesus," you say.

Exactly. That was Jesus, who laid aside His divine power[4] and was made like us—His brothers—*in every way*.[5] That was Jesus, who humbled Himself and did nothing on His own,[6] but allowed His Father to do it in Him.[7] Just as we are to do it. That was Jesus—the very Jesus who lives in me.[8]

And it is this same Jesus who gave us the authority to trample all over Satan and to overcome all the power of the enemy.[9] I'll say it again: we have the *authority* (the right and the duty) to utterly *stomp* Satan and to *overcome . . . all . . . the . . . power . . . of . . . the . . . enemy.* We must stop looking at our flesh and saying, "Weak!" We should look at the Greater One in us and say, *"Strong!"*[10] I won't waste my time holding a long conversation with the devil—I should just tell him, "The Lord rebuke you!"[11] Then I can go about the business of the Lord in power and victory.

We have no business being defeated,
because nothing can defeat the power of God.

---

[1] Luke 24:49   [2] Ps. 49:12–13   [3] Isa. 40:29   [4] John 5:30   [5] Heb. 2:17   [6] John 8:28   [7] John 14:10   [8] 1 John 4:4   [9] Luke 10:19   [10] Joel 3:10   [11] Jude 1:9

APRIL 7

Truly you are a God who hides himself,
O God and Savior of Israel.
Isaiah 45:15

To know that there is a God, that He is separate from and far above the material world, is knowledge available to all mankind. Everything around me declares there is a God—a God of power and wisdom.[1] It is so obvious, in fact, that to not comprehend the existence of God is utterly foolish.[2]

Yet there is a vast gulf of difference between knowing God *is*, and *knowing God*. Why is this so? Why is it so hard to find God? If He is not willing that any should perish, but that all should come to repentance,[3] then why does He not simply show up and show out? Though His voice roars and thunders[4] as loud as a trumpet,[5] why does He prefer to speak to us in such a still small voice[6] that most miss it completely or ignore it?

How does a God who fills heaven and earth[7] hide Himself? When I seek God, what do I look for? Where do I start? Remember, God is spirit,[8] and it is the Spirit who reveals Jesus to us.[9] I cannot see God with eyeball vision. But how do I get spiritual vision? I must be born again. "No one can *see* the kingdom of God unless he is born again."[10] God is hidden from the unsaved and the unspiritual. Jesus also said, "Whoever has my commands and obeys them, he is the one who loves me . . . and I too will love him and show myself to him."[11] God is hidden from the disobedient.

"Truly you are a God who hides himself." He is hidden from the wicked, from the rebellious, from the insincere. "You will seek me and find me when you seek me with all your heart. I will be found by you."[12]

When God is not just God—when He is *my* God; when my love for Him kindles a hunger in me that burns like a fire; when my spirit is at peace with Him in agreement—then my spiritual eyes shall see God all around me. I will see Him in every smile, every laugh, in beauty, in kindness, and in thousands of small acts of favor each day. I will see Him in every need and opportunity that comes my way. He will no longer be a God who hides Himself from me.

There is a vast gulf of difference between
knowing God is, and knowing God.

---

[1]Ps. 19:1–4   [2]Ps. 14:1   [3]2 Pet. 3:9 [KJV]   [4]Amos 1:2   [5]Rev. 1:10   [6]1 Kings 19:12 [KJV]   [7]Jer. 23:24
[8]John 4:24   [9]John 16:12–15   [10]John 3:3   [11]John 14:21   [12]Jer. 29:13–14

APRIL 8

*. . . as soon as the priests who carried the ark reached the Jordan
and their feet touched the water's edge,
the water from upstream stopped flowing. . . .*
Joshua 3:15–16

ollowing God in faith can be scary. It's as if He lets me see the path and its hazards, then blindfolds me and says, "Trust Me. I will lead you."[1] I must ignore what I've seen (or imagined), discount the facts and stand firm in the truth,[2] and to go forward in absolute trust that the truth of God overrides physical reality. Since I'm following a God who speaks a universe into existence out of nothingness–literally, "now you don't see it, now you do"–then the *facts* are only what *is* for the moment, and the truth is all the possibility and power of God in His Word. Facts are subject to change; truth is eternal.[3] Big thought, big philosophy–but what does that look like for me?

I thought about the Israelites camped on the edge of Canaan–the only thing between forty years' worth of wilderness wandering and the long-awaited Promised Land was a river. At full flood stage,[4] the Jordan might as well have been a solid stone wall. If you've never seen a river at flood stage, you need to obliterate any image you have of "Ol' Man River" rolling calmly by under a placid moon. Picture instead a tree-chewing, rock-rumbling, roaring wall of mud and water.

Those are the facts. The truth is, God said to go forward and take possession of the Promised Land. Tell the priests to take up the ark and step into the Jordan; I'll stop the water, and you'll cross on dry ground.[5] Sounds like a Red Sea replay. Except this time, God waited until "Their feet touched the water's edge" before He activated the miracle.

If I had to see if happen first, I would still be standing on the riverbank– *outside* the Promised Land—waiting for God to stop the water before I took a step forward.[6] If I could let go and trust God, I'd get the soles of my feet wet. *But only the soles.*

"When you pass through the rivers, they will not sweep over you."[7]

---

*Following God in faith means
discounting the facts to stand firm in the truth.*

---

[1]Isa. 42:16   [2]John 7:24   [3]Isa. 40:8   [4]Josh. 3:15   [5]Josh. 3:13   [6]Exod. 14:15   [7]Isa. 43:2

APRIL 9

Woe to you who long for the day of the LORD!
Why do you long for the day of the LORD?
That day will be darkness, not light.

Amos 5:18

The greatest need among believers today is for the heart of God to be manifested through us. There has been much talk of love, true love, unconditional love—and we still do not understand it. We long for Christ's coming, for the day of the Lord, because of what it means for us. But what does it mean for God, whose love is so overwhelming, it is not merely a part of Him, it *is* Him?[1] Remember, the Scripture says that God loves us with an *everlasting* love.[2] He loved us when we hated Him, which is why He went so far as He did to save us.[3] He did this for the *whole world*. Everybody. You, me, and all those people who are still hating Him, because they don't really know Him. All those people who are going to die an eternal death when Jesus comes back.

Yes, they brought it on themselves. But that is not going to make it any easier for God to destroy them. God is love. Destroying the objects of His love is such a terrible, heart-wrenching thing that the Bible calls it, "his strange work . . . his alien task."[4] Although the horrible roar of destruction will be beyond imagination, above all the cries of the condemned will be the anguished cry of God: "Why will you die, O house of Israel?"[5] "How often I have longed to gather your children together . . . but you were not willing."[6]

If I am ever to become one with God, I must hate what God hates and love what He loves. He hates sin, but He takes no pleasure in the death of anyone;[7] He does not gloat over their punishment.[8] If I long for the day of the Lord, then I should long to bring everyone with me! I can pray for them in passionate intercession,[9] crying out for them, "Mercy!"[10] I can love them with the kind of love that Jesus loved me with. The only way I can— with the loving heart of my Father God.

The greatest need in the among believers today
is for the heart of God to be manifested through us.

---

[1]1 John 4:8   [2]Jer. 31:3   [3]Luke 18:31–33   [4]Isa. 28:21   [5]Ezek. 33:11   [6]Matt. 23:37   [7]Ezek. 18:32
[8]Prov. 24:17–18   [9]Ezek. 22:30   [10]James 2:13

APRIL 10

My food . . . is to do the will of him who sent me . . .

John 4:34

I have cried out long and hard for discernment, for the knowledge of God's will for me, for my life. Yet God does not reveal His entire will, His complete plan for my life in one dramatic, 3D Technicolor vision. In this, as in all things, God leads me step by step. And at every step, I will be tested. I should expect it! God reveals His plans and purposes only to His chosen ones.[1] Who are His chosen ones? Those who love Him, and who show that love through willing, faithful obedience.[2] Before God ever reveals His specific will for me, He watches to see how faithful I am to His general will for all. He laid out this principle when He said, "Whoever can be trusted with very little can also be trusted with much."[3]

What is His general will? When I read the Bible, I discover His will—His overall will for everybody. "He has showed you, O man, what is good . . ."[4] "Of course," I say, "I know all that. But I want to know what *my* gifts are. Do You want me to teach? To preach? To be a missionary?" That was the question the rich young ruler had asked Jesus: "What must I do . . . ?"[5]

What has God already told me to do? Am I doing it? "One thing you lack," Jesus told him[6]—and directed him right back to God's general will: selflessness, care for others, and following Him.

I will not discover my specific purpose if I am not faithful to walk in His overall purpose to hear Him, know Him, and become like Him. I will spend a lifetime growing in perfection in His general will.[7] It is *only in this process* that I will fulfill my specific purpose. James 1:22: "Be doers of the word and not hearers only," is quoted so often, yet its power is not diminished. Do I really want to hear God? Do I honestly want to know His will? I must listen carefully and do whatever He tells me.[8]

God leads you step by step.

And at every step, you will be tested.

Expect it!

---

[1]Amos 3:7 [2]John 14:21 [3]Luke 16:10 [4]Mic. 6:8 [5]Mark 10:17 [6]Mark 10:21 [7]Heb. 10:14 [8]John 2:5

APRIL 11

When the cherubim stood still, they also stood still;
and when the cherubim rose, they rose with them,
because the spirit of the living creatures was in them.

Ezekiel 10:17

*I*n visions of God,[1] Ezekiel saw the glory of heaven's throne. The intricacy of its workings so amazed him that he went on at length, describing its beauty as if it were a perfectly choreographed ballet. As I read of glittering, chrysolite wheels and fantastical living creatures, I was impressed, but not particularly moved. How could all that help me today? Then I read this verse, and the Holy Spirit began to speak: "They move together as one, because *the spirit of the living creatures is in the wheels.*"

The Holy Spirit of the Living God is in me.[2] When I pray, "Your will be done on earth as it is in heaven,"[3] I, myself, am to be the answer to that prayer. I must learn to move in concert with the Holy Spirit, because the Spirit always does the will of God. The Holy Spirit is not given to me to empower *my* plans, but to enable me to do *His* will, to fulfill *His* plans.

I thought about the message given to King Asa by the prophet Azariah during a time of deep revival in Judah: "Listen to me . . . the LORD is with you when you are with him. If you seek him, he will be found by you . . ."[4] It is not a matter of God being on *my* side; the truth is, *I* must be on *God's* side. "He who is not with me is against me," Jesus said.[5] I must not ask God to bless *my* plans, *my* pre-conceived ideas, *my* will; I must seek *His* will, *His* path. The Bible tells me that for the one who fears Him, God will instruct him in the way chosen for him.[6] *God* chooses my path. The Lord does not change His direction to suit me. If I want to walk with God, I must walk in the direction He is going, moving in concert with His Spirit, which is in me. I must stand still when He stands still, and rise up when He rises up.

True worship is total surrender. "Do two walk together unless they have agreed to do so?"[7] Total surrender is a beautiful ballet, each partner perfectly in step with the other, moving with the beat of one heart.

The Holy Spirit is not given to us to empower our plans,
but to enable us to do His will, to fulfill His plans.

---

[1]Ezek. 8:3   [2]John 14:17   [3]Matt. 6:10   [4]2 Chron. 15:2   [5]Luke 11:23   [6]Ps. 25:12   [7]Amos 3:3

APRIL 12

. . . Because you have prayed to me concerning Sennecherib king of Assyria,
this is the word the LORD has spoken against him . . .
Isaiah 37:21–22

$\mathcal{W}$hat, *really*, is the purpose of prayer? God knows our needs before we ask.[1] So, praying *isn't* to keep God informed. Proverbs reminds us, too, that God's purpose *will* prevail.[2] So, how much do our prayers affect the course of events? How necessary is prayer? Jesus prayed, and He specifically taught us—not only to pray but how to pray and even what to pray about.[3] He even told a parable especially to teach us to always pray and not give up.[4] I have heard of people's experiences being prompted by God to pray for someone and of the amazing answers—even miracles—that followed.

When I think of those accounts, I always wonder, *What would have happened if they hadn't prayed?* Why does God ask us to ask Him to do something He already wants to do? What is it about prayer? Did King Hezekiah's prayer in today's verse change the course of history?

King Hezekiah got a miracle in response to his prayer about the Assyrians. Others have been healed . . . but many others have not. I know there is power in prayer. How much heartache could be avoided if we only prayed?[5] But I also know that God is not a puppet that can be forced to act because we pray. Is it that prayer changes *things* or that prayer changes *us*?

There is so much that God wants to accomplish in me and through me. Knowing Him is essential.[6] Knowing His will is a lifelong journey of seeking, testing, proving, and seeking some more. I have spent much of my life *out* of His will; learning to hear and understand what He wants in my life takes a lot of practice.

That is what prayer is: seeking to know God and to follow Him.[7] Although He can use me in spite of me, He wants me to be His child and become like Him.[8] Maybe Hezekiah's answer wasn't so much the miraculous delivery as it was the revelation of God's intentions, of His heart.[9]

"Call to me and I will answer you and show you great and unsearchable things you do not know."[10] *That* is what prayer is all about.

That is what prayer is:
seeking to know God and to follow Him.

---

[1]Matt. 6:8 [2]Prov. 19:21 [3]Matt. 6:5–13 [4]Luke 18:1–8 [5]Ezek. 22:30–31 [6]John 17:3
[7]Ps. 25:12, 14 [8]Ps. 32:8–9 [9]Gen. 18:17–19 [10]Jer. 33:3

APRIL 13

*His divine power has given us everything we need for life
and godliness through our knowledge of him who called us
by his own glory and goodness.*

2 Peter 1:3

*W*hat a wondrous statement! What tremendous, life-changing power this sentence contains! This is it. This is what Jesus meant when He roared, "It is finished!" from the cross. In that moment of supreme surrender, not only did the Son of God re-open the way to the Tree of Life and restore eternity to mankind, He gave us back the ability to live godly, to be holy. Everything we need for life and godliness has been bought, paid for, gift-wrapped, and given. Past tense. Done deal.

What do *I* need to live godly? More love? Some joy, perhaps? Peace and patience? (Those are top on most people's list, too.) It doesn't matter what is on my list; it's already in me. It's been given. He says so, and He doesn't lie.[1]

Jesus lived everything I need: love, compassion, mercy, boldness, wisdom . . . these are good things, and God says that He withholds no good thing from me.[2] The Holy Spirit is everything God is, and Jesus promised to send us the Holy Spirit and fill us with power.[3]

So why don't I feel it? Why can't I see it in my life? Because, like everything else in the kingdom of heaven, everything we need for life and godliness is accessed and empowered by faith. Ignorance has been a major roadblock.[4] I've been asking God to give me peace, to download some patience and kindness, to issue me some self-control and victory, and He's been saying, "I already have! It's in you! Use it. Trust me."

God knows I don't know what I'm doing. "Everything we need" also includes not only the instruction manual, but the Instructor Himself—the precious Holy Spirit.[5] "Everything we need" is manifested in my life *through my knowledge of Him*—exactly what the Holy Spirit teaches.[6]

Get to know Jesus. *He's* everything we need, and He's in us.

---

*Everything we need for life and godliness
is accessed and empowered by faith.*

---

[1]Num. 23:19   [2]Ps. 84:11   [3]Acts 1:8   [4]Hos. 4:6   [5]1 John 2:27   [6]John 16:14–15

APRIL 14

Who, then, is the man that fears the LORD?
He will instruct him in the way chosen for him.

Psalm 25:12

*G*od has a preordained purpose for everyone. I had heard this so many times that its impact had almost been lost. But the longer I walk with Jesus, the more I learn about purpose. Again and again the Bible tells us that God is sovereign, that He rules over the affairs of man.[1] We go our own way, make our own plans, but it is His purpose that prevails.[2] His purpose will be accomplished one way or another.[3]

It is that "one way or another" that shakes me to the core. I *used* to think that God required my cooperation in order to accomplish His purpose through me. But the Bible is filled with stories of people God used to get the job done in spite of themselves.[4] If God's plans could fail because of man's ignorance, resistance, or outright disobedience, then He is not God. In fact, all of the ways men tried to get rid of Jesus and prevent/deny the resurrection only served to fulfill the greatest plan of God.[5]

If God will accomplish His pupose anyway, do I still need to know what my purpose is? Yes and no. God's plans are deeper and more intricate than we can imagine. We may never know until eternity all that God accomplished through us.[6] The point is not that we need to see the big picture,[7] but that we see and do our part. *Our* part is that thing that God is showing, dealing with us about, or prompting us to do right now.

To be used in spite of myself is devastating to my soul. It means I am rebelling against God. Knowing that God has a purpose for me should drive me to seek Him. This is His pull in us. The same pull the rich young man felt[8] when he realized there was more to obeying God than following the law.[9] When Jesus said, "Follow me," the man was overwhelmed by the lifestyle changes it would require. To follow Jesus, I have to recognize His leading.[10] To obey Him, I have to know what He is asking me to do. The more I seek and obey, the more He reveals. To do less is to be unworthy of Him[11] and shows how much (or how little) I truly fear the Lord.

To follow Jesus, I have to obey His leading.
To obey Him, I have to know what He is asking me to do.

---

[1]Dan. 4:24–26 [2]Prov. 19:21 [3]Isa. 46:8–10 [4]Isa. 45:1–6 [5]Luke 24:44–48 [6]John 13:7 [7]Heb. 11:8
[8]Matt. 19:16–22 [9]Matt. 23:23 [10]John 10:4 [11]Luke 17:10

APRIL 15

... "Abraham believed God, and it was credited to him as righteousness,"
and he was called God's friend.

James 2:23

As I get to know God, I can see Him in several roles, or relationships, with me. When He saved me, I could cry out like Thomas, "My Lord and my God!"[1] As I began to experience His love for me, I could more readily call Him Father, and even more intimately, Abba.[2] As I learned to recognize His many favors, kindnesses and blessings He was pouring into my life, I could easily say He is my friend.

But as I was reading this passage of Scripture for the umpteenth time, it suddenly hit me what it really says. It isn't saying that God was Abraham's friend; it says that *Abraham* was *God's* friend! That is another whole story—a profound shift in perspective. It opens a door to a completely new and deeper level of intimacy with God.

The difference is that when God is my friend, I am the one mostly receiving, but when I am God's friend, *God* is on the receiving end. What an enormous concept, to think that *I* can be a blessing to *God*! Is it even possible? Of course! Remember: God is love.[3]—and love requires someone to love. So God made man—and the yearning cry of God's great heart is for fellowship with the creatures of His love. Fellowship is love returned; it is friendship. To be a friend requires commitment and selflessness. To be a friend to God means I love at all times[4]—in disaster as much as in prosperity.[5] A friend always has your best interests[6] at heart, like Moses did.[7] A friend believes you, believes in you, like Abraham did.

To be God's friend means I love Him, guard His honor,[8] trust His Word, and obey Him.[9] And above all, I fellowship with Him, sharing all the intimate moments of my life with Him.

Do you want this? Do you want to be God's friend, too?

When God is my friend, I am the one receiving . . .

but when I am God's friend, God is on the receiving end.

---

[1]John 20:28 [2]Mark14:36 [3]1 John 4:8 [4]Prov. 17:17 [5]Isa. 45:7 [6]Prov. 27:9 [7]Num. 14:10–19
[8]John 2:13–17 [9]John 15:14

APRIL 16

". . . Everything is all right," she said.
2 Kings 4:26

If I could paint a picture of faith, several scenarios leap to mind: Abraham and Isaac, hiking together up Mt. Moriah–Isaac carrying the load of wood;[1] Daniel on his knees before his open windows, praying;[2] Peter, arrested by King Herod and chained between two soldiers, likely to be executed–peacefully sleeping.[3] And this woman, known only as the Shunammite, prostrate before Elisha, clasping his feet in grief and desperation, saying, "Everything is all right."[4]

Faith is the only way she could've said such a thing–the kind of faith that takes hold of God's purpose, His character, and never lets go, no matter what darkness or disaster threatens to drag you under its overwhelming flood. Only a faith that trusts God in the darkenss[5] can hold her dying son until his last breath, and still say, "It's all right."

Faith is the utterly unshakable confidence that in God, "Everything is all right." "Faith is the substance of things hoped for . . ."[6] The Shunammite's faith was the stuff of her miracle. It was the substance, the raw material God used to create the very thing she hoped for–her son back from the dead.

"Faith is . . . the evidence of things not seen." The evidence of her faith was in her words, put to work in her actions–a long, hard donkey ride to the man of God.[7]

I have to ask myself, "What is challenging my faith right now?[8] What chaos, what disaster has struck my life today, trying to rip my confidence in God to shreds?[9] Can I grasp the goodness of God in the midst of my grief and say, 'Everything is all right?'[10] Can I rely on the love God has for me,[11] never wavering in the face of cruel circumstances, and absolutely insist on the overarching truth that everything is all right?"

Then God's purpose will prevail.

Faith is the utterly unshakable confidence that in God, everything is all right.

---

[1]Gen. 22:1–18   [2]Dan. 6:1–13   [3]Acts 12:1–6   [4]2 Kings 4:8–37   [5]Isa. 50:10   [6]Heb. 11:1
[7]James 2:17–26   [8]Isa. 50:7–9   [9]Heb. 10:23   [10]Lam. 3:19–26   [11]1 John 4:16

APRIL 17

The end of a matter is better than its beginning . . .
Ecclesiastes 7:8

I am an accomplished beginner. In my time, I have begun many excellent projects, launched laudable programs, initiated worthy causes. If I had only completed half of what I had begun, I would've been smarter, slimmer, faster, stronger, and probably wealthier than I am now. Somewhere along the way, my stick-to-itiveness came unstuck, my fast track got side tracked, and my fortitude got an attitude. I can really relate to Terah.

You know—Terah—Abraham's dad. Abraham, of Father-of-the-Faithful fame. Everybody knows Abraham. But Terah? Not exactly a household name. *But he could've been.* In Genesis 11:31, It says that Terah packed up his whole family "and together they set out from Ur of the Chaldeans to go to Canaan . . ."

Wait a minute—*Canaan*? The *Promised Land* Canaan? What could have prompted Terah to do such a thing? Is it possible that the call of Abraham had originally been the call of Terah? The Bible doesn't say. It *does* say that they started to go to Canaan, but ended up settling in Haran. Why? Who knows? Maybe the trip became harder than he thought;[1] maybe there were too many bandits. Maybe sickness plagued them. Maybe his wife complained too much about the heat, the camels, the constant packing and unpacking[2] . . . Maybe by the time they made it to Haran, the city looked a lot more inviting than some distant, unfamiliar country. Maybe they met a caravan coming from Canaan, whose masters told of giants and fierce-looking fortress-cities.[3] Maybe he thought he'd just stop for a short while—a few months, or a year at the most—then continue on his way.

Whatever the reason, Terah never made it to Canaan. He never saw the Promised Land. He started out. He even made some decent progress. He just never finished the journey.

I don't want to be like Terah. I want to finish what I start,[4] complete the work and bring glory to God.[5] I want to stand firm and end well.[6] I want to be like Abraham, who set out for the land of Canaan, and . . . *arrived* there.[7] Jesus won't ever say, "Well started!" He will only welcome his children home with a hearty, "Well done!"[8]

Jesus won't ever say, "Well started!" He will only welcome his children home with a hearty, "Well done!"

---

[1]Matt. 7:14 [2]Luke 8:14 [3]Num. 13:26–33 [4]Luke 14:29–30 [5]John 17:4 [6]Mark 13:13 [7]Gen. 12:5
[8]Matt. 25:21, 23

APRIL 18

The Word became flesh and made his dwelling among us. . . .
John 1:14

hat an incredible statement! It is hard to wrap my mind around such a concept—that God the Creator would willingly become a part of His own creation. The immortal, divine Word departed the Spirit world[1] and clothed Himself with the physical world. He became flesh and blood—human—living as a man among men. He sweated, bled, ached, grew tired, got hungry and thirsty, stretched and yawned, did His chores, and studied to learn what He Himself had inspired.[2] He outgrew things. He had to squint into the sun He had called into being, take shelter from the rain He had sent, and cough out the dust He had weighed in the palm of His hand.[3]

When I read the book of Job, I begin to get a glimpse of the depth of His condescension. This is the One who fixes limits for the oceans, gives orders to the morning, and shows the dawn its place. This is the One who reserves the hail in storehouses against the days of war and battle. This is the One who directs the tempest, who cuts a channel for the rain. He has journeyed to the springs of the sea and walked in the recesses of the deep.[4]

He who measured the expanse of the earth and marked off its dimensions[5] became the carpenter's son from Nazareth. Can you see Him with a measuring line in His hand—and a pencil behind His ear? Did He ever get a splinter, I wonder? How odd it must have felt for the Bread of Life[6] to have to earn His daily bread. Imagine the omniscient One having to learn; the omnipotent One needing someone to hold a board He was cutting, the all-seeing God having to turn His head in order to see behind Himself. Did He ever feel claustrophobic in our skin?

So—am I struggling? In pain? Weary beyond words? He knows what that feels like; He was made like us in every way.[7] He understands what I'm going through; He's been there—He's been here.[8]

Now that's a God worth serving.

It is hard to wrap your mind around the concept that God, the Creator, willingly became a part of His own creation.

---

[1]John 4:24   [2]John 1:1   [3]Isa. 40:15   [4]Job 38:8–25   [5]Job 38:5   [6]John 6:35   [7]Heb. 2:17
[8]Ps. 103:14

APRIL 19

Stop judging by mere appearances, and make a right judgment.
John 7:24

*W*hen life blindsides me and leaves me wounded and bleeding; when I'm down for the count, and the blows are still coming, it is hard to remember that *this* situation is working for me, for good. In the center of the storm, it is hard enough to hold onto belief in an over-all good, let alone that *this* disaster, *this* tragedy, will specifically turn out for good for *anybody*. But when God said that He would carry, sustain, and rescue me.[1] He meant it for situations exactly like mine. He meant it for sorrows and stresses;[2] He meant it for disappointments, damage, and disaster.[3] He meant it for rejection and reversals.[4] He meant it for my breakdowns, whether they are broken arms or broken hearts,[5] broken promises or broken hopes.[6] He meant it.

Perseverance is the key to seeing the good He promises.[7] I shouldn't look at outward appearances. I must wait until the end of the story. Have I ever left in the middle of a movie simply because the hero was in trouble, or thrown away a book because the problem wasn't solved by chapter three? Of course not. I know that somehow, eventually, the hero will figure it out and save the day.

"But that's only Hollywood," doubt says. "That doesn't always happen in real life." Yes, it does! I've seen the script. I've read the Book. God gives us a sneak preview of how the story ends,[8] and I've gotta tell you—we win! It all works out; the Hero saves the day!

When I have trouble believing there's anything good in my troubles, any triumph in my tragedy, I just haven't gotten to the end of the story! As long as this world continues—if I am still on the *until* side of the Second Coming of Jesus—I am not at the end of the story. I must not be too hasty to judge whether or not God has been faithful to His promise. I need to trust Him. He meant it.

---

*Perseverance is the key to seeing the good
that God promised.*

---

[1]Isa. 46:4 [2]Isa. 61:3 [3]Isa. 60:18 [4]Joel 2:25 [5]Ps. 34:18 [6]Num. 23:19 [7]Heb. 10:36
[8]Rev. 21–22

APRIL 20

*As they pass through the Valley of Baca,
they make it a place of springs . . .*
Psalm 84:6

he Valley of Baca. If I have set my heart on pilgrimage (Ps. 84:5), I will, indeed, pass through the Valley of Baca—the Valley of Weeping. It is a rough path, but worn—for many before me have passed this way. Our Savior Himself became intimately familiar with this valley.[1] It is holy ground. It is the way of the cross.[2]

If I try to avoid this valley, I am making a mistake. If Jesus Himself was made perfect through suffering,[3] what makes me think that I don't also need this discipline? There is much, much more to be gained in the Valley of Baca than on any Mount of Transfiguration. It is the Valley of Becoming, the Valley of Discipleship.[4] If I *wish* to avoid this valley, I do not realize the gift God is offering me.[5]

The gift of the Valley of Baca is not received by what God does in me. The beauty of Baca is embraced by what God does *through me*. As I pass through the valley, I *make it a place of springs*. (Again, it is not about us!) As I pass through the Valley of Weeping, I leave behind not pools of tears, but wellsprings of blessing, fountains of comfort, and bubbling springs of joy. The Valley of Sorrows, this Valley of Weeping, is a dark place, where God's light, His glory in me, shines out brightest.

I have learned that when I am passing through sorrows, Jesus wants me to reach out, comfort another, pray for another. When I am pressed down with troubles, I will reach out. I will let His quietness and trust be my strength,[6] and God's glory can touch another. When I feel darkness closing in, I will reach out. His light will always overcome.[7] Another will find hope in Him. The only way to pass *through* the Valley of Baca is to set my heart on pilgrimage, let the glory of God touch others. I will make the Valley of Baca a place of springs.

*If I wish to avoid this valley,
I do not realize the gift God is offering me.*

[1]Isa. 53:3 [2]Mark 8:34 [3]Heb. 2:10 [4]Ps. 119:67, 71 [5]Heb. 12:10–11 [6]Isa. 30:15 [7]John 1:5

APRIL 21

But in your hearts set apart Christ as Lord. . . .
1 Peter 3:15

*W*hat is Peter urging me to do when he admonishes me to set apart Christ as Lord in my heart? Isn't He already Lord? Then how (and why) do I need to set Him apart as Lord?

He tells me to do this in my heart: make it personal. Yes, Christ is Lord. And one day, every knee will bow . . . and every tongue will swear[1] this truth. Peter is urging me to *choose* to do this now, today[2] (out of desire), before I am *compelled* to do it later (out of necessity), when it's too late.

I am to *set apart* Christ as Lord, or *sanctify* Him (KJV). When I sanctify something, I make it holy, sacred—inviolable. Nothing is to touch it, remove it, or replace it. What I have declared sacred, I will not violate for any reason. So much of my struggle is that although I have declared Jesus our Lord, I have not *set Him apart* as Lord: I have not made His Lordship over my life sacred and inviolable. Instead, I continually challenge His Lordship at every juncture. With every temptation that presents itself, I find myself deciding all over again whether or not I will obey Christ's commands. I have not set Him apart as Lord.

I need to consider well what I mean when I make Christ the Lord of my life. By definition, a lord is a "ruler by hereditary right or pre-eminence to whom service and obedience are due."[3] Jesus has both hereditary right as the Son of God,[4] *and* He is Lord by right of pre-eminence:[5] He won His Lordship by supreme sacrifice.[6] *Webster's* also says that a lord is "one having power and authority over others."[7] This is the *ability* and the *right* to command. The people in Jesus' day saw this in Him. In amazement, they said, ". . . with authority and power he gives orders to evil spirits and they come out!"[8] Satan admitted Jesus' right to command him.

Can I? Do I? Does Jesus truly command my life, or am I trying to be co-regent—reserving the right to ratify or veto His commands? I must give up the throne. He deserves that seat of highest honor. In my heart (lovingly, desiring nothing else), I will set apart Christ as Lord. He will never command me wrong.

Much of our struggle is that although we have declared Jesus our Lord, we haven't set Him apart as Lord.

---

[1]Isa. 45:23   [2]Heb. 4:7   [3]*Webster's:* "lord"   [4]Heb. 1:8–9   [5]Heb. 1:1–4   [6]Rev. 1:18
[7]*Webster's:* "lord"   [8]Luke 4:36

APRIL 22

*Let us therefore come boldly unto the throne of grace,
that we may obtain mercy . . .*
Hebrews 4:16 [KJV]

or myself, I know that the moment I am least inclined to be bold is when I am most in need of mercy. I have sinned; the pain of disappointment in myself for having disappointed Him is intense. All I can usually manage is a hang-dog, cast-down, slow drag of shame only to the outer edges of His courts.[1] I have great difficulty imagining the confident step of boldness—right up to His throne, to ask Him to have mercy on me! God must have understood this feeling—which is why He made certain this statement was included in the Scriptures.

The boldness urged here is not cockiness, nor is it that highly offensive arrogance that makes light of sin and cheapens His grace.[2] Rather, it is the assurance of love; the strength that comes from an unshakable faith and trust in the compassion of a Father for His cherished—though errant—child.[3] It is knowing, even as my heart aches with the sorrow of my confession, that He will receive me, forgive me, and make me clean and pure.[4]

Maybe it would help if I looked at what the writer of the letter to the Hebrews meant when he chose this particular word, *boldly*. The Greek *parresia* means not only "boldness and confidence," but "frankness, in public, with openness (of speech)." In other places in Scripture, the same word is also translated as "plainly, fearlessly, with courage, assurance, and freedom."[5] When I come boldly unto the throne of grace, I should come frankly, with openness to lay bare my heart—and the truth—before God.[6] I can come fearlessly,[7] with assurance and freedom, to tell Him plainly that I have sinned—confident in His love and faithfulness to forgive me.[8]

When we come boldly, as such, truly we will not only obtain mercy, but we will find grace to help us in our time of need.

---

*When we come boldly unto the throne of grace,
we should come with openness
to lay bare our hearts before God.*

---

[1]Luke 18:13   [2]Ps. 36:1–2   [3]Mal. 3:17   [4]1 John 1:9   [5]*Strongest:* p. 1,581   [6]Prov. 28:13   [7]Isa. 54:4
[8]Ps. 27:13

APRIL 23

And God said, "Let there be light," and there was light.
Genesis 1:3

*C*ontrary to popular opinion, God did not create light first because He needed to see what He was doing! God Himself *is* light,[1] and the psalmist tells us, "Darkness is as light to you."[2] So what *did* He create when He called forth light on that first day, to the joy and delight of all the watching angels?[3] It was not the sun, nor the moon and stars. In fact, He waited three more days to create natural light![4] No, this light that shone forth on day one was something supernatural, a glorious, heavenly brightness from which darkness fled. It is the same light into which you were called out of darkness:[5] the light of knowing God. It is the Light by which we see light.[6] The book of Proverbs, in personifying Wisdom, tells us, "the LORD brought me forth as the first of His works."[7]

Wisdom and knowledge, being created, are not the same as truth, for God's truth is eternal.[8] Wisdom is the application of truth to our physical world. God created all knowledge and wisdom first, because wisdom is the foundation of all life, of all order. Without knowledge, understanding and wisdom, there is only chaos and anarchy.

By creating wisdom, God called into being every physical, spiritual, and moral law that governs our universe. With a mere word, every rule and principle of every science and discipline sprang forth, fully developed. From the laws that govern atomic structure to the inescapable rules of cause and effect, action and consequence, God forever filled the textbooks of genius. And all He had to do to establish the whole of this vast, intricately interconnected order was to speak two words (since in the original Hebrew—if that is what God spoke—it's only two words: "Light be!"). "Let there be light."

God did nothing without intelligence, without design. There were no prototypes, no going back to the drawing board to correct a few *oops*. He made wisdom, knowledge, intelligence and understanding first, because this is His way. "Wisdom is the principal thing; therefore get wisdom: and with all thy getting get understanding."[9] His ways are to be my ways, too. In my life, let there be light. Let me constantly be seeking His wisdom.

Wisdom is the application of truth to our physical world.

---

[1] 1 John 1:5 [2] Ps. 139:12 [3] Job 38:7 [4] Gen. 1:14–19 [5] 1 Pet. 2:9 [6] Ps. 36:9 [7] Prov. 8:22
[8] John 14:6 [9] Prov. 4:7 [KJV]

APRIL 24

Now he had to go through Samaria.
John 4:4

Jesus did nothing haphazardly, by chance, on the spur of the moment. From the beginning of all beginnings, every part of His life was ordained by God.[1] His lineage was pre-arranged,[2] His parents pre-selected,[3] His birthplace pre-announced more than seven hundred years before there was no room at the inn.[4] His ministry and rejection,[5] His betrayal,[6] His death (the manner of his death was intimately described nearly a thousand years before anyone ever conceived of crucifixion[7])—even the very words hurled at Him in insult were predicted.[8] Of all the clouds of witnesses[9] in the heavenly realms, only Satan was surprised by Jesus' resurrection! Jesus spoke no word and took no step apart from the command of His Father.[10]

When Jesus went to the region of Tyre and Sidon, when He had to go through Samaria, it was by divine appointment. It was not a matter of geography; it was a matter of deliverance, of salvation. One soul—how infinitely valuable, how supremely precious, is each soul to Him! For the sake of one broken, oppressed soul, Jesus left the country, abandoned the traditional trail, and went where no self-respecting Jew would go.

Jesus is still calling us out of our way. He wants to break into my plans and schedules to send me into the life of another, to minister to that one valuable soul. I may have to go where no self-respecting "Christian" wants to go. (Why am I concerned with respect?) The needs of that one may require much of me;[11] I may never be able to return to my previous plans and schedules. Is that really so bad?

Am I ready and willing to go through Samaria for the sake of one soul?

For the sake of one broken, oppressed soul,
Jesus left the country, abandoned the traditional trail,
and went where no self-respecting Jew would go.

---

[1]Gen. 3:15   [2]Gen. 49:10; Isa. 11:1   [3]Luke 1:26–38   [4]Mic. 5:2   [5]Isa. 53   [6]Ps. 55:12–14
[7]Ps. 22   [8]Ps. 22:8   [9]Heb. 12:1   [10]Luke 12:48   [11]John 14:11, 31

APRIL 25

. . . his word is in my heart like a fire, a fire shut up in my bones. . . .
Jeremiah 20:9

Comic books, crosswords and classical music; azaleas and auto-graphs; skydiving, skateboarding, and scrapbooks; race cars and rock stars; jelly jars and jelly beans and Jelly Roll Morton . . . What could such disparities possibly have in common? Passion. People everywhere spend themselves in pursuit of these and innumerable other interests equally temporal, equally passing.

When I spend a little time with someone, it's not hard to discover their passion.[1] It is conspicuous in their surroundings. Everywhere around them I'll see symbols and samples, tidbits and trophies of their passion. They wear it, display it, carry it in their wallets. Their conversation is saturated with whatever it is that has captured their heart.[2] One look at their calendar reveals it—where their time is, there is their treasure.[3]

Passion does not come instantly or by chance. Passion is a fire. It is a warmth that has been stoked, a flicker that has been continually fed until it is a fire raging in my bones. It is deliberately chosen;[4] it is an attraction ardently acted upon. It *must* be expressed; I simply cannot hold it in.[5] If passion is unchecked, it will entirely consume me.

What a glorious thing to be consumed by a passion for Jesus Christ! It is no waste to abandon all restraint and lose myself in attraction to the Son of God, ardently acted upon,[6] to pour myself out for the sake of the Sinless One. It is the highest praise, the deepest expression of zealous love. Jesus was consumed with just such a passion.[7]

So I ask myself, "What is my passion? What consumes me? What consumes my thoughts, my time, my energy, my resources?[8] When I look about me with the eyes of a stranger, what do my surroundings, my conversation, say about what my treasure is? What would my neighbor say my passion is?" If it is anything other than the Passionate One Himself, I need to let it go.

How wonderful to let the all-consuming fire of His ardent love capture my heart forever.

Passion is a warmth that has been stoked,

a flicker that has been continually fed

until it is a fire raging in your bones.

---

[1]Prov. 23:7 [KJV]   [2]Luke 6:45   [3]Matt. 6:21   [4]Josh. 24:15   [5]Jer. 20:9   [6]Matt. 10:39   [7]John 2:17
[8]Isa. 55:2

APRIL 26

Enter his gates with thanksgiving and his courts with praise . . .
Psalm 100:4

Oh, the riches to be found in the presence of God! Everything our heart and soul can ever desire, all that our spirit shall ever need, is found in the presence of God: fellowship, consecration, deliverance, mercy, favor, power, acceptance, fullness of joy, and pleasures evermore.[1] Do we lack knowledge? Do we have questions? All the answers we need are found in His presence.[2]

How do I get into the presence of God? What must I do? While I am urged to come boldly before the throne of grace,[3] I am also warned to worship God acceptably with reverence and awe, for our God is a consuming fire.[4] *Boldly* does not mean *blunderingly unprepared.* Considering the intense preparation of Esther to enter the presence of an earthly, pagan king,[5] how much more should we prepare our hearts to enter the presence of the Eternal King of kings and Lord of lords?

To enter His gates, I must purge myself of any hint of a complaining, ungrateful spirit.[6] I should take a moment to reflect on His blessings, His incredible mercy and forgiveness to me. My gratitude will throw open His gates to me, and I can enter into the public part of His castle, so to speak. Anyone with business in the King's household could come through His gates, but to enter His courts? To have access to His actual presence in His inner council chambers? That requires more! Thanksgiving is good and right, but thanksgiving is merely recognizing what He has done. You can enter His courts with praise, giving honor and glory to Him for who He is, not just for what He has done.

Beyond the blessings, there are those who worship and serve Him simply for who He is, praising the excellence of His being with unadulterated (unmixed with thoughts of gain) adoration and love. These are the ones who will make up His jewels and His treasured possession.[7] These are the ones for whom God's presence truly gives fullness of joy and pleasures evermore. They long for Him, and linger unhurried in His glory. They are not only His children; they are His friends.[8] Am I truly one of them?

Take a moment to reflect on God's blessings,
His incredible mercy and forgiveness to you.

---

[1]Ps. 16:11 [KJV]   [2]Exod. 28:30   [3]Heb. 4:16   [4]Heb. 12:29   [5]Esth. 2:12   [6]Ps. 50:20–23
[7]Mal. 3:16–17 [KJV, NIV]   [8]John 15:15

APRIL 27

Why should I forgive you? . . .
Jeremiah 5:7

The betrayal, the pain—how much another has hurt us! Our wounds are deep and raw, and we hold our bleeding hearts close, nursing the ache. To be blindsided by a moment of carelessness is pain enough, but for many of us, our wounds were no accident. Cold and calculated, deliberate and brutal abuse, neglect, treachery, and violence were aimed at our vulnerable bodies and souls. It is easy to see us asking this question; we ask it every time we are beaten or backstabbed. How can we forgive our tormentors?

But the question is not being uttered by a person, a human being. The question is being asked by God—to us.

He knows what betrayal feels like.[1] He understands neglect[2] and abuse. He's felt the fires of lies and treachery,[3] hatred and brutal violence.[4] He's been there. He was our victim.[5]

He is asking me now (as He will one day, from His great, white throne[6]), *"Why should I forgive you?"*

What will I answer? Before I name a single *should*, I need to remember: It was *my* lips that spoke the lies against Him, *my* hand that wielded the whips and rods; *my* hand that held the nails and pounded them through His flesh and lifted the cross and stabbed His side and rolled the dice for His clothes as He bled away above me. It was *me*—it was each of us. *Now* let me find something good in myself,[7] something that doesn't deserve the death penalty[8] for the murder of His only Son.

Why should God forgive me? There is no reason, except that He wants to, for the sake of His love and His Son's death. If I plead that, plead only that—He will be faithful to do it.[9]

Why should God forgive you?
There is no reason, except that He wants to
for the sake of His love and His Son's death.

---

[1]Ps. 55:12–14 [2]Mark 14:37 [3]Matt. 26:59–61 [4]Isa. 52:14 [5]Isa. 53:6 [6]Rev. 20:11–12 [7]Isa. 64:6
[8]Gen. 2:17 [9]1 John 1:9

APRIL 28

Deep calls to deep in the roar of your waterfalls;
all your waves and breakers have swept over me.
Psalm 42:7

*H*ave I waded in the shallows long enough? Have I tested the waters of commitment, getting wet only as far as the knees? How then will I ever know that the Lord can hold me up when I cannot?[1] I stand before a vast ocean of experiencing God, yet I barely dip my toe into the waters. Such shallowness is bound to disappoint and dissatisfy, because there are deep places in me that can only be filled from the deep places of God.[2] This is why, once I have truly tasted and seen that the Lord is good,[3] my soul will forever thirst for God.[4] I can never again be satisfied with less; I have been ruined for the superficial.

Listen. I can hear His voice in the roar of His waterfalls.[5] "Go deeper!" He cries out. "Don't just go to church, My child—*be* the church! Don't just say your prayers—pour out your heart and soul in intimate conversation with Me. I am speaking in your deep places. Can you hear Me?"

Religion is a shallow experience; friendship with God is deep.[6] "Forgive me, God," is surface; "Change me, Lord," is deep. *Knowing the way* is not the journey; *walking it* is. Recognizing my sinfulness is superficial; overcoming my flesh is deep. I was meant for more than a skin-deep, ritual morality; I am designed and destined for a deep, personal spirituality that penetrates even to the dividing of soul and spirit, joints and marrow.[7]

Soul (my mind, will and emotions) is religion. *Spirit* is God.[8] My spirit is the deep place in me that resonates only to the heartbeat of God. Mere outward religion is not enough to touch and fill my spirit. Only an intimate, personal relationship with the eternal God will satisfy. Only when I go deep with God—only when I allow the Infinite to invade my whole being—will I be so radically changed that I must be considered new-born all over again![9]

I will never be content again in the shallow end of this incredible ocean called God. Instead, I will go ahead and throw myself in *way* over my head. He is out there, waiting to catch me. He will never let me drown, though all His waves and breakers sweep over me.[10]

God is speaking to you in deep places.
Can you hear Him?

---

[1]Isa. 46:3   [2]Eccl. 3:11   [3]Ps. 34:8   [4]Ps. 63:1   [5]Rev. 1:15   [6]Job 29:4   [7]Heb. 4:12   [8]John 4:24
[9]John 3:3   [10]Isa. 43:2

APRIL 29

. . . His way is in the whirlwind and the storm,
and clouds are the dust of his feet.

Nahum 1:3

*J*esus said that if we come unto Him, He would give us peace–but He also said that He did not give peace as the world gives peace.[1] If I am waiting for all the storms and confusion in my life to quiet down before I look for God to manifest Himself to me, I have probably missed Him. God's way is *in* the storm; His path leads right into the tempest. His way is in the whirlwind. When things are seemingly out of control, God isn't.[2] He is the eye of calm. If I am following God, I need to watch for the storms, for He is intimately present with me in the midst of chaos. He will speak to me as He did to Job–out of the storm.[3] If I listen for His voice, often the very thunder of the storm will be His message to me.

God said, "If you falter in times of trouble, how small is your strength!"[4] Storms are not obstacles to be avoided; they are opportunities to experience a powerful manifestation of God in my life. The very clouds I pray away are the evidence of Him moving in my circumstances. His footsteps kick up some clouds; He stirs up the dust of deadness in the dark corners of my soul as He passes by.

Anyone can praise God beside the still waters and in the green pastures. But when I follow my Shepherd, His paths of righteousness often lead me through some very dark valleys.[5] What clouds are storming in my life right now? Is it raining some opposition?[6] Are there winds of change blowing hard and strong? Maybe I am being drenched by doubt, disease, or disappointment. I might be in a blizzard of abuse and betrayal; I could be facing a tempest of temptation, or even a full-blown hurricane of hell-fired hatred and hopelessness.[7] I can let these storms strengthen me in the ways of God, for He is, indeed, there in the midst.

What are the ways of God? Jesus spoke them from a mountainside in Galilee, beginning with a bunch of "Blesseds" and ending with several chapters of radical, midst-of-the-storm victory.[8] When I read this sermon, I can look at my storms in a different light: they are simply the dust of His feet.

If you wait for the storms of life to quiet down
before you look for God, you have probably missed Him.

---

[1]John 14:27 [2]Ps. 89:9 [3]Job 38:1 [4]Prov. 24:10 [5]Ps. 23:1–4 [6]1 Pet. 4:12 [7]Rev. 2:9–10
[8]Matt. 5:1–7:28

APRIL 30

. . . I will make myself like the Most High.
Isaiah 14:14

hat is original sin? Is it a sensual, sexual thing, as many seem to think? What difference does it make anyway? If original sin is nothing more than sexual immorality (as devastating as that is to the body, soul, and spirit[1]), then it makes no difference, it is not essential. But it *is* more than that. It is so much more that to misunderstand original sin is to misunderstand the essence of *all* sin. And if we do not understand the essence, the nature of sin, then we cannot understand the sacrifice of Christ, or comprehend our absolute need of a Savior.

Sin originated in heaven itself, with Lucifer,[2] the anointed guardian cherub,[3] whose very wings covered the throne of God Himself.[4] Beautiful, wise, and greatly honored, yet when his eyes should have been gazing upon the infinite glory of God, he turned them instead upon himself.

Pride is the original sin,[5] and it is the root, the substance, of every sin it spawned. Envy, jealousy, spite, greed, lust, hatred . . . all are driven by an unholy, inordinate opinion of self. Pride is never satisfied, demanding for itself the possessions, praise, and power that belong only to God.[6] The essence of pride is to unseat God as the supreme authority,[7] and to refuse to render Him due honor.[8] This can be done deliberately as a willful, considered defiance. But more often it happens carelessly, in giving no thought to spiritual things and relegating God to the bottom of my to-do list, making the Eternal about as important as dusting.

Is God truly Lord of my life? Do I recognize His authority? When He speaks, do I hasten to obey?[9] Do I seek His will, making no plans of my own, but instead standing in eager readiness for His direction?[10] Are my eyes upon Him, or am I always considering the consequences to myself?[11]

I need to give thought to my ways,[12] and beware of original sin in me.

Pride is the original sin,
and it is the root of every sin it has ever spawned.

---

[1]Heb. 12:16–17 [2]Isa. 14:12 [3]Ezek. 28:14 [4]Exod. 25:20 [5]Ezek. 28:17 [6]Acts 12:21–23
[7]Exod. 5:2 [8]Ps. 96:8 [9]Ps. 119:60 [10]Mark 14:36 [11]Job 35:3 [12]Prov. 14:8

MAY 1

*His daughter was Sheerah, who built Lower and Upper Beth Horon
as well as Uzzen Sheerah.*

1 Chronicles 7:24

*M*y father is the son of Hungarian immigrants, whose old-world ideas of women's work excluded just about anything that didn't involve an apron. I grew up resentful for being born female, someone not allowed to pursue whatever future her heart desired. I was even taught that this limitation was Biblical, that it was God's plan. But I didn't want to be June Cleaver, vacuuming her house in heels and pearls; I wanted to be like my cartoon heroine, *She-Ra, Queen of the Jungle!*

Imagine my surprise to discover that there was a *real* Sheerah! She wasn't exactly the Queen of the Jungle, but she was still a mighty woman, a force to be reckoned with. The Bible doesn't record anything more about her than this one verse—a mere footnote buried in those interminable lists of fathers and sons that most readers skip over to get to more interesting material. But God's Spirit inspired the Scriptures, and He made certain Sheerah was included for all time in our only guidebook for life.

It is only one sentence, but it says a lot. She had to have been an independent woman in a society that did not allow independent women; no husband, father or brother got credit for what she did. She must have been a woman of means and authority, because it takes money and a lot of help to build not just one, but *two* cities! She was definitely in charge, too. Not only does the Bible say that she built the cities, but one of them was even named for her! She had the force of character it took to face down every challenge, every voice—male *and* female—that tried to dissuade her from her destiny;[1] that told her it wasn't ladylike.

God has planted dreams within me.[2] He has empowered me with His Spirit to fulfill those plans.[3] I dare not let anyone tell me it is not to be; my gift will make room for me.[4] I may have to remind them of Peter's words: "If God gave them the same gift as he gave us . . . who was I to think that I could oppose God?"[5]

Like Sheerah—pursue your purpose. Fulfill your destiny!

. . . Let no one tell you your dream is not to be;
your gift will make room for you.

---

[1]Ps. 57:2   [2]Num. 12:6   [3]Acts 1:8   [4]Prov. 18:16 [KJV]   [5]Acts 11:17

MAY 2

Fear of man will prove to be a snare,
but whoever trusts in the Lᴏʀᴅ is kept safe.
Proverbs 29:25

Oh, how many sins can be laid at the feet of the fear of man! How many times have I done what I *knew* to be wrong—what I didn't even *want* to do—all because I wanted the approval of others?[1] Did I cherish their opinion, their acceptance? Some have even been willing to sacrifice their own conscience in order to win it or keep from losing it. To stand up for the right is to stand out from the crowd[2]—and that is a lonely position, even dangerous.

But sins of *commission*—our dirty deeds—are not the only behaviors driven by the fear of man. There are those conscience-searing sins of *omission* that James warns us about: "Anyone, then, who knows the good he ought to do and doesn't do it, sins."[3] Many times I hold back from doing good, from helping another. I hold my peace instead of speaking out for justice and for the truth.[4]

Fear of man is a terrible bondage. The favor and good opinion I hope to gain is fickle and fleeting. It's the enemy's game of bait and switch. The very compromises he says will earn my acceptance are the grounds people use to disrespect and reject me.[5] I am an unfaithful, untrustworthy crowd-pleaser.[6] When the tide of their approval ebbs, I am left high and dry—diminished and guilty.[7]

Fear of man is the reason whole armies have obeyed horrendous orders. It is the driving force behind every initiation rite and every delinquent dare. It is the power of mob mentality. It is the reason so many who had just been shouting, "Hosanna!" could so quickly change to crying, "Crucify!" And it was the reason Pilate gave in to their cries.[8]

But God says to strengthen our feeble hands and steady our weak knees and to say to our fearful hearts, "Be strong, do not fear."[9] Jesus tells me to follow Him, and He never followed the crowd. He refused to entrust Himself to men, because He knew what was in a man.[10] He stood true to the truth, and God Himself gave Him His seal of approval.[11]

Jesus tells us to follow Him,

and He never followed the crowd.

[1]1 Sam. 15:24 [2]Exod. 23:2 [3]James 4:17 [4]Job 31:33–34 [5]Ps. 7:14–16 [6]Prov. 11:3 [7]Prov. 13:15
[8]Mark 15:9–15 [9]Isa. 35:3–4 [10]John 2:24–25 [11]John 6:27

MAY 3

What other nation is so great as to have their gods near them the way the LORD our God is near us whenever we pray to him?
Deuteronomy 4:7

hat is the power of prayer? It is the *presence of God.* When we pray, God draws near.[1] But it is more than power; the presence of God is the *purpose* of prayer. Over and over God tells us to seek Him,[2] to seek His face, to seek Him with all our heart and soul.[3] He hides Himself,[4] then challenges us to desire Him enough to *earnestly* and *energetically* seek Him.[5] He draws us to Him;[6] He wants to be found.[7] When I am seeking someone who wants to be found, I call out to Him.

When I humble myself and pray and seek His face,[8] He is present. Beyond the things I want Him to do for me (we all have needs and desires), I need Him. His face—not just His hands. In His presence is all that He is, and I have so much to learn, to discover of Him. Knowing God is our supreme, sublime goal.[9] Unless I get into His presence, I will only know *about* Him secondhand. In His presence, He speaks to me. I ask, I hear, I learn, I grow. I discover my call and my purpose, His plans for me and how to fulfill them.

Will I feel it? Will I feel His nearness with tingles of electricity or like a sense or something like warm honey being poured over me . . . ? Maybe I will, maybe I will not. But God is spirit, and we worship Him in spirit.[10] Physical sensations reinforce the physical realm, and I am already firmly entrenched in the physical. His presence is perceived in my spirit and strengthens the spiritual in me. In His presence, I am changed. I begin to participate in His nature,[11] to think like He thinks.[12] I connect with God, and my soul begins to desire godly ways. Even when my prayer is over, my thoughts and my heart carry Him with me in the afterburn, and His grace is with me to do whatever He has asked of me.

All because the Lord my God is near to me when I pray.

What is the power of prayer?
It is the presence of God. When we pray, God draws near.

---

[1]Ps. 145:18 [2]Amos 5:4 [3]Jer. 29:13 [4]Isa. 45:15 [5]Heb. 11:6 [6]John 6:44 [7]1 Chron. 28:9 [8]2 Chron. 7:14 [9]Jer. 9:24 [10]John 4:24 [11]2 Pet. 1:4 [12]Isa. 55:7–9

MAY 4

By this all men will know that you are my disciples,
if you love one another.
John 13:35

I am not marked as a Christ follower by the clothes I wear, nor by my choice of music. It is not the little fish symbol on my car, nor the cross around my neck. Going to church does not make me a Christ follower, any more than going to a zoo makes me a monkey. But make no mistake: believer or not, I am marked. What I am cannot be hidden;[1] the abundance of my heart will spill out in my actions,[2] and all can know what—or *whose*[3]—I am.

God talks about marks. He warns all of us that those who do not worship Him will one day worship the beast, the false Christ—the Antichrist. He says they will be marked in their foreheads (their minds, or thoughts and attitudes) and in their hands (their actions).[4] The way they think will show in what they do.

But God also said that this mark will only be given to those who do not have the seal[5]—the mark—of God.[6] What is the mark of God, the mark of a true believer? Jesus said it plainly: If you love one another, you are marked as My disciples.

This mark is not merely a physical stamp, emblem, tattoo, or implant. Sure, the enemy will offer such a thing, but by the time the lines form to receive it, it will already be too late. Things always develop *inwardly* before they manifest *outwardly*. I am receiving my mark now, in the multitude of choices I make each day; choices to walk in love or in selfishness. Love is the fruit I bear, showing myself to be His disciple.[7] Love is the obedience He desires above all sacrifice,[8] showing myself to be His friend.[9] Love is His command.[10] *Love* is the mark of a Christ follower. The love of God, made possible in me by the Holy Spirit, is the seal of God.[11] By this—and this only—will all men know that I am His disciple.

Christ follower or not, you are marked.

What you are cannot be hidden.

---

[1]Matt. 10:26 [2]Luke 6:45 [3]John 8:38–44 [4]Rev. 13:16–17 [5]Ezek. 9:4, 6 [6]Rev. 7:3; 9:4
[7]John 15:8 [8]1 Sam. 15:22 [9]John 15:14 [10]John 15:17 [11]John 17:26

MAY 5

He trains my hands for battle;
my arms can bend a bow of bronze.
Psalm 18:34

*I*n the army of the Lord, every day is training day. No commander sends raw recruits to the front lines; every enlistee must go through various levels of training first. Why? Because even though he's signed up, sworn in and legally a soldier, he still thinks, talks, acts, and reacts like a civilian. He needs to learn the moves, the tools, and the strategies that will help him win the battle.

We are at war. There are no civilians, no non-combatants. There is only the choice of which side I will join.[1] When I decide to switch sides to God's, He begins my training, teaching me His thoughts and His ways and showing me how to get rid of *my* ways.[2] He begins to show me the strategies of the kingdom[3] and reminds me of the strategies of the enemy.[4]

My training will go much more smoothly and quickly if I consciously co-operate with God. I can learn to recognize when He is teaching me, and I am becoming a hungry, thirsty learner.[5] God uses many methods of instruction, especially for the alert and teachable spirit. He uses visual aids and repetition,[6] and object lessons from my surroundings[7] (if I'm wise enough to observe, ask, and pay attention). His strongest method is His Word, quickened by His Spirit, if I will put it before my eyes, *think* about it, and actually put it into practice![8]

His least-favorite, but often-necessary method is the furnace of affliction.[9] If the previous methods are not getting through, I leave God with little choice but to get my attention the hard way. My own stubbornness and rebellion bring God's discipline. Even then, I can pass through that valley faster if I stop kicking against Him and learn to *listen*. God promised that one day my teachers would not be hidden any more, but that His own voice would guide me.[10] If I keep the cotton out of my ears (and the stiffness out of my neck), that day can be now!

My training will go much more smoothly and quickly
if I consciously cooperate with God.

---

[1]Matt. 12:30 [2]Isa. 55:7–9 [3]Ps. 103:7 [4]Job 21:27 [5]Matt. 5:6 [6]Deut. 11:18–20 [7]Job 12:7–8
[8]Ps. 119:97–100 [9]Isa. 48:10 [10]Isa. 30:20–21

MAY 6

Go at once to Zarephath of Sidon and stay there.
I have commanded a widow in that place to supply you with food.

1 Kings 17:9

*H*earing the voice of the Lord—there is no more urgent desire in a child of God. This is the one thing that Mary chose above Martha.[1] In this there is healing,[2] joy,[3] life,[4] and one day—if we have listened well—a blessed resurrection.[5] There is no greater cause of angst and confusion among believers than this, yet God has promised that we would not only hear His voice, but we would *know* it, recognize it, and follow it—to the exclusion of all others.[6] This widow did just that. God had commanded her, and she obeyed—and all of their needs were miraculously met in the midst of famine.

My question is, how did God command the widow? It wasn't when Elijah told her. God had already commanded her before He told Elijah to go. She didn't seem to know anything about it when he showed up, yet *she obeyed the wordless command.*

God has many ways of speaking to His children—directly out of the thunder,[7] in dreams and visions;[8] through His Word;[9] and by the Spirit within our spirit.[10] I long to hear words, sentences, unmistakable direction—but that is not faith. Faith is not to seek to hear His voice so that I can be His sheep. I ought to seek to be His sheep, because His sheep do hear His voice.[11]

When I stop being busy, get quiet before Him and listen for what He is telling me, I will hear in my spirit His wordless command, too. When I truly want to do His will,[12] my spirit will know which direction to take. If I make a mistake, He'll correct me.[13] When I follow Him with all my heart, my Shepherd will keep me from straying.[14]

We long to hear words, sentences,
unmistakable direction, but that is not faith.

---

[1]Luke 10:42 [2]Exod. 15:26 [3]John 3:29 [4]Deut. 30:20 [5]John 5:25, 28–29 [6]John 10:3–5
[7]Heb. 12:18–19 [8]Num. 12:6 [9]Prov. 6:22–23 [10]1 John 3:24 [11]John 10:27 [12]John 7:17
[13]Isa. 30:21 [14]Ps. 55:22

MAY 7

Jesus said, "This voice was for your benefit, not mine."
John 12:30

As a child of God, I need to look beyond myself. The world does not exist for me alone; I do not exist for me alone. There is a song that says, "What God has for me, it is for me."* No, what God has for me is for others *through* me. God so loved the *world*, He reached out through Jesus, and He is reaching out still. I am His voice, His hands, His feet.

Yes, God blesses me—because He loves me and desires my happiness. Actually, He desires that I share my Master's happiness.[1] *His* happiness is outward; it involves others. If I want to share His happiness, I need to turn my vision outward. Jesus' vision, His focus, was always outward. He reminded the Pharisees of John the Baptist's testimony not for Himself, "But I mention it that you may be saved."[2] At Lazarus' tomb, His prayer was offered to help those around Him believe.[3] As He struggled and stumbled along with His cross, even then He paused for the wailing women, saying, "Do not weep for me; weep for yourselves and for your children."[4]

Jesus knew who He was and *whose* He was. He could let God have free rein to use His life to reach, teach, and bless others. As Jesus did, so should I. He is my example.[5] Believers who struggle through trials all the way to triumph can let God use their stories, their lives, to encourage and strengthen others.

If I stop thinking only of myself, God can display[6] His power in my life to be a witness to others.[7] I will choose to love others enough to gladly become a living object lesson to the mighty love of God.[8] I know I will be in good company.

Jesus knew who He was and whose He was,
so He could let God have free rein to use His life
to reach, teach, and bless others.

---

[1]Matt. 25:21   [2]John 5:34   [3]John 11:42   [4]Luke 23:28   [5]1 Pet. 2:21   [6]Isa. 60:21   [7]John 9:3
[8]John 17:23   *Biblio. p. 385

MAY 8

His mouth is sweetness itself; he is altogether lovely. . . .
Song of Solomon 5:16

*O*f all the Bible is, it is first and most the greatest love story ever written. The crowning act of the Genesis creation was . . . a wedding. And the final scene of Revelation is . . . the wedding supper of the Lamb! As His bride, I revel in the privilege of whispering sweet praises in my Beloved Bridegroom's ear. Oh, how it stirs my soul to praise Him!

Consider the names with which He is adorned: He is the Lily of the Valley, and the Rose of Sharon (Song 2:1). He is the Bright Morning Star (Rev. 22:16). He is the Wonderful Counselor, the Prince of Peace (Isa. 9:6), the Lamb of God (John 1:29). He is the Sun of Righteousness, rising with healing in His wings (Mal. 4:2). How awesome a vision!

Jesus is the tender Shepherd,[1] the abundant Vine (John 15:1), the Bread of Life (John 6:48). What lovely images of caring provision. He who feeds us is Himself our very food and drink. He is the Humble One of Gentle Heart, offering us His own peace, and rest for our souls.[2]

Although Isaiah tells us He had no beauty or majesty to attract us to him,[3] yet I find in Him that shining, unfading inner beauty of a gentle and quiet spirit,[4] and in His face I see the image of God made flesh,[5] all the radiance of God's glory.[6]

When the skirmishes in this spiritual war start to wear, I listen for His voice bidding me to "come with me by yourselves to a quiet place . . ."[7] Then oh, how alluringly He speaks to me.[8] He will remind me of who He is, and my soul will be stirred by the incomparable excellence of my Beloved!

I love to tell Him! What lover's heart doesn't beat faster to hear His beloved's praise? He is the gracious and compassionate God; He is Love and Truth and Beauty. Honor and glory surround Him, and even the trees clap their hands for joy at His presence![9]

What strength and gladness, what fierce and faithful devotion flames up within my spirit by the touch of the One who is altogether lovely.

In Jesus is a shining, unfading inner beauty of a gentle,
quiet spirit . . . the image God made flesh . . .

---

[1]Ezek. 34:11–16   [2]Matt. 11:28–29   [3]Isa. 53:2   [4]1 Pet. 3:4   [5]John 1:14   [6]Heb. 1:3   [7]Mark 6:31
[8]Hos. 2:14   [9]Isa. 55:12

MAY 9

Because of the LORD's great love we are not consumed,
for his compassions never fail.
They are new every morning; great is your faithfulness.
Lamentations 3:22–23

*Y*ou only really believe what you believe under fire.[1] What you cling to, what you find strength in when you are sorely tested, is what is truly in your heart.[2] This is what it means to *know* that you *know*.

I may believe God is good, but do I still believe God is good when the doctor says I have cancer?[3] I have read that God does everything for my good,[4] but do I believe that when I've just been fired? Does that verse still comfort me, give me strength to bear up? Or when the bad times roll, do I read it with a scowl that says, "Yeah, right!"?

Jeremiah's statement above sounds like one of those glib, "everything will be all right" platitudes that fall so easily from the lips of someone who has never really suffered.[5] If someone were to share it with me when I am sitting in a hospital waiting room after the doctor had just come out of the operating room shaking his head, would it still be true? Or would I feel that Jeremiah had no idea what he was talking about?

Yet Jeremiah *did* know. He'd been there. He'd preached and prophesied for over forty years to a nation that utterly refused to listen. He'd been rejected, assaulted, imprisoned, and threatened with death. He was even thrown into a muddy cistern and left to starve! He'd been lied about and lied to[6]—and worst of all, it seemed as if it had all been for nothing, because the people of Israel still were captured and exiled.

Either the Scriptures are true, or they aren't. What they say in the sunshine is still true in the storm. God is love, God is good, and God is faithful,[7] not only in the day, but even more so in the dark night of the soul. God doesn't ask me to understand how. He just asks, "Do you trust Me?"[8]

What do I *really* believe?

I only really believe what I believe under fire . . .

what I cling to when I am sorely tested.

---

[1] 1 Pet. 1:6–7   [2] Matt. 12:34   [3] Ps. 112:7   [4] Heb. 12:10   [5] Prov. 14:10   [6] Jer. 37 & 38   [7] Ps. 145:13   [8] Nah. 1:7

MAY 10

The enemy pursues me, he crushes me to the ground . . .
Psalm 143:3

*A*m I in earnest about growing in Christ? Am I hungrily seeking His truth, His purpose for me? Do I look daily for ways to express my love for Jesus? Have I ever prayed obediently and sincerely as Jesus did, desiring God's kingdom to come, His will to be done on earth as it is in heaven?[1] Then I have made myself very unpopular with the prince of this world.[2] I have a spiritual enemy who is known to be subtle, crafty, deceitful, cruel, merciless and unrelenting. By deciding for Christ, I have made myself a target.

This need not frighten me, however. Jesus is galaxies beyond the strength and power of Satan. Jesus Christ, the Son of the Living God, is hands-down the Greater One living in me.[3] He has delivered me for a purpose[4] and He *will* fulfill that purpose for me.[5] His own blood is an impenetrable force-field around me,[6] and He has encamped some really awesome angel-warriors around me to protect and deliver me![7] Fear is not in the believer's vocabulary.

But *wisdom* is. We are at war,[8] and there is no opting out of the battle. *I* can choose not to fight, but the enemy recognizes no détente and honors no truce. I must keep my wits about me, stay alert, and *expect* the enemy's attack.[9] Not in hand-wringing anxiety, but in a prepared awareness, standing ready to repel any tactic the enemy will use to hinder, harass, hamstring, and halt me.

He has many weapons. Some are more obvious than others, yet still prove effective all too often. Dissension and strife are two of his favorites.[10] "Divide and conquer[11] is his brainchild, and he has many other techniques. He will attempt to undermine any and every aspect of my walk with Christ. I can't afford to be caught off-guard! An attack anticipated is an attack thwarted.

Nothing and nobody can stop me fulfilling God's purpose for me as long as I resist the enemy, listen to Jesus, and never give up! I must remember–Jesus has already overcome the enemy and destroyed his works.[12]

Remember—Jesus has already
overcome the enemy and destroyed his works.

---

[1]Matt. 6:10 [2]John 14:30 [3]1 John 4:4 [4]Jer. 15:11 [5]Ps. 138:8 [6]Heb. 9:12, 14 [7]Ps. 34:7
[8]Rev. 12:7–12 [9]1 Pet. 5:8 [10]Hab. 1:3 [11]Jude 1:19 [12]1 John 3:8

MAY 11

It is not . . . honorable to seek one's own honor.
Proverbs 25:27

*H*ow much self-interest do I have? How much of my behavior is motivated by concern for my rights or reputation? How do I react when I am not treated as I feel I ought to be? Does it matter?

It matters very much, if I want to please God. You see, without faith it is impossible to please God.[1] Self-interest does not spring from faith, but is rooted in fear[2]—the opposite of faith. It is a fear of losing out, of coming up short. Self-interest does not want to surrender, to yield control to God, because it is afraid that God will not come through, that His promise will fail.[3] It does not truly believe that the Lord has good plans for us.[4]

Self-interest cannot turn the other cheek, nor go the extra mile.[5] Self-interest cannot stand to be wronged, and it cannot humble itself and trust that God will, indeed, exalt, as He said He would.[6] *I will be a doormat. I will be used. If I give, I will not have for myself.* Self-interest (pride) is overly concerned with what is fair, with getting what is owed.[7] It cannot simply let it go and trust that God will pour a generous measure back into my lap.[8]

A person of faith, on the other hand, looks at Calvary and believes the love the Father has for His children.[9] He knows that no one who puts his trust in him will ever be put to shame.[10] No one who lays up treasure in heaven will ever be short changed. A person of faith knows that Jesus Christ is faithful to treasure and reward whatever we sacrifice for Him, be it a reputation, hope, or life itself—body, soul, and spirit.

I can let my faith rest fully on the One who sustains all things—including me—by His powerful Word.[11] He will never disappoint me.[12]

A person of faith looks at Calvary and believes
the love the Father has for His children.

---

[1]Heb. 11:6   [2]1 Pet. 3:14   [3]Zeph. 3:5   [4]Jer. 29:11   [5]Matt. 5:39, 41   [6]1 Pet. 5:6   [7]Matt. 18:32–34
[8]Luke 6:38   [9]1 John 4:16   [10]1 Pet. 2:6   [11]Heb. 1:3   [12]Isa. 49:23

MAY 12

Let love and faithfulness never leave you . . .
then you will win favor and a good name in the sight of God and man.
Proverbs 3:3–4

*F*avor is powerful. Things *happen* for people with favor. Favor can change minds, cut red tape, engineer circumstances, and make the last first.[1] Favor *solves problems.*

Man's favor is fickle—only a fool would bet his life on it.[2] But God's favor is not based on His mood or whether someone else has bribed Him more.[3] God's favor can do things on a level that man's favor can't touch;[4] it is spiritual, supernatural. If it were for sale, we couldn't afford it. But God's favor is not for sale, nor is it given on the basis of money, looks, athletic ability, charm or connections.[5] It is given on the basis of *love and faithfulness.* Why these? It helps to understand what His favor is—and what it is not.

I used to think of God's favor as His blessing (Hebrew *beraka*[6])—the things He gives and does for me. But the Hebrew is not *beraka*; it is *hen*, which actually means "grace."[7] God's grace is His strength and power given to enable me to fulfill my purpose—*His* plans. That is why it takes love and faithfulness to move in the favor of God. They go together: love without faithfulness is mere sappiness. That kind of love is not love at all. It is sin-enabling and wishy-washy (cheap grace). Faithfulness (obedience) without love is harsh, intolerant legalism.

But love *and* faithfulness together—as a lifestyle—is enduring, willing obedience; it is the character of God.[8] If I choose to do God's will,[9] if I obey Him in spite of how daunting the task may seem, God's favor—His grace—goes before me to ensure that I can get the job done. Like the disciples on the Sea of Galilee, I will encounter storms (obstacles), but I *will get to the other side* if I don't give up.[10]

Loving God and faithfully letting Him love others through me wins His favor every time.

God's favor is not based on the mood He's in,
and if it were for sale, you could not buy it.

---

[1]Mark 10:31 [2]John 2:23–25 [3]Ps. 30:5 [4]Matt. 19:26 [5]Acts 8:20 [6]*Strongest:* p. 1,382
[7]*Strongest:* p. 1,406 [8]Ps. 25:10 [9]John 7:17 [10]Matt. 14:22–34

MAY 13

. . . One thing I do know. I was blind but now I see!
John 9:25

*T*don't have to be a theologian to witness to the power of the gospel of Jesus Christ. I don't need a degree, I don't need to be ordained; I don't really need training.[1] All I need to witness for Christ is to have had an encounter with Christ, a life-changing experience with the living Son of the living God.[2] I can say, "One thing I *do* know."

The man born blind was no orator, no evangelist, no powerhouse preacher with a multi-thousand-member congregation. He was nobody different than you and me, and he had been touched by the Master's hand. God trusted the flicker within him enough to call him to witness for Him before the whole ruling council! A heavy assignment, indeed.

Yet God graced him with courage and fanned that flicker into a passionate flame as he risked speaking the truth faithfully.[3] Starting out with a tentative telling of the bare facts, he grew in his boldness—declaring Jesus first a prophet, then himself a disciple—until he ended up standing as resolute as Elijah before the idolatrous King Ahab, reproving their unbelief.

What has Jesus done for *me*? That is my witness. It's the only testimony that matters, the only testimony that Jesus commanded. "Return home and tell how much God has done for you."[4] That's what John did. He wrote, "That which was from the beginning, which we have heard, which we have seen with our eyes, which we have looked at and our hands have touched—this we proclaim."[5] That was his testimony.

What is my testimony? What has God done for me? When I start telling others about the wonders of God in my life, God will grace me, too, with a holy boldness. I, too, may witness before kings and governors.[6] All I need to tell them is, "One thing I do know."

I don't have to be a theologian to share the gospel.
What has Jesus done for me? That is my witness.

---

[1]Matt. 21:16   [2]Ps. 66:16   [3]Acts 4:29   [4]Luke 8:39   [5]1 John 1:1   [6]Luke 21:12–15

MAY 14

Be exalted, O God, above the heavens;
let your glory be over all the earth.

Psalm 57:5

One of the greatest weapons in our spiritual arsenal is praise. When we're under attack with the enemy's flaming arrows landing all around us and we're standing boldly confident, praising our God *anyway*,[1] all heaven joins us in that instant. And don't you think the enemy is going to turn tail and run when he sees a legion or two of holy angels forming ranks on either side of us?[2]

The psalms are full of praise, and wonderful songs exalting the glory of God. The awesome thing about *this* verse is that David placed it smack in the middle of a major attack! The psalm opens with disaster (v. 1).[3] Men hotly pursuing him (v. 3)[4] until he's surrounded (v. 4)[5]. It's desperate, it's frightening—his enemies are ravenous lions . . .[6] "Praise God!" he shouts. "Be exalted above the heavens!"—even as the nets are being spread for his feet. He may be bowed down in distress (v. 6), but he can sing and make music (v. 7). He may be surrounded, cornered, treed, but he can praise the Lord (v. 9). The enemy is closing in, but he can glorify God (v. 11).

Why? How?

Because his heart is steadfast (v. 7). He has *kept* his heart steadfast the same way Peter walked on water . . . by keeping his eyes on God, not his enemies. And David's enemies were very real: King Saul and the entire army of Israel, hunting him down to kill him. To escape, David fled into the caves of En-Gedi. In 1 Samuel 24, the story of the physical encounter is told, but this psalm records the real battle—the spiritual battle.[7]

Am I under attack? It doesn't matter if the battle is physical (body), mental/emotional (soul), or spiritual; I can triumph the same way David did: ask and rely on God to help me (v. 1),[8] remember His promises to me (v. 2)—and praise His name *in the midst* of the battle, because the battle is already won![9]

One of the greatest weapons
in our spiritual arsenal is praise!

---

[1] 2 Chron. 20:22 [2] 2 Kings 6:17 [3] Ps. 37:19 [4] Exod. 15:9–10 [5] Luke 4:29–30 [6] Dan. 6:27
[7] John 6:63 [8] Isa. 41:10–14 [9] John 16:33

MAY 15

Do two walk together unless they have agreed to do so?
Amos 3:3

In the military, I learned the value and importance of keeping in step with those with whom I was marching. Getting out of step created chaos, causing myself and others to trip, stumble and fall. Staying in step got us from point A to point B in the least amount of time with the least amount of stress and energy expended. Everything worked faster and smoother.

As I was thinking about the idea of walking with the Spirit, God asked, "Have you ever tried to walk with a three-year-old where he didn't want to go?" I immediately recalled half-lifting, half-dragging my toddler daughter as she kicked and pulled and went limp, obstinately refusing to cooperate.[1] We certainly weren't walking together, because she *would not agree to do so.*

"That is what it is like when you do not cooperate and keep in step with My Spirit." How frustrating![2]

And yet keeping in step with the Spirit is not like marching: regimented, wearisome, and mindless. It is more like a dance: an exquisite ballet, a magnificent tango, where every move becomes a beautiful, creative expression of two spirits knit together as one. As in the dance, one leads, the other follows.[3] The leader knows the pattern of the dance, and His partner takes all her cues from Him.[4] To resist and reject His leading is to disrupt the flow. The dance becomes work, a battle, a contest of wills, and the pattern is ruined.[5]

Face it. In the dance, we cannot both lead. Someone's toes will get stepped on! I need to surrender and *let the Spirit lead me.* He is the only One who knows the intricate pattern of my dance.[6] All I have to do is keep in step with Him, and my life will become an eternal dance[7] of everlasting beauty—a joy forever.[8]

I need to surrender and let the Spirit lead me.
He is the only One who knows
the intricate pattern of my dance.

---

[1]Acts 7:51 [2]Isa. 5:4 [3]John 16:13 [4]Ps. 143:8–10 [5]Isa. 1:19–20 [6]Ps. 25:12 [7]Ps. 30:11 [8]Isa. 61:7

MAY 16

The manna stopped the day after they ate this food from the land . . .
Joshua 5:12

*Y*ou know, I have read the experiences of the Israelites in their journey from Egypt to the Promised Land and wondered, "What was *wrong* with these people? Why couldn't they just trust God and go forward?"

Israel fought every transition God brought them through, crying and complaining from their birth passage through the Red Sea to their infancy at Mt. Sinai, where God carried them in His arms.[1] In their childhood, God fed them and cared for them as their Father,[2] enrolling them in His Wilderness School until they were ready to graduate to the next level.[3]

We, too, struggle with our spiritual growth.[4] From the moment we are born, we cry and kick and fight against change, yet God continually draws us up and away from our familiar paths into unexplored heights and depths with Him.[5] The goal is fullness in Christ.

Am I going through some strange sensations in my spiritual life? Is there some unexplained yearning and discontent? Do I suddenly have some disturbing doubts, unanswered questions? Do the things that always gave me comfort before no longer satisfy my spirit? These are all typical growing pains—thresholds of transition. They are moments of opportunity disguised as crisis.

The Israelites struggled with this, too. Their freedom began with a doubled workload and plagues! They went from the fleshpots of Egypt[6] to a barren desert before they could eat the bread of angels.[7] And the day they crossed the Jordan River, at the threshold of the Promised Land, the comfortable security of supernatural manna suddenly stopped. They were growing up.

Challenges—transition—change—growth. The baby must be born, the child must mature.[8] I don't have to be afraid; I can trust God in my crisis/opportunity, and grow up in my salvation.[9]

---

*God continually draws us up and away
from our familiar paths into unexplored heights
and depths with Him.*

---

[1]Isa. 46:3 [2]Jer. 31:9 [3]Deut. 8:3–5 [4]Heb. 5:11–14 [5]Ps. 42:7 [6]Exod. 16:3 [KJV] [7]Ps. 78:25
[8]Heb. 6:1 [9]1 Pet. 2:2

MAY 17

When Simon Peter saw this, he fell at Jesus' knees and said,
"Go away from me, Lord; I am a sinful man!"
Luke 5:8

To encounter God is to experience a profound revelation. Just as the Word of God is a double-edged sword,[1] so also is that spirit-opening, soul-piercing moment of realizing that this is *God* I am seeing, hearing or feeling. It is the dumb-struck awe at the pure and absolute holiness of God, and it is the consuming shame of the extreme contrast between His purity and holiness and my utter sinfulness.

No one can bear a full and complete revelation of God and live.[2] There is no one who is righteous and never sins.[3] When God manifests Himself, mankind falls flat in abject terror and self-loathing: Job, Daniel, Isaiah, Ezekiel, . . . even John, the disciple whom Jesus loved.[4] To think we would do otherwise is to not know the holiness of God. But God is merciful, therefore we are given only glimpses, flashes of glory, moments of grace, when the Holy Spirit convicts us of sin and righteousness.[5]

That's what happened to Peter that astonishing day on the Sea of Galilee. Jesus had filled their nets with fish *because He was GOD*. In that one moment, Peter *knew* who Jesus was—and he *knew* who he himself was.

Salvation comes in such a moment—when it suddenly hits you that God is *real*, that He is *right*, and that you are wrong and without excuse. And when, in spite of all that, He reaches down and says, "Don't be afraid."[6]

God is love.[7] If it were not for this, nothing could ever bridge the yawning chasm between His amazing holiness and our complete sinfulness. The world would've ended before Adam and Eve swallowed. "But with you there is forgiveness, therefore you are feared."[8]

Salvation is in that third revelation: holiness, sinfulness and love. When the truth sinks in that it is because of the Lord's great love we are not consumed, for His compassions never fail,[9] who wouldn't fall down and worship the One who is good, whose love endures forever?[10]

Salvation truly comes when it suddenly hits you
that God is real, that He is right,
and you are wrong and without excuse.

---

[1]Heb. 4:12   [2]Exod. 33:20   [3]Eccl. 7:20   [4]Rev. 1:17   [5]John 16:8   [6]Luke 5:10   [7]1 John 4:8
[8]Ps. 130:4   [9]Lam. 3:22   [10]Ps. 100:5

MAY 18

Evil men do not understand justice,
but those who seek the LORD understand it fully.
Proverbs 28:5

There is something about standing at the foot of the cross that steals away my words. There is something about His blood, those nails, that anguished cry of forsakenness that excludes all my excuses, and reduces all my reasons to ashes on the ground. There is something about seeing the penalty for sin[1] fully carried out that leaves me speechless.[2]

In the midst of my sin, I thought myself justified. I was convinced I had cause; not a jury in the world would convict me. But it wasn't the world's jury I should've feared. I was called to account before the Judge of all the world.[3] I looked around me. There was no jury anywhere in sight.

Is God a God of justice? Ask Jesus. He paid the penalty for every sin ever committed. He took the punishment for every single act of disobedience, rebellion, selfishness, and evil ever contemplated and committed by human beings from, "In the beginning God . . ."[4] to "Amen. Come Lord Jesus."[5] He can tell you better than anyone that God's justice leaves no loopholes.

Pontius Pilate said it: "Behold the man!"[6] What could I tell Him? What reason could I give for my disobedience?[7] What excuse, what justification could I claim for my sin?[8] If any of my *buts* or *what abouts* were acceptable, were sufficient to justify sin, Jesus need not have died.[9]

But no. I came seeking God. I came to the cross, and I now understand justice. Only those who come to this place and look with fear and reverence into the face of the suffering Son of God can say, "Yes, Lord God Almighty, true and just are your judgments."[10] These are they who seek God, who understand justice.

And these are they who also discover the miracle of His truth: Mercy triumphs over judgment.[11]

Only those who come to this place and look with fear
and reverence into the face of the suffering
Son of God can say, "Yes, Lord God Almighty,
true and just are your judgments.

---

[1]Gen. 2:17 [2]Matt. 22:12 [3]Ps. 98:9 [4]Gen. 1:1 [5]Rev. 22:20 [6]John 19:5 [KJV] [7]John 15:25
[8]Luke 10:29 [9]Ps. 49:7–9 [10]Rev. 16:7 [11]James 2:13

MAY 19

Do not let this Book of the Law depart from your mouth;
meditate on it day and night . . .
Joshua 1:8

The Book of the Law was the written copy of all that God had spoken from the fiery summit of Mt. Sinai.[1] This was the clearest revelation of that time of this God who called Himself I Am. In all the previous times and ways that God had shown Himself and had spoken, this was the first time He had ensured that everything He had said was to be written down.[2] This revelation was too precious; not one word was to be lost, changed, or twisted.

And it was to be *available:*[3] Joshua was not a priest or a teacher of the Law. He was a soldier. He was called to lead the people, but as God laid out for him what he needed to do, He said nothing about military strategy, government councils, or even desert survival tactics. He told Joshua to meditate on His revelation, to keep it in his mouth day and night. Only then would he prosper and have good success.[4]

There is no true, lasting success outside of the will of God,[5] and the only way to know His will in every situation is to *know Him.*[6] For far too long now, people have allowed others to interpret God for them—letting others tell them who He is, what He is like, what He has said.[7] We have forgotten how to go to Him directly, to seek Him and hear Him for ourselves, as Jesus made possible.[8] God is directing us back to *His* words, back to the Source.

If I want to hear God's voice and know it is Him—to recognize His ways and His will—a good starting place is to find out what He has already said and done. God does not change;[9] The way He was then is the way He is now. I need to study the Scriptures—not just read them, but *meditate* on them. That doesn't mean sitting in a strange posture and chanting them, like many think of meditation. No, meditation means pondering them, thinking about their meaning, asking God what He is revealing about Himself, about me. Letting His Holy Spirit bring them to life, teaching me to understand how they fit in the kingdom of heaven here on earth.[10] Meditating on God's words is vital to knowing God.

There is no true, lasting success outside of the will of God.

---

[1]Exod. 24:3–4   [2]Exod. 34:1   [3]Deut. 31:10–13   [4]Josh. 1:6–9   [5]Ps. 73:2–20   [6]Jer. 9:24   [7]Deut. 5:27
[8]John 16:25–27   [9]Mal. 3:6   [10]John 16:13–15

MAY 20

Through these he has given us his very great and precious promises,
so that through them you may participate in the divine nature
and escape the corruption in the world caused by evil desires.

2 Peter 1:4

hroughout my life in Christ, I've sought to understand His promises—what they are and how to claim them. I was taught that if I
could find it in the Bible, I could claim it from God—always. It is that
always that is the crux of understanding His promises. The Bible is full of the
intense suffering of God's people, people of faith.[1] The promises are not that
we will never suffer; they are *because* we suffer. Suffering inherently involves
pain—and time. God's promises are His assurance that He not only knows our
pain, but that ultimately, He has a good purpose for allowing it.[2] Suffering is the
crucible that proves if our faith is genuine.[3] This test is not optional, because
faith—believing in Jesus—*is* the work that God requires.[4] *No other work* can
substitute for believing Him, especially when the chips are down.

Much of my struggle had to do with my motivation, my childish desires
to have, and to have it easy—to avoid the path of suffering.[5] But my Father is
helping me to change my desires from the stuff of this world to the ways of His
kingdom instead.[6] His promises are not given to make my life easy and trouble
free,[7] but to enable me to participate in the divine nature—to become like Him
in character:[8] loving, kind, generous, faithful, and compassionate. The hardest
lesson to learn is submission. The best way to teach submission is to say *no.* I
finally realized that God's *no* requires suffering; suffering for my own benefit.

Jesus' suffering was not for Himself, though, but for us. There is nothing
more Christlike than the way of the cross—to willingly suffer for the benefit
of others. This is what the better promises of the new covenant are for: to
write the kingdom of God on our hearts so that we can know God, directly
and personally.[9] Only those who know God can keep trusting Him even if it
kills them.[10]

> *God's promises are His assurance that He*
> *not only knows our pain, but that ultimately,*
> *He has a good purpose for allowing it.*

[1]Heb. 11:35–40   [2]1 Pet. 3:14–18   [3]1 Pet. 1:6–7   [4]John 6:29   [5]James 4:3   [6]Luke 12:33–34
[7]John 16:33   [8]1 John 4:17   [9]Heb. 8:6–12   [10]Job 13:15

MAY 21

And he gave them their request; but sent leanness into their soul.
Psalm 106:15 [KJV]

nswered prayer is not always a blessing! This is a radical thought that I really didn't want to consider. After all, if God gave me what I asked for, it must be good, right? It must be His will, right?

Not always.

The Israelites asked for meat, and God gave it to them—so much meat that it choked them, made them sick, and they loathed it.[1] They asked for a king, and God gave them a king, and they truly *did* become just like the nations around them—sinful, idolatrous and enslaved.[2] Hezekiah begged to live, and God granted him fifteen years more, which fed his pride and lured the conquering Babylonians into the heart of his kingdom.[3]

God has warned me, "Beware your strong desires." If I cannot accept a *no* answer, it is time to re-evaluate my motives.[4] There is a difference between persistence[5] and pestering. One comes from an attitude of faith, confidence and trust in God; the other from a dissatisfied, discontented, murmuring spirit. Persistence discerns God's will first, then asks and keeps on asking until His will is manifested in my life.[6]

Pestering, on the other hand, is being stubbornly immature, instead of seeking God's will.[7] It is deciding what *I* want regardless of what God may desire for me. It is easy to fall into this trap, for we all yearn for an easy, comfortable life with a minimum of challenges. I want to be surrounded with pleasant people who think and act just like I do, and have all my (self-defined) needs met instantly. I have even (sad to say) prayed away from me people I dislike! (What if God had been hoping *I* would be the one to love that person into the kingdom?[8])

Seeking God's will means putting His kingdom ahead of my comfort, God's plans ahead of my desires, seeking the lost ahead of serving myself. "Seek first His kingdom and His righteousness."[9] If my priorities are right, I need never fear an answered prayer.

If I cannot accept a no answer from God,

it is time to re-evaluate my motives.

---

[1] Num. 11:18–20   [2] 1 Sam. 8   [3] Isa. 38 and 39   [4] James 4:2–3   [5] Luke 18:1   [6] 1 John 5:14
[7] 1 Pet. 4:2   [8] 1 John 4:19   [9] Matt. 6:33

MAY 22

Then I will tell them plainly, "I never knew you. . . ."
Matthew 7:23

God wants us to know Him. Jesus said, "Now this is eternal life: that they may know you, the only true God, and Jesus Christ, whom you have sent."[1] There is nothing "New Testament only" about this yearning; God spoke it also through Jeremiah: "Let him who boasts boast about this: that he understands and knows me."[2] His heart has ached for this relationship, this fellowship, ever since Adam and Eve ran and hid from Him in the Garden of Eden.[3]

But the kind of *knowing* God has in mind is not a dry, dead studying of facts, as you would study the life of Caesar or Galileo or Abraham Lincoln. He's not assigning an essay; He's looking for a friend.[4] He sent Jesus to die for us and take care of that whole sin-and-death problem we had, so He could once again walk with us in the garden in the cool of the day.

And to have us walk with him—just as Enoch did.[5] Notice Jesus did not say, "You never knew *Me*." He said, "I never knew you."

You see, the kind of *knowing* God yearns for is *intimacy*. You get to know *about* someone by reading about them; you *get to know them* by talking to them, spending time with them, asking them questions, and listening for their answers. Conversation of this type is so much more than the usual laundry-list prayer of "Gimme, bless me, help me, thank you, bye." Intimate friends share their thoughts and dreams, their hurts and hopes, the funny things that happened to them today, and the things that made them mad. *True* friends need no masks;[6] they can let down their guard, let down their hair, and let it all hang out—the pretty, *and* the pretty ugly parts of themselves.

Do I really want to know God? Do I want God to know *me*? Then I need to break out of the old *thee* and *thou* mold and tell Him about my day—about my difficulties, disasters, my hopes and dreams.[7] And it's not a one-way conversation. I need to learn to ask, to get quiet and listen for what He wants to tell me. I may end up walking so close to God, I'll walk right into heaven—just like Enoch!

The kind of knowing that God yearns for is intimacy.

---

[1]John 17:3 [2]Jer. 9:24 [3]Gen. 3:8–9 [4]John 15:15 [5]Gen. 5:24 [6]Prov. 21:29 [7]Prov. 14:10

MAY 23

But rejoice that you participate in the sufferings of Christ . . .
1 Peter 4:13

*P*eople of all sorts come and go throughout our lives—most superficially, never growing any closer than a nodding acquaintance. Yet others manage to break through our defenses, get under our skin, and end up in our hearts. These are they with whom we have "gone through" together.[1] We know we can count on them to be there for us in our sorrows and our strengths. This fellowship of shared suffering is a bond deeper than any other.[2]

Not all of our pain is participating in the sufferings of Christ, however. "Life *is* pain . . . anyone who tells you differently is selling something,"* says the hero in one of my favorite movies. No one goes through life unscathed.[3] Physical pain, loss, betrayal, loneliness, and abandonment are but a few of the agonies of existence.[4] But to participate in *Christ's sufferings* is only available to believers; it is to suffer specifically because we are His, because we dare to follow in His footsteps. It is to suffer for doing good in the name of Jesus. It is to be ridiculed, mocked, beaten, cast out, imprisoned, and even killed, simply because we bear His Name and refuse to deny Him. In this we are told to rejoice.[5] For some, their suffering overwhelms them; they do not survive it. Others grimly endure, struggling through horrors, barely making it from day to day. But who *rejoices* for their suffering?

Jesus is not asking us to become pain-loving masochists. It is not the suffering itself we are to be happy about, but what it means. It is the experience of sharing Christ's suffering with Him.[6] When we truly suffer for the name of Jesus[7] (and not because of our own character flaws), we are walking with our Lord in the way of the cross. Rejoicing helps us to deal with feelings of betrayal or abandonment; our hearts sometimes forget that we are destined to be rejected by a world opposed to Christ.[8] Rejoicing keeps our eyes on Jesus,[9] and reminds us to react with blessing, not cursing.[10] Our rejoicing strengthens us to endure, to triumph. There is no deeper relationship with Jesus than to go through His sufferings with Him.

When we truly suffer for the name of Jesus,
we are walking with our Lord in the way of the cross.

---

[1]Ps. 23:4   [2]Heb. 13:3   [3]Eccl. 2:22–23   [4]Ps. 88:15–18   [5]Matt. 5:11–12   [6]Heb. 12:3   [7]1 Pet. 4:16
[8]John 15:18–25   [9]Heb. 12:2   [10]Luke 6:27–28   *Biblio. p. 385–6

MAY 24

*Just as it was in the days of Noah,
so also will it be in the days of the Son of Man.*
Luke 17:26

*I*n most apocalyptic visions and scenarios of the last days, times of up-heaval and complete revolution are imagined. Many are counting on dramatic events to give them advance warning, alerting them in time to repent and get serious with God. This attitude is permeating even believers, fed by various dramatic end-times books and movies.

Although Jesus painted a picture of wars, famines, and earthquakes, He said that these things must happen first, but the end will not come right away.[1] To be sure, there will be dramatic events, but just as many of the most revolu-tionary, history-making events occurred almost unnoticed and unrecognized by the world, so shall it be with the fulfillment of prophecy in the end. Many will never realize that the news they are watching is reporting the rise of the Antichrist;[2] they will never make the connection.

No—the picture Jesus actually painted is a much more subtle and dangerous delusion. He spoke of how it was in the days of Noah and Lot—people eat-ing and drinking, buying and selling, planting and building.[3] In other words, *business as usual.* Everyday folks going about their everyday tasks in their everyday lives, completely oblivious to the signs of Christ's return, and of how near disaster is.[4]

When the Twin Towers fell on September 11, 2001, all those people were busily going about their business as usual without a clue that in mere moments, they would be facing eternity. It will be the same in the days of the Son of Man.[5] Jesus said the delusion would be so powerful that if it were possible, it would deceive even the very elect.[6] Remember, subtlety is Satan's preferred approach.[7]

I don't dare count on headlines announcing the Antichrist; I absolutely must learn from the Holy Spirit how to discern truth from error,[8] right from wrong.[9] I will serve God passionately and wholeheartedly now, and fill myself with the truth and obey it fully. I will walk every day with God's business in mind, and business as usual will not catch me unaware and unprepared![10]

Remember, subtlety is Satan's preferred approach!

---

[1]Luke 21:9   [2]1 John 2:18   [3]Luke 17:28   [4]Judg. 20:34   [5]Luke 17:30   [6]Matt. 24:24   [7]Gen. 3:1
[8]2 Pet. 3:17   [9]Heb. 5:14   [10]Luke 12:42–46

MAY 25

. . . Then give to Caesar what is Caesar's, and to God what is God's.
Luke 20:25

*H*e was a model of grace, wisdom, dignity, skill and faithfulness. His loyalty was above reproach. This was remarkable, considering he was a captive in exile, forced to serve the enemy king! Was he a traitor? No, Daniel served his enemy, because he served God first.

Daniel was everything the devil hates. Of course he wanted to destroy him. *But he had no foothold.*[1] Daniel's enemies could not find a single compromise in his character or his work to use against him. They had to make an entirely new law just to get him![2]

So, who is *my* "Caesar"? He may be hard to recognize without the toga, but Caesar is my employer; my government (and all its representatives); the people with whom I buy and sell; my community. Caesar is the world, and although my citizenship is in heaven,[3] I am a resident alien here, and I have an obligation to fear God, and honor the king;[4] to be faithful in all I do.

Faithfulness, you see, is the *fruit* of faith;[5] it is faith with hands and feet.[6] It is integrity, diligence, and excellence in every act, understanding that every act reflects upon the character of the God I serve. It is doing the right thing well, because I cannot imagine doing things any other way. The faithful soul loves God supremely and yearns to honor Him through all things. There is no desire in his heart to cut corners, misappropriate materials, fudge numbers, mistreat equipment—to be sloppy, inconsistent, or undependable.[7] Lack of integrity displeases God, who grieves, "Many a man claims to have unfailing love, but a faithful man who can find?"[8]

What I do and how I do it reflects on my God. I want to honor Him with excellence, an unblemished offering.[9] I want to express His character through my actions.[10] If I am faithful, others may come to believe that my God is faithful[11] and put their trust in Him, too.

Faithfulness is understanding that every act reflects upon the character of the God you serve.

---

[1]John 14:30 [2]Dan. 6:3–9 [3]Heb. 11:13–16 [4]1 Pet. 2:17 [5]Matt. 7:16–20 [6]James 2:18
[7]Luke 12:42–46 [8]Prov. 20:6 [9]Prov. 14:35 [10]Matt. 10:25 [11]Ps. 33:4

MAY 26

. . . but the people who know their God will firmly resist him.
Daniel 11:32

*W*hen I was a kid, one of my fondest ambitions was to be a spy. There was one major hitch in my plans, however: I couldn't tell when people were lying to me. Being able to tell the false from the true is a vital skill for a spy. It might someday be a matter of life or death.

Discerning between true and false is crucial for another occupation as well: being a follower of Christ. It is matter of life or death. Our enemy has been described as being full of wisdom,[1] subtle, crafty,[2] and a masquerader.[3] He is a liar, and deception is his strong suit.[4] How will we ever be able to tell the difference between a deceptive miracle and a genuine one? A confirming sign and a counterfeit? A wonder, and a lying wonder?[5] They are all supernatural! But *supernatural* doesn't mean it's of God. After all, the devil is a supernatural being, too—and he has an agenda. He can appear shiningly beautiful and deceive those who believe that evil always looks ugly. How can we resist his siren song?

The thing is, it is not the miracle itself that is the problem. The problem is in what it leads us to accept and believe. All of the enemy's counterfeits are designed to get us to swallow his lies[6]—to follow his false teachers, his false teachings.[7] God warned us that even accurate prophecies are not a reliable measure.[8] Within His warning, however, is the key to true discernment: loving God with all our heart and soul. You see, loving God is not like loving a celebrity; not like being a fan. A fan knows a lot *about* their favorite star; they do not know them personally. Even the most devoted fan cannot act as a character witness for them.

How well do I *really* know God? Do I know His heart's desires?[9] Do I understand His goals, His plans, His methods?[10] Do I know Him enough to recognize Him in the midst of seeming contradictions?[11] Enough to argue with him *and win*?[12] Loving God means knowing God like that.

No matter how palatable or plausible the lie, only those who *know their God* will firmly resist.

Loving God means knowing God.

---

[1]Ezek. 28:12 [2]Gen. 3:1 [KJV, NIV] [3]Mark 13:21–22 [4]John 8:44 [5]Rev. 16:14 [6]Rev. 13:13–14
[7]2 Pet. 2:1–3 [8]Deut. 13:1–3 [9]Hos. 6:6 [10]John 15:15 [11]Gen. 22:1–19 [12]Exod. 32:7–14

MAY 27

*. . . let us throw off everything that hinders
and the sin that so easily entangles . . .*

Hebrews 12:1

If someone were to ask us what is it in our life that is keeping us from becoming all that God wants us to be, chances are, we would not name any gross sin. Our biggest stumbling block in going higher and deeper with God is more likely to be the very thing that choked the good seed of the Word: life's worries, riches and pleasures.[1] It is important to realize that two-thirds of those Word-choking thorns are *good things*: riches and pleasures! These are the things that hinder.

One of the enemy's greatest weapons is not outright temptation, but distraction. He is not only a liar, but a thief.[2] He steals our time and attention away from things eternal,[3] filling up our minutes, hours, days with so much temporal stuff, our schedules are too full to focus on God. The subtlety of this deception is that the devil lulls us into his trap of busy-ness without raising any red *Temptation!* flags. He uses those things that tie us up, tie us down, and hinder us—but are not in themselves sinful. They just are not beneficial, not constructive, not what Jesus has called us to do. They *dissipate* us.

Jesus, in speaking of His return, solemnly warned us to "be careful, or your hearts will be weighed down with dissipation . . ."[4] We think of dissipation as wild, immoral living—orgies and such—and we feel safe, because we're not like *that*. But the dictionary says that *dissipation* means not just "intemperate living," but a "wasteful expenditure." To *dissipate* means to "cause to spread out or spread thin to the point of vanishing," to "lose irrevocably," to "expend aimlessly or foolishly," and to "use up . . . heedlessly."[5]

Am I weighed down with dissipation? I can't let my faith be spread too thin and vanish. I must not lose His grace irrevocably, and I must not expend or use up my life aimlessly, foolishly or heedlessly. Whatever is hindering me from growing closer to God, I need to *throw it off!*

---

*One of the enemy's greatest weapons
is not outright temptation, but distraction.*

---

[1]Luke 8:14   [2]John 10:1, 10   [3]John 6:27   [4]Luke 21:34   [5]*Webster's:* "dissipate"

MAY 28

I will walk about in freedom, for I have sought out your precepts.
Psalm 119:45

*W*hat is freedom? Many seem to think that freedom is being able to do whatever they please, whenever and wherever they please. But the word translated here is not *deror* (liberty), but *rahab*, which literally means "spacious, broad, and roomy."[1] The psalmist is saying that because he has sought out God's precepts, he walks about in a spacious, broad and roomy place!

Dissidents rebel against rules, claiming they are too confining. But ask me—an inmate in an 8'x10' cell—if disobedience has put me in a spacious and roomy place. Too many of us learn the truth the hard way: rebellion is not freedom, it is confinement. And the *hard* truth is, the more we rebel, the smaller and tighter our confinement becomes!

Yet true freedom is not found in mere mindless or reluctant obedience. Oh, what a difference between just keeping the rules and actively, eagerly seeking out God's precepts! Precepts are not rules or laws, but the principles behind the laws. They are the ways of God.[2]

God's ways do not come to me in my easy chair; I will never understand His precepts if I am a spiritual couch potato.[3] David *sought out* (Hebrew *daras*) God's precepts—His way of *being* and *doing*. That means he put some elbow grease to it; he inquired, consulted, pondered, cared for, required, investigated, appealed to, studied and probed God's principles.[4] He changed his life to line up with them. They were his daily advice column,[5] his mentors, his guide.[6] When he learned something new about God's ways, he made it his way, too. He fell in love with doing right, and as result, he walked about in freedom, in a spacious, broad, roomy place of abundance.

When I found myself hemmed in, constricted, confined and shackled—when I lost my freedom—I realized it was because I was rebelling against the ways of God. I am learning now to seek out His precepts, for true freedom is found only within their boundaries.[7]

*True freedom is found in eagerly
seeking out God's precepts.*

[1]*Strongest:* p. 1,390; 1,489   [2]Ps. 25:4–5   [3]Prov. 12:24   [4]*Strongest:* p. 1,390   [5]Ps. 73:24   [6]Prov. 1:5
[7]Ps. 16:6

MAY 29

... For to see your face is like seeing the face of God ...
Genesis 33:10

Like David, my heart cries out, "Seek his face!"[1] The chronicler of Israel urges me to seek his face always.[2] Ever since He called me out of darkness into His wonderful light,[3] I have been like Solomon's beloved, searching for the One my heart loves.[4]

Where do I look? Where does one go to look for God? Where is He, that I may see His face?

"You cannot see my face, for no one can see me and live."[5]

Yet Jesus whispers in my spirit, "The pure in heart . . . will see God."[6] I had thought He meant that someday, in heaven, if I am pure, I will finally see God. Purity became all my desire—and holiness, for without holiness no one will see the Lord.[7] Who does not long to gaze upon their Beloved?

So I searched for Him on my bed—in prayer and meditation.[8] I sought Him in the streets and squares, and I got closer. And one day, as I bent to wash your feet, I saw the hem of His garment. In astonishment, I looked into your face, and I saw His face instead! Now, I see His face everywhere—in the weary face of my sister in her struggles. When I help her carry her burdens, I help Him carry His cross. I see Him in the teary eyes of my neighbor in her sorrows. When I wipe her tears, I am wiping His feet with my hair.[9] I see him even in the face of my enemy, for I, too, was once His enemy. When I love her and speak peace to her, my enemy, I begin to see the face of God in my own face.

I cannot see His face and live, except I see it veiled in your flesh. He has placed eternity—His image—in the hearts of men,[10] so pardon me if I look very deeply into your eyes. I am looking for my Beloved in you, for seeing your face is like seeing the face of God. What can I do for you, that I may serve Him?

Where does one look for God?

Where is He that we might see His face?

---

[1]Ps. 27:8 [2]1 Chron. 16:11 [3]1 Pet. 2:9 [4]Song 3:1–2 [5]Exod. 33:20 [6]Matt. 5:8 [7]Heb. 12:14
[8]Ps. 63:6 [9]Matt. 25:40 [10]Eccl. 3:11

MAY 30

. . . Rather, it is the Father, living in me, who is doing his work.
John 14:10

*M*y struggle to follow Christ is never more than when it is just that—*my* struggle. The harder I try, and grit my teeth, and work at it in spite of all my flesh wants to do otherwise—following Jesus is very hard work.

But Jesus indicated it shouldn't be that way. He said, "Come to me, all you who are weary and burdened, and I will give you rest. Take my yoke upon you and learn from me . . . and you will find rest for your souls. For my yoke is easy and my burden is light."[1]

If anyone could have claimed the ability to do God's will by His own power, it was Jesus. But even Jesus said, "By myself I can do nothing."[2] *And He was perfect.* How can it be? Because doing the will of God is not so much in the physical execution; it is in the relationship of communing with His Spirit. God's will can only be done by God's Spirit. For me to do God's will, I must not hinder His Spirit in me and allow Him to work in and through me. But I am like a toddler, insisting that I can do it. As long as I think I can, I will use my own strength, knowledge, and discipline. I am separate from God's power; His Spirit is not involved, and therefore His will is not done, no matter how well I perform. I must come to know and admit that I cannot do it by myself *at all.*[3] Only then can I come to God and ask Him honestly to do it in me, through me—for me. That is when I finally enter His rest—by resting from my own work.[4]

God does not need me; He is omnipotent. He can raise up children of Abraham from rocks.[5] If He needed something done, He could do it Himself.[6] The goal is not primarily to get something done. The goal is to grant me the opportunity to become His child,[7] to become one with Him as Jesus was,[8] to experience the glory of His perfect unity by acting in union with Him. For this, I choose to set aside my *I, me, mine* and accept His will as my own.[9] The *I, me, mine* in me fears becoming lost. What I find, though, is that I become so much *more* with God in me than anything I could ever be alone.

God's will can only be done by God's Spirit.

[1]Matt. 11:28–30   [2]John 5:30   [3]John 15:5   [4]Heb. 4:9–10   [5]Matt. 3:9   [6]Ps. 50:9–12   [7]John 1:12   [8]John 17:20–23   [9]Mark 14:36

MAY 31

Then Samuel took a stone and set it up . . . saying,
"Thus far has the LORD helped us."
1 Samuel 7:12

God well knows man's tendency to forget. We all suffer from short attention spans. Too many times we fall into trouble and immediately forget all the blessings and providences of God.[1] As soon as we are safe and secure, we forget the miracles and wonders He worked to get us through.[2] It's the cliché of jailhouse religion to make vows in our valleys that we quickly deny in our deliverance.[3]

That's why nearly twenty-five times in Deuteronomy alone, God urges the Israelites to "Remember–!" and "Do not forget–!" He instituted the Passover and the feasts of Tabernacles, Trumpets, and Firstfruits[4] to set aside specific times to remember His power, His protection, and His provision. He even gave them the Israelite version of the string around the finger, He had them put tassels on their garments to remind them to think of His commands.[5] They made an altar out of stones from the dry Jordan riverbed to remember their miraculous crossing.[6] They gave names to places where God had stepped into their lives, both for judgment and for deliverance. We have a drive placed within us by God to do this, to erect memorials to major events in our lives.

When we think back over *our* walk with the Lord—what memorials would we erect along that journey? We may not be able to build an altar on the site, but there are ways we can keep alive the memory of God's hand in our lives. (A spiritual journal might be an excellent and effective means, especially if we frequently re-read it.) We need to take the time–often–to remember the deeds of the Lord and to meditate on all His works.[7] In the wisdom of times and seasons, we are admonished, "There is a time to build . . . a time to gather . . . a time to keep."[8] We can build our relationship with God by gathering experiences and moments one by one, keeping them deep in the memory of our heart so when our next valley comes, we will remember thus far has the Lord helped us.

I should take the time—often—

to remember the deeds of the Lord.

[1]Exod. 14:10–12   [2]Deut. 8:10–18   [3]Ps. 66:13–14   [4]Lev. 23   [5]Num. 15:38–39   [6]Josh. 4:20–23
[7]Ps. 77:11–12   [8]Eccl. 3:3, 5–6

JUNE 1

Your promises have been thoroughly tested, and your servant loves them.
Psalm 119:140

hroughout my life in Christ, I have struggled to understand His promises. It may sound like a simple matter, but I haven't found it so easy. What *are* His promises? Are they all meant for me? Always, in every situation, just find it in the Bible and claim it? It's a popular teaching these days that God wants us to be healthy, wealthy, and prosperous in every aspect of our lives, and that He has promised all of this to every believer everywhere, if we would only have enough faith to claim it. I am a prisoner. The Bible says, "The LORD sets prisoners free."[1] If I believe hard enough, will the gates open for me? But what about John the Baptist and James?[2] What about all the martyrs? Is it freedom from physical prison, like Peter,[3] or freedom from the prison of sin and hopelessness?[4]

That is what testing the promises is all about. Everything in my life is supposed to drive me to seek His face, to discover the path of His will for me. It's not about my comfort or my desire.[5] It's about doing the will of God and fulfilling His purpose for me, whether that purpose calls for fire or flood. Seeking His face is seeking His desires: to be healed, rescued, delivered–or to bear through suffering by His grace and thus bring Him glory.[6] His promise is that whether it be fire or flood, it will not overwhelm my soul.[7] He will be with me in it all; He will never leave me nor forsake me.[8]

Jesus promised us trouble,[9] persecution, betrayal, arrest, even death–but He also promised that not a hair of our heads will perish.[10] To Peter, He spoke a promise of martyrdom. When Peter asked about another disciple, Jesus said, "What is that to you? You must follow me."[11] I must find out what He is speaking *to me* about *my* path. Following Jesus is not a get-rich plan for living comfortably in this world. Following Jesus should loosen my grip on the things of this life.

Testing His promises is my journey deep into His heart. This is how I learn His thoughts and His ways, and surrender my own. This is where I discover His will for me. What He promises, He will deliver.

His promise is that whether it be fire or flood,
it will not overwhelm my soul.

---

[1]Ps. 146:7 [2]Acts 12:1–2 [3]Acts 12:3–11 [4]John 8:36 [5]1 Pet. 4:1–2 [6]John 12:27–28
[7]Isa. 43:1–2 [8]Heb 13:5 [9]John 16:33 [10]Luke 21:12–18 [11]John 21:18–22

JUNE 2

Why should any living man complain when punished for his sins?
Lamentations 3:39

What do we deserve? Respect? Fair treatment? Rewards? Life, liberty, and the pursuit of happiness? In America, these are thought of as God-given, inalienable rights. We consider them our due as human beings, and we take it poorly and personally when we are not accorded what we "deserve," when someone steps on our "rights."

Thomas Jefferson did have this correct, though: the playing field is level. All are equal. We began that way, created by God in His image, and valuable because of it. And we have ended up that way—equally sinful and guilty. There is no one who does good, not even one.[1] It really doesn't matter what our crimes against God are. The truth is, we have all—every single one of us—earned the death penalty for what we've done, what we've thought about doing, what we would've done if we'd had half a chance.[2] Whether I murdered, you stole, or he lied, dead is just as dead.

Until I truly felt the weight of that death sentence,[3] however, my entire life was out of perspective. God's mercy was not my very life's breath; His forgiveness was not my heart's beat. Until I knew all the way to the marrow of my soul that death and destruction are *all* I deserve,[4] all I have a right to expect,[5] grace was not the absolute, no-other-way lifeline to me that it should have been.[6] I thought I had options, and I continued to negotiate my obedience to God: "I'll do that, if You'll do this . . ."[7]

Ending up in prison was my wake-up call, my reality check. Only then did I realize that every breath I take is a miracle of grace. Every day that dawns, every single blessing of God is a gift[8] I don't deserve, given only because He loves me.[9]

If we don't have everything we think we deserve, thank God!

It doesn't matter what our crimes against God are.
Dead is dead.

---

[1]Ps. 53:3   [2]Ezek. 18:4   [3]Luke 23:40–41   [4]Ezek. 9:7–10   [5]Lev. 26:21   [6]John 8:24   [7]Mic. 6:6–7
[8]James 1:17   [9]Ps. 103:10–11

JUNE 3

Whoever claims to live in him must walk as Jesus did.
1 John 2:6

WJD. What would Jesus do? In spite of the over-worn trendiness of the acronym, this is *the* question. By this, the Holy Spirit renews our mind,[1] guides our steps, and directs our path. It echoes Mary's wisdom: "Do whatever he tells you."[2]

So what *would* Jesus do? How *did* He walk? "In obedience" is usually the first thing that comes to mind.[3] But obedience was the fruit, the result, of an even higher principle by which Jesus walked. You cannot simply walk in obedience; you must walk in obedience *to* something, *because* of a choice you've made. Jesus walked in obedience to the law of love[4] because He chose to love His Father above all else. Everything He did was done *in* love, *because* He loved.[5] Obedience for any other reason is warped, tainted with selfishness and fear, and is dead. A slave obeys with his heart full of fear, rage, and hatred toward his master. Such a one would never be happy in heaven serving a God he does not love.[6]

Love is not optional. God does not merely love, He *is* love.[7] We are to be like Him.[8] We are to be so filled with and driven by love that it defines us.[9] Jesus loved. He treated all with dignity, respect, kindness, grace and mercy, no matter how they treated Him. He pushed no one away—not the liars, the cheats, the ungrateful, the unholy. He touched the untouchable, welcomed the outcasts, ate with the sinners. He had the grace and mercy to tell them the hard truth, even as He embraced them. He rescued them from their circumstances, yet commanded, "Go, and sin no more[10] . . . or something worse may happen to you."[11]

Am I mistreated? Misunderstood? Disrespected and abused? Lied about, lied to, ignored, unappreciated? What should I do when my brother or sister sins against me?[12]

What would Jesus do? Let's go and do likewise.[13]

Jesus chose to love His Father above all else.
Everything He did was done in love.

---

[1]Heb. 4:12 [2]John 2:5 [3]John 8:29 [4]Matt. 22:37–40 [5]John 13:1 [6]Luke 16:13 [7]1 John 4:8
[8]1 John 4:17 [9]John 13:35 [10]John 8:11 [KJV] [11]John 5:14 [12]Matt. 18:15–18 [13]Luke 10:37

JUNE 4

My soul finds rest in God alone; my salvation comes from him.
Psalm 62:1

After all the fear and hurt and stress and striving to make our way in the world; after all the trying and reaching and straining to find peace and happiness; after settling for the quick fixes that fixed nothing and giving up on ever satisfying that hungry hole inside us, coming to Christ is the ultimate rest. It is finally being able to exhale, to relax what we hadn't even realized was tight and tense.

Jesus said, "Come to me, all you who are weary and burdened, and I will give you rest."[1] The enemy discourages people from accepting Jesus, from choosing God's way, by fooling them into thinking their life will be so hard, that God makes impossible demands, and that they will never have fun or be happy.

But don't you know it? The Big Daddy of All Liars has struck again! The truth is, Jesus' yoke is easy and His burden is light.[2] It is the way of the unfaithful that is hard,[3] and many are the woes of the wicked.[4] With God, nothing is impossible![5] When God's people obeyed Him and were ruled by a righteous king who loved the Lord, were their lives miserable and rigidly controlled? Hardly! The Bible says, "The people of Judah and Israel were as numerous as the sand on the seashore; They ate, they drank, and they were happy."[6] God blesses His obedient people with peace,[7] sweet sleep,[8] a good future,[9] and greater joy than abundant wealth could ever give.[10]

Think about it: before you came to know the Lord, was your life easy? Smooth sailing? No ruffles, no pain, no bills, no envy, jealousy, rage, hatred, malice, slander and misery? Was it all a bed of roses that salvation really messed up for you? Was the fun you had lasting, and were your friends as true in the bad times as when the good times were rolling?[11]

People have to fight to stay lost, for God's Spirit draws all souls inexorably to His cross and to His heart. Why struggle so much, when we can find rest in God alone?

Obedience to God does not make a person miserable.
His yoke is easy and His burden is light!

---

[1]Matt. 11:28 [2]Matt. 11:30 [3]Prov. 13:15 [4]Ps. 32:10 [5]Luke 1:37 [6]1 Kings 4:20 [7]Ps. 29:11
[8]Prov. 3:24 [9]Ps. 37:37 [10]Ps. 4:7 [11]Prov. 20:6

JUNE 5

He who falls on this stone will be broken to pieces,
but he on whom it falls will be crushed.
Matthew 21:44

There is no avoiding the issue: no one can encounter Jesus Christ and come away unchanged. Take note as well: whether we accept or reject him, we *will* be broken. Whether it is a brokenness that heals or destroys us is up to us. God warns us that His Word is like a hammer that breaks a rock in pieces.[1] Both the demolitions man and the sculptor use hammers to break rocks. The blows of the first shatter and ruin, but those of the second create and refine.[2]

Unlike rocks, however, we are brought face to face with Jesus Christ, the Living Word, with the gift of choosing what He will be to us: sculptor or de-molitions expert. It is not that we come to him whole and He breaks us; we are already broken. Only those who recognize their brokenness, the wrongness of their ways, can fall on Him and be broken to pieces and can be healed.[3] Those who fool themselves, thinking they are fine the way they are, feel no need of the Cornerstone.[4] They encounter Jesus Christ, but they refuse to ac-cept His correction.[5] The stone of His Word, the Rock of His sacrifice, falls on them and crushes them.[6]

Stiffness—being rigid, inflexible, unmalleable and unmoldable—is what breaks even a thing as strong and hard as granite or steel. And what did God call those who refused correction? Stiff-necked.[7]

Are we willing to suffer a little now, so we need not suffer eternally? Believe me, humbling ourselves is no easy task. Putting down our pride—admitting our way is wrong and God's way is right[8]—is painful. Oh, but the life and beauty born of such pain is absolutely miraculous!

We need to stop bucking God's discipline and let the Holy Spirit soften that stiffness in our neck. We can yield to the Rock of our salvation. We need to fall on the stone before *it* falls on *us!*

Only those who recognize their brokenness
can fall on Him, be broken to pieces, then healed.

---

[1]Jer. 23:29   [2]Heb. 12:5–11   [3]Ps. 32:1–5   [4]Matt. 9:12   [5]Jer. 6:27–30   [6]Prov. 29:1   [7]Exod. 33:3
[8]Rev. 2:21

JUNE 6

As long as it is day, we must do the work of him who sent me.
Night is coming, when no one can work.

John 9:4

*H*ow much of my life have I really lived? Too many of us have been duped into putting our lives on hold—waiting to *do* and to *be* until some other event takes place, until conditions are right. And in our waiting, time slips by—moments of grace, opportunities, our very lives.[1] But life is never on hold; moment by moment, breath by breath, I am living. I am not given tomorrow's life; I am only presented with the gift of *now*. What am I doing with the life I am given *right now*?

When you consider God's purpose for you, what comes to mind? A ministry, a career, an avenue of service,[2] something in your future? We usually connect our purpose with God's promises in Jeremiah 29:11. "I know the plans I have for you . . . plans to give you a hope and a future." Yet consider how this promise was given. This reassurance came only *after* the exiles to Babylon were told to settle down, plant, build, marry and have children *in the land of their captivity*.[3] Basically, they were warned: "Don't put our lives on hold! Don't wait for freedom before you live. Live every day, right now where you are."

Knowing that we are commanded to redeem the time, to make the most of every opportunity,[4] ask God *not*, "What is my purpose?" but, "What is my purpose *right now*?" How can I serve You right now, in this moment? In what way can I manifest (make visible) Jesus's love to the person I am with *right now*?

God is our source. For all that we are given, God will require an accounting:[5] our money and possessions, of course. But I will also be asked what I have done with my words,[6] with the needs and opportunities that were presented to me, and with my time.

"Time is short," we are warned. I want to pay attention and fulfill the purpose of every moment. *Now* is a very short time!

Ask God not, "What is my purpose?"
Ask, "What is my purpose right now?"

---

[1]James 4:14   [2]Matt. 25:34–36   [3]Jer. 29:4–7   [4]Eccl. 9:10   [5]Matt. 25:19   [6]Matt. 12:36

JUNE 7

. . . I do believe; help me overcome my unbelief!
Mark 9:24

*H*ow much faith does it take to have faith? When you hear someone's testimony, do you ever wistfully think, "I could never do that.
I just don't have that much faith"? *How much faith does it take?*
When the disciples couldn't cast a demon out of a boy, they asked Jesus what
had happened, why had they failed? Jesus chided them, saying it was because
they had so little faith and went on to say that faith as tiny as a mustard seed
could cast a mountain into the sea.[1]

That makes a lot of us nervous, to say the least! If it only takes a minis-
cule, mustard seed-sized faith, and the disciples themselves didn't have it,
then how is little ol' me supposed to do it? Yet the disciples *did* have enough
faith! Not too much earlier, these same disciples had returned from their first
missionary trip, excitedly reporting to Jesus: "Lord, even the demons submit
to us in your name."[2] God enables us to believe.[3] Can you even imagine that
our loving Father would give us less than a mustard seed of faith?[4] Less than
we *need*? Remember: "His divine power has given us everything we need for
life and godliness."[5]

Yet several times, Jesus rebuked His disciples for having so little faith, and
He commended a Gentile woman–a Canaanite, no less–for having great faith![6]
The difference is that the woman *used* her faith, and the disciples *didn't*. Yes,
God has given us everything we need in the same way He has given a baby
everything he needs to become a pro athlete. If that baby never grows up *using*
those muscles, sinews, tendons and brains, he will never be a pro athlete. If
we do not exercise our faith, we will never have great faith, nor will we ever
move mountains.[7] Jesus never agreed to increase the disciples' faith,[8] but He
did respond to that desperate father when he cried out for help–not to have
more faith, but to overcome the doubts that were keeping him from using the
faith he had!

Faith works when it is faith *in God*, not faith in our faith. So, how much
faith does it take? All that we have–and we have enough.

If we do not exercise our faith,
we will never experience having great faith.

---

[1]Matt. 17:20 [2]Luke 10:17 [3]John 6:65 [4]Matt. 7:11 [5]2 Pet. 1:3 [6]Matt. 15:28 [7]Mark 4:25
[8]Luke 17:5

JUNE 8

For your Maker is your husband . . .
Isaiah 54:5

Just how intimate a relationship with God do we want? When Moses asked Him His name, God thundered His reply: "I Am!" I Am so far above all things that I cannot be limited to any *one* thing. I Am everything your needs require; everything you can possibly desire.

Think of all the relationships God can be for us. He is our Creator, Counselor, and our King and Lord. He is our Judge *and* our Lawyer—and our Ransomer. He is our Priest, Teacher, Doctor, Accountant, Biographer and Builder. He is our Father, our Brother and our Friend.

Are we satisfied with this kind of closeness, this level of intimacy? Do we realize that God is not? *Friend* is good, and *family* is better, but God is not satisfied with merely a platonic relationship with us. He wants to marry us![1] "I will betroth you to me forever,"[2] He says. Listen close, as He woos: "How beautiful you are, my darling! Oh, how beautiful![3] The king is enthralled by your beauty.[4] I will never leave you; I will never forsake you.[5] Therefore I am now going to allure her; I will lead her into the desert and speak tenderly to her.[6]

But we have been disappointed in love before. I am tired of being used, abused, lied to and cheated on. I have longed to be loved by someone who truly knows me, appreciates me, honors me and treats me like royalty. God knows how to love. After all, He *is* love! "I will betroth you in faithfulness."[7] God wants more than a master/slave relationship—even more than a parent/child fellowship.[8] He wants to be one with me in the same way He and His Father are one.[9] He is longing to hold me in His arms, to whisper His secrets in my ear,[10] and to have me love Him back just as deeply.

"In that day," declares the LORD, "you will call me 'my husband.'"[11]

How intimate a relationship with God do *you* really want?

God knows how to love. After all, He is love!

---

[1]Isa. 62:5   [2]Hos. 2:19   [3]Song 4:1   [4]Ps. 45:11   [5]Heb. 13:5   [6]Hos. 2:14   [7]Hos. 2:20   [8]John 17:11   [9]John 17:20–26   [10]Jer. 33:3   [11]Hos. 2:16

JUNE 9

. . . Zacchaeus, come down immediately. I must stay at your house today.
Luke 19:5

As a captain of the drill team for Sheppard Air Force Base in Texas, I marched in a lot of rodeo parades. Of all of them, one in particular stands out in my memory: Jacksboro, Texas, 1978. The team was especially sharp that day and performed better than we ever had before. The drum and bugle corps played one rousing march after another, and the color guard bore Old Glory with spit-shined pride. And the horses! Fine-spirited and ridden by true cowboys in full regalia! It was the finest parade that nobody saw. Nobody. As we marched down the main thoroughfare, I was astonished that *not a single soul* was sitting on the sidelines or lining the street. No one was watching the parade, because *everybody was in it*! The entire town—young, old, even the disabled in decorated wheelchairs—was a part of the celebration.

How many times are we like Zacchaeus instead—a spectator, watching the Jesus parade go by.[1] We hope to figure it all out from our safe perch above it all. Ah, but the kingdom of God is like Jacksboro, Texas; there are no spectators, only participants.[2] To those of us still trying to stay above it all—watching Christianity from the back pew[3]—Jesus calls out, "Come down! Get elbow to elbow with the crowd following Me. Get dusty, get sweaty, get down to the nitty-gritty.[4] I'm coming to your house today. Will you have Me?"[5]

Take note: most of the crowd won't be happy for you.[6] They didn't like Zacchaeus, either. They thought it terribly shameful that Jesus would even *think* of eating with one of *those people* (you know the kind).[7]

Jesus didn't care. And once Zacchaeus climbed down from his self-appointed high position to everybody else's level, he didn't care, either.[8] He stopped watching the parade and joined it, and salvation came to his house that day.

In the kingdom of God,
there are no spectators, only participants.

---

[1]James 4:11–12 [2]Matt. 12:30 [3]Eccl. 11:4 [4]James 1:23–25 [5]Rev. 3:20 [6]John 15:18
[7]Luke 7:39 [8]Matt. 23:12

JUNE 10

But my righteous one will live by faith. And if he shrinks back,
I will not be pleased with him.
Hebrews 10:38

Shrink back from what? From doing the will of God,[1] which is usually a daring, uncomfortable, frightening, and solitary act. God's will cuts directly across human nature and what our flesh is used to. Our flesh understands the way things *are* and the way things have always *been*. Only our spirit can understand the way things *can be*. Doing the will of God means stepping out in a new direction, acting and reacting like complete aliens and strangers. It means doing different things differently. Such oddness is risky; be prepared to stand alone. Consider it par for the course to be misunderstood,[2] to have your motives unappreciated and your actions berated.[3] Face it; those on the other side of the cross cannot comprehend selflessness.

Jesus taught us—commanded us—to love:[4] love the one who borrows and doesn't repay,[5] who steals from you,[6] who slaps you in the face,[7] and sins against you seventy times seven times in the same day.[8] Not merely tolerate, but actively love, pray for, and bless[9] the rude, the abusive, the liar,[10] and the thief. Such love looks outrageous, idiotic, dangerous and futile to the natural mind. Consider what such love might lead you to do! Yet love like this *is* the will of God.

Jesus said this, making no allowance for our dignity, respect, or reputation, nor for our being only human. He never said, "Try to do this, but it's understandable if you can't."[11] He said, "Love."

Everyone around you is an opportunity to love. We must live it by faith and not shrink back.

Consider it par for the course to be misunderstood,
to have your motives unappreciated,
and your actions berated.

---

[1]Heb. 10:36 [2]John 14:17 [3]John 16:2–3 [4]John 13:34 [5]Luke 6:34–35 [6]Luke 6:30 [7]Matt. 5:39
[8]Matt. 18:22 [KJV] [9]Matt. 5:44 [10]Matt. 5:11 [11]Matt. 5:48

JUNE 11

Surely the wrath of men shall praise thee:
the remainder of wrath shalt thou restrain.
Psalm 76:10 [KJV]

*G*od is so amazing, so in control, that even when men rage and plot against Him, He only uses it for His glory! The psalmist well understood this, which is why he said not to fret because of evil men;[1] they only rage in vain.[2] When we face roadblocks and opposition, we don't need to get agitated and worried. God is actually *laughing* at their futile attempts to stop us,[3] to interfere with His work.[4] If we stand firm and rest in the Lord, we will watch Him turn their plots back on them. When God ordains something to be done, it will be done!

Consider the rebuilding of His temple in Jerusalem. When the area governors wrote a complaining letter to the king, hoping to stop the work, *their very request* made the king search his records for the original order.[5] The result? Not only were their enemies told to stop harassing the Jews, but they were ordered to *supply all their needs* for the building, and provide the sacrifices—daily![6]

Think about all the ways men have tried to ensure their plots wouldn't fail, and they only ended up increasing the glory of God's miracle! Nebuchadnezzar had the fire heated seven times hotter (it even killed his own soldiers when they got close), so no one could say that the three Hebrews didn't burn because there wasn't enough flame![7] King Darius had the lion's den sealed, and therefore, no one could claim Daniel wasn't eaten because he'd somehow escaped.[8] The Jewish leaders demanded that Pontius Pilate seal *and* guard Jesus' tomb, lest the disciples steal the body.[9] This made such a feat impossible, and therefore only added convincing proof of the reality of the resurrection. And persecution? It only spreads the gospel more.[10]

And of course, the cross of Christ is the ultimate proof that the wrath and plots of men only serve to fulfill the plans and purposes of God.[11]

Is the enemy trying to stop you from doing the will of God? Don't fret. Get quiet and listen closely. That laughter you're hearing is your heavenly Father—our sovereign Lord—working it all out for His glory!

Men have tried many ways to stop God's plan,
but only ended up increasing the glory God received!

---

[1]Ps. 37:1 [2]Ps. 2:1 [3]Ps. 37:13 [4]Ps. 2:4 [5]Ezra 5:7–17 [6]Ezra 6:1–12 [7]Dan. 3:19–27 [8]Dan. 6:16–22 [9]Matt. 27:62–66 [10]Acts 8:1–4 [11]Luke 13:31–32

JUNE 12

For it is commendable if a man bears up under the pain
of unjust suffering because he is conscious of God.

1 Peter 2:19

*E*nding up in prison was my wake-up call, my reality check. Until then, I thought I knew about God—but I never let that knowledge interfere with how I lived my life.[1] Suddenly, I was face to face with consequences, and revelation hit me. I became conscious of God: *that* He is, *who* He is, *how* He is, and that I was supposed to be becoming like Him.[2] I realized that the way I was living my life denied Him and everything I said I knew about Him. I repented, acknowledged His right to rule me, and began to change.

I was in prison. Painful, but not unjust. Bearing up under that isn't especially commendable,[3] but following Jesus and living His way now brings me up against all the choices I naturally made before. Being conscious of God means I now trust Him instead for justice, reputation, strength, a good outcome.[4] Being conscious of God means believing that His way works, that there is more than meets the eye, that there is an eternity. Being conscious of God changes everything.

Which, of course, makes me different—and different people are targeted by the world.[5] When doing things God's way risks loss, being conscious of God gives me the power of humility to let it go, to bear up under injustice,[6] and give the power of love. It enables me to reach out to my tormenters and break the cycle.[7]

Being conscious of God, I know that the challenge of suffering unjustly is when the rubber meets the road, when what I say I believe is tested.[8] Passing the test glorifies God. What a powerful testimony to the reality of eternity and all the rewards that Jesus promised to those who take up their crosses and follow Him![9] It is commendable, silently shouting that there is something worth losing everything to gain.[10] It gives others a chance to also become conscious of God.

Being conscious of God changes everything.

---

[1]Luke 6:46   [2]Matt. 10:25   [3]1 Pet. 4:15   [4]Matt. 19:27–29   [5]John 15:18–19   [6]1 Pet. 4:19
[7]Matt. 5:43–48   [8]Matt. 13:20–21   [9]Matt. 10:37–39   [10]Luke 9:25

JUNE 13

Peace I leave with you; my peace I give you. . . .
John 14:27

*P*eace and rest: two of the most beautiful words in any language. Jesus left us His peace as a blessing to strengthen our hearts and take away our fear. Not just any peace, but *His* peace–and His peace came because He lived in constant, unbroken fellowship with His Father.[1] Our task and privilege is to learn from Him and walk in His peace.[2] Jesus grieved over Jerusalem because His people refused to know what would bring them peace.[3]

Peace is not automatic to a Christ follower; I must seek peace, pursue it.[4] To have His peace, I must learn to walk in that same constant communion with God that Jesus did and avoid the things that interfere with it. How did He do it? *He sought Him out.* He rose early, got away from the crowds, and spent time talking with His Father.[5] He was always careful that the weeds and thorns of this life didn't choke out His Father's voice.

Some of those weeds and thorns are not just external circumstances, but my internal thoughts and attitudes. Breaking the patterns of a lifetime of fallen thinking is difficult, but I can make it less so by feeding the good and starving the bad. Jesus said to consider carefully what I hear[6]–not just His words, but everything I am stuffing into my heart through my ears, eyes, and imagination. Garbage in, garbage out–but godly in, godly out, too! The Word judges my thoughts and attitudes,[7] and teaches me that gratitude, gentleness, integrity, kindness–all the things He is–draw Him near to me. How much easier it is to follow Him when I know He is right here with me!

Hearing (and seeing) is one thing, but doing it is another.[8] Obedience is walking together with God; disobedience instantly breaks fellowship. "There is no peace . . . for the wicked."[9] When I am in His will, doing what He has planned for me and submitted to Him, I have peace even in the midst of chaos.[10] I see Him working in my life, and my trust in Him grows. The essence of peace is trusting God in spite of chaos. When I fix my eyes on Jesus,[11] I have His peace.

To have His peace, I must walk in the
same communion with God that Jesus did.

---

[1]John 8:29   [2]Matt. 11:29   [3]Luke 19:41–42   [4]Ps. 34:14   [5]Mark 1:35   [6]Mark 4:24   [7]Heb. 4:12
[8]Matt. 7:24–27   [9]Isa. 57:21   [10]Job 22:21   [11]Heb. 12:2

JUNE 14

"You have answered correctly," Jesus replied. "Do this and you will live."
Luke 10:28

To be an eager student, hungry for knowledge and thirsty for wisdom, is a very good thing.[1] It can also be a very dangerous thing, depending on what all that learning produces.[2] There are pitfalls; as with anything good, the enemy is always seeking to undermine our efforts in growing in God. Scripture warns us of his traps.

One of his tricks is to sidetrack us with trivial matters, things that do not build up our spirit or anyone else's. We should be on our guard against becoming quarrelsome and divisive[3] over meaningless words or arcane arguments that have nothing to do with doing the will of God.[4] It is helpful to ask ourselves, "How will this help me to know God better and to become more like Him?"

Similarly, Satan's second snare is to promote an unhealthy desire to know that which God has not revealed. This was Adam and Eve's sin—to know good and evil, and thus be like God.[5] The Scriptures say, "The secret things belong to the LORD our God, but the things revealed belong to us and to our children forever."[6] Much of this "secret knowledge" is mystical in nature and often promises unique powers to those initiated into its realm (gnosticism). Yet, if God Himself has chosen to conceal it,[7] then who, indeed, would be trying to whisper it in our ears? In His message to Thyatira, Jesus commended and encouraged those who have not learned Satan's so-called deep secrets.[8]

Yet the biggest snare, the most dangerous pitfall in the pursuit of learning, is storing up knowledge that we never put into practice. It is being a hearer only and not a doer.[9] Like the teacher of the law in today's verse who answered correctly, we know what God requires.[10] If we ignore what we already know, what's the point of learning more?

Since we know that Jesus' commandment is to "love each other as I have loved you,"[11] then we know enough to keep us overwhelmingly busy for the rest of our lives—and eternity. Do this and you will live.

The most dangerous pitfall in the pursuit of knowledge is storing up learning we never put into practice.

---

[1]Prov. 2:1–5   [2]2 Pet. 1:5–8   [3]Prov. 22:10   [4]Matt. 7:21   [5]Gen. 3:4   [6]Deut. 29:29   [7]Prov. 25:2   [8]Rev. 2:24   [9]James 1:22   [10]Mic. 6:8   [11]John 15:12

JUNE 15

Anyone, then, who knows the good he ought to do and doesn't do it, sins.
James 4:17

This is the infamous sin of omission that is glossed over in many prayers, relegated to the *et cetera* part of asking forgiveness—kind of like adding, "and any other sin I forgot to mention" at the end, just to be sure we're covered.

But what, really, have we omitted? It is hard to imagine punishment for *not* doing something—but God calls it *sin* to not do the good we know to do. What is this good we know to do? There are two kinds, basically. The first kind is that which is required of all of us, the good that means being kind, generous, unselfish, merciful, and loving to everyone who crosses our path.[1] Jesus taught us quite clearly that to truly do the will of God, we must do more than merely refrain from doing wrong; we must radically seek to do right, to love others actively.[2] Going through our days with our eyes focused only on ourselves (*our* schedules, *our* goals, *our* needs) makes us blind to the many opportunities we have to do something for someone else. If I slow down and pay attention for chances to spread some kindness,[3] to tangibly share God's love, I won't miss out on doing some of the good I know to do.

But the second kind of good comes directly from our closeness to God. It goes beyond His general will for all and involves the direct and specific things God asks of us as individuals.[4] To accomplish His purposes, His plans, God commands certain people at just the right times to do specific tasks.[5] His Spirit guides each of us in the path He has chosen for us.[6] When God speaks to our hearts to move our hands and feet, not doing it is disobedience—sin. It is easy to think that our contribution is too small to matter;[7] we rarely are shown the other puzzle pieces of His purpose and how our portion fits. That does not relieve us of the responsibility of obedience.[8] Yes, God may find someone else to do it, but more often than we imagine, that hole left by our disobedience causes greater suffering than was necessary.[9]

We are God's children, Jesus's brothers and sisters, who do the will of God[10]—with great joy.

There are many acts of kindness God is calling us,
His representatives, to do for Him to others.

---

[1]Luke 6:27–36 [2]Matt. 5:43–48 [3]Prov. 14:31 [4]Matt. 21:28–31 [5]Mark 13:34 [6]Ps. 25:12
[7]John 6:9 [8]Luke 5:5 [9]Ezek. 22:30 [10]Mark 3:35

JUNE 16

*Whether you turn to the right or to the left, your ears will hear
a voice behind you saying, "This is the way; walk in it."*
Isaiah 30:21

The issue believers seem to struggle with most is hearing from God. "How can I hear His voice? How can I know that it is God and not me—or the devil?" So many believers are wallowing in guilt and frustration over this, because they are convinced that they do not hear God. Yet Jesus said unequivocally that His sheep know His voice, and that they will never follow a stranger, because they do not recognize a stranger's voice.[1] If we are truly His sheep, we hear His voice, and we obey Him. We cannot follow Him any other way! "No one can come to me unless the Father who sent me draws him."[2] We were drawn by the Father speaking in our heart, and we understood what He was saying, because the Holy Spirit made it clear. It takes the Spirit of God to open our understanding. Jesus's words are spirit; they are not understood by the flesh.[3]

Remember Peter's confession of Christ? Jesus told him that man had not (could not have) revealed it to him, but God.[4] Peter had heard the voice of God within his spirit, had understood the message, yet had not recognized it for what it was. We do the same thing! Do we understand some Scripture? (No one understands all Scripture.) It is only because God spoke it into our spirit.[5] The Holy Spirit taught us,[6] not the preacher, teacher or writer—and it certainly wasn't our own intellect, either. Human beings are merely one of the channels among many that God uses to speak to us.

Recognizing when God is speaking to us begins with faith: believing that He is, indeed, speaking and has been all along. It involves paying attention[7]—we often realize it was God only after the fact. And it comes with the understanding that God speaks *inside* us[8] (it is rarely audible), using *our own voice*, not some strange, deep accent. Often, He uses no words at all. That flash of insight? That strong "knowing"? That Bible verse that suddenly popped into your mind?[9] That is God.

Listen closely, for He is, indeed, speaking.

---

*Recognizing when God is speaking to you
begins with faith.*

---

[1]John 10:4–5 [2]John 6:44 [3]John 8:43 [4]Matt. 16:17 [5]Ps. 71:17 [6]1 John 2:27 [7]Luke 8:18
[8]John 14:17 [9]Ps. 119:130

JUNE 17

. . . "Not by might nor by power, but by my Spirit,"
*says the L*ord *Almighty.*
Zechariah 4:6

*O*h, the incredible stopping power of "I can't!" God alone knows how many noble plans, great purposes, and worthy causes have died unfulfilled because those He called quailed saying, "I can't." The perplexing thing is, it's true! We can't. Nobody can do what God calls us to do. Even if I were amazingly talented, highly skilled, or eminently knowledgeable, I can do nothing effectively for the kingdom of God on my own.[1] "With man this is impossible," Jesus asserts, "But not with God; all things are possible with God."[2]

I have struggled, procrastinated, and feared the task, because I keep forgetting that I am not supposed to do it in my own power and knowledge, but by His Spirit. He reminds me, "Do not worry about what to say or how to say it. At that time you will be given what to say."[3]

When I read the faith chapter of Hebrews 11, I see a whole list of flawed, seemingly insignificant people whose weakness was turned to strength[4] in the hands of the Lord. The Bible is full of the opposite, too: people and nations who fought against God. They don't exist anymore. "There is no wisdom, no insight, no plan that can succeed against the Lord."[5] When God ordains something, it only takes one person to put a thousand to flight.[6] The entire population of the world could not complete the Tower of Babel, but a handful of Jewish refugees could rebuild the walls of Jerusalem in a mere fifty-two days.[7] "If their purpose or activity is of human origin, it will fail," Gamaliel warned the Jewish leaders. "But if it is from God, you will not be able to stop these men."[8]

Jesus is my example; I am to walk as He walked.[9] He willingly set aside His divinity—all His own personal power and ability—and allowed His Father to live in Him and do His work through Him.[10] As He did it, I can, too. When He calls me, I can step up, trusting that He will provide the know-how, the strength, the resources and opportunities . . . whatever it takes to get the job done. Only then will it bear fruit for the kingdom . . . fruit that will last forever.[11] "Let the weakling say, 'I am strong!'"[12]

If Jesus allowed His Father to live in Him
and do His work through Him, I can, too.

---

[1]John 15:5   [2]Mark 10:27   [3]Matt. 10:19–20   [4]Heb. 11:34   [5]Prov. 21:30   [6]Deut. 32:30
[7]Neh. 6:15–16   [8]Acts 5:38–39   [9]1 John 2:6   [10]John 14:10   [11]John 15:16   [12]Joel 3:10

JUNE 18

But if anyone does not have them, he is nearsighted and blind,
and has forgotten that he has been cleansed from his past sins.
2 Peter 1:9

*M*any are the tales of home-grown heroes—small-town folks who made good. The ones especially beloved are those who, in their success, never forget where they came from. These people are humble, approachable, honestly grateful, and gracious to others who are struggling. Self-pride, on the other hand, is an ugly thing.[1]

In Adam and Eve's sin, they tried to be as God, and in their banishment from Eden, God reminded them of their roots, of where they came from. "For dust you are and to dust you will return."[2] It wasn't that He was throwing their past in their faces, but a healthy awareness of who and what you are apart from God is very humbling. Humble is good; humble is teachable, renewable, re-creatable.[3] Pride is hard as flint, and just as unyielding.

"But wait," you say. "Aren't we told to forget the former things?[4] To consider the future God has for us, our expected end?[5] If God doesn't remember our sins any more, why should we?"[6]

Wallowing in guilt and regret over your past wickedness is not what God has in mind. That kind of remembering is debilitating, crippling. That's how the enemy wants us to feel. But to acknowledge just how bad off we really are apart from God, where we would be without Him, is simply being honest.[7] Such remembering humbles us, and humility is the cure for a judgmental, critical, holier-than-thou spirit. It is hard to point fingers when we pray "God, have mercy on me, a sinner."[8]

It will drive us closer to God, keeping us deeply grateful for—and sincerely dependent upon—His mercy.

To acknowledge just how bad off we really are
apart from God, where we would be without Him,
is simply being honest.

---

[1]Deut. 8:11–14   [2]Gen. 3:19   [3]Ps. 25:9   [4]Isa. 43:18   [5]Jer. 29:11 [NIV, KJV]   [6]Isa. 43:25
[7]Job 40:9–14   [8]Luke 18:13

JUNE 19

But the LORD provided a great fish to swallow Jonah,
and Jonah was inside the fish three days and three nights.
Jonah 1:17

*W*hat does deliverance look like? There have been times when I have been in desperate straits and cried out to God for help—or been confounded by circumstances for which I earnestly sought a solution from God. How many were the times I had expected His answer to come from a certain direction or had some idea of how I thought He would fix my problem! I have finally figured out that He rarely does the expected.[1] God is a God of surprises.

I'm sure Jonah, on the verge of drowning, did not regard the gaping jaws of a humongous fish as his heaven-sent rescue. Elijah was carried to heaven, all right—but his transport was on fire the whole way![2] Rescue does not come riding in on a white stallion accompanied by armies of angels until the end of time itself![3]

God's deliverance often involves some mud and sweat. Noah and his family (and the Whole-Earth Zoo) were miraculously preserved from destruction—after he had spent years building the boat.[4] God delivered Israel from the Edomites by miraculously making water flow into the valley and appear blood-red, but only after the Israelites had spent a long, hard night digging ditches.[5] How many of them, I wonder, thought their commander was crazy when the order to start digging was announced? Remember, God didn't tell them *why* He wanted them to dig. My answer from God may not make much sense to me, either. It may sound about as crazy as filling jars with water when what you really need is wine,[6] rounding up five loaves and two fish to feed over 5,000 people,[7] or hitting a rock to get water.[8] When I expect a boat, God may send a fish.

Putting God in a box can limit the means for our miracle. If He tells us to go dip seven times in the Jordan,[9] we should not argue; we should just do it. We can trust Him; He knows how to rescue.[10]

God's deliverance often involves some mud and sweat.

---

[1]Isa. 64:3   [2]2 Kings 2:11   [3]Rev. 19:11–14   [4]Gen. 6   [5]2 Kings 3   [6]John 2:1–10   [7]Matt. 14:16–21
[8]Exod. 17:6   [9]2 Kings 5:10   [10]2 Pet. 2:9

JUNE 20

Why do you look at the speck of sawdust in your brother's eye and pay no attention to the plank in your own eye?

Matthew 7:3

There's a saying that when you point your finger at someone else, you have four more pointing back at yourself. I am horrified to discover how very true this is. More and more, Jesus confronts me with my hypocrisy whenever I scowl at, scold, or condemn another. And Jesus—who knows me better than I know myself—is always right. I do the same things. Sometimes exactly as those I am condemning![1] "Clean up your own back yard," Jesus tells me.

The question is not, "Am I my brother's keeper?"[2] Jesus *does* want us to care about each other, to love each other as He loves us.[3] But there *is* a persistent lure for us to promote ourselves, to set ourselves above others. We hear it all the time. "Be a leader!" We have countless leadership books, seminars, and retreats.

But you know what? Jesus never once said, "Be a leader." In fact, to His disciples who spent so much time arguing and jockeying for the position[4] of greatest in the kingdom,[5] He told them that the greatest was the one willing to be the least . . . the servant . . . no, the *slave* of all![6] Jesus isn't looking for man's defintion of leaders; He's looking for followers.[7] It was the Pharisees, the religious *leaders*, who loved titles and power and recognition. "But you are not to be like that," Jesus told the disciples.[8] ". . . you are not to be called 'Rabbi,' . . . 'Father,' . . . 'Teacher . . .'"[9]

Speaking into someone else's life is a *dire* responsibility I *dare not* take upon myself, on my own. How can I claim to see clearly?[10] I must not attempt to remove the speck in *your* eye before I clean the beam out of my own. What makes me think I am in any position to fix you? I am not called to be your leader, to display a holier-than-thou attitude of superiority or condemnation.[11] I am called to love and serve you. If He *does* call me to speak into your life, I must make certain I am only speaking His words.[12] And I need to apply those words to my own life before I speak them into yours.

Jesus isn't looking for man's definition of leaders; He's looking for followers.

---

[1] James 4:11–12 [2] Gen. 4:9 [3] John 15:12 [4] Matt. 20:20–21 [5] Luke 22:24 [6] Mark 10:41–44
[7] John 12:26 [8] Luke 22:26 [9] Matt. 23:5–10 [10] John 9:41 [11] Isa. 65:5 [KJV] [12] 1 Pet. 4:11

JUNE 21

But go and learn what this means . . .
Matthew 9:13

"Learn what this means . . ." Jesus ended almost all of His parables by saying, "He who has ears, let him hear."[1] Essentially, He was warning us to pay attention, *think*—there's more than meets the ear here. Don't stop at the obvious. It's like a spiritual code to alert the true God-seeker to a deep truth hidden in a simple story.

I had to learn this about the Lord: He still speaks in parables. He truly is a God who hides Himself.[2] He is willing to be found—but I had to learn to seek.[3] I am learning still—when He tells me something, I should not just run with it.[4] I need to sit down and ask questions, like, "Does this mean what I think it means? Is there more?" And most importantly, "What do you want me to do with this?"

These deep truths are not new truths, for God does not change.[5] What He is trying to tell me is not something He's never told anyone else. Back in the psalms He promised, "I will open my mouth in parables, I will utter hidden things, things from of old—*what we have heard and known* . . ."[6] He's not telling me something new; He's trying to give me a deeper understanding of what I already thought I knew!

So how do I "learn what this means" when I think I already know what it means? It goes back to the difference between knowledge and wisdom. Jesus tells me over and over that until I'm walking in it, I do not truly know it. I have the knowledge, but not the wisdom. Wisdom is the application of truth (knowledge) to my life. Wisdom is *doing*, and doing is far more important to God than head knowledge.[7] God does not play trivia games; He sends His Word to *accomplish a purpose*.[8] His greatest purpose for me is to restore His image in me—to help me become like Christ.[9] That is only a hands-on experience.

"Learn what this means . . ." Head knowledge will only condemn. I have to learn what He means *by heart*: with my hands and feet.[10] Walking it out is the best teacher, the purest and quickest route to true revelation.

Head knowledge will only condemn.
I have to learn what He means by heart . . .

---

[1]Matt. 13:9 [2]Isa. 45:15 [3]2 Chron. 15:2 [4]2 John 1:9 [5]Mal. 3:6 [6]Ps. 78:2–3 [7]Matt. 21:28–31 [8]Isa. 55:11 [9]1 John 4:16–17 [10]1 John 3:18

JUNE 22

. . . Surely the Lord is in this place, and I was not aware of it.
Genesis 28:16

*I*s there a place, a location here on earth, where God is? Where was Jacob when he uttered these words? Was it that particular plot of ground, that stopping place for the night, where he lay with a stone for a pillow? What if he had taken a slightly different route or pressed on a little farther that night and had camped somewhere else? Would Jacob have missed the place where God is?[1]

Where was Jacob? Physically, he was near a small town called Luz, on his way to Paddan-Aram.[2] It wasn't where he was in his body, however, but where he was in his soul. He was on the run, fleeing from his own brother, in terror for his life, having lost the very thing he had lied to get. He was alone, driven by guilt, and full of despair. Jacob was broken.[3]

And that is where God is:[4] in the very place I least expected.[5] In the midst of my turmoil, God is there.[6] In my darkness and lonely despair,[7] God is there. In my fear and my terror, He has not left me, He has not forsaken me.[8] In my unbelievable circumstances,[9] He is there. He always has been, and I was not aware of it—of Him. It is in my brokenness that I can most clearly hear God.[10]

How did Jacob recognize God "in this place"? He dreamed of a ladder—a bridge—between earth and heaven, between man and God, between desperate need and infinite grace. In Jacob's most desperate hour, without a clean heart to offer, he did *not* see a judge's bench, nor did he hear condemnation.[11] Wonder of wonders! He heard God speak blessing—the very blessing he thought he'd lost.[12]

Where are you today? Have chance and choice conspired against you and driven you from all you'd ever hoped for? Are you broken and wondering where in the world God is?

He is right there where you are—even if you, too, are not aware of it. If you rest a moment and listen, you will find Him.

God is in the place where you least expect Him to be.

---

[1]Prov. 19:2   [2]Gen. 28:19   [3]Ps. 147:3   [4]Isa. 65:1   [5]Ps. 139:7–12   [6]Ps. 65:7   [7]Ps. 18:11
[8]Deut. 31:6   [9]Jer. 15:11   [10]Ps. 34:18   [11]Lam. 3:22–23   [12]Gen. 28:13–15

JUNE 23

*The LORD said, "If as one people speaking the same language
they have begun to do this, then nothing they plan to do
will be impossible for them."*
Genesis 11:6

This is truly an amazing verse. Not only does God declare that these men would find no goal, no project impossible, but even more astonishing is that He was speaking of *unbelievers*! Those outside the circle of faith. Men with *no access* to the supernatural can-do power of the Holy Spirit! How is it even possible?

Unity. Never underestimate the power of minds and wills in one accord, all working together for a common purpose. If mere unsaved, human minds in unity can perform the impossible, *how much more* can the Body of Christ, one in spirit and infused and anointed with *the* Spirit, accomplish for the kingdom of God? Why do you think Jesus prayed so earnestly—not just once, not twice, but *four times in one prayer*—that his followers would be one just as He and His Father are one?[1] Why do you think it took ten days for the Holy Spirit to be poured out on the disciples in the upper room? Could it be it took that long for those disparate, squabbling, who-is-the-greatest, position-jockeying followers of Christ to finally come to one accord?[2] Oh, but when the rich harmony of spiritual unity filled that locked room, all heaven exploded with the glory and grace of God Almighty! Heaven's power was so strong, it was literally visible and audible. Souls by the thousands were cut to the heart, called into the kingdom, and converted to Christ.

Unity! Why do you think Satan works so hard to cause strife and division?[3] Because it dismembers the Body of Christ.[4] It gives our enemy great pleasure to wound Christ, and even greater joy to tease, offend, and provoke us into doing it for him.[5] The psalmist teaches us that the anointing *and* the blessings of God are poured out when brothers live together in unity.[6]

Unity isn't easy; it demands humility. I can let go of insisting on my way and, instead, develop a servant's heart.[7] The more we seek to serve each other, the less the enemy can drive a wedge between us. As Christ-followers filled with the power of the Holy Spirit, we can out-impossible unbelievers any day![8]

Never underestimate the power of unity.

[1]John 17:11, 21–23   [2]Acts 2:1 [KJV]   [3]Jude 1:19   [4]3 John 1:9–10   [5]Luke 22:3–4   [6]Ps. 133:1–3
[7]John 13:14–17   [8]John 14:12

JUNE 24

If your brother sins against you, go and show him his fault, just between the two of you. If he listens to you, you have won your brother over.
Matthew 18:15

How much pain and heartache we avoid when we put this principle into practice! Yet most folks deal with a hurt by taking the long way around—going to everybody and anybody else *but* the one who wronged them.[1] We've been hurt; we want the sympathy of others. We want to be reaffirmed; we want someone to agree with us and tell us we were right.[2] (How we hate to be wrong!) Unfortunately, instead of feeling better, our rehashing the incident and their sympathy only serves to magnify the hurt and drive the wedge deeper. It's like pulling off a scab; the wound takes so much longer to heal, and it ends up leaving a scar.[3]

But going directly to the one who hurt us is stressful and even scary for some. It's confrontation, and few enjoy conflict. Done incorrectly, the world's way, it usually ends up hot, raw, and bleeding worse than before.[4] To win your brother (or sister) over, you must do it God's way.[5] That's why Jesus gave a whole chapter of instruction about this. The lesson didn't start at verse fifteen; it started with the disciples' question about who was the greatest (the very attitude of pride that is the root of most conflict[6]). Jesus talked about humbling myself like a little child. Before I can go to my brother, I need to get real with myself: I'm not perfect, either.[7] Then He gave some shockingly graphic commands about the lengths we should go to get sin out of our lives.[8] That means I must go to God first and ask Him if there is anything I need to get right with Him myself.[9] I must spare no pain to get right in my heart and spirit before God first.

Then Jesus talked of lost sheep and the Father's love. I need to remember that the one who hurt me is desperately loved by God. I should think about that love and how much it hurts Him to see His children angry with each other.

Then I can go—humbled, clean, with earnest, sincere love[10]—directly to the one who hurt me. I refuse to play the enemy's game of gossip, slander, strife and division. I will trust God's way.

Jesus talked about humbling yourself like a little child.
Do things God's way!

---

[1]Prov. 17:9 [2]Prov. 27:6 [3]Matt. 5:23–26 [4]James 1:20 [5]Ps. 81:13–14 [6]Prov. 13:10 [7]Prov. 20:9
[8]Matt. 18:8–9 [9]Prov. 18:17 [10]1 Pet. 1:22

JUNE 25

Everyone will be salted with fire.

Mark 9:49

"Let the weakling say, 'I am strong!'"[1] In our triumphs, we are glorious: kingdom-conquering, lion-taming, flame-quenching, sword-dodging, army-routing, dead-raising, heroic champions of the faith. In our persecutions, we shine even more gloriously. Though tortured, jeered, flogged, chained, imprisoned, and even sawed in two,[2] we rise triumphant, for absolutely nothing the world can do to a child of God[3] can ultimately harm him.[4] We come from heavenly stock, holy seed,[5] royal blood. Don't let the meekness of love fool you. We are an invincible army, mighty in power, terrifying to demons, and wielding as a weapon a Word[6] so powerful, its use alone flung a whole universe into existence.

Do we feel it when we look in the mirror? Or do we feel more like Satan's punching bag than his nemesis? When we hear the divine call, do we shout like Isaiah, "Here am I! Send me!"[7]? Or do we feel more like Moses, "O, Lord, please send someone else!"?[8] Don't worry, don't fear; be strong, take heart! Be of good courage![9] God knows our fainting, terrified hearts can't handle the call. He remembers that we are but flesh.[10] God Himself is our armor, our personal trainer. He sends no one into battle unprotected, untrained, unfit to fight the good fight. We will go through training. It looks suspiciously like trials.

You see, the hardest (and the most precious) things are formed under intense pressure, in the hottest fires: fine steel in the furnace and on the anvil; diamonds in the rock-melting heat and crush of the earth.

Salt, too—the pure, heavenly variety—is formed the same way. "Don't be surprised at your fiery trials," we are told.[11] We are in basic training, being salted. Let's set our hearts and minds and say with Job, "When he has tested me, I will come forth as gold!"[12]

---

*The most precious things
are formed under intense pressure.*

---

[1]Joel 3:10   [2]Heb. 11:33–37   [3]Luke 21:16–18   [4]Luke 10:19   [5]1 John 3:9   [6]Heb. 4:12   [7]Isa.6:8   [8]Exod. 4:13   [9]Josh. 1:9   [10]Ps. 78:39   [11]1 Pet. 4:12   [12]Job 23:10

JUNE 26

*I was ashamed to ask the king for soldiers and horsemen
to protect us from enemies on the road, because we had told the king,
"The gracious hand of our God is on everyone who looks to him . . ."*
Ezra 8:22

e live in a world of spin doctors, media manipulation, and so much hype that few really believe what anyone says.[1] The gap between our talk and our walk has grown to a seemingly uncrossable chasm of hypocrisy.[2] Oh, for an Ezra today! Oh, for someone willing to put their money where their mouth is!

There he was, leader of a band of exiles returning from Babylon to Jerusalem, carrying with them *tons* of silver, gold, and temple treasures.[3] Their four-month-long journey[4] would take them through rough, bandit-infested terrain. Logic and reason would ask the king for a full military escort. But Ezra was more than just a priest or a teacher of the Scriptures.[5] Ezra *believed* the Scriptures with all his heart. Logic and reason were never his foundation; absolute faith in God and His Word guided his every thought and action. He had boasted of the power of the Lord, and he had given Him glory for His protection. He was not about to negate all that by asking for an armed escort.

Maybe we have never been in a position so impossible that only the hand of God could deliver us. Maybe we have been okay trusting in man, in natural solutions, in logic and reason.[6] Life has a way of doing that—lulling us into an unchallenging, faithless existence, never stretching beyond normality. And when disaster strikes, we suddenly have no idea how to trust in God and in His promises. So we do what we have always done: look to natural, human solutions,[7] and the world lets us down.

Faith is trusting that an invisible, untouchable God will actually, literally help us.[8] It's not natural, it's not reasonable, and the world calls it crazy.[9]

Do I really want to be a powerful person of faith? I need to get crazy enough to act as if what I say about God is really true. God didn't let Ezra down, and He won't let me down, either.

---

*Faith is trusting that an invisible, untouchable God
will actually help you.*

---

[1]Matt. 5:33–37 [2]Matt. 23:2–3 [3]Ezra 8:24–27 [4]Ezra 7:9 [5]Ezra 7:12 [6]Isa. 2:22 [7]Ps. 78:22
[8]Matt. 9:28 [9]Mark 3:21

JUNE 27

. . . but the righteous will live by his faith . . .
Habakkuk 2:4 [NASB]

orldly thinking says *seeing is believing*. The truth is, *believing is seeing.* Until I experienced the life-changing power of God, I could not understand that there is so much more than just this physical world.[1] There is another, higher realm—a realm not bound by the limits of what I thought was the only reality. Faith doesn't mean that I ignore the world around me; I eat and drink, sleep, use gravity and generally rely on the laws of physics to maneuver. But having faith means I also am aware that when God's purpose requires it, the spiritual realm can break through and miracles can occur. Living by such faith means that I account for that in order to obey His voice.[2] If Jesus tells me to feed over 5,000 people with what's in my lunchbox, He can make it happen.[3] If He calls me out of the boat, mere water will hold me up.[4] If He tells me nothing can harm me,[5] I need not be afraid to die. Whatever Jesus tells me to do—no matter how outrageous, impractical, or impossible it may seem—I can do it.[6]

There is no room for *but . . .* when I live by faith. When I am doing what He has called me to do, my faith says that He who knows the end from the beginning[7] knows everything that will be needed to accomplish the task. Moreover, faith trusts that God has already worked out those details and will present them each at the proper time, as long as I keep seeking His directions and moving forward.[8]

Living by faith like this does not mean obstacles and opposition will never hit me. I should never be surprised or dismayed that the enemy would try to stop God's plan;[9] he opposes God at every turn. My faith puts my money on God in such a contest! The Lord has a way of turning even opposition to His glory.[10]

Living by faith also does not measure success by the usual standards. By all the world's measures, the ministry of Jesus was a total failure: His right-hand man denied knowing Him, all the rest deserted Him, and He was executed as a criminal. Faith sees the bigger story, and knows failure (even death) is not the end. Living by faith is obeying God no matter what, and leaving the results up to Him.

---

*Living by faith is obeying God
no matter what, and leaving the results up to Him.*

---

[1]John 6:61–63 [2]John 14:11–12 [3]Matt. 14:16–21 [4]Matt. 14:28–29 [5]Luke 10:19 [6]Mark 10:27
[7]Isa. 46:10 [8]Ps. 119:105 [9]Ps. 2:1–6 [10]Exod. 14:4

JUNE 28

But seek first his kingdom and his righteousness,
and all these things will be given to you as well.

Matthew 6:33

God's Word makes no allowances. God's Word is truth.[1] Truth is truth for rich or poor, healthy or sick, free or bound. It doesn't matter if you're black, white, red, yellow, or any shade in between. Truth doesn't change with your address, your age, or your gender. Truth is still truth, with or without a degree. Truth is still truth when it's inconvenient.

I am not talking about rites and rituals,[2] or the do's and don'ts we've come up with.[3] I am talking about *sin*. There is no circumstance, no need, no desperation, that excuses disobedience. Man will never be able to stand before a holy God and honestly say he had no choice. There are no exemptions to obedience. If there were, Christ need not have died. Mercy is *needed*, because the truth is absolute;[4] Mercy is *available*, not because Jesus set the truth aside, but because *we* did, and He paid the penalty demanded. Mercy—the cross—proves that there is no excuse.

To seek His kingdom and His righteousness *first*, before all worries, fears, doubts, or reasons, is to agree with God: "I would rather die than disobey." And God's blood-bought mercy gives Him the right to give us all His power,[5] will,[6] and wisdom[7] to do just that. To the one who determines in his heart that nothing shall move him, that no matter how impossible a situation may appear, he will not depart from the truth,[8] God steps in and makes all things possible.[9] He Himself dwells within, supplies the strength *and* does the work![10] For extraordinary circumstances, He grants extraordinary grace.

Agree with God. Make His kingdom and His righteousness first in your life. *Believe*, and you will see the glory of God![11]

Determine in your heart that nothing will move you,

that you will not depart from truth,

no matter how impossible your situation seems.

---

[1]John 17:17   [2]Luke 6:1–4   [3]Matt. 15:1–7   [4]Matt. 5:17–20   [5]Isa. 53:12   [6]Ps. 40:8   [7]James 1:5   [8]Josh. 1:8   [9]Mark 10:27   [10]John 14:10   [11]John 11:40

JUNE 29

. . . Come with me by yourselves to a quiet place and get some rest.
Mark 6:31

Life is busy. I know, I know—that's an understatement if ever I heard one! Nobody needs to tell you that there are not enough hours in the day to do what you need to do,[1] and somehow you just know that if God miraculously stretched out the daily cycle by a few hours, the world would quickly find a way to fill those to overflowing, too.[2]

The airlines have the right idea. In the midst of those repetitive safety briefings about various possible disasters, there comes an instruction straight from heaven: "Be sure to place the oxygen mask securely *on yourself first*, before assisting the person next to you."

What am I talking about? I'm talking about the law of renewal. Basically put, this law says that we will not be any good to anyone else if we are worn out, broken down, burnt out, or unconscious. We are not bottomless buckets. If we pour ourselves out in endless activities and service—no matter how good, necessary, or even spiritual those activities may be—and do not stop to refill the bucket, we will run out, empty ourselves, and dry up.[3]

Jesus felt this need for renewal keenly.[4] He was in constant ministry, and it took something out of Him every time He healed or blessed or taught.[5] He literally felt power had gone out from him.[6] He spent His days pouring Himself out, but He knew to separate Himself from the crowds to spend time in prayer and communion with the source of His power.[7] He knew that if He abided in His Father and let Him direct His every step,[8] He would never run dry.

We, too, need to listen for the Master's voice. He bids us to "come with me by yourselves to a quiet place and get some rest." When we renew ourselves in Him daily, we can serve both effectively and joyfully.

---

*The law of renewal says we will not be any good
to anyone else if we are worn out and broken down.*

---

[1]Eccl. 2:22–23 [2]Luke 21:34 [3]Matt. 11:28–29 [4]Matt. 14:13 [5]Luke 6:19 [6]Mark 5:30 [7]Luke 5:16 [8]John 14:31

JUNE 30

The fear of the Lord is the beginning of wisdom,
and knowledge of the Holy One is understanding.
Proverbs 9:10

*I*t may surprise you, but the goal of wisdom is not to know things. It is to know *Him*. Things—even good things like guidance, direction, discernment, and understanding of how to effectively use what God has given us to advance His kingdom—are all just the fruit of our knowledge of God. The more we know God—personally, intimately—the more in tune we are with His Spirit. Have you ever tried to pick up a television or radio station that kept fading in and out? The signal—the voice—is constantly drowned out by the static.[1] Our knowledge of God is what keeps us tuned in to Him.

Although God can work *through* anybody or anything—a burning bush,[2] a donkey,[3] a pagan[4]—He wants to work *with* us. Jesus told His disciples in the upper room, "I no longer call you servants, because a servant does not know his master's business. Instead, I have called you friends, for everything that I learned from my Father, I have made known to you."[5] *Then* He said He'd chosen them to bear lasting fruit.

All the fruit we will ever bear for the kingdom—if anything we do is to be effective and lasting at all—must flow from our relationship, our knowledge of God, not our knowledge *about* Him.

Knowing God causes us to reflect Him, to be like Him.[6] Peter talked about what it takes to be effective and productive *in our knowledge of Jesus*: a character like His, full of goodness, kindness, self-control, and love.[7]

I will let the Holy Spirit—the Spirit of wisdom and revelation—help me to get to know God, and I will grow in my relationship to Him. To know Him is truly to love Him.[8]

The goal of wisdom is not to know things.
It is to know Him.

---

[1]Matt. 13:22 [2]Exod. 3:4 [3]Num. 22:28 [4]Isa. 10:5–6 [5]John 15:15 [6]1 John 1:5–7
[7]2 Pet. 1:5–8 [8]John 8:42

JULY 1

. . . Do not be afraid of what you are about to suffer.
Revelation 2:10

*N*obody likes to suffer. Too many times, we have the impression that God will always intervene to prevent His people from suffering. Oh, we know about how "A righteous man may have many troubles," but we glide quickly over that to get to the next part: "but the LORD delivers him from them all."[1] I'm not sure what we're expecting about His deliverance, except that the space between *having trouble* and *being delivered* is mere seconds long—or maybe a minute or two if we're feeling especially spiritual. We simply do not expect to suffer—which, by definition, involves time.

Yet there are those Scriptures like, "To this you were called, because Christ suffered for you, leaving you an example, that you should follow in His steps."[2] God's people throughout the centuries have suffered.[3]

They suffered for doing good,[4] yet they did not crumble, crying, "Why me?" They kept their focus, considering their afflictions as badges of honor,[5] a participation in the sufferings of Christ,[6] a prelude to sharing His glory.[7]

I should never let suffering cause me to lose my focus. God is true. I *will* be delivered. Peter encourages us to "Resist [the devil], standing firm in the faith, because you know that your brothers throughout the world are undergoing the same kind of sufferings. And the God of all grace . . . after you have suffered a little while, will himself restore you and make you strong, firm and steadfast."[8]

Yes, Jesus comforts us in our suffering, because He knows how it feels. At the same time, though, He reminds us that we are at war. He encourages us to get tough, to strengthen our feeble arms and weak knees.[9] To be counted worthy to suffer for His sake is a sacred trust, a blessing.[10]

Never let suffering cause you to lose your focus.
God is true. You will be delivered.

---

[1]Ps. 34:19 [2]1 Pet. 2:21 [3]Heb. 11:35–40 [4]1 Pet. 2:20 [5]Acts 5:41 [6]1 Pet. 4:12–13 [7]1 Pet. 5:1 [8]1 Pet. 5:9–10 [9]Heb. 12:12 [10]Matt. 5:10–12

JULY 2

. . . Lord, teach us to pray . . .
Luke 11:1

*T*he disciples thought they knew how to pray. They were godly men. They'd gone to the synagogue all their lives. They knew what to pray during the morning and evening sacrifices; they understood the prescribed prayers for meals and births and deaths and for all the significant events of life. They knew the proper posture and the correct placement of the *talit*, their prayer shawl. But one day, watching Jesus pray, they suddenly realized they didn't have a clue about prayer.[1]

Maybe it was the personal way He addressed the Almighty Creator. Abba[2] (Daddy) just didn't sound like the dignified chanting they were used to. Was it possible that you could just talk to God[3] like you could talk to your daddy?[4] Jesus never "said His prayers"; He *prayed*. It was not a ritual, it was a conversation, and it was not one-sided. Could they—could we—actually have a conversation with God?

Maybe it was the fact that Jesus truly *enjoyed* praying, that it filled Him with strength and energy,[5] that He came away from prayer renewed.[6] He could work all day, climb a mountain and pray all night, come down in the morning and go all day on the strength of His communion with God.[7] There's something about being in the presence of God that imparts and sustains life beyond what natural flesh can handle.[8]

Maybe it was the fact that Jesus' prayers got *results*. He got answers, He got power. Wherever He went, whatever He touched[9]—and whatever touched Him[10]—was instantly and fundamentally changed. Darkness was driven back, demons were driven out, and disease was defeated. Death itself bowed to the power of His command and touch.[11] So they asked Him, "Teach us to pray."

Jesus, teach me, too.

Yes, we actually can have a real conversation with God!

[1]Mark 9:28–29   [2]Mark 14:36   [3]Job 23:3–7   [4]Dan. 10:17   [5]Isa. 41:10   [6]Ps. 103:5   [7]Luke 6:12
[8]Exod. 34:28   [9]Luke 6:18–19   [10]Luke 8:44–46   [11]Luke 8:54

JULY 3

. . .You have been weighed on the scales and found wanting.
Daniel 5:27

*A*s much as man might argue it, the standard of right and wrong, good and evil is not for man to decide. Postmodernism, moral relativism, and many other *-isms* all contend that there is no absolute right and wrong–that right is right if it is right for you. "Right for you" usually means "whatever is convenient or gets you what you want."[1]

God swept away all such arguments in the midst of a drunken feast in the court of a pagan king. As Belshazzar, his nobles, and even his harem drank in sensual abandon from the holy vessels of God's temple–and dared to lift them in toasts to their idols–the Eternal I Am carefully and precisely measured them against His holy standard, His law. With His own hand, He wrote His findings on the wall of Babylon's palace: "You have been weighed on the scales and found wanting."[2] Your chance to prove yourself has passed, O king, and you do not measure up.

Do not be deceived. God's standard is absolute, and it applies to all.[3] If He holds a pagan ruler responsible for knowing and following His law, how much more will He demand obedience from those who have seen His light? Peter warns us: "It is time for judgment to begin with the family of God; and if it begins with us, what will the outcome be for those who do not obey the gospel of God?"[4]

Grace does not make obedience optional; grace makes obedience possible.[5] No one will have any excuse for their sin, least of all those on whom the shadow of the cross has fallen. "From everyone who has been given much, much will be demanded."[6] I have to search my heart, examine my rationalizations. What standard am I measuring myself by? I often compare my behavior to another's,[7] and sometimes my life now, by my past–and both make me feel justified by the contrast. It's easy to minimize my sin by imagining how much worse it isn't. But victory in one area does not atone for wickedness in another, as shown by every *nevertheless* warning Jesus gave to the churches of Revelation. "Woe to those who call evil good and good evil . . ."[8] I need to take sin seriously, especially in the light of His grace–and what it cost Him to make grace available.

Grace doesn't make obedience optional;
grace makes obedience possible.

---

[1]Isa. 57:12   [2]Dan. 5:1–27   [3]Ps. 96:13   [4]1 Pet. 4:17   [5]James 4:5–7   [6]Luke 12:48   [7]Luke 18:9–14
[8]Isa. 5:20

JULY 4

The Spirit of the Lord is on me, because he has anointed me
. . . to proclaim freedom for the prisoners . . .

Luke 4:18

uring the anti-slavery movement in the 1800s in America, many abolitionists in the North actually bought slaves from the South—in order to set them free. What a perfect picture of the truth of redemption through Christ![1] To redeem something is to buy it back. What had belonged to God by right of creation was sold into slavery to sin and Satan.

Too many view the way of holiness and righteousness as restrictive, inhibiting their freedom. They don't want anyone, not even God, to tell them what to do. They want to say, like the poet, "I am the master of my fate/I am the captain of my soul."*

I was that blind, and so were the Jews of Christ's day. When Jesus told them that knowing the truth would set them free, they indignantly replied, "We . . . have never been slaves of anyone"[2]—even as Rome brutalized their country. Far worse than Roman slavery, however, is the truth that Jesus pointed out: "I tell you the truth, everyone who sins is a slave to sin."[3] No one has ever been their own master.[4]

Without the Spirit of Jesus, we are all slaves of sin.[5] The enemy tricked us, promising us wonderful things in exchange for our souls—wisdom, wealth, long life, popularity, etc. . . . But he is the master of the bait and switch. "You were sold for nothing." God mourns, but He promises, ". . . without money you will be redeemed."[6]

Without money, indeed! To buy us back required blood[7]—nothing less than the blood of God Himself, in the body of His Son.[8] Jesus infiltrated the slave market of Satan, and in the flesh of a man, He paid for all flesh. He redeemed us—bought us back at a shocking price—to be able to set us free.

Do not sell yourself back into that slavery again.[9] Walk in His ways, and enjoy all the freedom He paid so dearly to give you.

Without the Spirit of Jesus, we are all slaves of sin.

To buy us back required blood.

---

[1]Heb. 9:15   [2]John 8:32–33   [3]John 8:34   [4]2 Pet. 2:19   [5]Heb. 2:15   [6]Isa. 52:3   [7]Heb. 9:22
[8]1 Pet. 1:18–19   [9]1 Pet. 4:3–5   *Biblio. p. 386

JULY 5

. . . You will leave me all alone.
Yet I am not alone, for my Father is with me.
John 16:32

earning to lean on God as my source is a lot more than singing, "He's Everything to Me" on a sunny day. It is so easy to say that Jesus is my all in all when I'm all filled up. But what about when I'm running on empty? The difference between what I sing in worship and what is really in my heart is often a shock to me when put through the fire. "You are my witnesses. Is there any God besides me? No, there is no other Rock, I know not one."[1]

He wants to be my Rock—my *only* Rock. Anything or anyone other than God is but shifting sand, a poor foundation, a deceitful support system.[2] He knows that He alone can hold me, lift me, keep me, protect me, and provide for me *unfailingly*. When others fail me, I am hurt, bereft, and wounded. God is too loving a Father to let me lean on anything that will disintegrate when I need it most!

That is why it so often happens as I grow in my walk with Jesus, that He —one by one—knocks[3] out from under me every crutch I lean on, be it man, money, or material things.[4] I, too, have had seasons when my finances were suddenly turned inside-out. He reminds me then that He is *Jehovah-jireh*, my Provider. He calls me to serve Him, and He is faithful to provide all I need to be able to do it.[5]

Then there are the times I have suffered the pain of disappointment, or even betrayal by someone near and dear.[6] In those moments, He wants me to trust that He is the friend that sticks closer than a brother[7] who will never leave me, never forsake me.[8]

When all forsake me,[9] when everyone I leaned on leaves me, I am learning to lean on Jesus; to lean on God. I am never all alone.

Who is God to you when you're running on empty?
How about when your faith is put under fire?

---

[1]Isa. 44:8 [2]Matt. 7:24–27 [3]Isa. 31:1–3 [4]Matt. 6:33 [5]Isa. 41:10–14 [6]Ps. 146:3 [7]Prov. 18:24 [8]Heb. 13:5 [9]Ps. 27:10

JULY 6

But the Lord replied,
"Have you any right to be angry?"
Jonah 4:4

*I*s it wrong to be angry? The Bible tells us that anger resides in the lap of fools.[1] It says that anger is cruel and fury overwhelming,[2] and that wise men turn away anger.[3] Jesus taught that anyone who is angry with his brother will be subject to judgment.[4]

But if it is wrong to be angry, what about Jesus? Mark, in telling of the healing of the man with the shriveled hand, said that Jesus looked around at them in anger.[5] In fact, on one occasion, He was so angry that He made a whip out of cords and drove all from the temple area, both sheep and cattle. He scattered the coins of the money changers and overturned their tables.[6] Wow! That doesn't sound like what you'd expect from lowly Jesus, meek and mild! If He is our example, then why can He be angry, but we have to get rid of it? And what about all those references to the wrath of God? What's different about God's anger and ours?

James tells us that everyone should be slow to become angry, for man's anger does not bring about the righteous life that God desires.[7] There is a difference between godly anger and man's anger. Godly anger is spiritual; man's anger is soulish. As children of God, our spirit is reborn,[8] but our thoughts, attitudes, and emotions[9] are still being made holy.[10] Godly anger—righteous indignation—is stirred up at the hardness of men's hearts, and when God's honor is profaned; it is God-focused. Man's anger is inflamed when pride is hurt, when we are ill-treated; it is self-focused. Jesus never got angry for *Himself*.

When I feel anger rising, I need to ask myself, *"Why* am I angry?" If it is wounded pride, I should let it go. Remember Jesus, and "Do not repay evil with evil or insult with insult."[11] I need to ask myself, "Have I any right to be angry?"

There is a big difference between
man's anger and God's anger!

---

[1]Eccl. 7:9   [2]Prov. 27:4   [3]Prov. 29:8   [4]Matt. 5:22   [5]Mark 3:5   [6]John 2:15   [7]James 1:19–20
[8]John 3:6   [9]Heb. 4:12   [10]Heb. 10:14   [11]1 Pet. 3:9

JULY 7

*For I desire mercy, not sacrifice, and acknowledgement of God
rather than burnt offerings.*

Hosea 6:6

$\mathcal{S}$acrifice! A reminder of failure. Forgiveness, yes, but a forgiveness necessary only because I have sinned, broken fellowship, disobeyed. Forgiveness needed only because I did not choose to walk in mercy.

This mercy—Hebrew *hesed*—is not what we usually think of when we think of the mercy of God. It is not the canceling of debt; it is not pardon. This *hesed*-mercy is faithfulness, unfailing love, loyal love, devotion.[1] This mercy that God so longs for is the cure for sacrifice. *Hesed* is walking with God with a heart that loves Him freely, deeply, with eager and willing obedience. *Hesed* toward God is *hesed* toward man, the first and second greatest commandments of all.[2]

God's mercy is gracious and compassionate, abounding in love and forgiveness. When He declared His glory, He announced Himself as the God who was slow to anger, forgiving wickedness, rebellion, and sin.[3] He paid a very high price[4] for the privilege of offering forgiveness.[5] He is faithful to forgive. All we need do is ask.[6]

But forgiveness is not His first choice. Forgiveness is His *redemptive* will—His blood-bought choice to redeem what would have otherwise been fatal. His redemptive will is necessary only when we disregard His perfect will, when we disobey. His redemptive will should never be taken for granted. His perfect will is victory.

"To obey is better than sacrifice, and to heed is better than the fat of rams."[7] Obedience is victory. Obedience is triumph. Obedience is more than conquering;[8] it is pleasing our Abba-Father God with the desire of His heart. We ask Him all the time to fulfill the desires of our hearts, as He promised He would.[9] How wondrous a thing it would be to delight ourselves so much in the Lord that the desire of *our* heart is to fulfill the desire of *His* heart!

---

*Let us delight ourselves so much in the Lord that
the desire of our heart is to fulfill the desire of His heart.*

---

[1]*Strongest*: p. 1,407 [2]Mark 12:30–31 [3]Exod. 34:7 [4]Ps. 49:7–9 [5]1 Pet. 1:18–19 [6]1 John 1:9
[7]1 Sam. 15:22 [8]Heb. 11:33 [9]Ps. 37:4

JULY 8

Why should I wait for the LORD any longer?
2 Kings 6:33

God promises many good things to those who endure, who persevere, who *wait for Him*: They will renew their strength,[1] they will see His goodness,[2] they are delivered from death and kept alive in famine,[3] they will be exalted and will inherit the land,[4] and they'll get answers from God.[5] These promises and many more are written in the psalms—by the same one who also wrote, "*How long* must your servant wait?"[6]

Waiting is not our strong point; we are an impatient people. If we don't see results on *our* timetable, we readily give up. How many times have we tossed in the towel on the very brink of our breakthrough? When Israel was surrounded by enemies, God sent Isaiah to tell them to trust in Him in spite of how it looked. He would defend them. Their enemies were only men; He was the sovereign Lord. He challenged them: "If you do not stand firm in your faith, you will not stand at all."[7] Standing is perseverance; standing is endurance; standing is outlasting the enemy, outlasting doubt, outlasting fear, and outlasting discouragement. Standing in the face of all evidence to the contrary is living by faith. *The last man standing is the winner*!

Jesus told a parable specifically to teach us that we should always pray and not give up.[8] He knows our hearts, and He knows how hard it is for our flesh to keep going when it seems pointless, endless, fruitless, or too late. But Jesus is the Word of God, and He knows more than anyone that the Word of God *does not fail*.[9]

Why should you wait on the Lord any longer? Because your only two options are death or life; the god of the break*down* or the God of the break*through*! How long must we wait? Until He says otherwise; until the end.[10] Until then, stand!

*How many times have we tossed in the towel
on the very brink of a breakthrough?*

---

[1]Isa. 40:31 [2]Ps. 27:13–14 [3]Ps. 33:18–20 [4]Ps. 37:34 [5]Ps. 38:15 [6]Ps. 119:84 [7]Isa. 7:9
[8]Luke 18:1 [9]1 Kings 8:56 [10]Matt. 24:13

JULY 9

And David was greatly distressed . . .
but David encouraged himself in the LORD his God.
1 Samuel 30:6 [KJV]

how me one who has never felt distressed, disappointed and discouraged, and I'll show you someone in a coma! We all feel this
way at times in our lives. It is especially hard on believers because
somehow we think we should always be happy and bouncy, ready to jump up
and shout, "Hallelujah!"

When we feel our weakness;[1] when the world does to us what Jesus already
told us it would—when we're misunderstood, rejected, mocked, or even attacked,[2] we feel guilty for the sorrow and loneliness we experience.

But isn't the joy of the Lord our strength?[3] Aren't we supposed to rejoice
—even leap for joy—when we are persecuted?[4] Didn't Jesus endure everything
He endured—even the cross—for the joy set before Him?[5]

Yet Jesus was a man of sorrows, familiar with suffering. The greatest, most
penetrating prophetic revelation of the work of the Messiah is full of words like
despised, rejected, stricken, smitten, afflicted, pierced, crushed, and *oppressed.*[6]
Though all men die, Jesus was *specifically* born to die, and he lived His whole
life knowing it. The shortest verse in the Bible is, "Jesus wept."[7] It didn't need
to be longer; it says enough. He knows tears, He understands sadness. But it
is also the shortest verse in the Scripture, because Jesus never *stayed* down;
His weeping endured for a night, but His joy truly came in the morning![8]

Like David, He knew how to encourage Himself in the Lord His God.
Joy, you see, is not the happiness found in convenient circumstances. Joy is
found *within* us, for it is the abiding in Jesus,[9] who dwells in us. When I am
distressed, I can draw on that joy, by faith. It is there, and faith will make it
manifest. I can stir my own spirit; encourage myself in the Lord. Sorrow may
come, but it need never *overcome*!

The joy of the Lord is our strength. We can, like David,
learn to encourage ourselves in the Lord!

---

[1]Mark 14:38   [2]Luke 21:16–17   [3]Neh. 8:10   [4]Luke 6:23   [5]Heb. 12:2   [6]Isa. 53:3–7   [7]John 11:35
[8]Ps. 30:5   [9]John 15:9–11

JULY 10

Then Jesus, still teaching in the temple courts, cried out,
"Yes, you know me and you know where I am from . . ."
John 7:28

Oh, the excuse of ignorance! How much I put off doing what I know I must, by convincing myself that I *don't* know.[1] How often have I excused my bad behavior by arguing that I didn't know—against the accusations of my conscience.[2]

The Jews argued all day long, pitting their treasured traditions and expectations of the Messiah[3] (the voice of their flesh) against the evidence of the truth laid out plainly before their eyes.[4] Jesus cut through all the sophistry and debate and aimed His words directly at their conscience (the voice of their spirit): "Yes, you *do* know Me." Deep inside, in their heart of hearts, they *knew*. The blind could see, the deaf heard, the lame walked, and the dead lived again. The devil was cast out from where he had taken root; order, sanity and peace had been restored.[5] From His gentle hands, bread was multiplied, seas calmed, and blessings bestowed. From His lips, truth unfolded in revelation after revelation of purity, holiness, and service.

And love. Extravagant, all-inclusive, merciful love. To heal what was hurt and to restore what had been stolen. Wherever the Spirit of the Lord is, captives are set free, the oppressed are released.[6]

To even think that such could be the fruit of a lie,[7] the work of the enemy, is pure foolishness.[8] The spirit within recognizes the Spirit and knows it must submit.[9]

And to that, the flesh rebels. But I know the truth; I know what is asked of me, and I know what I must do. I know who He is, and I know where He is from. I will make no more excuses, but I will follow the truth.

I know who He is, and I know where He is from.
I will make no more excuses, but I will follow the truth.

---

[1]James 4:17   [2]Heb. 9:9   [3]Mark 7:7–8   [4]John 14:11   [5]Mark 5:15   [6]Luke 4:18   [7]Matt. 7:16–18
[8]Ps. 14:1   [9]1 John 3:24

JULY 11

. . . your will be done on earth as it is in heaven.
Matthew 6:10

*H*ow exactly is God's will done in heaven? Have you ever thought about it? What are we praying for when we ask this of Him? Understanding is vital, because we are the answer to this prayer! Who does the will of God on earth? We do. People. You and I. I am not praying this prayer for everyone else . . . *am I?*

If God's will is to be done at all, it will be done by us. *Us* starts with me, and it starts with you. It's more like praying, "Let me do Your will on earth as it is in heaven."

So, how is God's will done in heaven? The psalmist wrote: "Praise the LORD, you his angels, you mighty ones who do his bidding, who obey his word."[1] Can you picture it? God on His throne, and all the angels of heaven standing before Him praising His name and His glory. Yet even as they sing, their eyes never leave His face. They pay close attention, watching for that almost-imperceptible nod, the slightest indication that the King of kings and Lord of lords has a task that needs doing. There is no lack of volunteers. "Your commands are my delight."[2] *God's will is done eagerly.*

Once the assignment is made, there is no delay, no procrastination, no hesitation. The angels do His bidding in swift flight.[3] *God's will is done instantly.*

Prophecy said that the Messiah, the Christ, would come to do the will of God.[4] Jesus said, "The world must learn that I love the Father and that I do exactly what my Father has commanded me."[5] He also prayed, "I have brought you glory on earth by completing the work you gave me to do."[6] Exactly. To the finish. *God's will is done accurately and completely.*

Eagerly. Instantly. Accurately. Completely. When we love the Lord with all our heart and soul and mind and strength,[7] His commands are not at all burdensome[8]–they are truly our delight!

"Your commands are my delight." God's will is to be done eagerly, instantly, accurately, and completely.

---

[1]Ps. 103:20   [2]Ps. 119:143   [3]Dan. 9:21   [4]Ps. 40:8   [5]John 14:31   [6]John 17:4   [7]Mark 12:30   [8]1 John 5:3

JULY 12

In those days Israel had no king; everyone did as he saw fit.
Judges 21:25

Anyone who has contended with governmental bureaucracy and come away crushed by its callousness, bruised by its bullheadedness, and tangled up in red tape, might think that the Israelites had it made back then. No king, no government, no taxes, no forms in triplicate—just everyone free to do as he saw fit. Heavenly!

And it would've been, if everyone saw fit to do things like they do in heaven![1] But as I read these chapters in Judges, I see what happens when we forsake God's thoughts and heaven's ways and lean on our own understanding.[2]

Israel had no king. Sad, but true. God was their king,[3] but they refused to acknowledge Him as their rightful ruler.[4] They would not listen to His counsel, they would not obey His laws. They thought that as long as they had the tabernacle set up and they offered up the required sacrifices, then they could do as they pleased otherwise. The book of Judges is a sad history of idolatry, debauchery, chaos, and bondage. Doing as they saw fit left them wide open to being conquered by their enemies.[5]

Proverbs tells us that all a man's ways seem innocent to him.[6] We are truly the masters of manipulating excuses and justifications for our behaviors. We long to be free—to have no one tell us what to do. No king but self! Yet self unruled by the Spirit is subject to Satan—a horrible bondage, indeed! True freedom is not freedom *from* God, but freedom *in* God—in Christ. "If the Son sets you free, you will be free indeed."[7] Not freedom as a cover-up for evil, but freedom to serve God as we were meant to do.[8]

Israel had no king; everyone did as he saw fit. The results were idolatry, assault, gang rape, murder, and a very bloody civil war.

So I ask myself, "Do I only do as I see fit, or is Christ truly my king?"

True freedom is not freedom from God,
but freedom in God—in Christ.

---

[1]Matt. 6:10 [2]Prov. 3:5 [3]Judg. 8:23 [4]1 Sam. 8:7 [5]Judg. 2:12–14 [6]Prov. 16:2 [7]John 8:36
[8]1 Pet. 2:16

JULY 13

The voice spoke from heaven a second time,
"Do not call anything impure that God has made clean."
Acts 11:9

I know about impure. I know about envy and lust, promises broken, and lies told. I know about the sludge collecting in the soul from a lifetime of selfishness and rebellion. I know about being unacceptable, grimy with guilt, and completely unclean. From the bottom of the mud pit, purity seems as possible as airborne pork. In shame, I—*we*—hide from God.

But God is not easily put off. "Come let us reason together," He says.[1] "I know all about your dirt. I can make you clean." And He does—whiter than snow. The enemy tried to use my dirt against me, telling me God didn't want someone like me. "Too filthy," he hissed. "Too guilty!" Failing that, he does the next worst thing: "Maybe you're saved, but God can't use you. You're no good to Him; He only tolerates you."

David battled this very thing, too. "For I know my transgressions, and my sin is always before me."[2] With adultery and murder in his past, he could go on only by asking for God's mercy and cleansing, then moving forward to teach others to do the same.[3] Consider, too, Mary Magdalene, who had danced to the devil's tune seven times over[4]—or Matthew, the treacherous, cheating tax collector, who had profited off the misery of his own people by working for the Roman enemy!

But if anyone was the target of the devil's accusing schemes,[5] it would've been Peter. His *sworn-with-an-oath* denial of the very Lord he'd just declared he'd go to prison and death for had to have rung in his ears over and over again. Yet he chose instead to agree with what Jesus had said about him.[6] He would not call himself impure when God had made him clean.

And neither should I. Not about myself, and not about others. God can turn a persecutor into a preacher, a murderer into a deliverer,[7] and an idolater into His anointed high priest.[8] He can use me. He can use that one slinking into the back pew, and that one just released from prison. He can use the tax collectors and the prostitutes.[9]

Call no one unclean whom God has made clean.

God says, "Come let us reason together.
I know about all your dirt. I can make you clean!"

[1]Isa. 1:18   [2]Ps. 51:3   [3]Ps. 51:1–13   [4]Mark 16:9   [5]Rev. 12:10   [6]Matt. 16:18–19   [7]Acts 7:24–25
[8]Acts 7:40–41   [9]Matt. 21:31–32

JULY 14

Turn from evil and do good; seek peace and pursue it.
Psalm 34:14

ow can I know that I'm in the will of God for my life? What if I miss His direction? How will I know if I step off the path?[1] I'm afraid to make a decision, because I don't know if it's the choice He wants me to make.[2]

If you have ever asked (or are asking now!) these questions, you are in with a good crowd, because every sincere believer I've ever met has struggled with these very issues. The fact that these questions deeply concern you scores you an A on the first test for hearing from God: you want to please Him!

So, how do we know that we are pleasing Him?[3] *He will let us know!* One of the greatest gifts He gives us as proof of His approval is His peace. His peace is not like the world's, based on circumstances.[4] I'll be able to say, "I don't know why, and I can't figure it out, but I have such peace about this decision." God says, "There is no peace . . . for the wicked."[5] He also promised that if I stray off His chosen path, either to the right or to the left, He'll tell me so![6] He will nudge me and poke me until I simply have no peace about it. It is like an itch in my spirit.

Trust God.[7] He is intimately involved in our walk.[8] It is not just us striving and straining and struggling to figure out this thing called following Christ, while He sits up in heaven like a Roman emperor, thumbs up or thumbs down on our performance! He has invested everything He is and everything He has to make sure we succeed. There is no way He is going to just let one of His blood-bought children fall,[9] get lost, wander into enemy territory, and die without doing everything His almighty arm can do to get our attention and pull us back![10]

We need to seek His peace. Pursue it. Hunt it down, track it, and stay in it. If we lose the track, we must stop what we're doing and find it again. He promises peace to us as long as we seek Him and don't return to folly.[11]

God has invested everything He is and has
to make sure we succeed.

---

[1]Ps. 25:12 [2]Ps. 32:8 [3]1 John 3:21–24 [4]John 14:27 [5]Isa. 48:22 [6]Isa. 30:21 [7]Ps. 25:14
[8]Isa. 42:16 [9]Ps. 55:22 [10]Ezek. 18:31–32 [11]Ps. 85:8

JULY 15

Love and faithfulness meet together;
righteousness and peace kiss each other.
Psalm 85:10

When two streams meet together, they become one—a river. There is no telling which is which, because their waters are mingled together and inseparable. Love and faithfulness are two streams, and when they meet together, they become a river of righteousness.[1] Righteousness *is* love and faithfulness mingled and inseparable. You cannot truly have one without the other.[2] All of man's attempts to do so end in strife, confusion, and heartache. Unfaithfulness is a betrayal of true love.[3] God has designed it that way. He Himself is a jealous God,[4] because He knows that a relationship cannot be built on divided affections.[5] Righteousness is right-doing (faithfulness): God's Word says, "He who does what is right is righteous."[6] The bad news is that no one is righteous, not even one.[7] The good news is that anyone can *become* righteous, because righteousness is also right-*being*, right standing, being in a right relationship with God. This righteousness is based on love—love that repents and receives His gift of grace: the righteousness of Jesus Christ given to an undeserving you.[8] This frees you to be able to also become faithful—something you could not do before. In Christ, love and faithfulness meet together, and your life is now a river of righteousness![9]

"Righteousness and peace kiss each other." I don't know about you, but peace in my life is more precious to me than prosperity. There is no joy without inner peace, and since the joy of the Lord is my strength,[10] a lack of peace and a lack of joy leave me drained, exhausted, weak, stressed, and eventually—sick and dead! Isaiah tells us that peace is the *fruit* of righteousness, and that the *effect* of righteousness is quietness and confidence forever.[11] Confidence is that calm assurance of having studied for a test and knowing the material; it's that total trust that what I am depending on will come through, do His part and work for me when it counts the most.

Love and faithfulness. Righteousness and peace. They are God's will for *you*.

When the two streams of love and faithfulness meet,
they become a river of righteousness.

[1]Amos 5:24 [2]Ps. 89:14 [3]Ps. 88:11 [4]Josh. 24:19 [5]Luke 11:17 [6]1 John 3:7 [7]Ps. 14:3
[8]Isa. 61:10 [9]Isa. 48:18 [10]Neh. 8:10 [11]Isa. 32:17

JULY 16

. . . You do not stay angry forever but delight to show mercy.
Micah 7:18

*T*he patience and mercy of God leave me breathless. Everywhere I turn, I see great sin, rebellion, selfishness, and thoughtless foolishness. I see our sins catching up with us and calamity hanging over our heads. I see the foolish woman of Proverbs, tearing down her house with her own hands,[1] and when it falls, I hear the cries for mercy.

I am astonished at our presumption, our boldness, our *arrogance*–to sin repeatedly and yet dare to expect mercy when the consequences hit us in the face. I tremble inside, wondering what suffering will be necessary to teach us a lesson . . . yet God continues to show mercy.

God keeps on forgiving, and lifting, canceling debts, and letting us go.[2] One of these days, He will rise to judge the wicked, but today is still His day for mercy.[3] The door is still open, and He not only holds back His wrath, but His eyes are constantly searching for someone–*anyone*–who will step up and intercede for others so He will not have to punish sin just yet,[4] so He *can* show the mercy He delights in.

Yet for all this, God is not a patsy. He fully understands tough love, and He knows how to let consequences teach us.[5] How much better it is to suffer a little now, while there is still a chance to repent, than for someone to gain the whole world, yet forfeit his soul![6] And God, in all this extravagant, audacious, undeserved compassion, is posting billboards, writing it in the sky, shouting it with fireworks: "I am a good and gracious God![7] I love you! I don't want to have to punish you. I want to be able to bless you and see you happy, if you'd only let Me! Come home!"[8]

Oh, let His mercy touch us, let His grace change us! *Today*–in the day of His favor[9]–let's tell Him thank you and love Him back.

God keeps on forgiving and lifting,

canceling debts, and letting us go.

---

[1]Prov. 14:1   [2]Matt. 18:27   [3]Heb. 3:13–15   [4]Ezek. 22:30   [5]Num. 14:33–34   [6]Mark 8:36
[7]Exod. 34:6–7   [8]2 Pet. 3:9   [9]Isa. 49:8

JULY 17

. . . I delight in your commands because I love them.
Psalm 119:47

he greatest safeguard against sin in a Christian's life is a love of doing right. When we truly delight in pleasing God,[1] we will not only do all He asks of us, we will eagerly seek out what makes Him happy.[2] Loopholes, excuses, and justifications[3] for wrongdoing won't even be attractive. Our eyes will be opened to see compromise for what it is: a deception of the enemy to get us out of the will of God and into *his* territory.[4]

A love of doing right never attempts to measure the "badness" of this wrong or that wrong.[5] Small matters are esteemed as opportunities to demonstrate faithfulness. It always bears in mind that Jesus declared, "Whoever can be trusted with very little can also be trusted with much, and whoever is dishonest with very little will also be dishonest with much."[6] When we love to do right, we cherish that awesome feeling of peace and freedom we have. We never have to worry about who's watching us[7] or about those things done in the dark that *will* be brought to the light.[8] We also get to share our master's happiness.[9] When we do right, we please God, and when God is happy, He shares His joy with us!

A love of doing right also protects us from legalism. Legalism only does right for fear of the consequences.[10] It tries to do just enough good to cancel out its bad and earn heaven as a reward. Legalism obeys out of a fear of the power of God. There is no love—not for God, not for His ways. When we love God for who He is, we love His ways. We imitate Him in all we do, because we want to be just like Him. When we truly love God, we love to do right, and His Spirit gives us the power.[11] Let us love to do right, because it's right, whether anyone else does it right or not!

When we love to do right,
we cherish the feeling of peace and freedom we have.

---

[1]John 5:30   [2]Ps. 19:14   [3]Luke 16:15   [4]John 14:30   [5]Jer. 3:9   [6]Luke 16:10   [7]Ps. 56:5–6
[8]Luke 8:17   [9]Matt. 25:21   [10]1 John 4:18   [11]Zech. 4:6

JULY 18

. . . And lead us not into temptation.
Luke 11:4

*T*rust God, my sisters and brothers. He does not set you up to fail. You are led by the Spirit, and wherever the Spirit leads, there is victory.[1] We do not wage war as the world does. God has no spiritual counterpart to the world's concept of cannon fodder. He does not secure a beachhead against sin by sacrificing His own people, by leading the weak into temptation.

When it comes to sin, *just don't go there*. The wise man in Proverbs paints us a picture of a wrong place/wrong time situation: a young man, no judgment, going down the street where temptation lives—just as the dark night is coming on.[2] Don't fool yourself. God warns us, "The spirit is willing, but the body is weak."[3] If you are prone to gossip, don't go down the street where Gossip lives. If you struggle with an addiction, don't hang out where the addicts do their thing. If you do, you can bet that the dark night is coming on! The old saying about playing with fire? It's from the Bible—Proverbs—the book of wisdom itself.[4] Wisdom also tells us that the prudent see danger and take refuge, but the simple keep going and suffer for it.[5]

Jesus told us to pray that we would not be led into temptation, and He is quick and sure to answer that prayer. The Holy Spirit will not only not lead us into temptation, into enemy fire, He will jump up and down, waving a whole parade of red flags if we start to go that way on our own!

Trust Jesus. Jude gives Him glory as the One who is able to keep you from falling.[6] He is able, but we must be willing. I don't want to be foolish and tempt the enemy to tempt me or God to rescue me.[7] But if temptation comes looking for me, I can stand up against it by crying out to Jesus. He will not let me fall.[8]

When it comes to sin, just don't go there.

---

[1]Ps. 44:3   [2]Prov. 7:6–9   [3]Matt. 26:41   [4]Prov. 6:27–28   [5]Prov. 27:12   [6]Jude 1:24   [7]Matt. 4:7
[8]Ps. 55:22

JULY 19

My people are destroyed from lack of knowledge.
Hosea 4:6

Lack of food will kill you in weeks; lack of water, in days. A lack of oxygen only takes minutes. All are terrifying ways to die. We fight and kick and strive against such horrors. But a lack of knowledge? What do we say? "Ignorance is bliss," and "What you don't know can't hurt you."[1]

But God says that a lack of knowledge can not only kill you (the body), it can destroy you (the soul). Am I kicking as hard against ignorance as I would fight to breathe? I can't know everything;[2] just how much ignorance is safe?[3]

It isn't the amount; it is the substance—the what. Or more specifically, the who. The people were destroyed because they didn't know God (v. 1—"no knowledge of God in the land"), and they didn't know His ways (v. 6—"you have forgotten the law of your God").[4] The Jews knew the law: summarized, divided, categorized, and defined down to the straining of a gnat.[5] But they missed the point—just as I do if I can rattle off Bible facts and quote verses[6] but never let the words get down into my thoughts and attitudes, never actually do them. If I never let my religion draw me close enough to God to change my life.[7] If I do not seek Him—to know Him[8] enough to talk to Him about everything I encounter—and listen for His response. If I don't know Him enough to recognize Him in my life.

What good is it to know all sixty-six books of the Bible (in order), the longest verse, the shortest chapter, etc.—but not understand that God is love,[9] therefore His people also love?[10] That to love Jesus is to love others. with acts of deliberate compassion, every day, everywhere?[11]

His mercy is not to overlook my ignorance. He who knows my heart wants me to know His—intimately enough that we will become one: walking, working, living, and loving together in harmony.[12] True knowledge is knowing God.

How can anyone be content to lack such knowledge?

True knowledge is knowing God.

---

[1]Eccl. 1:18   [2]Ps. 131:1   [3]Luke 19:41–44   [4]Isa. 1:3   [5]Matt. 23:23–24   [6]John 5:39   [7]Isa. 1:11–17   [8]John 17:3   [9]1 John 4:8   [10]1 John 4:19   [11]Matt. 25:35–40   [12]John 17:22–23

JULY 20

For your love is ever before me, and I walk continually in your truth.

Psalm 26:3

*J*esus never asks dumb questions. Asking two blind men what they wanted Him to do for them[1] and asking a cripple if he wanted to get well[2] were not dumb questions. Desire is the foundation of victory; we have to *want to win*. But we don't just want something; we want something *for a reason*. What motivates or drives our desire is what keeps us going when the going gets tough. We can want victory for a lot of reasons, but only one is strong enough to carry us through the darkest valley. Only one motivation is a living force strong enough to defeat death:[3] "Love the Lord your God with all your heart and with all your soul and with all your mind and with all your strength."[4] In the battle against sin, love is the first line of defense.

If we've been struggling against sin for any other reason—because we're supposed to, because we fear the consequences, because we're dissatisfied with the results of sin so far—we do not have a strong enough motivation. Even wanting heaven is not enough, if heaven is nothing more to us than streets of gold and a personalized mansion; if heaven is simply *not hell*.

Only love is stronger than death. Everyone—every single person—will one day submit to God.[5] Only those who do so willingly—now—because they love Him for who He is—will ever experience the freedom, peace and joy He offers: freedom from the bondage of sin,[6] peace in the victory over sin,[7] and joy in a communion with Him unhindered by sin.[8] Love is better than *supposed to* any day!

When I fall, it is love that picks me up and keeps me going. When temptation hits, it is love that lets me say, "I don't want to hurt Him like that." I don't do it to make Him love me; I do it because He already loves me. "We love, because He first loved us."[9]

Desire is the foundation of victory;

we have to want to win.

---

[1]Matt. 20:29–34 [2]John 5:6 [3]Song 8:6 [4]Mark 12:30 [5]Isa. 45:23 [6]John 8:34–36 [7]2 Pet. 3:14
[8]Ps. 66:18 [9]1 John 4:19

JULY 21

But you will receive power when the Holy Spirit comes on you . . .

Acts 1:8

*I*f loving God with everything in us is our motivation to overcome sin, the Holy Spirit in us is the power to do what we now desire. Without the Spirit, we can't even understand the things of God, let alone obey them.[1] God's ways are so different from ours, from our natural inclinations,[2] we have to have an interpreter—someone who not only knows what the Scriptures say, but knows Him to the very depths of His being.[3] Jesus laid out for us the ways of God in His Sermon on the Mount, and our natural minds say, "Whoa! God couldn't have meant that the way it sounds!" But Jesus is not a "do as I say, not as I do" kind of teacher. His every step, every act, every word demonstrated His sermon in real life. Only as we grow in Him do we even begin to get it, and to get it on deeper and deeper levels. Jesus meant what He said, but it is only by the power of the Holy Spirit in us that we can learn to live like that.

It is only by the Spirit that we can overcome our weak flesh[4] that can do nothing but give in to sin. Apart from the Spirit of God, apart from Jesus, we can do nothing.[5] It is the Spirit that gives even the desire to follow God, to obey Him.[6]

Only when we fall in love with God are we ready to take the steps needed to win the victory over sin. James tells us to submit first to God, then resist the devil.[7] All the resistance in the world will only make the devil laugh at us if we are not submitted to God. Submitting to God is submitting to His will, and His will is in His word. Without the Spirit's power in us, we cannot submit to God.[8]

Submission is not slavery; it is agreeing that God's way is better. It is choosing life and not death.[9] The Holy Spirit opens our minds to see the truth in this, and the moment our spirit says, *yes*, He makes it possible. The secret is to love God, receive His Spirit, and submit to Him. All power comes from this.

---

*Only when we fall in love with God are we ready
to take the steps needed to win the victory over sin.*

---

[1]John 8:43–47 [2]Isa. 55:8–9 [3]John 15:26 [4]Mark 14:38 [5]John 15:5 [6]Ezek. 36:27 [7]James 4:7
[8]John 14:15–17 [9]Deut. 30:19

JULY 22

But I have stilled and quieted my soul; like a weaned child with its mother,
like a weaned child is my soul within me.

Psalm 131:2

*T*here is peace in knowing that I don't have to know everything, because He knows everything. When I realized—finally—that I was not in control, that Jesus holds the reins of my universe firmly in His capable and loving hands, my frantic world stopped spinning, and I could finally breathe. It was like that scene in *The Hunt for Red October* when the hero suddenly realized that he didn't have to solve the problem of how to get the crew off the Russian submarine. The defecting captain already had a plan . . . he just needed to figure out what had already been determined!

When I am faced with a choice, a crisis, I don't need to come up with a solution. God saw the whole thing coming,[1] and He already knows what needs to be done to navigate safely through,[2] for me to come out on top—a conqueror. I just need to figure out what He has already determined, what His plan for me is.

To do that, I must still and quiet my soul, not panicking, but getting quiet and turning to God.[3] I may think I know what is going on, what the best response is, but I am a child. I don't see as He sees, nor do I know the end from the beginning. He has resources and solutions I can hardly imagine[4]—help He wants to give me if I would only let Him. He wants to take me by the hand and walk me through the fire, through the flood[5]—but I have to trust Him and step where (and when) He says to step, no matter how unstable or even invisible the path seems. If I remember that I am a child (okay, I'm not a baby, but I'm not done growing), then I can stop leaning on my own understanding[6] and listen for His instructions.[7]

The more I still and quiet my soul before Him, the more I wait on the Lord,[8] the more Jesus can speak to my spirit, can open my eyes and ears, can give me light for my path.[9] As a weaned child, I'm not looking for milk. He can start feeding me solid food.[10] He can take me to new heights and depths. As a weaned child, still and quiet in my trust, I can look to the hand of my Maker and grow.[11]

The more I still and quiet my soul,

the more Jesus can speak to my spirit.

---

[1]Ps. 139:16 [2]Eccl. 3:1–8 [3]Ps. 37:7–9 [4]Job 38 & 39 [5]Isa. 43:1–2 [6]Prov. 3:5 [7]Ps. 32:8
[8]Ps. 27:14 [9]John 1:9 [10]Heb. 5:11–14 [11]Ps. 123:2

JULY 23

I tell you the truth, unless you change and become like little children,
you will never enter the kingdom of heaven.
Matthew 18:3

The world trains us from birth to crave recognition and respect, to measure success by rewards and position. "Climb the ladder! Become somebody!" The desire for rank ate up the disciples, making them constantly argue over who was the greatest.[1] What were they measuring this by? Ability? Time in service? Special access to Jesus?[2] Membership in His inner circle (those privileged three . . .)?[3] Maybe they expected to be rewarded according to who had sacrificed more, who desired it more. Jesus was ushering in His kingdom, and they all wanted the top spots, the best titles. Referring the whole thing to Jesus, they were dumbfounded when He set a little child before them as His ideal for the greatest.

"You won't even get into the kingdom, unless you change completely, unless you are willing to be a nobody."

This hits me hard, too. I'm not unlike most people; I want to be someone special—approved, respected, honored.[4] I build my self-worth around my abilities. I don't want to admit that I am not smart enough, capable enough, or good enough to be in the kingdom of God,[5] let alone operate in it, to admit I can't do it. I have to let go of every shred of self-confidence, every desire for self-promotion I have. Leaders must have followers, but who should follow me?[6] "He must become greater; I must become less."[7] How much less?

Jesus asks, "How low will you go? The last will be first and the first will be last."[8] Are you willing to be last, to be the least of all?[9]

As a child, I have no status; I am not independent. I can't do anything on my own.[10] I must depend completely on Jesus. No matter how much I learn, no matter how much I have grown in Him, I will never outgrow this.

Becoming like a little child means I no longer desire position, power, or honors. I renounce my titles; I don't want to be in the spotlight. I want Jesus to have center stage—all eyes on Him, the only One worthy to be followed.

I have to let go of every shred of self-confidence,
every desire for self-promotion I have.

---

[1]Luke 9:46; 22:24   [2]John 13:23–25   [3]Mark 14:32–33   [4]John 5:41–44   [5]Eccl. 7:20   [6]John 10:4–5
[7]John 3:30   [8]Matt. 20:16   [9]Luke 9:48   [10]John 15:5

JULY 24

. . . then Manasseh knew that the L*ORD* *is God.*
2 Chronicles 33:13

*F*or those who have ever felt their lives beyond hope, their guilt too great, their sin unforgivable[1]—for those especially, God made sure this story was recorded in Scripture. Manasseh's life proves the vastness of the mercy of God. It can encourage and give hope to the worst of sinners. You have done evil? Manasseh did worse.

He had so much going for him. As crown prince of Judah, he had wealth and all the advantages that brings and the powerful example of a godly father (King Hezekiah) to follow. Some of us might say we didn't know any better, but Manasseh was raised around priests and prophets, prayer and miracles.[2] He well knew of how the Lord had rescued Jerusalem by putting to death 185,000 besieging Assyrians in one night—without Judah lifting a finger.[3] He himself existed only because the Lord had healed his father through Isaiah the prophet and had sent a miraculous sign to confirm His Word to him. Oh, he knew better.

But as a twelve-year-old king, he lost no time casting off "all that religion" and doing everything his rebellious heart desired. He got into the occult through sorcery and witchcraft, worshipped pagan gods, and actually dared to put their images in the holy house of God. His rebelliousness became bloodthirsty, and the Scriptures say he shed so much innocent blood, he filled Jerusalem from end to end. As if mass murder were not enough, he performed human sacrifice, starting with his own son. The Lord sent him warning after warning—all of which he ignored.

For all this sowing, his day of reaping most assuredly came. God sent the Assyrians, and Manasseh was captured, taken to Babylon with a hook in his nose and shackles on his feet, and thrown into prison.[4]

And there—oh, there!—this child-killing, devil-worshipping mass murderer suddenly realized how wrong he'd been. He doused his pride, begged God for forgiveness, and began to worship the One True God.

And the Lord God Jehovah forgave him. *And* opened his prison doors. *And*—get this—gave him back his kingdom.[5] Now *that's* an awesome God!

Who says jailhouse religion isn't real?[6]

The mercy of God can encourage
and give hope to the worst of sinners.

[1]Mark 3:28   [2]2 Kings 20:1–11   [3]2 Kings 19:35   [4]2 Kings 21:1–18   [5]2 Chron. 33:1–20
[6]Ps. 107:10–22

JULY 25

But Jesus asked him,
"Judas, are you betraying the Son of Man with a kiss?
Luke 22:48

*H*ave I betrayed the Son of Man with a kiss? What a question! How could I have done what Judas did?

What did Judas do? He pretended to be a loyal follower, a friend, while his actions sided with the enemy. He spoke words of fellowship, even as he walked in darkness.[1] He called Jesus *Rabbi* (Teacher), yet refused to learn from Him and to live by His teachings.

Have I done this? Have I ever worshipped with malice in my heart?[2] Have I ever shouted praise with a tongue that has cursed, backstabbed, or gossiped about my neighbor?[3] What of the times I've prayed so earnestly for mercy for myself, yet harbored unforgiveness in my heart against another?[4] Have I not kissed Him and betrayed Him in the same breath? Is it not a betrayal to claim God's vast, unconditional love for myself and deny it, withhold it from others?[5]

Judas used his standing as a disciple to personally profit, to accomplish his own purpose rather than submit to the purpose of Christ.[6] Whatever his motives were, I'm sure he convinced himself that he was doing the right thing. He might even have thought he was helping Jesus. I doubt he saw it as a treacherous betrayal—until afterward.[7]

Maybe I have thought the same way. After all, kissing Jesus and calling Him Lord while doing things our own way is, unfortunately, common.[8] He calls this being lukewarm;[9] He'd rather I'd be His enemy than a fake friend. Cold or hot, no pretense. An enemy attacks directly; only a friend can betray.

Apparently, Jesus was not what Judas expected. The kingdom was not what he expected. Both challenge my assumptions, too. Will I follow Jesus on His terms, or will I, like Judas, insist on religion my way? Is Jesus my Lord, or only a name on my lips?[10] Will I surrender to the lover of my soul, or will I betray the Son of Man with a kiss?

Is it not a betrayal to claim God's vast, unconditional love
for myself and deny it, withhold it from others?

---

[1] John 1:6   [2] Prov. 26:24–26   [3] James 3:9   [4] Mark 11:25   [5] Matt. 18:33–35   [6] Luke 22:3–6
[7] Matt. 27:3–5   [8] Luke 6:46   [9] Rev. 3:15–16   [10] 1 John 2:4

JULY 26

. . . And God said, "Ask for whatever you want me to give you."
1 Kings 3:5

*I*f God were to bend close and whisper to *you,* "Ask for whatever you want me to give you," what would you ask? As a child, I remember playing Ali Baba and imagining what wishes I would command the genie in the magic lamp to grant for me. I remember imagining myself as suddenly the wealthiest,[1] most glamorous,[2] most sought-after person on the planet.[3] I sorted through many options, including the ones God was pleased that Solomon had *not* chosen: long life, riches and vengeance on enemies. I may have wasted my first two wishes on such things, but I figured out that the *one* thing I wanted more than anything else was knowledge and the wisdom to apply it.[4] I knew that if I had that, I could always get the rest!

The Bible tells us the same thing, actually. "Blessed is the man who finds wisdom . . . long life is in her right hand; in her left hand are riches and honor."[5] And wisdom and understanding are exactly what Solomon asked of God. His request pleased God especially, because Solomon asked it from that poor-in-spirit[6] state of heart that places no confidence in the flesh. He asked it for the sake of God's glory, that he might govern God's people wisely and justly.

Yet even this supernatural dose of knowledge and understanding could not keep Solomon from falling into great sin.[7] Knowledge alone is not the answer. What Solomon forgot is that the fear of the Lord is the beginning of wisdom[8]—and the middle, and the end! He had it, he knew it—he was the one who wrote that proverb! Yet in all his getting, he did not keep the fear of the Lord. He ended badly, bitterly, and in despair—you can read his sad regret in every line of his other book, Ecclesiastes.

What if God were to ask *you*? He *has.* "Ask and you will receive."[9] Wisdom? Yes, Lord. But for me, far above all knowledge, give me a heart that beats for You alone.[10] You above all,[11] forever.[12]

Knowledge alone is not the answer. We need wisdom.
The fear of the Lord is the beginning of wisdom.

---

[1]Prov. 17:16 [2]Prov. 31:30 [3]Prov. 19:6 [4]Prov. 4:7 [5]Prov. 3:13, 16 [6]Matt. 5:3
[7]1 Kings 11:1–9 [8]Prov. 9:10 [9]Matt. 7:7 [10]Ps. 86:11 [11]Mark 12:30 [12]Ezek. 11:19–20

JULY 27

Simon, Simon, Satan has asked to sift you as wheat.
But I have prayed for you, Simon, that your faith may not fail.
And when you have turned back, strengthen your brothers.
Luke 22:31–32

Just as Jesus spoke of plowing and planting good seed in our heart,[1] and as He taught about watering it by the Holy Spirit to make that seed grow;[2] even as He urged us to produce fruit—a harvest of righteousness—He also warned us that our season of threshing, winnowing and sifting will come.[3]

Oh, think of it! The process is not pleasant: our grain is beaten out, shaken vigorously, tossed about. Such confusion and chaos! And all of this must be done on a *windy day*, not in the calm of untroubled times. It is the beating and shaking that separates our precious grain from the useless chaff. Chaff—the hard shell of the old self, our worldly ways, sinful habits, rebellions and hard-headedness[4] will not separate by itself. It takes effort, struggle, pain, even violence to get rid of it.[5] God's Word has been doing its work. God says His Word separates straw from grain, that it is a fire and a hammer.[6] Jesus Himself said that the Vinedresser prunes—cleans—His vines with His Word.[7] Once His Word has done its work[8] the winds (which have thus far been held back)[9] are let loose, and into our beaten and shaken soul blows the storms of life.

Do not flinch, do not despair, though it seems like troubles on top of troubles come in the midst of your very soul's anguish. It is your season of threshing. Both the piercing within of His Word and the tumult without of your troubles are necessary,[10] for though your chaff is separated, the dregs and husks still cling to the grain. The winds must blow it away. In the midst of your threshing, however, remember: Jesus has prayed for you, that your faith may not fail. And when the storms pass—as they always do[11]—your testimony will strengthen your brothers.

It is the beating and shaking
that separates precious grain from useless chaff.

---

[1]Matt. 13:23   [2]Mark 4:26–29   [3]Isa. 28:27   [4]Heb. 12:1   [5]Matt. 18:8–9   [6]Jer. 23:28–29
[7]John 15:2–3   [8]Heb. 4:12   [9]Rev. 7:1   [10]Lam. 3:31–33   [11]Ps. 34:19

JULY 28

Let everything that has breath praise the LORD. Praise the LORD.
Psalm 150:6

*T*here are so many ways to praise the Lord—so many different expressions of worship—one person can spend an entire lifetime exploring them all! We may have our own style, our own preferences, but it would be a mistake to assume that God has His favorites, too.

Psalm 150 commands praise, starting with us (those in His sanctuary) and including all the heavenly host. It gives us two infinitely deep reasons to praise our God: for what He's done (His acts of power) and for who He is (His surpassing greatness). The first will get us through His gates, but the second will bring us into His very courts—the throne room itself, His immediate presence.[1] We will never run out of things for which we can worship, shout, sing, dance, clap, stomp, jump, sigh, cry, rejoice, and prostrate ourselves before Him.

Every act driven by grateful surrender is an act of worship, whether it be loud and boisterous or calm and reverent. Every heart that recognizes and welcomes the sovereignty of God *worships*. It can do no less. The psalmist urges us to praise God with music—both the big, brassy kind and the soft, ethereal sort. Ecclesiastes tells us to be quiet before Him and stand in awe.[2] David leaped and danced before the Lord;[3] the twenty-four elders fall down prostrate.[4] Israel leaned on his staff;[5] the priests and Jehoshaphat praised Him with a very loud voice.[6] So many ways to worship—so many reasons to wait no longer!

If we have breath, we are commanded to praise the Lord. Just as the psalmist tells us to, "Sing to the LORD a new song,"[7] we can worship the Lord in a new way.[8] We can lift our hands and our voice. We can speak out or sing and shout for joy to the Lord.[9] We can praise Him with loud hallelujahs or get quiet before Him and let our hearts be moved in silent reverence and awe at His wonders.

However we choose to worship, let's make it real. God isn't interested in fake, heartless worship.[10] Let it flow from our hearts and from the depths of our souls. God will take great delight in us.[11]

Every act driven by grateful surrender is an act of worship,
whether it is loud and boisterous or calm and reverent.

---

[1]Ps. 100:4   [2]Eccl. 5:1, 7   [3]2 Sam. 6:16   [4]Rev. 4:10   [5]Gen. 47:31   [6]2 Chron. 20:19   [7]Ps. 96:1
[8]Heb. 10:20   [9]Ps. 98:4   [10]Matt. 15:8   [11]Isa. 62:4

JULY 29

The secret things belong to the LORD our God,
but the things revealed belong to us and to our children forever . . .
Deuteronomy 29:29

There is so much mystery in life, so many things for which we can only guess the explanation, and that is just the natural world. For any man to claim to know all there is to know about the spiritual world would be foolishness. Jesus told Nicodemus, who had trouble grasping the concept of the new birth, "I have spoken to you of earthly things and you do not believe; how then will you believe if I speak of heavenly things? No one has ever gone into heaven except the one who came from heaven—the Son of Man."[1] There is a whole realm of mystery waiting for us beyond our natural understanding!

To claim to know God—to know all there is to know of who He is and How He is, is dangerously deceptive. God is infinite, and infinity simply cannot fit into a finite mind. Have you ever wondered how a God who is all light with no darkness in Him[2] can make darkness His covering?[3] If man cannot even understand the way of a man with a maiden,[4] how can he expect to comprehend an eternal God? Who has understood the mind of the Lord?[5]

Such mystery and incomplete knowledge are no hindrance to faith, however.[6] God has revealed enough of Himself,[7] of the enemy,[8] of the great drama of creation that is yet ongoing[9] and of the ultimate outcome of that drama[10]—for us to choose whose side we want to be on.[11] If God does not always do as we expect when we expect, there is still the undeniable truth that one side tricked us into loss, sorrow, bitterness, and death, and that the Other Side gave everything, to the last drop of His own blood, to rescue us from that death.[12]

God does not promise us life on our terms. He does not guarantee that choosing Him will give us a trouble-free life.[13] He simply promises that for all of that, it will be worth it.

He has revealed Himself as I AM WHO I AM.[14] He asks, "Will you trust Me?"

God is infinite,
and infinity simply cannot fit into a finite mind.

---

[1]John 3:12–13   [2]1 John 1:5   [3]Ps. 18:11   [4]Prov. 30:18–19   [5]Isa. 40:13   [6]Heb. 11:1, 13
[7]Isa. 43:10–12   [8]Rev. 12:7–12   [9]Job 1:6–12; 2:1–7   [10]Rev. 21–22   [11]Deut. 30:19   [12]Rev.5:9
[13]John 16:33   [14]Exod. 3:14

JULY 30

I have brought you glory on earth
by completing the work you gave me to do.
John 17:4

I want to be able to say this, too. I want to come to the end of my life in triumph, to stand before Jesus unashamed.[1] I want to stand firm to the end.[2] A good beginning is nice. To burst forth from the gate like a thoroughbred does me no good, however, if I never cross the finish line.

So many of the leaders of Israel started well: Gideon, Samson, Saul, Solomon, Asa, Joash, Uzziah—even Hezekiah. Yet over and over again, they turned away from the Lord once God had blessed them with peace and prosperity. To avoid their fate, I can learn from their mistakes.

Compromise took out many. Deviating even a little from the will and the ways of God,[3] or tolerating evil and sin around me and in me is a sure death sentence. Purity and obedience honors God.

Poor counsel swept away several.[4] Those who fell did not listen to good advice from older and wiser men,[5] but let flattery and ego-stroking advisors pull them off course.[6] I need to beware of counsel that appeals to my pride—godliness and success is found in humility. Note to self: He who walks with the wise grows wise.[7]

Complacency conquered others.[8] It is easy to press in, cry out to, and rely on God when things are impossibly against me, but I must continue to diligently seek God and depend on Him when I am abundantly blessed and strong.[9] I must not rest on my laurels, but continue to do the things I did at first.[10]

Conceit—or pride—is the greatest faith killer and the worst idolatry.[11] Pride claims God's glory for itself, saying, "I did all this. I don't need God." I should always remember where success comes from[12] and give God the glory.

We should strive to be humble, diligent, and wise in our choice of companions and counselors. If we keep ourselves pure through continual obedience, we, too, will say, "I have completed the work you gave me to do."

To burst forth from the gate like a thoroughbred
does me no good if I never cross the finish line.

---

[1] 1 John 2:28   [2] Matt. 10:22   [3] Judg. 8:27   [4] 2 Chron. 22:4   [5] 1 Kings 12:6–15   [6] Prov. 12:5
[7] Prov. 13:20   [8] Heb. 6:11–12   [9] 2 Chron. 16:7–9   [10] Rev. 2:5   [11] 2 Chron. 26:16   [12] Deut. 8:17–18

JULY 31

Though my father and mother forsake me, the LORD will receive me.
Psalm 27:10

*R*ejection is a deep wound that often festers into bitterness. When the ones who should be your strongest supporters, your greatest encouragers, and your most understanding comforters fail you[1]– when they are the very ones who reject you–the damage can be devastating.[2]

As followers of Jesus Christ, we understand why the world rejects us.[3] We are different, something *other*, and this world has ever rejected, pushed out, and even savagely attacked anything that did not fit it. The world rejects what it cannot understand, and drives away what exposes its *wrongness*.[4]

Knowing why it happens does not take away the pain, however. Most of us are still in the process of healing the wounds and scars of our sin-damaged lives. We have a past–we are not *condemned* for our past once we are in Christ,[5] but we have a past nonetheless. It takes time soaking in the Word of God, wrapping our brokenness with the love and promises of God,[6] to staunch the bleeding of our hearts and to knit together the fractured foundations of our selves.[7] The more we grow in Christ, experiencing His love and acceptance, allowing His wisdom and grace to heal and restore us, the more the influences of our past fade and fall away. We must come to understand our newly reborn selves,[8] our "new man," our strength and beauty and worth in Christ.

Rejection sometimes comes from within the Body of Christ itself because we are all growing, learning,[9] healing–we sometimes thoughtlessly wound each other. (Sometimes, not so thoughtlessly; hypocrisy can be brutal.) When that sideswipe comment tears at an old scar, reopened pain can rip sisters and brothers apart. I tell myself to let mercy rule;[10] forgive[11]–and I remind myself that I am *not rejected*. My tongue can bring life or death;[12] I should be sensitive to the hurts of others.

Always remember, the Lord receives you. Though *all* forsake you, the Lord receives you.

The world rejects what it cannot understand and drives away what exposes its wrongness.

---

[1]Ps. 55:12–14 [2]Matt. 10:35–36 [3]1 John 3:12–13 [4]John 3:20 [5]John 8:11 [6]Ps. 147:3
[7]Amos 9:11 [8]John 1:12 [9]Heb. 5:12–14 [10]James 2:13 [11]Matt. 18:21–22 [12]Prov. 18:21

AUGUST 1

You will not have to fight this battle. Take up your positions;
stand firm and see the deliverance the Lord will give you . . .

2 Chronicles 20:17

T he battle is the Lord's.[1] When the situation starts out impossible
and only gets worse, the battle is the Lord's. When you don't know
what to do, whom to trust, where to turn–the battle is the Lord's.
When problem after problem piles up one after another or threatens to drown
you all at once[2]–the battle is the Lord's.

When He says to you, "Not by might nor by power, but by my Spirit,"[3] He
is telling you that your weakness is no worry,[4] your lack is no loss,[5] and your
ignorance is no obstacle.[6] *He* is going to do the work, so it does not matter
if you are a 98-pound weakling with bad credit, if you have no cash and no
clue. *He* is going to do it. He saw it coming and already has a plan in place
to take care of your emergency. God's idea of crisis management is, "before
they call, I will answer."[7]

Yet the angels are not going to slug it out with your enemies while you sit
back and sip lemonade. *You* must take up your positions. *You* must stand
firm. You will not have to fight, but you must march out to the battlefield.
Why? *Because that is faith in action.* Faith activates the power of heaven.
No faith, no power.[8]

When God tells you, "Don't worry, I've got this," He is telling you to step
out in faith, counting on Him to back you up. He will send you out like David
to face your Goliath. It will look dangerous, overwhelming and absolutely
impossible, but God laughs at impossible odds. Remember David,[9] Gideon,[10]
and Jonathan.[11] Remember eleven terrified disciples against the might and
power of Rome. Remember one Man against the sin and curse of the entire
world *and* all the concentrated powers of hell itself.

The battle is not yours. God will fight for you when you show up, march
out, take up your position, and stand firm.[12] He has never lost.

Your weakness is no worry, your lack is no loss,

and your ignorance is no obstacle.

---

[1]2 Chron. 20:15 [2]Job 1:13–22 [3]Zech. 4:6 [4]Luke 10:21 [5]Ps. 50:9–11 [6]Acts 4:13 [7]Isa. 65:24
[8]Matt. 13:58 [9]1 Sam. 17:50 [10]Judg. 7:7 [11]1 Sam. 14:6 [12]Ps. 27:1–3

AUGUST 2

As for you, O watchtower of the flock. O stronghold of the
Daughter of Zion, the former dominion will be restored to you . . .

Micah 4:8

hat is the former dominion? I used to think it was the earth: when God created mankind, He said, "Let them have dominion over . . . all the earth."[1] When Adam and Eve fell, they forfeited that dominion to the enemy, and Satan became the prince of this world.[2] But it is a deep truth that everything first develops in the *in*ternal, in the spiritual, before it ever manifests in the *ex*ternal, in the physical. Adam and Eve lost dominion of their internal world—over their spirit. They no longer ruled themselves, but had become slaves of sin.[3] They have passed this down to every generation since.[4]

If the Son sets us free, we will be free, indeed,[5] . . . free to take command over our souls. That is the former dominion: the ability to master yourself, to choose good, to become righteous. The proverb says that better is he who rules his spirit than he who takes a city.[6] Why? Because only the one who rules himself can keep what he is given, and it will stay a blessing. If we were to regain dominion over the earth without having mastered ourselves, we would make a hell of Eden all over again. After all, what good is it for a man to gain the whole world, yet forfeit his soul?[7]

Beware of desiring *only* an outward blessing—even if it has a chapter-and-verse reference for its promise. One of the main differences between the old covenant and the new is that the old was expressed in externals—the Presence, the Spirit, the law, even the kingdom. The new covenant is so much better, because all of these are now within us! He has put His Spirit in us[8] and has written His law on our hearts.[9] The kingdom of God is within us.[10]

The one who rules his spirit is free, no matter what his circumstances are. No one can take his peace; no one can touch his joy. It is his crown, and only he can lay it before the One who sits on the throne[11] and acknowledge that Jesus has truly restored the former dominion.

If the Son sets us free, we are free, indeed, . . .

free to take command over our souls.

---

[1]Gen. 1:26 [KJV]   [2]John 14:30   [3]John 8:34   [4]Ps. 14:1–3   [5]John 8:36   [6]Prov. 16:32 [NKJV]
[7]Mark 8:36   [8]Ezek. 36:27   [9]Jer. 31:33   [10]Luke 17:21   [11]Rev. 4:10

AUGUST 3

. . . May they be brought to complete unity
to let the world know that you sent me . . .
John 17:23

*H*as the idea of unity ever made you grimace, picturing a monochromatic Futureworld of mindless yes-men? Does *unity* really mean sameness, and does coming into *one accord* mean subjugating (and erasing) individuality and variety?

Webster's tells us that although *unity* means "not being multiple," it is also "a condition of harmony," "continuity without deviation or change (as in purpose or action)"—and my favorite, "a totality of related parts: an entity that is a complex and systematic whole."[1] These definitions allow for different notes, yet one harmony; different phases, yet one future; different sheep, yet one flock with one shepherd.[2]

We should be asking, "Unity in what?" Unity is not necessarily uniformity. We are united in one purpose,[3] not one method. We are united in one Person,[4] not one personality type. We are united in one drama, not one role.[5]

We should also ask, "Unity with whom?" With each other, we automatically assume—and we are easily defeated. There are too many voices pushing too many agendas. Does unity mean we must tolerate hypocrisy or heresy in order to have harmony? Jesus gave us the answer in this same prayer: "I in them and you in me." Unity is unity with Christ, being one with Him as He is one with the Father.[6] We have struggled for unity—and failed—because we are focused in the wrong direction. Unity with each other is not the seed; it is the fruit of being in unity with Jesus Christ.

We must seek Him. Immerse ourselves in Him. When we surrender our will to His, we will be conformed to Him.[7] When our goals, desires, loves, and hates are one with His, we will find ourselves in harmony with others of the same spirit. We will have fellowship with each other,[8] and we will be one.

Unity with each other is not the seed;
it is the fruit of being in unity with Jesus Christ.

[1]*Webster's:* "unity"   [2]John 10:16   [3]Luke 19:10   [4]Matt. 23:9–10   [5]1 Pet. 4:10–11
[6]John 17:21–22   [7]Luke 6:40   [8]1 John 1:7

AUGUST 4

Then David was angry
because the LORD's wrath had broken out against Uzzah . . .
1 Chronicles 13:11

*H*as God ever made you angry? Has He done things that shocked you, that you have trouble reconciling with your image and expectations of Him? Or maybe He *hasn't* done something that you thought He would—or should?

We can connect with David, who thought he was doing a wonderful thing. Who could not imagine that God would be anything but pleased with all the celebrating, all the joyful noise being made in His honor as the ark was being carted to Jerusalem? But right in the middle of the loudest hallelujahs, God struck a man *dead* who only tried to steady the ark and keep it from falling![1]

We can connect with Joshua, too. Fresh from the conquest of the stronghold of Jericho, he is shaken, shocked and stunned by their utter defeat at the hands of the villagers of tiny Ai![2] Prostrate, he complains to God—and *blames Him!* "Why did you ever bring this people across the Jordan to deliver us into the hands of the Amorites to destroy us?"[3]

Hell is going to shock far too many people, too, who suppose that God is too loving to destroy anyone. They are betting their eternal destiny on a faulty concept of love, or a mistaken expectation of what "God is love"[4] really means. They would do well to heed God's response to Uzzah's presumption and to Joshua's accusation: "Stand up! What are you doing down on your face? *Israel has sinned.*"[5]

I can only be offended by God's harsh response to sin if I do not see sin as all that bad.[6] Life in this world desensitizes us to sin[7]—we are so used to it that it hardly even shocks us, let alone grieves our hearts and souls.[8] God is our Father, our Abba (Daddy); it is easy to forget that He is also the Holy One, so pure no one can look on Him and live.[9]

Because so much sin goes by apparently unpunished, sudden judgment shocks us.[10] If I'm angry, I need to re-examine my attitude toward sin, my own in particular. Sincerity will not replace obedience.[11]

We can only be offended by God's harsh response to sin
if we do not see sin as all that bad.

---

[1]1 Chron. 13:7–10   [2]Josh. 7:2–5   [3]Josh. 7:7   [4]1 John 4:8   [5]Josh. 7:11   [6]Lam. 3:39   [7]1 John 2:11   [8]Gen 6:5–6   [9]Exod. 33:20   [10]Eccl. 8:11   [11]Isa. 58:1–4

AUGUST 5

Whoever tries to keep his life will lose it,
and whoever loses his life will preserve it.
Luke 17:33

I am not trying to save my life; I want to lose it. I'm ready to lose it and preserve myself in Him, in His life. All of my effort, passion, and focus is to live for Jesus Christ—learning what that means step by step. Old habits die hard, but He has set the example, walked the path,[1] and now He takes me by the hand and says, "Trust Me."

Every day is an ongoing lesson living for Christ, living His life and not my own. I am determined that as long as I have breath in my body,[2] as long as my heart is beating, I will lose my life to live for Jesus. This means that where He sends me, I will go—carrying the gospel with every step,[3] even if those steps are merely to my job, to the store, to the gym. I know that I must keep my eyes and ears open for His promptings. I am His representative,[4] whether it be to some far-flung mission field or simply to my neighbors.

Losing my life, I am finding out, means surrendering all of my parts for His exclusive use: my eyes, my ears, my mouth . . . I will see as He sees, I will hear His truth, I will speak His words. My hands are to be His hands—to lift, to comfort, to pull up higher, to push a little further, to help another.[5] I will seek His desire and consider it my highest joy to fulfill it.

The beauty of losing my life is that from now on, I am His and He is mine.[6] Every moment of such a life becomes worship. Praise comes easier with every breath.[7] Obeying Him is not a burden,[8] it is truly a joy! It is true—no one has ever known love, has ever *loved*, until he loves Christ. No one has ever lived until he lives Christ.

He is teaching me to live in Him, and I will gladly spend myself for Him. With all the strength He gives me, I will run this race;[9] I will walk and not faint,[10] and I will crawl, if I must, to continue in Him. When at the last I close my eyes, my sleep will be sweet, for I will awake satisfied to see His face.[11] I would lose the whole world,[12] yes—I would lose my life gladly for the One who gave me His.

I will seek His desire and consider it
my highest joy to fulfill it.

---

[1] Pet. 2:21   [2] Job 27:3–4   [3] Isa. 52:7   [4] John 20:21   [5] 1 Pet. 4:10–11   [6] Song 2:16   [7] Ps. 150:6
[8] 1 John 5:3   [9] Heb. 12:1   [10] Isa. 40:31   [11] Ps. 17:15   [12] Mark 8:35–36

AUGUST 6

. . . I have not found your deeds complete in the sight of my God.
Revelation 3:2

*I*ntention is not completion. It is the *doing* that is obedience, not the *meaning to*. What if Jesus had every intention of going to the cross but somehow got distracted along the way and never quite made it? What if He had *meant* to start His ministry but decided to settle down first, get married, and have kids? He could've said, "Yes, Father, but can't I have a bit of my own life first?"[1]

No, Jesus brought glory to God by *completing* the work God gave Him to do.[2] He told a parable of two sons whose father gave them a command: one said, "Yes," but didn't go. The other said, "No," but went. Jesus made it clear—the son who went was the obedient son; intention counted for nothing at all.[3] Over and over, Jesus warned that it is not what I say, but how much I really believe it.[4] Talk is only talk, but belief is *walked*; it is lived out, demonstrated in my life, and obvious to others. This is so profoundly true, He even told us we could look at the fruit of someone's life and tell if they are true or false.[5]

I need to take heed! He who searches hearts and exposes motives[6] is not fooled. Partial obedience and delayed obedience are disobedience. If I *meant to* but never quite *did*, I have not done the will of God. I cannot excuse myself by saying, "But He knows my heart." Jesus said, "Not everyone who says to me, 'Lord, Lord,' will enter the kingdom of heaven, but only he who does the will of my Father who is in heaven."[7]

I cannot divide belief and obedience any more than I can separate love from obedience. If I say I love Jesus, but I do not do what He commands, I am a liar.[8] Those are not *my* words; they're His! Jesus also said, "If you love me, you will obey what I command."[9]

If our deeds are not complete in His sight, we need to repent and take hold of His grace to finish the work. Only then can we receive His promise: "Now that you know these things, you will be blessed if you do them."[10]

You cannot divide belief and obedience,

any more than you can separate love from obedience.

---

[1]Luke 9:59–62 [2]John 17:4 [3]Matt. 21:28–31 [4]Matt. 17:20 [5]Matt. 7:15–20 [6]Prov. 16:2 [7]Matt. 7:21 [8]1 John 2:4 [9]John 14:15 [10]John 13:17

AUGUST 7

*I looked for a man among them who would build up the wall
and stand before me in the gap on behalf of the land
so I would not have to destroy it, but I found none.*
Ezekiel 22:30

*P*ay attention! God is telling us that our wall of protection is broken down, breached, and not only are we vulnerable to the attacks of the enemy, but we have even made ourselves subject to His wrath. "Build up the walls!" He says: "Fill in the gaps before it is too late!"

What are the walls? How do we build them up?

Consider well the children of Israel: whenever they were obedient and faithful to God, He Himself was their protection. When they were in right standing with God, He overthrew cities, destroyed giants, and slaughtered whole armies that dared to come against them or stand in their way.[1]

But when they forsook the truth and made a lie their refuge and falsehood their hiding place,[2] they were pillaged, conquered, and made captive. Truth is not what our flesh wants to hear. Unrepentant souls want to hear that all is well, nothing need change.[3] Comfort and abundance only are what they want to hear.[4] God blasted such false teachers and prophets as builders of flimsy, unreliable walls; their teachings, like whitewash, look pretty and sound nice, but they are no protection from the wrath to come. It is desperately serious, for God Himself says that by false teaching, we have killed those who should not have died and have spared those who should not live.[5] False teachings are the breaches and gaps in our wall.

We must rebuild the wall. We must know the truth[6] and teach the truth,[7] no matter how unpopular it may be. We must not whitewash sin or compromise with wickedness. We must stand on the pure Word of God, for this is what the Lord says about modernism: "Stand at the crossroads and look; ask for the ancient paths, ask where the good way is, and walk in it."[8] He promises: "Your people will rebuild the ancient ruins and will raise up the age-old foundations; you will be called Repairer of Broken Walls."[9]

---

*We must know the truth and teach the truth,
no matter how unpopular it may be.*

---

[1]Num. 14:9 [2]Isa. 28:15 [3]Jer. 6:13–14 [4]Mic. 2:11 [5]Ezek. 13:1–19 [6]John 8:31–32 [7]Matt. 5:19
[8]Jer. 6:16 [9]Isa. 58:12

AUGUST 8

. . . You must be born again.
John 3:7

There is a big difference between choosing good and choosing God. Many people, frustrated with their lives and unhappy with the results of their choices, come to the conclusion that they need a change. There is an emptiness in them; it's easy to see that their lives are not working.

The enemy quickly tells them it's because they've done wrong–they should start doing right. Yes, I said the *enemy*–because the problem isn't that they've *done* wrong; it's that they *are* wrong. You can't change *being* wrong by *doing* right.[1] That is why so many so-called conversions don't stick, why so much of jailhouse or foxhole religion fails.

It's the difference between choosing good and choosing God. When someone whose life is in a shambles says, "I need to start going to church. I should quit cussing too, . . ." the enemy has deceived them. He is sidetracking the work of the Holy Spirit,[2] who is speaking to the eternity in their soul[3] and is drawing them to the cross of Christ,[4] bringing them to the only One who can make the change they desperately need.

"This is what the LORD says: 'Your wound is incurable, your injury beyond healing.'"[5] We don't need bandages; we need to be born again! No matter how much good we choose, no matter how many changes we make in our life, if we do not choose God,[6] it is as effective as makeup on a dead man.[7] Maybe we won't look so pale, but we're still not breathing, and we're fooling ourselves.

Choosing God instead, means giving up on every other way.[8] It means acknowledging that He is right and I am wrong. It means asking Him to come in and change me, because I cannot change myself. Asking Jesus to be my Savior is also surrendering to His right to be my Lord.

It is being born again, an entirely new way of being from the inside out.[9]

---

*There is a big difference
between choosing good and choosing God.*

---

[1] Jer. 13:23 [2] John 16:8 [3] Eccl. 3:11 [4] John 12:32 [5] Jer. 30:12 [6] Prov. 1:29–31 [7] Matt. 23:27–28 [8] John 14:6 [9] John 1:12–13

AUGUST 9

. . . Why do you look for the living among the dead?
Luke 24:5

*W*hen you lose something, you tend to go back to the last place you knew it was. When you've forgotten something, you go back to the last thing you knew. That's what these women were doing. They thought they'd lost their Lord, and they were looking in the last place they knew He'd been. Based on normal thinking and on their whole past experience, they knew that *crucified* meant *dead*, and *dead* meant *tomb*. Dead was dead, and resurrection was for someday far off. The Last Day, the judgment. It was what everybody knew. In spite of Lazarus, the *meaning* of what Jesus had said—"I am the resurrection and the life"[1] had not really registered. So they trudged to the tomb, looking for the living among the dead.

Jesus had told His disciples over and over that He would die *and on the third day* would rise again.[2] And He told them that when He did, He would meet them in Galilee.[3] Their tradition-trained minds could barely get past the horrible first part: He would die.[4] They had just declared Him the Christ—the Messiah—the Son of the Living God;[5] it was inconceivable that God would allow His Son to die. "He must've been speaking metaphorically," they decided.[6]

When facing the unknown, we look for answers from what is known. But what if what you know is wrong? How do you find out it is wrong? How do you learn what is right? God said, "Forget the former things; do not dwell on the past. See, I am doing a new thing!"[7] How can you be open to His new thing? Jesus said He couldn't pour His new wine into old wineskins.[8] How can you be sure you are a new wineskin? Old wineskins filter everything through rigid rules and assumptions. New wineskins open themselves up to what God is really saying. Old wineskins went to the tomb; new wineskins would've gone to Galilee.

Dead thinking does not produce a living relationship. The angels at the tomb asked the question, because Jesus had already given the answer. What has He been telling you? Why keep turning back to the dead, old-wineskin way that has left you dry, thirsty, and confused?[9] Why look for the living among the dead?

How can you be sure you are a new wineskin?

---

[1]John 11:25   [2]Matt. 16:21; 17:22–23; 20:17–19   [3]Matt. 26:32   [4]Matt. 16:22   [5]Matt. 16:16
[6]Mark 9:10   [7]Isa. 43:18–19   [8]Luke 5:37   [9]Acts 15:1–11

AUGUST 10

". . . but do this with gentleness and respect."
1 Peter 3:15

ruth can sometimes be more dangerous than a lie, and more deadly. All too often, we excuse our harshness,[1] cruelty,[2] and thoughtlessness[3] by saying, "It's the truth!" Truth, without a heart of prayerful love behind it, is not so much spoken as it is spewed out, slammed down, and spiked into place like a conqueror's flag. Truth flung out with no care or concern for its victim sets no one free[4]—it only adds to the weight of their humiliation, discouragement, bitterness,[5] and rejection. It is an aberration, and becomes as much a lie as any deliberate falsehood.

Truth is sharper than any two-edged sword. It may cut even deeper than bone, for truth will slice straight through the heart and divide even soul and spirit.[6] Spoken with gentleness, truth cuts as a surgeon's scalpel: skillfully and carefully, designed to repair, to mend, to heal. Never more than necessary, never without the purpose of making the patient whole. Without love, truth just hacks and slashes like a madman in a shop of horrors.

Truth may also be blunt, like a hammer. God says, "Is not my word . . . like a hammer than breaks a rock in pieces?"[7] Some of us are tough nuts to crack, and even the Holy Spirit has to hit home hard before He gets our attention. If love is truly behind such bold bluntness, that hammer will shatter the shell and leave the soul intact. Without love, who can bear the crushed spirit that has been hammered flat?[8]

Warning: opinions are not necessarily truth. Scripture says that only fools delight in airing their own opinions.[9] Jesus is the Truth,[10] and only He can reveal another's truth to you. If He does, His grace is available to enable you to speak it in love, gently or bluntly, to heal and not harm. Think twice before you speak that "truth." If you cannot speak it in love, consider, instead, the discipline of silence,[11] for gracious compassion overlooks many faults.[12] If truth must be told, speak it only in love—for love is the power of God.

Truth must have a heart of prayerful love behind it.

[1]Jude 1:15   [2]Prov. 12:10   [3]Matt. 12:36   [4]John 8:32   [5]Heb. 12:15   [6]Heb. 4:12   [7]Jer. 23:29
[8]Prov. 18:14   [9]Prov. 18:2   [10]John 14:6   [11]Prov. 10:19   [12]1 Pet. 4:8

AUGUST 11

Where there is no revelation, the people cast off restraint . . .
Proverbs 29:18

*T*he King James version says, "Where there is no vision, the people perish . . ." I thought vision was dreams and goals, and I had jumped on the world's self-improvement bandwagon. "Dream big," it says. "Set a goal, make a plan. Drive your own life."

But the Hebrew *hazon* is not a self-produced vision of earthly desires. It is not a goal to be achieved. *Hazon* is supernatural, spiritual truth.[1] It is a God-given eye-opener, a life-changing moment of utter clarity such as Isaiah[2] and Ezekiel[3] saw and that Peter confessed.[4] It set their feet on the path of their calling and Peter on the Rock against the gates of hell. It wasn't until this revelation hit that Jesus could finally begin to explain His purpose as the Messiah—and their purpose as His disciples.[5]

Without this vision, the people perish. And yes, perishing as we normally define it *is* the ultimate result. But the word is not any of the Hebrew words meaning "perish," "die," or "be destroyed." The word is *para*, meaning truly "to cast off restraint," literally to be out of control,[6] to run amok, like the Israelites at Mt. Sinai, dancing and reveling before the golden calf—the image of absolute, debauched abandon.[7]

The purpose of this revelation of God, is—well, *purpose*. Without the utter clarity that there is a God, there is no purpose to life;[8] there is only survival of the fittest. All that remains (if there is no God) is to "eat, drink, and be merry, for tomorrow we die." There is no reason for restraint. Revelation changes everything.

Knowing God revealed in Jesus Christ is why we keep pressing forward when the darkness presses in.[9] It's perspective, it is purpose. The truth of a holy God claims our souls, calls us out of selfish pettiness[10] into something far grander than we could imagine.[11] It is the rhyme and reason to the do's and don'ts, to suffering and selflessness. It is why we get back up again and again.[12] Because He is, we are, too.

Where there is the revelation of God, there is purpose. And where there is purpose, there is hope.

Where there is the revelation of God, there is purpose.

[1]*Strongest:* p. 1,403   [2]Isa. 6:1–8   [3]Ezek. 1:1   [4]Matt. 16:15–18   [5]Matt. 16:19–27
[6]*Strongest:* p. 1,476   [7]Exod. 32:25   [8]Eccl.1:1–11   [9]Luke 9:51   [10]Luke 9:23–25   [11]Matt. 19:27–29
[12]Prov. 24:16

AUGUST 12

*Moses said to Pharaoh, "I leave to you the honor of setting the time
for me to pray for you and your officials and your people that you
and your houses may be rid of the frogs." . . . "Tomorrow," Pharaoh said . . .*

Exodus 8:9–10

omorrow is the most momentous day in the story of mankind. It is
a day of power, of total victory. Tomorrow is the day that multitudes
live in—the Day of Decision.[1] Tomorrow is the day of every good
intention, every habit kicked and formed, every "new you" ever imagined.
Tomorrow is the day we knuckle down and do it.[2] For every soul ever fueled
by wishful thinking, tomorrow is the first day of the rest of their life. Tomorrow is the greatest day that never was.[3]

Consider Pharaoh sitting on his throne before Moses and Aaron, pushing
frogs from his armrests, kicking them from his footstool, and plucking them
from his robes. He slaps away one that dares to plop onto his crown, and he
determinedly ignores the constant twitching of his officials as they vainly try
to rid themselves of the creatures. Attempting to maintain his kingly calm, he
reaches for his cup, but nearly gags as a frog stares back at him from his wine.[4]
Everywhere he looks there are frogs, except on Moses and Aaron.

A simple request—a word of prayer—and this problem, this persistent irritation, this besetting plague will be gone, done with, delivered.

Tomorrow is not surrender.[5] *Tomorrow* means, "I'm still hoping to find
another way so I will not have to admit you are right." *Tomorrow* does not
mean "Yes," *tomorrow* means, "Not today."[6] *Tomorrow* is the same as someday,
which really means *never*.

When a heart is truly convicted and repentant, there is no such thing as
tomorrow. The soul is so desperate for God, *today* already feels too late.[7] Regret
for every wasted yesterday is only expiated by the glory of His promise, "From
this day on I will bless you."[8] Not tomorrow, not someday. Today.

There is no such thing as tomorrow; there is only today, the day of His
salvation,[9] the time of His favor.[10]

*When a heart is truly convicted and repentant,
there is no such thing as tomorrow.*

[1]Joel 3:14 [2]Prov. 12:24 [3]Prov. 27:1 [4]Exod. 8:1–4 [5]Exod. 9:30 [6]Prov. 3:27–28 [7]Acts 22:14–16
[8]Hag. 2:19 [9]Heb. 3:13 [10]Isa. 49:8

AUGUST 13

But the pot he was shaping from the clay was marred in his hands;
so the potter formed it into another pot, shaping it as seemed best to him.
Jeremiah 18:4

The finest Ming vase, the most delicate Limoges porcelain, and the sturdiest stoneware pitcher[1] all started out the same way—as dirt. A mix of minerals and detritus. The same stuff of earth from which man himself was formed.[2] We have a lot in common with that Ming vase; the processes that shaped it have shaped us, also.

Before the clay could ever begin to be shaped at all, the potter had to remove all its impurities[3]—an astonishingly brutal process involving mashing, pounding, pulling, kneading, beating, and cutting.[4] The clay is washed[5] and pressed over and over, then thrown down vigorously untold numbers of times[6] until all debris and air pockets are gone. If even the tiniest amount remains, the vessel will not survive the firing. It may crack, or even explode, damaging all the vessels around it.

Once the clay is ready, the potter begins to shape it. He works it carefully, measuring exactly the right amount of pressure with his hands.[7] Yet even the most experienced potter has encountered stubborn clay that simply refuses to yield in his hands, to take the shape the potter intends. Sometimes it is a small piece of debris left behind—a bit of the pit from which it was dug still clinging to the clay. Sometimes it is an air pocket, an emptiness unfilled.[8] Whatever the reason, the vessel the potter imagined is not to be.[9] It is marred in his hands.

God sent Jeremiah to the potter's house to watch this happen, because it does happen all too often in our lives. He needs us to see that when we mess up His plan, His vision for us, He does not throw the clay away. He just starts again, and shapes us into another pot, a different pot, but just as beautiful, just as useful.

If you are not on God's Plan A for your life, don't give up![10] He is the God of second chances. Let Him reshape you today.[11]

Even the finest Ming vase started out as dirt.

---

[1]Isa. 22:24   [2]Job 33:6   [3]Isa. 1:25   [4]Isa. 41:25   [5]Isa. 4:4   [6]Lam. 3:1–3   [7]Job 10:8–9
[8]Matt. 12:43–45   [9]Lam. 4:2   [10]Isa. 45:9–11   [11]Isa. 64:8

AUGUST 14

You are the salt of the earth . . .
Matthew 5:13

*H*ow salty are you? Salt does a lot of things, and much has been written about its flavoring and preserving qualities. I want to talk about two others, however: salt melts ice, and salt makes you thirsty.

When it comes to spiritual things, this world is in a deep ice age. The heart of the unsaved is frozen—cold and desolate. Their response to the heated passion of our heavenly lover is frigid. You and I, as followers of Christ, are the salt of the earth. We are God's contact points for an ice-bound world.[1] When unbelievers encounter us, they touch the love of God, and our salt starts to melt their frozen sensibilities. The more we live *in* the world but are not *of* the world,[2] the more our saltiness melts their hearts. The world knows nothing of faith; they need to *see* and *hear* and *feel* God's love in order to believe.[3] God draws souls to Jesus through loving kindness[4]—be salty enough that those who touch your life feel that draw.

Salt makes people thirsty, and thirst is a good thing! Jesus said, "Blessed are those who . . . thirst."[5] When the lost world starts getting a good taste of our saltiness, it will stir up a thirst for more—a thirst for heavenly things, for eternity, for the kingdom of God. Salt in a box on a shelf (or a pew in church) does not make anyone thirsty, however. Salt has to be opened, shaken out, mixed in.[6] Salt has to infiltrate in order to influence. When we actually rub elbows with the world, they'll know if our salt is kosher or not. If we've lost our saltiness, there is no substitute. Nothing other than true *agape* (unconditional God-love) salt makes a soul thirsty for the living water that only Jesus can give.[7] Salt is the seal of the covenant;[8] it is the signature that makes it binding. It is the mark of the reality of the promise in our life.

We are the salt of the earth. We do not *have* the salt—we cannot give it out dose by dose. We *are* the salt. We can only share it by sharing ourselves. Let's go melt some ice and stir up someone's thirst for the water of life!

You are the salt of the earth.
Salt has to infiltrate in order to influence.

---

[1]Isa. 6:8 [2]John 17:14–18 [3]John 20:24–29 [4]Jer. 31:3 [5]Matt. 5:6 [6]Luke 15:1–2 [7]Rev. 22:17
[8]Lev. 2:13

AUGUST 15

To fear the LORD is to hate evil.
Proverbs 8:13

*W*hat does it really mean to fear the Lord? How can you fear the One you love? It has been explained before that the fear we are commanded to have is not a knee-knocking, hair-raising, run-the-other-way terror, but that it is a deep awe and reverence, a holy respect for God. Yet the original Hebrew word, *yare* could literally mean either, depending on the circumstances. Throughout Leviticus and Deuteronomy, the Israelites were commanded to fear (*yare*) the Lord. In Genesis, Jacob–in great fear (*yare*) and distress–divided up his people and flocks as the brother–who, years before had sworn to kill him–drew near.[1] It is fair to say that Jacob had a deep respect for the damage Esau could do, and he was terrified.

When God showed up at Mt. Sinai, He came in a thick cloud, with thunder so loud it shook the entire mountain. Lightning flashed everywhere, and the trumpet of God (the same one that will wake the dead later!) blasted through billows of rolling smoke.[2] His holiness is so burningly pure, none could even touch what He had touched; those who dared had to be put to death from a distance.[3] Through the smoke, God spoke His law in a voice that drove people to their knees in terror.[4] The Israelites were paralyzed by fear. God did this purposefully, that the fear of God would be with them to keep them from sinning.[5]

Perhaps we should not so quickly dismiss the terror of God. He is not comfortable, He is not soft. "Consider this, you who forget God, or I will tear you to pieces, with none to rescue."[6] He is the same God who slew Herod for stealing His glory,[7] who struck down Ananais and Sapphira for lying to His Spirit,[8] and who still holds the Lake of Fire in reserve for that Day.[9]

Standing in awe of God[10] *is* fear–a healthy, reverent terror of His holiness and power. It is *hating* evil, because *He* hates evil. It is another sensible paradox of Jesus's kingdom: if you fear God, you will hate evil, and if you truly hate evil, you will never need to fear God!

We should not so quickly dismiss the terror of God.
He is not comfortable. He is not soft.

---

[1]Gen. 32:6–7   [2]Exod. 19:16–19   [3]Exod. 19:12–13   [4]Exod. 20:18–19   [5]Exod. 20:20   [6]Ps. 50:22
[7]Acts 12:21–23   [8]Acts 5:1–11   [9]Rev. 20:11–15   [10]Eccl. 5:7

AUGUST 16

The watchman opens the gate for him, and the sheep listen to his voice.
He calls his own sheep by name and leads them out.

John 10:3

I am not the Shepherd.[1] The sheep do not listen to my voice. They *must* not listen to my voice. *They must not follow me!* My job is to open the gate for the Shepherd so the sheep can hear *His* voice and follow *Him.*

We are simply servants, for there is but one Shepherd. "I am the good shepherd," Jesus declared.[2] The sheep are His. He is the One who calls for them by name, and He is the One who leads them out. He is the One who laid down His life for them. There is one flock and one Shepherd only.[3]

My job is to *watch for the Shepherd* then open the gate for Him. I need to keep the eyes of my spirit open to see Him coming, my ears to hear Him knocking on the door of someone's heart. I must pay attention to those moments of grace when souls are softened to His touch and open to His call. A true servant makes the most of every opportunity,[4] keeping himself tender to the long-suffering of the Holy Spirit, who has wooed this heart and drawn this soul[5] with great patience and lovingkindness.[6] I need only to open the gate for the Shepherd.

But what does it mean to open the gate? How do we do it? We open the gate in many ways—usually in those surprise opportunities that come disguised as interruptions, distractions and disturbances. If I learn to listen to the Spirit, He will lead me to comfort the hurting, calm the angry, work for justice, and show the curious the ways of God. His prompting will fill unspoken needs, and my neighbor will discover there is a God who knows and cares.

We need not *all* preach; we cannot convict.[7] We are simply those whose thoughtfulness will open the gate and step aside for the Shepherd. We must speak *only* the words He gives us,[8] then trust the Shepherd to take those words and speak them into hearts. The sheep will hear, the goats will not.[9] If we do our job, the Shepherd can do His.

We must speak only the words God gives us,
then trust the Shepherd to take them
and speak them into hearts.

---

[1]Ezek. 34:11–16 [2]John 10:14 [3]John 10:16 [4]John 9:4 [5]John 12:32 [6]Jer. 31:3 [7]John 16:8
[8]Luke 21:15 [9]John 10:26

AUGUST 17

Jesus answered, "If I want him to remain alive until I return,
what is that to you? You must follow me."
John 21:22

*M*y concern should not be about how the Lord is working in you. The call *you* have does not determine the call upon *me*. The discipline He directs toward you may not be at all like the methods He uses with me.[1] I am a unique individual;[2] my *self* has been wrought and shaped unlike any other.[3] The same is true of you. You are not me, and can never be me, and I cannot be you.[4]

Yet too many times, I measure myself by you.[5] You pray a certain way, maybe I should too. You spend your time with Jesus so differently than I. Am I doing something wrong? Sometimes the comparison is favorable, and I pat myself on the back for my level of spirituality. Often it is not, and I not only batter myself emotionally for my density, but I start to question my Lord. Why does Jesus not speak to me like that?[6] Do I even *have* a spiritual gift?[7] Doesn't God love me as much as He loves you?[8]

I hear of others' experiences in the Lord, and I feel a yearning that comes dangerously close to jealously. I want to be touched like that, to feel the electricity, the fire, the brush of angels' wings. I long for Him to speak to me in dreams, visions, complete and clear sentences. Oh, to be transported by an overwhelming sensation of the fullness of His presence! To fall into a trance like Peter, to be carried away by the Spirit like Philip!

I feel the Lord's conviction–the weight of His discipline as He teaches me,[9] and I assume that everyone is spoken to this way as well, that the same requirement is laid on them. I fought my fight a certain way; everybody else should, too. If Jesus saw fit to let me struggle against my flesh in this temptation, why does He simply take *your* craving away?[10] Yet, what is it to me anyway?

I must walk as my path is laid and remember to let you journey on yours. My Lord knows me best and loves me truly.[11] I will follow Him!

The call you have does not determine the call upon me.
The discipline He directs toward you may not be at all
like the methods He uses with me.

---

[1]Heb. 13:20–21   [2]Song 6:9   [3]Ps. 139:13–16   [4]Prov. 14:10   [5]John 8:15   [6]Num. 12:6–8
[7]Luke 11:13   [8]John 16:27   [9]Heb. 12:5–11   [10]Heb. 12:4   [11]Ps. 139:1–4

AUGUST 18

. . . Get rid of the foreign gods you have with you, and purify yourselves . . .
Genesis 35:2

*H*ow many foreign gods do we have with us? We may be surprised at the answer. Consider the verse's circumstances: Jacob had been worshipping God for many years. He had seen visions, dreamed dreams, built altars, and wrestled an angel. His new name, given by God Himself, became the name by which all of God's chosen people were to be called.[1] He had served God for more than twenty years and had been greatly blessed by the Almighty. Yet after all this, God suddenly called Israel to a new level in their relationship—one for which he must (finally) get rid of his foreign gods!

What are *our* household gods? Among them might be the myths and superstitions[2] that still hold a place in our life. Superstition is a stronghold in many believers' lives, as real as any carved stone figure, any golden teraphim on a personal altar. We may not burn incense to them, but how much do we order our lives by itchy palms, twitchy eyes, burning ears, and tingly feet? The women of ancient Israel aroused the anger of God with their many charms and amulets to ward off evil,[3] and He promised to tear them off their wrists and ankles.[4] How dare they trust in trinkets for protection[5] and not in His loving, saving care?

We shake our heads at their ignorance, even as we tuck our four-leafed clovers into our Bibles, smiling at our "good luck." Have you ever dreaded a Friday the 13th? Some places won't even number a thirteenth floor. Why?

The word *luck* does not appear in the Bible, but the word *witchcraft*[6] does, as does *idolatry*.[7] Superstition is deeply rooted in both. It denies the power and purposes of God for us and steals our trust[8] from where it should be—the Great I Am. Anything that takes our eyes off Jesus is a very dangerous thing! Superstition chooses fear over faith and refuses to believe that nothing touches our lives unless God allows it.[9]

Let's walk in the light of truth, and get rid of our foreign gods.

---

*Superstition denies the power of God for you
and steals your trust from where it should be.*

---

[1]Gen. 32:28   [2]Isa. 2:6   [3]Isa. 3:20   [4]Ezek. 13:18, 20   [5]Job 8:14   [6]Deut. 18:10   [7]1 Pet. 4:3
[8]Isa. 47:11–15   [9]Prov. 26:2

AUGUST 19

God is spirit, and his worshippers must worship in spirit and in truth.
John 4:24

*T*ruth may be stronger than fiction, but it is definitely more real than fact. Facts belong to the physical world, but truth rules the spiritual realm. Truth is not just another reality; it is a higher, a greater reality. Creation–our physical world–is finite, bound to time, place, and substance. The spiritual realm is infinite; it pre-existed creation,[1] and it will long outlast it as well.[2]

What does this mean for me, though? "God is spirit," Jesus declared. Worshipping God in spirit and in truth means that I must learn to walk in spiritual reality, remembering always that what I can see, taste, and touch is not the final answer. Faith is taking into account spirit and truth and believing in possibilities. It is realizing that all I have ever known is not all there will ever be. This life is but a copy and a shadow[3]–there is more going on that I can see or feel.[4] Faith is the bridge between the two.

Faith takes the confusion out of Jesus' paradoxical teachings, because faith is believing that God is more powerful than natural forces and bigger than my circumstances. When I am walking in spirit and in truth, I may not know *how* something can be done, but I know it *will* be done if God commands it.[5] It is the difference between Zechariah's "How–?" and Mary's.[6] Zechariah's meant, "No way!" Mary's meant, "Okay–how do we proceed?" That's the kind of faith that sees God as He is: omnipotent. There is nothing He cannot do.[7] When I worship God in spirit and in truth, His truth can trump my facts every time to accomplish His will.

Worshipping God in spirit and in truth is believing that what He said is true[8] and that His reality is worth losing everything I think I possess–not just stuff, but reputation, even my life[9]–in order to gain what He promised.[10] In spirit and in truth means worshipping from the inside out, not just lip service and rituals, but with a changed heart. I can answer all my doubts and hesitations by remembering to say, "You, O Lord, are strong, and You, O Lord, are loving."[11] And that is truth.

God's truth can trump facts to accomplish His will.

---

[1]Heb. 11:3 [2]Matt. 5:18 [3]Heb. 8:5 [4]2 Kings 6:13–17 [5]Job 42:2 [6]Luke 1:18, 34 [7]Jer. 32:27
[8]Ps. 119:160 [9]Luke 14:26, 33 [10]Matt. 19:28–29 [11]Ps. 62:11–12

AUGUST 20

The kings of the earth did not believe, nor did any of the world's people,
that enemies and foes could enter the gates of Jerusalem.
Lamentations 4:12

For centuries, God through His prophets warns us of certain doom for refusing to walk in His ways.[1] From Abel's blood crying out for vengeance[2] to the souls under the altar in Revelation,[3] God's people speak of judgment to come. Over and over again, the Lord graphically describes the consequences of rejecting Him.[4] He leaves out no detail and glosses over none of the pain and horror our disobedience will bring upon ourselves. He tells us, too, that we cannot blame Him, for it will be our own fault for failing to listen.[5] He is not a God to say, "I told you so," but, He *has* told us so!

He is a God of great patience, therefore, He sets the time of judgment,[6] the expiration of our last chance, far beyond the limits of what *our* patience would put up with.[7] Too many times, we take this to mean He will never call us to account.[8] We take His *not no*w to mean *never*, and we consider sin to be no big deal.

The weakest defense man can ever offer the Judge of All the Earth is, "I didn't think You really meant it."[9] Yet that is precisely what man is betting on. God cannot be faulted. He has told us what is required, then came in person to demonstrate what He meant. Even admitting that we cannot do it by ourselves, He offers to live within us and do it for us, if we'll let Him![10] Calvary not only paid our debt to Him, but it is conclusive proof that God *does, indeed, punish sin.*

If a pure and holy Jesus, submitting to the will of God and voluntarily taking on the guilt of all our sin, could not be spared the consequences, what makes us think *we* can?[11] Unrepentance, which shows up as a shrugging, casual attitude toward our sins, is not covered by the blood, the forgiveness of Jesus.[12] Your sins are on your own head, and so will be the penalty.[13] How can we be like Jerusalem's people, who did not think it could ever happen to them?

Sin kills. Repent, resist it, and rely on God's power to get rid of it.

Unrepentance is not covered by the blood. Sin kills.

---

[1]Ezek. 33:1–5 [2]Gen. 4:10 [3]Rev. 6:9–10 [4]Deut. 28:15–68 [5]Jer. 17:4 [6]Heb. 9:27 [7]2 Pet. 3:8–9
[8]Ps. 10:11, 13–14 [9]Ps. 50:21 [10]John 14:10, 12 [11]1 Pet. 4:17 [12]Heb. 10:26–31 [13]Ezek. 33:12–13

AUGUST 21

The LORD will guide you always;
he will satisfy your needs in a sun-scorched land . . .
Isaiah 58:11

*H*e is a big God. The sun is big, too, but we can block it out of our sight with just our thumb—because the closer an object is to us, the bigger it seems. Our problems are very close to us, and they tend to block our line of sight to God. In the confusion and desperation of our circumstances, God can feel very far away, indeed.[1] But He is a very big God; He fills all of creation and beyond;[2] He is the One who flings worlds into existence with a word,[3] who numbers not only the hairs on our head,[4] but the grains of sand on the seashore, and knows their total weight down to the micronanogram.[5] He commands the wind and waves;[6] all things serve Him.[7] He does not need ingredients at all to make anything He desires,[8] to call forth anything we need. And He has promised to satisfy our needs.

Maybe it isn't distance that makes God seem small, unable to help us through. Maybe it is silence. We pray, we bring Him our problems, but food, money, healing—our *needs*—are not suddenly satisfied. So we give up believing that God is our source.

I have been there. But—I am still here. I have not shriveled up nor wasted away. Somehow, some way, I made it through—because God was never as distant or as silent as I'd thought.[9] His grace was always there, and eventually, my needs were met. Not always the needs I'd thought I had, and rarely in the way I'd thought He'd do it, but looking back, He was always faithful.

He is still a big God. Bigger than my circumstances, bigger than the storm. Jesus has promised that if I keep seeking Him and His ways, He will keep me.[10] Even if I first must go through a sun-scorched land. He is and always will be my source.

What is your need? What is your problem? How big is your God?

What is your need? What is your problem?
How big is your God?

---

[1]Ps. 22:1   [2]1 Kings 8:27   [3]2 Pet. 3:5   [4]Matt. 10:30   [5]Isa. 40:12   [6]Mark 4:41   [7]Ps. 119:91
[8]Heb. 11:3   [9]Ps. 77:19–20   [10]Matt. 6:33

AUGUST 22

*Abide in Me, and I in you. As the branch cannot bear fruit of itself,
unless it abides in the vine, neither can you, unless you abide in Me.*
John 15:4 [NKJV]

"Abide in me." Abide—from the Greek *meno*—means "to stay, remain, live, dwell, endure, belong, hold on, keep on, stand, survive, make a permanent place, and last." It means, "to be in a state that begins *and continues*."[1] Abiding in Christ means to connect and to stay connected. I am to be so connected that, like a grapevine, you can't tell where the trunk ends and the branch begins. It means I am so bound up with Christ, that we two have become one.[2] This is the deepest heart cry of Jesus, of God Himself.[3] He has already done His part. He has paid my ransom,[4] reached through to my helpless and hell-bound soul, and lifted me out of the clutches of Death. He took my charges, suffered my sentence, and set me free. He has promised—with that Word that is forever settled in heaven[5]—that He will never leave me . . . never forsake me.[6]

All He was waiting for was for me to decide. You see, abiding doesn't automatically happen once I accept Christ as my Savior. It is a day-by-day, moment-to-moment decision. I must constantly, continually choose to be aware of His presence,[7] alert to His prompting,[8] in agreement with His purpose,[9] and active by His power[10] to walk as Jesus would walk.[11] Abiding is having a heart so in love with Jesus, so tender toward God, that I would rather die than hurt Him.

Two concepts drive the lifestyle of abiding: pervasiveness and consistency. When pleasing Jesus is pervasive in my life, I am conscious of Him in everything. When my walk is consistent, obedience is not reserved for only the comfortable commands or only for the ones I understand. I cannot truly call Him Lord and keep the option open to say, "No," to anything He commands.[12]

The more pervasive Jesus is in my life, the more consistent my walk becomes. That is what abiding in Him means.

---

*Abiding is having a heart so in love with Jesus,
so tender toward God,
that I would rather die than hurt Him.*

---

[1]*Strongest:* p. 1,570 [2]Gen. 2:24 [3]John 17:21 [4]Hos. 13:14 [5]Ps. 119:89 [KJV] [6]Heb. 13:5 [7]Matt. 28:20 [8]John 16:13 [9]Amos 3:3 [10]John 15:5 [11]1 John 2:6 [12]Luke 6:46

AUGUST 23

I also could speak like you, if you were in my place . . .
But my mouth would encourage you;
comfort from my lips would bring you relief.
Job 16:4–5

*W*hen my house is burning down around me, the last thing I need is a fire prevention lecture. I need water—lots of water, rolled-up sleeves, and strong hands to help. When my business has gone under, when the diagnosis is terminal, when I'm bleeding and the sharks are circling closer, I do not need some self-righteous pew-sitter to quote me chapter and verse on the causes and effect of sin. I need a lifeline.

I am no omnipotent, enthroned-above-the-flood knower of the end from the beginning. If the Holy Spirit has not given me a prophetic word revealing the specifics of someone's situation, how can I presume to root out their causes on my own? Job's experience alone should clue us in to a major, hidden plot line and a few more characters that have a hand in our story.

Which means that when someone is struggling, we need to take our cues from Jesus. Although He had plenty of ammunition, He did not come to shoot us down, but to treat our self- and Satan-inflicted wounds and rescue us.[1] He did not go around with a pointing finger, but with a healing hand. He did tell people to stop sinning, but he first set them free. He filled their stomachs with bread before He explained about the Bread of Life.

God's command and the merciful Spirit say to "Rescue those being led away to death; hold back those staggering toward slaughter,"[2] and to "snatch others from the fire and save them; to others show mercy, mixed with fear."[3] We will be better able to do this if we remember that convicting people of guilt, sin, and judgment is the Holy Spirit's job.[4] God's Word is a sword,[5] and a sword takes skill to wield effectively. It is not a blunt object for beating people! It is by *His* Word that souls are reborn.[6] *Our* words should be gentle,[7] pleasant,[8] full of grace and Jesus' wisdom.[9] To a soul bent with sorrow, the best words are often no words at all[10]—just silent companionship and shared tears.[11]

Let us use our mouths to comfort and encourage others, to be merciful and offer the grace of God.

Our words should be gentle, pleasant,
full of grace and Jesus's wisdom.

---

[1]John 3:17   [2]Prov. 24:11   [3]Jude 1:23   [4]John 16:8   [5]Heb. 4:12   [6]1 Pet. 1:23   [7]Prov. 15:1
[8]Prov. 16:21   [9]Luke 21:15   [10]Prov. 25:20   [11]Job 2:11–13

AUGUST 24

But God said to him, "You fool! This very night your life will be demanded from you. Then who will get what you have prepared for yourself?"
Luke 12:20

ealth is one of the trickiest substances known to man. It is a *thing*, neither good nor bad in itself. But oh, what it does to the souls of men! It is a powerful addiction. Starting with a genuine need, it is so easy to slide from making money *for* a purpose to *making money your purpose*. Solomon, one of the wealthiest men ever to live, said it best: "Whoever loves money never has money enough; whoever loves wealth is never satisfied with his income."[1] That addiction takes a downward path: "You cannot serve both God and money."[2]

The hallucination of wealth is that it is the kiss of God's approval. That's why the disciples were so astonished when Jesus said it was almost impossible for a rich man to enter the kingdom.[3] Wealth distorts reality. It makes you think you can easily fit through the eye of a needle!

Money is seductive; it takes all the grace of God to keep it from possessing us. God's blessing does, indeed, sometimes include wealth.[4] Sometimes, not always. It definitely should never be a barometer whether something is or is not of God. Wealth, like anything, is a test. God is searching for those who can use money without money using them. Any resources God gives us should be used to push back the darkness and advance the kingdom. There are souls to be rescued; bodies to be fed, clothed and healed;[5] neighbors to be loved with actions and in truth.[6]

God is looking for stewards—those who will remember not only the true *source* of all blessings,[7] but the true *purpose* as well: to bless others.[8] You can see it in the rebuke God gave the rich man in Jesus' parable: "Who will get what you have prepared for yourself?" His need was not bigger barns, but a bigger heart. Just count how many times he had said, "I, me, mine . . . ," echoes of the sin of Lucifer.[9]

As stewards of God, we are not so much receivers as distributors—pipelines—of His resources: from heaven, through us, to the world. And when our lives are demanded from us, it will be a good accounting.

God is looking for stewards who remember the true purpose of blessing is to bless others.

---

[1]Eccl. 5:10   [2]Matt. 6:24   [3]Luke 18:24–25   [4]Prov. 10:22   [5]James 2:15–16   [6]1 John 3:18
[7]Deut. 8:18   [8]Gen. 12:2   [9]Isa. 14:12–15

AUGUST 25

So you also, when you have done everything you are told to do, should say,
"We are unworthy servants. We have only done our duty."

Luke 17:10

*W*e are told to seek God with all our hearts.[1] Seeking God is an all-consuming career. It takes everything I have: my thoughts, time, energy, abilities, and desires.[2] To reserve even a portion of any of these for myself alone is a hindrance. It is taking back my surrender to God in order to retain control over my life.[3] That's a strong statement, but consider what *holding back* means. I would be saying, "God, you can have those hours but not these. I will serve you until I get tired. I'll do anything you ask, as long as I can still do these other things, too." *That* is setting limits on what or how much He can ask me to do. What if what He is trying to accomplish requires letting go of everything else I do . . . for a season, or even for good? Is seeking God still worth it?

But what *does* seeking God with all my heart look like? What kind of life would I have? What about work? What about relaxation? Can't I seek God and still do the things I enjoy?[4]

Wow! Do I realize what those questions are saying about myself and God? Why am I—are we—asking such questions?

From day one with Jesus, He has been peeling off the layers of *self* in me, the ridiculously entrenched, "What about me?" attitude[5] that hinders my ability to submit to Him. Deeper and deeper, item by item, He asks me, "Will you give me this?"

Do I truly believe that God is good, and that serving Him is as deeply satisfying as I claim? Deeper yet, am I still serving Him only for what it means for *me*? (And yet, there *is* a glorious reward . . . *I will find God!*[6])

Seeking God with all my heart and soul is irrevocably wed to obeying Him.[7] We do what He asks because He asks it. There is nothing to boast about. Nothing that demands special recognition or repayment. It is simply the whole duty of man.[8]

Do I truly believe that God is good,
and that serving Him is as deeply satisfying as I claim?

---

[1]Jer. 29:13   [2]Luke 14:33   [3]Luke 17:33   [4]James 4:2–3   [5]Matt. 19:27   [6]2 Chron. 15:2   [7]Isa. 58:2
[8]Eccl. 12:13

AUGUST 26

*Through Jesus, therefore, let us continually offer to God
a sacrifice of praise—the fruit of lips that confess His name.*
Hebrews 13:15

*H*ow can it possibly be a sacrifice to praise God? I used to wonder about this verse when my life was smooth and relatively trouble free. But when trouble came crashing down upon me, I caught a glimpse of the meaning of a sacrifice of praise. Then came the desperate hour and a fiery, piercing, hate-filled letter from someone I greatly loved and had greatly hurt. Even as I crumpled to the floor, my hands tearing at my hair in agony and my heart desperately wanting to stop beating, through my tears I heard my voice speaking words that astonished even me: "Thank you, Jesus. Thank You, God! Thank You, Jesus."

Even sinners love those who love them, Jesus said.[1] Anyone can dance when the music is merry, and it is nothing at all to shout *hallelujah* when the tidings are good. Yes, when God blesses us, we need to shout it out. Give Him thanks and praise His name. After all, we don't want to be out-shouted by a rock, do we?[2]

We want to truly bless the Lord at all times,[3] right? Praising the Lord *always* means praising the Lord *anyway*. Like Job, "The LORD gave and the LORD has taken away; may the name of the LORD be praised."[4] *Anyway*. Like Habakkuk, "Though the fig tree does not bud and there are no grapes on the vines, though the olive crop fails and the fields produce no food, though there are no sheep in the pen and no cattle in the stalls, yet I will rejoice in the LORD, I will be joyful in God my Savior."[5] *Anyway*. Like Jesus: "Now my heart is troubled and what shall I say? 'Father, save me from this hour'? No . . . Father, glorify your name!" *Anyway*. When we are persecuted, we endure it—*anyway*. When we are cursed, we bless[6]—*anyway*.[7]

When your tears are your food day and night,[7] when trouble is so thick, it threatens to suffocate you,[8] when all you have is swept away,[9] bless the Lord *anyway*. *That* is the sacrifice of praise. And God says, "He who sacrifices thank offerings honors me, and prepares the way so that I may show him the salvation of God."[10]

Praising the Lord always means praising the Lord anyway.

---

[1]Luke 6:32   [2]Luke 19:40   [3]Ps. 34:1 [KJV]   [4]Job 1:21   [5]Hab. 3:17–18   [6]John 12:27–28   [7]Luke 6:28
[8]Ps. 42:3   [9]Ps. 31:9–13   [10]Heb. 10:34   [11]Ps. 50:23

AUGUST 27

"He . . . puts his servants in charge, each with his assigned task . . ."
Mark 13:34

*W*e have a divine assignment, a position to fill and a mission to accomplish on behalf of the King of kings.[1] We are each now a full-blooded member of the heavenly family, and that comes complete with a critically important position in the family business! Jesus did not simply deliver us, He delivered us for a *purpose*.[2]

Notice also that the work for which we have been especially chosen[3] is *not up to us*. Abraham did not pick the land of Canaan out of a places-to-inherit prospectus. Moses did not select Deliverer of Israel from a wide variety of potential career choices, and John the Baptist did not get to bargain with God over his appointment as the forerunner to the Messiah. In fact, Scripture says, "He will instruct him in the way chosen for him."[4]

God has not only called us and assigned us, but He has also fully equipped us to do whatever He has required of us. The Holy Spirit has poured Himself into us as a particular gift—or several gifts—which gives us the ability to do the work with the power and authority of heaven.[5] We *can* do whatever He calls us to do!

Would I choose otherwise if it were up to me? Limited knowledge, tunnel vision, and outright fear often make us hesitate and draw back from enthusiastically accepting our assignment. If we could but see from heaven's perspective![6] How gladly and gratefully we would embrace the privilege He offers. The basic issue is *trust*. Do I trust that God—who made me and knew me before I was born[7]—knows and cares about the desires of my heart?[8] Is He wise enough to know I can't do the job without supernatural help? Does He really know what He's doing?

We need to trust God—to let Him show us all we have been assigned to do. Let us learn to submit to Him fully, that He might work unhindered through us to accomplish His will.[9]

God has not only called us and assigned us,
but He has also fully equipped us to do
whatever He has required of us.

---

[1]Mark 16:15   [2]Jer. 15:11   [3]John 15:16   [4]Ps. 25:12   [5]1 Pet. 4:10–11   [6]Ps. 33:13–15   [7]Jer. 1:5
[8]Prov. 10:24   [9]Ps. 40:8

AUGUST 28

. . . My heart is changed within me; all my compassion is aroused.
Hosea 11:8

*H*ow fierce is the love of God! How tenacious is His passion that will not let us go! Man will abide only so much; we draw the line so close, we set the bar so high. Relationships are fragile at best. At worst, they are doomed to constant disappointment.

But God—oh, how amazing His mercy; how everlasting His compassion![1] Though we pierce Him, spurn Him, turn our backs, and burn Him, *nothing* we do ever douses His love.[2] Jeremiah preached warning and woe for forty years and witnessed only hardness of heart, repeated rebellion, and eventually, the destruction and desolation of his people. Yet, he could cry over the captivity of Israel, "Because of the LORD's great love we are not consumed, for his compassions never fail. They are new every morning; great is your faithfulness."[3]

Now is the morning; *now* is the time of new compassions and great faithfulness. The times are evil,[4] and sin has infected even the very ground, creation itself. Evil, terror, wickedness, and vileness are bold and epic,[5] and everywhere, there are souls giving up, overwhelmed with the magnitude of what they have done. Too much, too far, too late—their sins rise up like a terrible dragon they are helpless to slay.

We need to let everyone know the day is still here, the night has not yet fallen.[6] God has promised for a little while longer, "I will not carry out my fierce anger . . . For I am God, and not man—the Holy One among you. I will not come in wrath."[7] For yet a little while, we have the light;[8] truth and salvation are available. They need to hear His invitation: "Come. Whoever comes to me I will never drive away."[9] One day, the door of mercy will close. Then, indeed, God will do "his work, his strange work, and perform his task, his alien task"[10]—punishing sin and the sinners who cling to it. Today, all can seek the Lord while He may be found![11] It is yet morning but for a few hours more. His compassions are still new. His love has not yet let us go!

*Now is the time of new compassions
and great faithfulness.*

---

[1]Ps. 136 [2]Jer. 31:3 [3]Lam. 3:22–23 [4]Amos 5:13 [5]Mark 13:12–13, 19–20 [6]John 9:4 [7]Hos. 11:9
[8]John 12:35 [9]John 6:37 [10]Isa. 28:21 [11]Isa. 55:6

AUGUST 29

. . . You who call on the LORD, give yourselves no rest, and give him no rest till he establishes Jerusalem and makes her the praise of the earth.

Isaiah 62:6–7

God is actually saying, "Come on! Pester Me! I want you to bring this issue up over and over. Don't stop, don't give up until it really happens." Why? Why does it take so much? Does God really need all that reminding, all that nagging, before He'll get around to it?

Have you wondered why Jesus told that parable about the persistent widow and the unjust judge?[1] What was He really saying? The lesson was not so much about the character of God as about the power of persistence. When it comes to prayer, persistence is the proof, the evidence of faith, and Jesus made much of faith. He forgave and healed the paralytic because He saw his friends' faith.[2] He told the bleeding woman,[3] blind Bartimaeus,[4] and the Samaritan leper[5] that their faith had healed them. He healed two other blind men according to their faith,[6] and He told the sinful woman who washed His feet with her tears and anointed them with perfume that her faith had saved her.[7] *Faith* changes *facts.*

Faith is a precious and powerful thing. Faith pleases God more than any good work,[8] because faith chooses God above all the lies with which the devil has smeared Him. Love touches the heart of God. Faith touches His throne, His sovereignty, His power. Faith pushes back the darkness and nullifies the strategies of the enemy. Faith frustrates the opposition!

The enemy is persistent; he does not give up easily. He held up Daniel's answer for three whole weeks, fighting the messenger of God.[9] Because Daniel did not simply ask once and give up when he didn't get an immediate response; because he persisted, backing up his faith with fasting and prayer, he received what he asked for.

I don't want to let the enemy rob me of my answer. I will keep up the pressure! God does not get weary or worn out;[10] I can give Him no rest. He is the source of all patience, He will not get irritated if I give Him no rest until His will is manifested.

Faith chooses God above all the lies
with which the devil has smeared Him.

---

[1]Luke 18:1–8 [2]Matt. 9:2–7 [3]Mark 5:34 [4]Mark 10:52 [5]Luke 17:19 [6]Matt. 9:29 [7]Luke 7:50
[8]Heb. 11:6 [9]Dan. 10:12–14 [10]Isa. 40:28

AUGUST 30

. . . You would have no power over me
if it were not given to you from above . . .
John 19:11

*H*ow big is our God? Is He big enough for His throne? Does He truly rule our life,[1] or does *Lord* not mean what it says? As children of God, we are safe in the palm of His hand.[2] Receiving salvation is surrendering my life—both now and for eternity—into His care.[3] His hands are big and strong; He has never dropped a soul committed to Him.[4] Neither does He ever leave one of His beloved children at the mercy of a merciless enemy.

Jesus understood this. He knew that everything in His life came only through the plan and permission of His Father in heaven. Nothing could touch His life that wasn't measured, monitored and restricted by the will and purpose of God.[5] Total surrender to that will and not to His own freed Him from the bondage of fear. Everything Jesus taught, He first walked out in His own life. When He told His disciples, "Nothing shall by any means hurt you,"[6] He was not saying there would never be unpleasant consequences. He was saying that no hurt or harm the devil could throw at us could ever have a lasting impact. God can be trusted. The enemy cannot touch me beyond what God allows.[7]

Submitting to God means following His thoughts and His ways no matter what our circumstances may be. This will require that we hold very lightly and loosely the physical stuff of this world and remember that the Spirit gives life; the flesh counts for nothing.[8] Flesh thinks that suffering, sickness, and death is harm; Jesus said that even though they could kill the body, they could do no more.[9]

Resisting the devil, therefore, is to reject all that is not of God, to refuse to do the *natural* thing or to follow the ways of the world, no matter what the consequences may look like. Since God is sovereign over our life and allows only what is necessary for His purpose and goal for us, then kicking against our circumstances is not allowing them to work God's purpose in us. That includes building a genuine faith,[10] perseverance, character,[11] hope—the image of Christ in us.

The devil can't hurt us. He has no power over us except what is given him from above.

The enemy cannot touch you beyond what God allows.

---

[1]Ps. 22:28 [2]John 10:28–29 [3]1 Pet. 5:7 [4]Ps. 31:5 [5]Prov. 19:21 [6]Luke 10:19 [KJV]
[7]Job 1:12, 2:6 [8]John 6:63 [9]Luke 12:4 [10]1 Pet. 1:7 [11]2 Pet. 1:5–7

AUGUST 31

And without faith it is impossible to please God . . .
Hebrews 11:6

*B*elieving that God exists is one thing, but believing that He will reward me is quite another. The first is that kind that believes and trembles, like the demons, yes,[1] but also like the neighborhood kids of the grizzled old man that lives alone in the house at the end of the path in the woods. They know he exists; they've seen glimpses of his overcoat-shrouded form[2] every now and then. Some have even heard his strange, whispery voice.[3] But the stories! Others have told terrible tales of evil eyes,[4] murderous intent,[5] frightening details of past encounters. The old man is talked about only in whispers and avoided at all costs.

Unfortunately, many believers in Christ have this kind of belief about God. He exists—of that they are certain. But they've heard some pretty frightening things about the Ancient of Days: fire and brimstone, judgment and wrath. They speak of Him in hushed tones, uneasy about those undotted *i*'s and uncrossed *t*'s in their lives, waiting for His lightning bolts to strike. . . . They serve Him in fear, as the pagans placated their hungry gods, the idea of *loving Him* too dangerous and impossible to grasp. Jesus, they can handle; He was meek, and gentle, and humble in heart.[6] He blessed children; He didn't condemn sinners. But God? Too cloud-shrouded and scary! No one can even look at Him and live![7]

But faith that believes He *rewards* you is a faith that says, "I've heard the stories, but I've dared to slip up outside Your window and I've peeked inside Your house. I've heard You crying for Your lost children,[8] and I've caught glimpses of You working on marvelous things, whispering, 'How much he'll love this,' or 'She'll smile when she sees this.'[9] I believe You are not at all like they say. I believe You are good, kind and generous. I want to hear Your side of the story. Can I get to know You?"

If your faith is going to sustain you,[10] heal you,[11] move your mountain,[12] and *please God*, it must be faith that God is good, that He is able *and* willing—that He *loves you*.

Dare to seek Him. Dare to delight Him.

You must possess the type of faith that believes
God is good and that He loves you.

---

[1]James 2:19   [2]Ps. 18:11   [3]1 Kings 19:12   [4]Job 14:3   [5]Num. 17:12–13   [6]Matt. 11:29
[7]Exod. 33:20   [8]Isa. 50:2   [9]Mal. 3:10   [10]Isa. 46:4   [11]Matt. 4:23–24   [12]Matt. 17:20

SEPTEMBER 1

*In your struggle against sin, you have not yet resisted
to the point of shedding your blood.*

Hebrews 12:4

*H*ow hard do we really fight for our victory?[1] How hateful is sin, really, to us?[2] A drowning man will fight for breath with a strength that would shame a body builder, but we do not fight our dying soul with the same fierce desperation. To quote Dylan Thomas, we do not "rage, rage against the dying of the light," preferring instead to surrender, to "go gentle into that good night."* We slide under the surface of a still pool with hardly a kick or a flutter, complaining all the while of the strength of the current.

We rail at Eve for being so gullible, for not resisting in even so small a matter as a piece of fruit. Yet we believe the same lie she did: "You will not surely die."[3] We do not kick and scream and wrestle against our temptations or besetting sins,[4] because we do not feel the sting of death in succumbing.[5] "It is a small matter," we rationalize.

Maybe it's perception. The words we use to mean *sin* take the sting out of it. Sin is disobedience deserving of punishment, but mistakes, stumbles, slips . . . well, that's just being human! Maybe if we called it *sin* instead of some excusing euphemism, it would eat at our hearts more. Maybe we would even repent.

How much do we resist sin?[6] Do we shake our heads a time or two, but give in when it insists? Are we able to withstand for a day? An hour? Ten minutes? Do we hold out through sweats, shakes, tremors, and torture, or do we cave in when we feel the first pang of discomfort?

Through the ages, believers have suffered cruelty, torture, exile, and death, steadfast in their faith—even to love their persecutors. We can do the same.[7] Much of what we face as temptation is not nearly so overwhelming or heinous. God is merciful. He knows how to rescue us from temptation when we call on Him.[8]

That is what resisting is: recognizing our weakness and crying out for God's power to overcome. Resist. All of heaven stands ready to help![9]

*God knows how to rescue us from temptation
when we call on Him.*

[1]James 4:7   [2]Prov. 8:13   [3]Gen. 3:4   [4]Heb. 12:1   [5]John 8:24   [6]1 Pet. 5:8–9   [7]Rev. 2:10
[8]2 Pet. 2:5–9   [9]Heb. 1:14   *Biblio. p. 386

SEPTEMBER 2

The bed is too short to stretch out on,
the blanket too narrow to wrap around you.
Isaiah 28:20

*T*he beautiful thing about a religion of relationship is that it *covers* you![1] No matter what the circumstance that comes against me, no matter how complex the situation, when I trust in my relationship with Christ (the Cornerstone)[2] I will always find the right path through.

Not so those whose religion is a religion of ritual, of rules, of do's and don'ts.[3] We cannot reduce a relationship to a formula.[4] We cannot prescribe a dose of so many prayers and such-and-such number of "good" acts to cancel out our "bad" acts, nor can we restore a fractured relationship by a rehearsed equation of rites and sacrifice.[5] If we try, there will always arise a situation, a disaster—an overwhelming scourge[6]—that will simply defy all the rules and formulas. The philosophy, the 1-2-3-step doctrine[7] we trusted in will be too narrow to wrap around us securely; that resting place will not hold all of our needs. We will need to stretch, and our feet will stick out. We will try to get comfortable, but our rituals will not let us. They will not have an answer for the disaster we are facing.

When this comes upon us—as it surely will, if we are trusting in anything but a living, dynamic, two-way relationship with that tested and precious stone, Jesus—it is our opportunity to throw off that old cover, to rise up from that too-small bed, to *wake up* to what He offers us.[8]

Believing in Jesus is not a go-to-church, don't-smoke/drink/dance/cuss religion.[9] Believing on Jesus is the family of God restored; it is the Father teaching His children what is good. It is the chasm crossed, the breach repaired, that we may once again talk to God and listen to Him, and follow Him as He goes before us to level the mountains, break down the gates and cut through whatever bars our way.[10]

We must consider carefully on what we base our confidence,[11] or we may find ourselves with a too-short bed and a too-skimpy blanket to cover our calamity.

Believing in Jesus is the family of God restored.

---

[1]1 Pet. 4:8   [2]Isa. 28:16   [3]Isa. 28:10–13   [4]Matt. 15:7–9   [5]Amos 5:21–24   [6]Isa. 28:15, 18
[7]Matt. 23:16–28   [8]John 1:12   [9]Matt. 23:25–26   [10]Isa. 45:2   [11]2 Kings 18:19

SEPTEMBER 3

He has showed you, O man, what is good . . .
Micah 6:8

The biggest obstacle to the Holy Spirit's work in us is the hardness of our heart.[1] Ignorance can be taught, weakness can be strengthened, but a cold, unwilling heart is harder than stone. A sculptor can work with stone to shape it into something beautiful. God engraved His law in stone, writing it with His own finger[2]—but an unwilling heart simply refuses to be shaped.

The hardness of our heart can be measured by what it takes to convict us. How must God speak to me to get my attention?[3] What must He do to show me what is good? To the soft heart, to the soul sensitive to the tiniest whisper of the Spirit, a flashing message across the heavenly marquee is not necessary.[4] God need not hit me upside the head when He wants to tell me something. A soft soul needs only to hear Him whisper it. A true lover does not wait for his beloved to beg; a true lover takes great delight in searching out what pleases his beloved.[5]

God has taken great pains to reveal Himself to us, to make Himself known.[6] He has wooed and warned, urged and prompted, and driven men and women over thousands of years to write down everything He wants us to know about what He is all about.[7] What pleases Him, what angers Him, what breaks His heart has been laid out in songs and stories, poetry, parables, and prophecies, history, and revelation—all bound together in a book called the Holy Bible. It required much blood, sweat, tears, and miracles to put this gift into our hands—all so we would know what is good, what makes our Beloved smile.

For a true God lover, that is all it takes to convict of sin and righteousness.[8] This book is not impersonal, but a deeply impassioned letter of love and longing, written especially to *me*. Therefore, I do not wait to feel convicted before I line my life up with what He has already showed me.

He has showed *you*, O Christ follower, what is good. How soft is your heart to receive it?[9]

A true lover takes delight in searching out
what pleases his beloved.

---

[1]Zech. 7:12   [2]Exod. 31:18   [3]Isa. 42:19–20   [4]Mark 8:12   [5]John 8:29   [6]Ezek. 38:23   [7]Luke 1:1–4   [8]John 16:8   [9]Heb. 4:7

SEPTEMBER 4

. . . the LORD is with you when you are with him . . .
2 Chronicles 15:2

There is no playing around with God. He is a refuge, a fortress, a strong tower, a shelter in times of trouble[1]–*if* He has been my shelter in times of plenty as well. He is not merely a 911 service, standing by to rush to my rescue in times of emergency, but otherwise not a part of my life. We humans are far too guilty of this.

God has blessings and goodness piled up in the storehouses of heaven for us[2]–blessings He greatly desires, even longs to give us. *Shalom* is God's idea of peace; *shalom* in the Hebrew means more than an absence of war. *Shalom* means fullness, satisfaction, wholeness–nothing missing, nothing broken. Anyone who has lived in anxiety and chaos can easily see that there is more to a full, satisfying life than mere *stuff*.[3] *Shalom* peace is the abundant life Jesus promised us.[4] It is not Cadillacs and swimming pools; it is wisdom, honor, freedom, peace, and purpose. God, who *delights* in the well-being of His servant,[5] wants us to enjoy His blessing. But never at the cost of our soul.[6]

Far above our material prosperity, God desires our peace–peace with Him. Not an on-again, off-again relationship. He does not want to date us, seeing us once or twice a week, but otherwise living apart. He wants to *marry* us![7] He wants *all* of us, *all* the time.[8] He promises no less of Himself to us.

Why such intensity? It seems so demanding! What about what *I* want? But all I ever wanted, dreamed of, and desired is found in its purest state in God. He wants my undivided loyalty because He wants me to have undivided joy.[9] I can only have it in Him.

Let's take God out of our emergency-use-only kit and make Him at home in our home. If we are with Him, He will always be with us!

God wants us to enjoy His blessing.
But never at the cost of our soul.

---

[1]Ps. 61:3–4   [2]Ps. 31:19   [3]Deut. 28:1–14   [4]John 10:10   [5]Ps. 35:27   [6]Mark 8:36   [7]Isa. 54:5
[8]Luke 9:62   [9]Isa. 48:17–19

SEPTEMBER 5

O my God, I cry out by day, but you do not answer,
by night, and am not silent.

Psalm 22:2

The psalmist was not afraid to say the things I am afraid to say. He railed in anger when evil and wickedness seemed to be winning.[1] When he was ill treated, slandered and scorned, he complained vigorously to the Most High, imploring Him to pour out His wrath and vengeance upon his enemies.[2] Sometimes the images are so shockingly raw,[3] it makes me wonder how such vehemence can come from a righteous soul. The religious part of me says, "Oh, my. I would rather he'd pray mercy and blessings on them."[4]

Yet there is a place within me, too, that cries out, "Yes! Do it, Lord. Do it to them and teach them a lesson!" There are times when I get tired of loving people I do not like,[5] tired of being kind to those who are not,[6] tired of walking when it feels like I'm going nowhere.[7] There are times when I feel like a phony, a fake, a hypocrite, because I do what He says to do and do not feel it in my heart.

There are times I cry out day and night. What do I want? Anything. A touch, a word, a tingle, a jolt. An answer. But the skies are shut, and I am left in my groaning.

I am not alone in my drought and famine.[8] The psalmist's words assure me that others have felt exactly as I do. He felt forsaken, alone, and ignored, too.[9] Yet he, as I, never gave up. He refused to believe—against all the evidence his desperation conjured—that God had abandoned him. He may have railed in anger and wailed in anguish, but he always ended in praise.[10]

Weariness is often our portion. That's why there are so many promises about renewal and rewards for persevering.[11] Yes, we get tired. Yes, our feelings do not always line up, but we do it anyway, by faith.

He is here, though I feel Him not.[12] He answers, though I hear Him not. I believe, though I see Him not.[13] I will wait on Him, and He will renew my strength.[14]

Weariness is often our portion.
That is why there are so many promises
about renewal and rewards for persevering.

---

[1]Ps. 73:12–16 [2]Ps. 59:9–13 [3]Ps. 137:7–9 [4]Luke 6:27 [5]Matt. 5:44 [6]Luke 6:32–35
[7]James 1:3–4 [8]Amos 8:11 [9]Ps. 22:1 [10]Ps. 22:31 [11]James 1:12 [12]Heb. 13:5 [13]John 20:29
[14]Isa. 40:31

SEPTEMBER 6

So Abraham called that place The Lᴏʀᴅ Will Provide.
And to this day it is said, "On the mountain of the Lᴏʀᴅ it will be provided."
Genesis 22:14

Jehovah-jireh: The Lᴏʀᴅ Will Provide. Abraham was well able to say this, to claim this, as he knelt upon Mount Moriah before the altar he had built, with his arms around the son he had been prepared to sacrifice in obedience to the Lord.[1] All the long journey from Beersheba to Moriah with the fire, the wood, and Isaac by his side, there was no indication of the Lord's provision. There were no flocks nearby, bleating. There was no lamb laid across the donkey's back. Just fire, wood, and Isaac—and the command of God: "Take your son, your only son, Isaac, whom you love, and go . . . Sacrifice him there as a burnt offering."[2]

There was no hint of the Lord's provision, except the certain faith that Abraham had in the truth of his God. He declared that faith aloud when he told his servants, "We will come back to you."[3] He affirmed that faith again when he answered Isaac's (worried?) question with, "God himself will provide the lamb for the burnt offering, my son."[4] His faith in the Lord's provision did not waver, even as he bound his beloved son, the child of promise, and laid him upon the altar. It did not stop him from drawing the knife. There was still no sign of the lamb the Lord would provide, but it did not stop him from obeying the Lord, from sacrificing the one thing on earth dearest to his heart.

It took the direct intervention of heaven itself to stop him from sacrificing Isaac.[5] Yet heaven only stopped the physical act, for Abraham had already sacrificed his son in his heart. Then—and only then—was the provision of the Lord made manifest.[6]

Do we claim that the Lord is our *Jehovah-jireh*? We can do so; He has promised it[7]—when we stand where Abraham stood. We are all, each and severally, called to Mount Moriah. We are, every one of us, commanded to sacrifice there the one thing on earth dearest to our heart.[8] Only when we've drawn our knife is the promise fully ours. When we do this, we make His kingdom and His righteousness first over all,[9] and the Lord will be our *Jehovah-jireh*.

Do we claim the Lord is our Jehovah-jireh?
We can do so . . . when we stand where Abraham stood.

---

[1]Gen. 22:1–19   [2]Gen. 22:2   [3]Gen. 22:5   [4]Gen. 22:8   [5]Gen. 22:11–12   [6]Gen. 22:13   [7]Isa. 58:11
[8]Luke 14:33   [9]Matt. 6:33

SEPTEMBER 7

The apostles said to the Lord, "Increase our faith!"
Luke 17:5

*I*s it the amount of faith that makes the difference between our mess and our miracle? If I am not getting what I ask for in prayer, do I need to ask Jesus to increase my faith? After all, Jesus told the disciples that they couldn't drive a demon out of a boy because they had so little faith.[1] But He commended an enemy soldier[2] and a foreign woman[3]—neither of whom were Jews, let alone disciples of Jesus—for their *great* faith. And *they* both got *their* requests granted.

Jesus did not tell the disciples, "Sure! Glad you asked! Here's a super-faith infusion. You're going to need it." Not at all. In fact, He actually told them that if they had faith as small as a mustard seed, they could uproot mountains.[4]

I have struggled with this and other sayings of Jesus, such as: "Ask and it will be given to you . . ."[5] "You may ask me for anything in my name, and I will do it."[6] And the currently popular, ". . . whatever you ask for in prayer, believe that you have received it, and it will be yours."[7] Do I still have no faith?[8]

Perhaps when I do not see the results I think I should see in my situation, it is not a question of having no faith, little faith, or great faith. Perhaps it is not even a question of using what faith He has already given me. Perhaps it is all about what I am using my faith *for*.[9] Am I even asking Jesus what He wants to do in each situation? Am I asking the right questions? Do I truly want *His* will to be done,[10] or only what I *hope* His will is? Am I building *His* kingdom with my faith and prayers . . . or my own? I need to stop assuming I know what God's will is for everyone and every situation. But if I *truly* want to serve Him, I also need to seek to learn His will so I can pray effectively. When I am fulfilling *His* purpose, I can ask Him for anything at all to accomplish the task. I can have faith that hell or high water will not stop me from reaching the other side.[11]

*Am I building His kingdom
with my faith and prayers . . . or my own?*

[1]Matt. 17:19–20 [2]Matt. 8:5–10 [3]Matt. 15:21–28 [4]Luke 17:6 [5]Matt. 7:7 [6]John 14:14 [7]Mark 11:24 [8]Mark 4:40 [9]James 4:2–3 [10]Matt. 6:10 [11]Luke 8:22–25

SEPTEMBER 8

You should not look down on your brother in the day of his misfortune.
Obadiah 1:12

To truly love my enemies, I must learn to stop seeing them as my enemies. There is a strong pull from my flesh to see an enemy suffer, to rejoice and to gloat when our enemy falls.[1] When Jesus said, "Love your enemies,"[2] He meant for us to love them with all of the impossible, outrageous, extravagant love of God, who makes His home in us.[3] This kind of love is overflowing, overwhelming, and overcoming: nothing can stand against His unfailing love.[4]

The psalmist tells us that God does not take pleasure in evil.[5] To love your enemy with the heart of God is to see that person through the eyes of the One who died to give them life, who longs to wrap His arms around them in a joyous embrace.[6] It is to see myself in them: an enemy of God, helpless against a justified death sentence—yet *justified* anyway. My enemy is but a step of grace away from being a brother. And love is the door that grace steps through.[7]

To love an enemy is not merely to be kind to him. It is possible to do a kindness with hatred in our heart.[8] I should beware of hidden selfishness:[9] do I want my enemy to change just so they will leave me alone? Would I take delight if misfortune should strike them? Would I be disappointed if they were forgiven? What thoughts and feelings surge through me when my enemy is blessed?

Can I love an enemy? Can I forgive them and truly pray that God does, too? Of course! I can do *anything* God asks—commands—me to do.[10] I can do even as the psalmist did for his enemies, those who repaid him evil for good and left his soul forlorn. He fasted for them and truly prayed blessings for them—and honestly mourned when blessings didn't come.[11] Why? How? He allowed God's love to be made complete in him.[12]

This perfect, fear-chasing, all-encompassing, unconditional, never-failing love is already in us, because *God is in us.*[13] Let's let Him love all people through us.

Love is the door that grace steps through.

---

[1]Prov. 24:17   [2]Matt. 5:44   [3]John 14:23   [4]Ps. 13:5   [5]Ps. 5:4   [6]Luke15:20   [7]Jer. 31:3   [8]Ps. 26:3
[9]Prov. 26:24–26   [10]Luke 18:27   [11]Ps. 35:12–14   [12]1 John 2:5   [13]1 John 4:4

SEPTEMBER 9

. . . You will be king over Israel, and I will be second to you . . .
1 Samuel 23:17

*A*m I still trying to figure out God? Do I still look as a man looks, on the outward appearance (or circumstances)[1]—the things that seem right to me? Do I still make decisions based on common sense and ask God only when my mind can't come up with a logical answer? Is prayer my first thought, or my last resort?

What does that have to do with the king of Israel?

Consider: Why would God not choose Jonathan? We cannot answer the question, except with a list of maybes, because according to the scriptural record, Jonathan was every bit as much a man after God's own heart[2] as the ruddy-cheeked giant-slayer. Jonathan was as bold as a lion in his faith and trust in God[3], and humble enough not only to accept, but embrace the loss of his kingdom to a shepherd boy because it was the will of God. Jonathan was not only a humanly logical choice (being the crown prince) but a spiritually excellent choice as well.

Beware of common sense—it is often relied on instead of heartfully seeking God's will. Saul's common sense suited up David in armor to fight Goliath; faith took it off.[4] Gideon's common sense rallied 32,000 men to battle the Midianites; God's plan sent home all but 300.[5] Martha's common sense said four days was too late for Lazarus; Jesus said, "Take away the stone."[6]

Common sense looks at the natural and says the task is impossible; it will take too much time, cost too much money, require more talent than we have, and drown us in red tape. God's plan *has* a plan for all of that.

We must be led by the Spirit to know God's will. We must not be tempted to substitute even spiritual common sense for His direction, or we'll choose Jonathan instead of David. The Word of God warns us twice but in Proverbs alone that the way that seems right to a man leads straight to death.[7]

God has a plan that man can never figure out on his own. If we listen to the Lord, He'll tell us![8]

---

*Beware of relying on common sense
instead of a heartfully seeking God's will.*

---

[1] 1 Sam. 16:7   [2] 1 Sam. 13:14   [3] 1 Sam. 14:6   [4] 1 Sam. 17:38–39   [5] Judg. 7:1–8   [6] John 11:38–40
[7] Prov. 14:12; 16:25   [8] Ps. 25:14

SEPTEMBER 10

He who walks with the wise grows wise,
but a companion of fools suffers harm.
Proverbs 13:20

"*Even* those of us who struggle with self-confidence still tend to believe we are wiser and stronger than we are."[1] We usually overestimate our abilities and our willpower. I have known dieters who successfully resist the temptation of an ice cream sundae—then reward themselves for their resistance with a chocolate milk shake! The hell of relapsed addiction is filled with enslaved souls who thought they were strong enough to face temptation.

Jesus knew how weak human willpower really is. That's why He told the drowsing Peter, James and John in Gethsemane, "Watch and pray so that you will not fall into temptation. The spirit is willing, but the body is weak."[2] That is also why He included this request in His model of the perfect will-of-God prayer: "Lead us not into temptation."[3]

If we pray that God (who *knows* what we can and cannot handle) should not lead us into temptation, then we should be sure we (with a woefully inadequate understanding of ourselves) do not lead *ourselves* into it! God warns us about the danger of continual fellowship with bad company.[4] Yet we insist, "That may be true for others, but I am stronger than that. *I* won't be corrupted." We are being duped, misled. Our flesh is weak against temptation but strong in its desires. It is a constant battle to not give into our old ways. The influence of the world finds a strong answering pull within us. But who wants to be like the proverbial cleaned-up sow that goes back to wallowing in the mud?[5]

One look at our history of failed New Year's resolutions ought to convince us that our willpower and self-discipline are not as strong as we'd like to think. Keeping our steps on the narrow path is challenge enough when we surround ourselves with godly fellowship;[6] why would we make it even more difficult by drowning ourselves in a sea of temptation?[7]

We become careless and inured to sin when we choose to hang out with those who do wrong—evil deceives and ensnares us.[8] It is one thing to be kind to others; it is *entirely* another to be drawn to what is evil and fellowship with it![9]

If we pray that God should not lead us into temptation,
then we should be sure we do not lead ourselves into it!

---

[1]Jer. 17:9   [2]Mark 14:38   [3]Matt. 6:13   [4]Prov. 24:1–2   [5]2 Pet. 2:22   [6]Heb. 10:25   [7]Exod. 23:2
[8]Prov. 5:22   [9]Ps. 141:4

SEPTEMBER 11

*Simon Peter answered him, "Lord, to whom shall we go?
You have the words of eternal life."*

John 6:68

*J*esus taught in such a way that brooked no wishy-washiness. Following Him is an uphill, hate-provoking, face-slapping, self-emptying, all-or-nothing proposition. He never said, "I know it's hard, but try your best." He never said that His teachings, His *commands*, were not for everyone. Straight up from day one, He told us what was *expected*: Hike that extra mile; let them sue the tunic off of you (and throw in your cloak for good measure!)—and love. Love in the face of anger, love at the hands of hatred, love enough in the instant of violence to turn the other cheek.[1]

Jesus did not hold back, sugarcoat, or spoon feed the truth. The disciples were no more spiritual than you or I, as they followed Him around for three-and-a-half years still arguing about who was the greatest.[2] Yet Jesus taught them at the highest level, holding up a standard that is not going to be lowered just because it seems impossible to reach. No one can say that Jesus duped people into following Him by hiding the difficulty and the demands of discipleship. "Take up your cross," He said. "Put if above your own family if it comes to a choice betweeen the two.[3] Lose your wealth, lose your life if it comes to that.[4] If you look back, you're not fit for the kingdom."[5] He promised us trouble.[6] He told us of persecution. He said they'd kill Him, and they'd kill us, too.[7]

And He said we'd never die.[8] We'd have joy unspeakable,[9] life more abundantly,[10] authority over all the power of the enemy,[11] and life eternal. He taught hard, then said, "Rejoice![12] Be of good cheer!" The gospel *is* good news! Like my Hungarian grandmother, who overrode all of my whining objections with, "Is *good* for you! Put hair on your chest! Make you strong like bull!"

Jesus left you no options: He is *the* way. He alone has the words of eternal life. He taught it straight, forged the path, and provided the strength. Now go and do it!

*Jesus did not hold back,
sugarcoat, or spoon feed the truth.*

[1]Matt. 5:38–48 [2]Luke 22:24 [3]Luke 14:26–27 [4]Luke 9:24–25 [5]Luke 9:62 [6]John 16:33
[7]Luke 21:12–17 [8]John 11:26 [9]John 15:11 [10]John 10:10 [11]Luke 10:19 [12]Matt. 5:11–12

SEPTEMBER 12

I am the LORD your God, who brought you up out of Egypt.
Open wide your mouth and I will fill it.
Psalm 81:10

*O*pen wide your mouth and I will fill it . . . with your needs. "You would be fed with the finest wheat, with honey from the rock I would satisfy you."[1] Like a mother bird and her nestlings. Helpless, blind, nearly naked—all they need do is open wide their mouths. She brings them everything they need to grow strong. They need not look to any other source. "But seek first His kingdom and His righteousness and all these things will be given to you as well."[2] These things: food, clothing, shelter, nitty-gritty needs for a nitty-gritty world.

Open wide your mouth and I will fill it . . . with My words, My wisdom. "I will give you words and wisdom that none of your adversaries will be able to resist or contradict."[3] . . . This is no light promise! I dare not let any other fill my mouth with careless, unheavenly words that will be called to account.[4] False words curse my life and the lives of those around me.[5] "No, the word is very near you; it is in your mouth and in your heart so you may obey it."[6] Filling my mouth with the words of the living God is vital to my faith, because my words direct my thoughts and attitudes.[7] By my words, I lead myself to hope and belief or to doubt and despair. God's words do what they say; they accomplish His purpose.[8]

"Open wide your mouth and I will fill it . . . with laughter.[9] The joy of the Lord is your strength."[10] More than food, clothing, and shelter, our soul needs forgiveness, healing, and restoration. "You turned my wailing into dancing; you removed my sackcloth and clothed me with joy."[11]

Whatever your need, open wide your mouth. An open mouth is faith; a mouth opened wide is great faith! When we look to our Source—our Abba-Daddy—He will not leave us empty, nor turn us away unsatisfied.[12]

Whatever your need, open wide your mouth. He will not
leave you empty, nor turn you away unsatisfied.

---

[1]Ps. 81:16   [2]Matt. 6:33   [3]Luke 21:15   [4]Matt. 12:36   [5]Prov. 18:20–21   [6]Deut. 30:14   [7]Heb. 4:12
[8]Isa. 55:11   [9]Job 8:21   [10]Neh. 8:10   [11]Ps. 30:11   [12]Ps. 63:5

SEPTEMBER 13

*. . . To him who overcomes, I will give the right to eat from the tree of life,
which is in the paradise of God*
Revelation 2:7

*E*phesus had it together! This was a church on fire—vibrant, active, doctrinally pure, a defender of the truth, a model to follow. Jesus commended them for their hard work, perseverance, intolerance of wicked men . . . for having tested false apostles, and for not growing weary in hardships. For all that, however, Jesus had a problem with the Ephesians: "You have forsaken your first love."[1]

Seriously? This church is a shining example! Surely its imperfections will be overlooked.[2] Surely, "Jesus, you know my heart—?"[3] I'm not even doing as much as the Ephesians; isn't my stuff good enough?[4]

But love—! Love is the one thing that transforms routine into relationship.[5] Love is the power and presence of God in every act, every attitude. Without love, we are left cast out, crying, "Lord, Lord—!"[6] Love is so indispensable, Jesus told this busy, enduring, defending church, "If you do not repent, I will come to you and remove your lampstand from its place."[7] He would pluck them right out of His presence. *And* He made the promise in today's focus verse.

Wait! What if I don't overcome, or get back to the height from which I'd fallen? There is no compromise in Jesus' words. I must, absolutely must, return to my first love, which is a constant struggle in my life—trying to love other people. That is, until I realized that my first love is not other people, or even myself. My first love is Jesus.[8] Everything I do, I do for love of Jesus.[9] To serve other people is to serve my Jesus. What a perspective change! It is the heart of the parable of the sheep and the goats in Matthew 25.

My first love is You, Lord, and I fall in love with You all over again, every moment of every day.

My first love is not other people, or even myself.
My first love is Jesus.

---

[1]Rev. 2:1–4   [2]Jer. 49:12   [3]Jer. 17:9–10   [4]Ezek. 33:13   [5]John 14:21   [6]Matt. 7:21–23   [7]Rev. 2:5
[8]Matt. 22:36–40   [9]1 John 4:7–12

SEPTEMBER 14

You will keep in perfect peace him whose mind is steadfast,
because he trusts in you.
Isaiah 26:3

Stress is chaos—constant motion with no rhyme or reason, no purpose or pattern. Chaos is completely ineffectual; it accomplishes nothing. Chaos is a destroyer, a sapper of strength,[1] an eater of dreams.[2]

Peace is not only the absence of chaos, it is the presence of righteousness.[3] "Righteousness and peace kiss each other," the psalmist says.[4] The prophet also connects the two: "The fruit of righteousness will be peace, the effect of righteousness will be quietness and confidence forever."[5]

Unrighteousness produces chaos.[6] Chaos has many children, among them worry and anxiety. Consider the picture of worry: aimless pacing, nail-biting (talk about a destroyer!), brain-stuttering helplessness, exhaustion, and nightmares.[7] Sounds just like our definition of chaos!

God tells us He will not only grant peace, but *keep* in peace the steadfast, trusting soul. Steadfast: unmovable, firm, unshakable, constant, steady, faithful and loyal. We cannot be any of these without a rock-solid base, without a foundation,[8] without a *reason*. Steadfastness comes from trusting in God. He'll never give way under us; our foundation will never collapse. God is faithful—the only One worthy of trust.[9]

Trusting God means knowing with certainty three things: He knows,[10] He can,[11] and He will.[12] Whatever might normally move us, shake us up, or unsettle us (like the hopeless and godless[13]), whatever disaster suddenly storms through our life, we can have peace because we *know* He knows all about it, He can fix it—and *He will*. That's why the psalmist could say so assuredly of the righteous, "He will have no fear of bad news." Why? Because "his heart is steadfast, trusting in the Lord."[14]

When chaos threatens our life, we don't need to let it shake us. Remember: He knows, He can, and He will! Trust God, and be in perfect peace.

Trusting God is understanding that He knows,
He can, and He will.

---

[1]Prov. 5:7–9   [2]1 Sam. 28:6   [3]Ps.119:165   [4]Ps. 85:10   [5]Isa. 32:17   [6]Deut. 28:20, 28
[7]Matt. 6:25–34   [8]Luke 6:46–48   [9]Heb. 10:23   [10]John 21:17   [11]Gen. 18:14   [12]John 14:14
[13]Job 27:8   [14]Ps.112:7

SEPTEMBER 15

. . . Prepare the way for the Lord, make straight paths for him.
Every valley shall be filled in, every mountain and hill made low.
The crooked roads shall become straight, and the rough ways smooth.
Luke 3:4–5

nder construction. The sign along the highway evokes mixed feelings. There is the "It's about time!" sigh of relief that something is finally being done about all those ruts and potholes—but there is also the dread of all the inconvenience and disruption it will cause. Face it: renovation and repair work are messy. It is always more costly than you expected[1] and takes more time than you'd hoped.[2] But the results of diligent effort are definitely worth the trouble!

When we accepted Jesus, our spirit was instantly reborn—a new birth into a living hope.[3] We are made perfect forever—while our soul (our mind, will, and emotions) is being made holy.[4] That "being made holy" is our soul under construction. We need to change like little children,[5] until what is going on in our soul matches what has happened to our spirit. It's getting our reality rearranged to match the blueprint, the perfect standard of our heavenly Father.[6]

There are valleys to be filled in. The low places of our lives need lifting. Negative events in our life shaped negative thoughts, which solidified into negative attitudes and overflowed into negative words,[7] which manifested in negative behavior. All of that negativity built the circumstances we are in today. Fill those low spots in with the positive promises and power of the Word of God. Let His love lift you up.

There are also some mountains and hills that need some lowering. Pride exalts itself, raises its throne above the stars of heaven.[8] We can't go anywhere if we think we've already arrived! God promises to do some amazingly awesome things for the humble. We can't bless ourselves like God can bless us.

Our rough ways need some smoothing, too. Harshness grieves the Spirit— we need to learn Jesus' gentleness and meekness.[9] Kindness is smooth, and smoothness catches no snags!

Under construction is a process. It takes more time and costs more than you think—but the results are worth every effort!

We need to change like little children, until what is going on in our soul matches what has happened in our spirit.

---

[1]Luke 21:12–19 [2]2 Pet. 3:9 [3]1 Pet. 1:3 [4]Heb. 10:14 [5]Matt. 18:3 [6]Matt. 5:48 [7]Prov. 18:21
[8]Isa. 14:13 [9]Matt. 11:29

SEPTEMBER 16

When he found one of great value,
went away and sold everything he had and bought it.
Matthew 13:46

*W*hat is the kingdom of heaven worth to me? How valuable must that pearl be for me to decide to sell all I have to win it? If the kingdom of heaven were put up on the auction block, what would I be willing to bid for it—if it were for sale?[1]

More revealing than that would be to ask, "What of all that is me and mine would I *not* be willing to bid, to exchange, for a chance to have the kingdom of heaven?"[2]

It depends on what I think the kingdom of heaven is. If I picture it as a bunch of white-robed, swan-winged harp-pluckers sitting around on clouds all day, every day, for eternity—I certainly wouldn't bid too much. You wouldn't either. If I imagine the kingdom of heaven as a lot of stern-faced finger-pointers with a long list of do's and don'ts,[3] I doubt anyone would bid anything at all to own it.

But if I see the kingdom of heaven as the most soul-cleansing amnesty ever offered;[4] as the chance to be adopted into the family of the King of kings and Lord of lords;[5] as a chance to be loved so completely by God that He makes His home in me,[6] as the *power* to become all I was ever meant to be[7]—I'd *sell my very soul* for such a thing!

And that is exactly what it costs: everything I have.[8] It is not available for any less. It is the most costly free thing ever offered.[9] Anyone not willing to pay all can never enjoy the kingdom.[10] I tried the enemy's cut-rate, knockoff version; it does not deliver the goods. It does not cleanse the soul nor give me peace or joy. A filthy-rag self-righteousness[11] can never been substituted for the pure righteousness of God—and there's something about those adoption papers that stinks of forgery. And the dead giveaway that I was swindled? No power supply.

If we want the real thing, we have to pay the real price. We have to sell out to God completely. Even if it costs us our life, we will never have paid too much.[12]

What would you not be willing to give in exchange
for having the kingdom of heaven?

---

[1]Mark 8:37 [2]Matt. 10:37–38 [3]Mark 7:6–7 [4]Luke 14:33 [5]John 1:12 [6]John 14:23 [7]Ps. 139:16
[8]Luke 14:33 [9]Isa. 55:1–2 [10]Matt. 10:28 [11]Isa. 64:6 [12]John 11:25–26

SEPTEMBER 17

Leave your gift there in front of the altar.
First go and be reconciled to your brother; then come and offer your gift.
Matthew 5:24

*Y*ou cannot worship God with a hatchet in your hand. Jesus teaches us that any gift we would offer to God is unacceptable as long as there is strife in our heart. "Go bury the hatchet," He says. It doesn't matter who is at fault. In this passage, we've offended our brother. Later, He teaches us to reconcile with the one who has offended us. "Hurry!" He says. "Do it now—don't wait. Interrupt your worship if you must."

Haste is vital, because every moment we delay is time that the deadly root of bitterness is growing. Bitterness is worse than a cancer, because Scripture says it spreads from one to another quickly and defiles many.[1] An offense is like cement: The longer we wait, the harder it sets. Anger and strife and hurt feelings are stones mortared by that cement. Every one not dealt with helps to build our prison walls. And make no mistake—when we hold a grudge against someone, we're the ones imprisoned.[2]

Strife is the fruit of denying God,[3] doing things our way instead of God's way.[4] This is what it means to walk in the flesh. We cannot walk in the flesh and worship in the spirit at the same time. We cannot love God and hate our brother.[5] If I ignore this, I am fooling myself—and my worship is worthless.[6]

God sent Jesus to reconcile the world to Himself.[7] He was not the One at fault, and our offense against Him was more than anything anyone has ever done to us. But God went to the limit and beyond to be reconciled, to be at peace with us. He commands us, too: "Love your enemies . . . that you may be sons of your Father in heaven."[8]

I can't make someone be at peace with me—but I am called to do everything even remotely possible to help them do so. I must cleanse my *own* heart of strife. I must forgive—and learn to walk in the love of God, the love that is patient and slow to anger[9] in the first place. Then I can go and worship the Prince of Peace in spirit—and in truth![10]

We cannot walk in the flesh
and worship in the Spirit at the same time.

[1]Heb. 12:15 [2]James 5:9 [3]Prov. 22:10 [4]Isa. 55:7–8 [5]1 John 2:9 [6]James 1:26–27
[7]John 3:16–17 [8]Matt. 5:44–45 [9]James 1:19 [10]John 4:24

SEPTEMBER 18

Blessed are those who have learned to acclaim you,
who walk in the light of your presence, O LORD.
Psalm 89:15

*A*cclaim is not a quiet matter. According to *Webster's*, it involves some shouting and a lot of joy. I did not grow up shouting in church, however. I grew up reverencing reverence—treasuring the deep, quiet stillness of awe before God.

I've been through a lot of changes since then, and although I still crave those incense-drenched moments of hushed expectancy, I have learned the exhilaration of singing, laughing, clapping and yes, shouting for joy to the Lord.[1] There is life and energy and renewal in such loud and joyous praise.[2] I could never have imagined the elevation of the soul[3] that comes from giving voice to gratitude[4]—my spirit is truly lifted into the company of heaven's angels as they stand around His throne crying out, "Holy! Holy! Holy!"[5]

God says that those who have learned to acclaim Him, those who have found the power in loudly proclaiming His praise, are *blessed*. Do we need a blessing today? Do we have situations that we need God to touch with the kiss of heaven? Are we in desperate need for *Jehovah-jireh* to be *our* Provider? Do we want to be blessed?

"Blessed are those who have learned to acclaim you." Acclaim does not come naturally. It is not the same shout or wave or dance[6] that we do for a rock star or Hollywood celebrity. The excitement of a club or concert is rooted in our flesh, in sensual and sensory delight.[7] It drains—it does not enliven. It degrades—not ennobles.[8] We must *learn* how to acclaim the Lord from our spirit, not our flesh. When our spirit shouts His glory, demons tremble and darkness scatters.[9] When our spirit praises God, the kingdom of light advances.

God's presence is His power for us. He does not make merchandise of His blessing; if we want His power, we must have *Him*. Acclaim—joyous, loud praise from the depths of our spirit—escorts us into His very presence,[10] and we are truly blessed.

When our spirit shouts His glory,
demons tremble and darkness scatters.

---

[1]Rev. 19:5–7   [2]Ps. 150:1–6   [3]Job 5:11   [4]Ps. 50:14–15   [5]Isa. 6:3   [6]Ps. 149:3–5   [7]1 Pet. 4:3–4
[8]James 3:15   [9]Num. 10:35   [10]Ps. 100:4

SEPTEMBER 19

Your path led through the sea, your way through the mighty waters,
though your footprints were not seen.

Psalm 77:19

I have been in the valley of the shadow of death, and I was afraid because I could not see the Lord who was with me.[1] I knew little of faith; I wanted to see footprints. I wanted the assurance of His hand warm upon my shoulder and His presence smoky with the glory.[2] He led me through, in spite of my whimpering, in spite of my fear. When I look back over all the troubled times in my life, I realize it was the Lord who led me through every time—but I had never seen His footprints.[3]

Dark times, troubles—those mighty waters—come to all of us.[4] His way does not avoid them. His path leads right into the sea—we have to get wet.[5] We do not always discern His steps—but we walk[6] We will not always feel His hand—but we walk. We cannot always hear His voice for the roaring of the waves, but He is speaking nonetheless—walk on! Press on, though the problem is deep; the waters will not sweep over us.[7] Continue, though the mountain is steep; we will make it to the top. We will break through the clouds that block our view, that keep us from seeing His leading, His footprints. Keep on, don't quit.[8]

The path of God does not turn aside, does not turn back, does not avoid the troubled water, for healing is found when we face our problems, not when we run away. His path will lead us into the waters so we can be cleansed.[9] Be strong! Take courage![10] Face it with faith in the Lord our God—especially when we cannot see His footprints. We *know* He will never leave us nor forsake us.[11] We *know* He covers us with His feathers, and under His wings we take refuge.[12] We *know* He will never let the righteous fall.[13]

His path leads into the waters—and keeps going *through*. When we come out on the other side cleaner, stronger, and more like Him—we will know it was the Lord who led us through.

Even though His footprints were not seen.

The path of God does not turn aside,
turn back, or avoid the troubled water.

---

[1]Ps. 23:4 [2]Acts 2:19 [3]Hos. 11:3–4 [4]Job 5:7 [5]Matt. 3:11 [6]Isa. 50:10 [7]Isa. 43:2 [8]Mark 13:13
[9]2 Kings 5:13–14 [10]Josh. 1:6 [11]Heb. 13:5 [12]Ps. 91:4 [13]Ps. 55:22

SEPTEMBER 20

This is what the Lord Almighty says,
"It may seem marvelous to the remnant of this people at that time,
but will it seem marvelous to me?"
Zechariah 8:6

*C*hildren are easily astonished. Soap bubbles, butterflies, a coin from behind the ear—all spark wide-eyed wonder and amazement. Then comes science and experience, and what was seen as wizardry is revealed to be nothing more than a man behind a curtain pushing buttons and pulling levers. A sign of jaded age is that it takes too much to make us gasp with wonder and awe.[1]

Then we encounter Christ. In the instant of an answered prayer, the child returns.[2] We clap for joy, dance in our excitement, and eagerly share our amazement.[3] It's like a dream come true—because our souls are made for the supernatural. Eternity is in our hearts, placed there by God[4] so we would never be content with what we could merely touch and see; so we would yearn for that indefinable *something more* that is the stuff of God.

Our disappointment with magic has made us skeptics, constantly suspecting a levers-and-buttons explanation for the miraculous. We are afraid of being duped once again, made to look like gullible children.[5] This makes faith—surrender to the reality of the supernatural—hard. But with faith comes the reward:[6] God Himself, living, breathing, and caring for us enough to do more than just pull a coin from behind our ear. God—answering, healing, providing, protecting. Things that had been broken for so long we can't imagine what *fixed* looks like are suddenly restored. Situations so dead even their bones have crumbled to dust are resurrected, made whole. And we gasp in wonder and awe.[7]

We have been so long without the supernatural, we forget what God can do. We don't ask for half of what could be[8] because we don't understand what *omnipotent* means. Miracles should never surprise anyone who believes in *El Shaddai*—God Almighty. *We* might be flabbergasted, but God eats impossibilities for breakfast and looks around for more![9] *Nothing* is too hard for Him.[10] Stop limiting God—ask!

We don't ask for half of what could be,
because we don't understand what omnipotent means.

---

[1]Jer. 2:19   [2]Luke 18:17   [3]Luke 24:41   [4]Eccl. 3:11   [5]Acts 12:13–16   [6]Heb. 11:6   [7]Isa. 29:23
[8]James 4:2   [9]2 Chron. 16:9   [10]Gen. 18:14

SEPTEMBER 21

For the eyes of the LORD range throughout the earth
to strengthen those whose hearts are fully committed to him . . .
2 Chronicles 16:9

God is continually on the lookout for someone He can encourage! He is actively seeking someone—anyone—who loves Him wholeheartedly, just so He can pour out His power on them. If I am totally sold out and surrendered to Jesus Christ, I will never have to pound on the portal of heaven to get His attention. I have not been looking for Him—He's been looking for me![1]

The soul that has laid itself upon His altar is His prized possession, His soldier, His champion. He will give me everything I need to stand firm against the enemy:[2] the authority of His name,[3] the power of His Spirit,[4] the promise of His protection,[5] and incontrovertible wisdom.[6] If I need boldness, my prayer will shake the earth itself.[7] If I am knocked down, He will lift me up and set me on my feet, infused with the very life of Jesus.[8]

God has a purpose for my life. He has called each and every one of us to have a part in fulfilling His plan. Accomplishing this task requires perseverance. When we give Him our all, He gives us His. He will never let a committed soul fall.[9] His eyes range throughout the earth to strengthen our hearts.

Fully committed means not backing down or giving up in the face of obstacles. It means knowing there is an enemy trying to hinder us but trusting in Jesus to deal with him. Fully committed means no compromise: It's God's way or no way.[10] It's refusing to fight fire with fire—as the world does—but battling the enemy's hatred with God's unfailing love.

Fully committed is not for the average weekend warrior; it is a 24/7, sold-out burning down of any and every bridge to our dead *before*. Jesus will not fail us; when we need Him, He is there. It is Him living in us who is doing the work[11] When He says, "Let's go to the other side," hell or high water will not be able to stop us![12]

Are we fully committed to Him?

The soul that has laid itself upon His altar

is His prized possession.

---

[1]John 15:16   [2]2 Pet. 1:3   [3]Luke 10:19   [4]Acts 1:8   [5]John 17:11   [6]Luke 21:15   [7]Acts 4:24–31
[8]Dan. 10:10, 19   [9]Ps. 55:22   [10]Isa. 55:7–9   [11]John 14:10   [12]Mark 4:35–41

SEPTEMBER 22

Israel cries out to me, "O our God, we acknowledge you!"
But Israel has rejected what is good . . .

Hosea 8:2–3

*W*hat am I trying to acknowledge? What do I mean when I cry out to God? How much do I really want Him? What am I asking Him for?

There is more of God than we can imagine,[1] more than we could ever exhaust.[2] If we are living without power in our life,[3] if all our religion bores us—it is because we have not been hungry enough to let go of everything that is not God. Our hands are too full to receive Him.[4] We are Israel—giving God a nod, maybe even begging Him for help, but rejecting the good He speaks to us.

What does it mean to acknowledge God? It is much more than admitting He exists, or even that He is powerful. We can drive by a magnificent castle and know that a mighty king is there, but that doesn't make us residents of the castle with him. Acknowledging God is submitting to Him. *Webster's* says to acknowledge means "to recognize the rights, authority, or status of; to express gratitude or obligation for"[5] When we acknowledge God, we not only agree that He *is*, but we recognize His authority over us, His status as God: Lord of all creation. We realize that He has the right as Ruler to tell us what to do, and that we have an obligation to obey.

Acknowledging God is not just a nod in His direction then business as we please. We acknowledge God with our life, or our words don't mean a thing.[6]

God doesn't tell us what to do because He's bigger than we are; He tells us what to do, because He's *smarter* than we are. He *has* the right, because He *is* right! Only a fool would turn down that kind of instruction.

Think about it. How many ways can we acknowledge God other than with our mouth?[7] What is the good He is telling us today? What has He showed us already?[8] To reject what is good is to turn our back on God, regardless of what our words say.

Choose good.[9] Acknowledge God.

Acknowledging God is much more
than admitting He exists. It is submitting to Him.

---

[1] 1 Kings 8:27   [2] Heb. 1:10–11   [3] Matt. 13:58   [4] Luke 1:53   [5] *Webster's:* "acknowledge"   [6] Isa. 29:13
[7] Hos. 6:6   [8] Mic. 6:8   [9] Deut. 30:19

SEPTEMBER 23

Before they call I will answer, while they are still speaking I will hear.
Isaiah 65:24

hen our whole being is in love with God, we need never scrape our prayers off the ceiling. Our cries to God are much more precious to Him than dead plaster; no ceiling can stop our prayers. The Lord loves us so much, He not only carries our load, but He made sure we knew that He *daily* bears our burdens.[1]

He is the infinite God; time is His creation. He alone can stand apart from time and not be bound to its restrictions. He is the One who is, and who was, and who is to come[2]—all at the same moment. He makes known the end from the beginning,[3] and He knows well in advance what our needs, desires, and prayers will be. He said He loves to give good gifts to His children.[4] He is like a doting Father preparing birthday surprises for His beloved. Long before the day arrives, He has selected the gift, wrapped it up and hidden it—only to present it with a flourish at the perfect moment. What pleasure He takes in our excitement and delight![5]

Consider the planning and engineering it took to ensure that all the cosmic forces involved—all the physical stuff, all the people and the places—came together at precisely the right moment to place our answer in our hand exactly when we needed it. All that preparation is going on long before we even know we have a need or think to pray about it! He moves on hearts to go places, do things, speak words—all accomplishing His purpose,[6] all for the sake of our prayers![7] Such is His amazing love.

It is happening as you breathe this breath, as you read these words. You may never know how many prayers you had a part in answering—or how many you may yet fulfill![8] Your own answers to prayers you will pray years from now are already being prepared.

In God, there is no such thing as coincidence. What is serendipity to us is, in reality, a beautifully wrapped present that our Father prepared for us!

He who makes known the end from the beginning
knows in advance what our needs,
desires, and prayers will be.

---

[1]Ps. 68:19 [2]Rev. 1:8 [3]Isa. 46:10 [4]Matt. 7:11 [5]Zeph. 3:17 [6]Exod. 12:36 [7]Neh. 2:1–9
[8]Isa. 45:4–5, 13

SEPTEMBER 24

When you reap the harvest of your land, do not reap
to the very edges of your field or gather the gleanings of your harvest.
Leviticus 19:9

The first sign of separation from God is selfishness. The world is caught up in the kingdom of *I*—considering others only when *I* can benefit. Its mantra is *I, me, mine.* God's way of selfless giving is incomprehensible to the world; they understand giving only when they can get something in return.[1]

"The ways of the Lord are loving . . ."[2] When we love God, we are filled with His love,[3] and it spills over to everyone around us. Selfishness has no place in us. One who walks in the reality of God's love is marked by a profound respect and consideration for others. They will do much more than merely mouth the words; they will say, "I love you" in their walk, their talk, and in the myriad little things that oil the years of life and make our ride smoother.[4] What they use up, they replace. What they mess up, they clean. What they drop, they pick up.

Love regards everything as a sacred trust from Him to whom belongs the earth and everything in it.[5] What I have did not come from my hand,[6] and He who gave it to me has enough to spare, enough to share. The root of selfishness is fear: "I must keep it all, because there may not be any more." The foundation of selflessness is faith: "My Father loves me. He holds back nothing that is good for me."[7]

Blessed is he who has regard for the weak,[8] who considers that not everyone knows how to be gracious. One who truly loves is not put out when someone treats them poorly,[9] rather, they take pleasure in demonstrating maturity and grace under pressure. Love considers, too, the timing of all things, being sensitive to the Holy Spirit to know the proper time and procedure for every matter.[10] Love remembers that if a man loudly blesses his neighbor early in the morning, it will be taken as a curse.[11]

I may not have land to harvest, but to be generous[12] and considerate of others is well within my reach. I can open my heart to the selfless love of God, consider how I might have regard for the weak, and share my harvest with others.

Love regards everything as a sacred trust.

---

[1]Matt. 6:1–4 [2]Ps. 25:10 [3]John 17:26 [4]1 John 3:17–18 [5]Ps. 24:1 [6]Deut. 8:17–18 [7]Ps. 84:11
[8]Ps. 41:1 [9]Luke 6:27–31 [10]Eccl. 8:5 [11]Prov. 27:14 [12]Prov. 22:9

SEPTEMBER 25

. . . Have you not read what God said to you . . . ?
Matthew 22:31

hat does it really matter what happened to a bunch of stiff-necked desert tribesmen thousands of years ago? I mean, God did all those amazing miracles, and it may seem to us as though Israel was pretty dense not to "get it"–but what does that really have to do with me?[1] God spoke to Moses out of a burning bush, so sure–Moses knew what was expected of him. But I haven't seen any smoking shrubs lately, so how can I know what God is telling me? Is He ever telling me anything? What's the point of reading about all those people with unpronounceable names who did such strange things long, long ago in a country far, far away?

The world, in its more sophisticated moments, admires the Bible for its beauty of form and expression, finding poetry in its imagery and language.[2] They may even value it as a glimpse of social customs and historical reference, although they tend to choke on the idea that all of it actually happened. But its relevance to our world today is completely lost on them.

It is a mistake to consider the Bible a done deal, past history, a tale all told. The Word of God is living and active,[3] it is not a story book of what was said and done once upon a time. It is an active interface between God and man, a living organism through which God is constantly speaking.[4] Jesus said as much! He did not ask the Sadducees about what God had said to *Moses*; He asked about what God said to *them*.

Scripture is the Word of God–not the *words* of God that He happened to say once to a few people here and there. Scripture is the Word of God spoken to all men everywhere and speaking to *us* today. The book of Hebrews constantly points to events of the Old Testament as examples for us.[5] An example is a definition of relevancy; it is how God's words to others *then* become God's words to us *now*.[6] It is another way of saying, "What He said to them, He says to us."

Read the Scriptures and listen to what God is saying to *you*.[7]

The Word of God is living and active,
not a story book of once upon a time.

---

[1]2 Kings 3:13   [2]Ezek. 33:32   [3]Heb. 4:12   [4]Prov. 6:22   [5]Heb. 4:1–11   [6]Heb. 12:25

SEPTEMBER 26

". . . Lord, even the demons submit to us in your name."
Luke 10:17

*A*m I afraid of the enemy, or is the enemy afraid of me? As I pondered this, I realized . . . it is not me he is afraid of; it is *Jesus in me*. The demons submit, not to me, but to the power and authority of the Name of Jesus.[1]

The Name we bear carries such power and authority that demons will beg us not to torture them[2]—if we know who we are and whose we are. If we carry that Name in spirit and in truth,[3] no devil in hell can withstand our command to leave and never return.[4] After all, it's not who *we* are, but who *He* is: Jesus, King of kings and Lord of lords,[5] Son of the Living God, the Lamb that was slain and lives forevermore![6] He is the One who already has met the enemy, took him on toe to toe, verse for verse, to the death—and utterly defeated him.[7] His Name and His Word have been exalted above all things.[8]

To bear that Name in spirit and in truth is no casual affair. It is not a half-way thing, taken on because we got uncomfortable being wrong and figured we needed to make a few changes in our life. Bearing that Name has nothing to do with sitting in a pew for an hour or so a week and singing pretty songs. It has nothing to do with being dipped in the river; if it isn't in our heart and soul, we're just wet.

Beware the unauthorized use of that Name above all names![9] An unsurrendered soul is not covered by the power of that Name. We may deceive others, we may even deceive ourselves—but we won't fool hell for long. God makes a distinction between those who obey and serve Him and those who do not,[10] —and the devil knows exactly who is who. He may let us shout and stomp for awhile, but when it's no longer a matter of emotion—when we come face to face with the darkness, he'll challenge our right to use that Name. Only a soul surrendered to the will of Jesus Christ and vitally connected to Him[11] will stand. The power of the Name of Jesus backs up all who are His, and hell itself must obey.

---

*The demons submit, not to me,
but to the power and authority of the Name of Jesus.*

---

[1]Luke 9:49–50 [2]Mark 5:7 [3]John 4:24 [4]Mark 9:25 [5]Rev. 19:16 [6]Rev. 5:12 [7]Matt. 28:18
[8]Ps. 138:2 [9]Exod. 20:7 [10]Mal. 3:18 [11]John 15:4

SEPTEMBER 27

*Now faith is being sure of what we hope for
and certain of what we do not see.*

Hebrews 11:1

*A*sk any believer what faith is, and you will likely hear this verse. The King James Bible calls faith "the substance of things hoped for . . ." Both of these translations are powerful presentations of faith. Faith is a noun: a *substance*, the stuff of which our hopes are made. Faith is the material God uses to build and shape the things we are hoping for. Little faith: little things.[1] Great faith: great things![2]

But the compilers of the New International Version chose to translate this not as a noun, but a verb: faith is *being* sure of what we hope for. The *-ing* part of the verb means that the action (and the sureness of our faith) is not a one-time deal and it's done. It is a continu*ing*,[3] endur*ing*,[4] persever*ing*,[5] believ*ing*—the kind of sureness and certainty that doesn't quit just because God is taking a longer while than we expected to shape the substance of our faith into its manifestation.

Faith is *being* sure. It is not *having* sureness and certainty. It is not something outside of ourselves. Faith is a state of being, a whole way of thinking, an attitude. We've come to know God—who He is and *how* He is.[6] We love Him; He's loved us and proved it over and over.[7] He has not changed, He does not change, He will not change.[8] We're convinced of this; we know we can rely on Him.[9] We trust Him. And because we trust Him, we can handle whatever we don't understand—like why some prayers are answered *no*—or *wait*.

Trusting faith is sure and certain that the Father truly knows best, and that when He says *no*, it is not because He's mean and doesn't want us to have good things. His *no* really means, "I have something better in mind." Faith can handle it even when *wait* seems like one of God's thousand-year days.[10]

Faith, being *sure*, never gives up, never gives in, never settles for less. That kind of faith says what we really think about God. That kind of faith pleases Him immensely.[11]

---

*Faith is a state of being,
a whole way of thinking . . . an attitude.*

---

[1]Matt. 13:58 [2]Matt. 15:28 [3]James 1:25 [4]Ps. 19:9 [5]Heb. 10:36 [6]Ps. 25:10 [7]1 John 4:19
[8]Mal. 3:6 [9]1 John 4:16 [10]2 Pet. 3:8 [11]Heb. 11:6

SEPTEMBER 28

*If you have raced with men on foot
and they have worn you out, how can you compete with horses?*
Jeremiah 12:5

It is time for the body of Christ to knuckle down; get determined. It is time to set our faces as flint,[1] to strap on our gear[2] and to cinch up our belts. It is time to stop whining about how hard it is to follow Christ—we have been racing with men on foot and eating their dust. The heat is about to be turned up; perilous times are upon us.[3] Our adversaries are increasing both in numbers and in strength, for the devil knows that his time is short.[4]

Tenderfoot, get tough! We can no longer afford to let the petty distractions of life's worries, riches, and pleasures[5] keep us entangled in this world. We have let the lightweights beat us up; we surrender far too quickly to every wind of temptation that blows our way.

God is saying, "Wake up![6] You are not on a picnic. This is not the summer games; this is for real!" It is not about our comfort, our convenience. Horses are coming—strong, sleek, and swift. The competition is about to get rough on another whole level.[7] We can no longer afford to be overrun by the enemy. Everything that has been hindering us must be thrown off. Every sin that has so easily entangled us must be overcome.[8] We can no longer afford to give in—we will be swept away. We are in the semi-finals now. Everywhere around us, champions are being chosen. They have learned how to dodge the enemy's punches, how to avoid his tricks and traps. They have some victories under their belts, and now they're hungry for more.

They know it takes training, and they're willing to submit to some sweat. We can, too. Our personal trainer, the Holy Spirit, is ready to guide us through a regimen of diet (feeding on Christ and His Word[9]) and exercise (*doing* the Word[10]).

Let's not whine about it being tough, nor quit because it's not a cake walk. Let's get that gleam of victory in our eye—and when the enemy growls, we'll growl louder!

Let's run against the horses—and win!

---

*God is saying, "Wake up! You are not on a picnic.
This is for real!"*

---

[1]Isa. 50:7 [2]Heb. 13:21 [3]Rev. 2:10 [4]Rev. 12:12 [5]Luke 8:14 [6]Rev. 3:2 [7]Rev. 9:7–19
[8]Heb. 12:1 [9]John 6:53–58 [10]James 1:22

SEPTEMBER 29

He said to his disciples, "Why are you so afraid?
Do you still have no faith?"
Mark 4:40

I have been in that boat many times. We may shake our heads at the disciples, but have we done any better? We should ask ourselves why Jesus rebuked them for their fear. These were experienced fishermen in their home waters—they knew the power and danger of these sudden squalls. Boats had been sunk before; lives had been lost. Fear was only natural.[1] And that is the first reason Jesus rebuked them. Faith is not natural. Faith responds to natural circumstances with supernatural calm, supernatural power. If my response to trouble is only natural, I am not walking in Holy Spirit-powered, all-conquering, nothing-can-harm-me faith.[2] He has given me a His powerful Spirit . . . not fear.[3]

They had also forgotten why they were in the boat to begin with: to get to the other side![4] Jesus had a destination in mind—and nothing can prevail against the purpose of God.[5] If God sends me on a mission, though hell and high water should rise up against me, God has promised me they will not sweep over me.[6] Faith remembers the destination, and trusts Jesus to get us there.

Not only did they forget why they were in the boat, they forgot who was in the boat with them. When the storm hit, they did all they knew to do—reef the sail, drop the anchor, and aim the bow into the waves. As the sea rose angrier, they grabbed buckets and bailed like madmen. They reacted to the storm in their own strength and knowledge while Jesus (who they had just witnessed performing miracles), slept in the stern undisturbed.[7] When trouble strikes, do I react[8]—running from breach to breach with patches and Band-Aids, only thinking to call on Jesus when my *fixes* don't hold?

The *real* source of their fear, however, was their nagging doubt—not that Jesus could do it, but that He would do it *for them*: "Teacher, don't you care if we drown?" I may know His promises, I know of His power—but will He do it for *me*?[9] Does He care if I drown?

Do we *still* have no faith?

Faith remembers the destination
and trusts Jesus to get us there.

---

[1]Luke 1:74 [2]Luke 10:19 [3]Acts 1:8 [4]Mark 4:35 [5]Isa. 55:11 [6]Isa. 43:2 [7]Mark 4:38
[8]Jer. 1:17–19 [9]John 14:14

SEPTEMBER 30

The Lord said, "Surely I will deliver you for a good purpose . . ."
Jeremiah 15:11

ough circumstances challenge my ability to focus on God's purpose in my life. When I am in trouble, all I want is to be rescued.[1] In the midst of pressure, it's hard to submit to the idea that God is using these bad times to accomplish something good.[2] I just want relief!

Of *course* God promises to deliver me from trouble[3]—in His time, once it has accomplished His purpose.[4] Cooperating with God's design in every aspect of my life means I need to seek Him constantly, asking for His step-by-step directions to keep me on the right path.[5] This requires patience and trust through the heat, in the storm, even without the explanations that would make it all so much easier to bear.[6] *Especially* without the explanations. It is hardest to follow God in the dark, when He seems silent,[7] when His footsteps are not seen.[8] To trust Him in these times anyway is what it means to live by faith.

As I write this, I am in prison serving the sentence my choices brought upon me.[9] Thank God He didn't simply give me up to those choices but came and rescued me from myself! He delivered my spirit and soul and set me free. Do I still want to be physically free? Of course! For God to cut through these bars of iron[10] was my goal, my dream for a long time—until I realized that God would not so much deliver me *from trouble*, from prison, as *into my purpose*. When He sets me free, it will be to serve Him in a way His plan requires. So my focus instead has become preparation—this sentence and all its challenges it brings are meant to prepare me to be able to fulfill all of His purpose for me.[11]

Trouble is less troubling, knowing that God will deliver me for a good purpose!

God does not so much deliver me from trouble . . .

as into my purpose.

---

[1]Ps. 69:17   [2]Ps. 119:67, 71, 75   [3]Ps. 34:17–19   [4]James 5:10–11   [5]Prov. 3:5–6   [6]Isa. 50:10
[7]Job 30:20   [8]Ps. 77:19   [9]Lam. 3:39   [10]Ps. 107:16   [11]Isa. 57:14

OCTOBER 1

And Jesus said to him, "The foxes have holes and the birds of the air
have nests, but the Son of Man has nowhere to lay His head."
Luke 9:58 [NASB]

ife in prison has forced me to take a hard look at *things*, as in material possessions. I live in an 8'x10' cell without closets, attic space, or a basement. Limited space is one factor, limiting rules are another. I am only allowed a certain amount of each item, and most of what I considered indispensable on the outside is contraband in here. After all these years on the inside, I am learning how little I really *need* to live.[1] Of course, I dream of returning to freedom, to "normal" life and all that I would once again be able to have.

But what if I could live *out there* like I live *in here*? What if I decided to be content with less in order to make more of myself available to Jesus?[2] How much more time, energy, and money might I have to offer Him if I required so much less for myself? How much more spontaneous could my life become if I am not tied down to my *stuff* and all that it takes to maintain it?[3]

Jesus lived in such a way that He called no place on earth home. He used whatever was willingly offered to reach into and touch the needs and lives around Him. He borrowed a boy's lunch, and in His hands, it multiplied into a feast.[4] He borrowed a donkey, and it became the carrier of the King.[5] He borrowed a tomb and left it tidied up for the next person.[6] When He died, His only possessions were divided up among the soldiers, who played dice for his robe.[7]

I once heard someone try to teach that Jesus was not poor, since He had a treasurer in charge of a money bag full enough to tempt a thief.[8] In truth, Jesus *was* rich . . . rich in all that mattered. The money people gave to Him, however, was for ministering to others, and Jesus respected that *so* much, He would not touch it for Himself to pay the temple tax.[9]

Jesus has taught me to simplify, to let go of *things* and invest in *people*.[10] If I loosen my hold on this world, this world has less of a hold on me.[11] In here or out there, the less it takes to fill my needs, the more I have to touch other lives with His love.

What if I decided to be content with less,
in order to make more of myself available to Jesus?

---

[1]Luke 10:41–42 [2]Luke 12:15 [3]Matt. 19:20-24 [4]John 6:5–13 [5]Mark 11:1–10 [6]John 19:41–42
John 20:6–7 [7]John 19:23–24 [8]John 12:4–6 [9]Matt. 17:24–27 [10]Luke 12:20–21 [11]Mark 4:18–19

OCTOBER 2

. . . I am the LORD; in its time I will do this swiftly.
Isaiah 60:22

*W*e love the *swiftly* part of this verse—it's the *in its time* part we have trouble with. Our greatest arguments with God usually involve timing: His versus ours. Jesus had problems with this among His own family as they tried to manage His campaign for Him, urging Him to present Himself as the Messiah at what they thought was the perfect time: the Feast of Tabernacles. Devout Jews from all over the world would be gathered in one place; it made perfect sense to them. But Jesus shook His head. "The right time for me has not yet come; for you any time is right."[1]

Adam and Eve could never have imagined that the promised seed of the woman who would crush the enemy's head[2] would not come directly from Eve's womb, but that "just the right time" would be thousands of years later.

Abraham and Sarah could not have realized when God promised whole nations would come from him[3] that they would have to wait twenty-five more years before they held the child of promise.[4] Short-term thinking is the plague of our times. There are not many left today who would plant an olive tree, who would invest time and sweat in something that only their grandchildren or great-grandchildren might enjoy. Even if we lived Adam's 900-year life span, we would have trouble living in God's sense of timing.

The first step toward oneness with the plan and timing of God is to remember that He is God—omniscient and omnipotent.[5] He *has* a plan; He *is* in control. When our answer is not forthcoming, when it waits while we mark *x*'s on our calendar, don't listen to the liar who whispers, "He's forgotten you. He doesn't care. He's tormenting you until you give up." Second, trust God.[6] Even in the face of an answerless death, we can say with Job: "I know that my Redeemer lives . . . yet in my flesh I will see God."[7] And finally, we must surrender *our* timing to His. Say with the psalmist, "You are my God. My times are in your hands."[8]

Though it be ten thousand years, His time is always just the right time.

The first step toward oneness with the plan and timing of God is to remember that He is God.

---

[1]John 7:6 [2]Gen. 3:15 [3]Gen. 12:2–4; 17:6 [4]Gen. 21:5 [5]Ps. 46:10 [6]1 Pet. 2:6 [7]Job 19:25–26
[8]Ps. 31: 14–15

OCTOBER 3

Anyone who runs ahead and does not continue
in the teaching of Christ does not have God . . .

2 John 1:9

*P*atience is not only a virtue, it is an absolute necessity. Immaturity does not know how to harness its impatient eagerness to the yoke of training.[1] First-belt karate students want to break boards—they do not want to sit and stretch for hours. Newborn believers want to preach to thousands—they do not want to cross-reference and compile Scriptures[2] or meditate on the teachings of Christ. Many want the power, but they do not want to be holy. We long for God to speak to us in dreams, visions and prophecy, but brush off the multitudes of His still, small whisperings nudging us toward righteousness. We want the glory, but not the grit.[3]

To be in the will of God, we must do everything by the *power* of God. Without it, nothing we do will be effective or bear lasting fruit.[4] God anoints His servants to do whatever good works He has prepared in advance for them to do.[5] If I am in Christ, I am appointed for a specific purpose, for which the Holy Spirit is training and preparing me. The key, however, is that His power in me only flows by faith. The stronger our faith, the more the power of God can flow. God has planted faith in us as a seed—it is up to us to grow it.

Growing our faith is the nitty-gritty work of believing, as Jesus said.[6] Growing our faith is *doing* the Word. Growing our faith is walking in love no matter who, what, when, or why. It is the basic training of obedience. If we do not learn obedience, we cannot walk in true faith[7]—and without faith, we cannot please God.[8]

Since we are following Christ, we must become like Christ.[9] We will love righteousness and love righteously. Holiness is not optional—why would we want it to be?[10] We must not run ahead of the Holy Spirit's teaching, but knuckle down and learn every lesson, no matter how small it may seem. If we are faithful in little, and He will use us in much.[11]

If we are in Christ, we are appointed

for a specific purpose

for which the Holy Spirit is training and preparing us.

---

[1]Matt. 11:29 [2]John 5:39 [3]Mark 10:35–38 [4]John 15:16 [5]Mark 13:34 [6]John 6:29 [7]James 2:17
[8]Heb. 11:6 [9]1 John 2:6 [10]Heb. 12:14 [11]Luke 16:10

OCTOBER 4

When they hurled their insults at him, he did not retaliate;
when he suffered, he made no threats.
Instead, He entrusted himself to him who judges justly.
1 Peter 2:23

The most treasured possession of the flesh is reputation. To let an insult go unanswered is the hardest task; to suffer in silence goes against our very nature. If we cannot confront our slanderer directly, we will rip him apart with our tongue to others. One way or another, we will be sure to let everyone know that the insult is undeserved, unfair, untrue—or, at the very least, that the mudslinger is far worse than we ever have been.

All for the sake of standing, our image in the eyes of man. "But God doesn't want me to be a doormat, does He?" Whether He does or does not, He does *not* want me to be the one concerned about it.[1] He wants me to obey, regardless of what it may do to my so-called reputation. He says, "Let them sue you, let them curse you—bless them anyway.[2] Turn the other cheek.[3] If they steal from you—so what? Let them have it.[4] I've got plenty more where that came from."[5] And the hardest of all: "Humble yourself."[6]

"Humble yourself" is the embodiment of all of the above. It means not only to let go of all that I consider to be my rightful due, all that I think to be fair; it means to do it without blowing my trumpet[7] to announce how wonderfully generous I am in doing so![8] *Humble* comes from the same root word that *humiliate* does. To humble myself is to accept humiliation in the eyes of man—all men—and not count my reputation so dear. I can entrust it to God, for He says He will not only deliver me, but He will honor me.[9] He sees and knows the truth, and He has promised not only to avenge me[10] but to exalt me! (I believe God can exalt me better than I can.) If I look like a doormat, if men laugh at me and dismiss me as nothing—so what? They have no crown to place on my head, and all of their approval is as fickle as a feather in the wind, anyway.

Just as Jesus could say to His Father, "Into your hands I commit my spirit,"[11] we, too, can do the same. He will never drop what we put in His hands.

To humble myself is to accept humiliation
in the eyes of men and entrust it to God.

---

[1]Isa. 45:9–11 [2]Luke 6:28 [3]Matt. 5:39–40 [4]Luke 6:29–30 [5]Ps. 31:19 [6]James 4:10 [7]Matt. 6:2 [8]Prov. 27:2 [9]Ps. 91:15 [10]Heb. 10:30 [11]Luke 23:46

OCTOBER 5

But the wisdom that comes from heaven is first of all pure;
then peace-loving, considerate, submissive,
full of mercy and good fruit, impartial and sincere.
James 3:17

*I*n Eden, the tree of the knowledge of good and evil was forbidden. Why? Isn't knowledge a *good* thing? Eve was tempted when she saw that the fruit was desirable for gaining wisdom.[1] She believed the enemy's lie. The Hebrew word for *wisdom* here is *sakal*, which actually means success, skill, and ability to prosper in life.[2] She believed that what God had withheld was necessary for her to survive and succeed in life. But *sakal* was not what the fruit imparted. The knowledge of good and evil was *da'at*–facts, or learning.[3] Disobedience would teach her what evil really was–by experience. That kind of knowledge is not wisdom.

The wisdom of God produces the character of God in those who are led by His Spirit. Am I filled with the Holy Spirit? Am I becoming more like Jesus? His wisdom is pure; do I still cling to crudity, raunchiness, immodesty, and similar vices?[4] Or are my conversation and habits marked by purity?[5]

God's wisdom is also peace loving. Do my words and actions stir up anger and strife? Strife and confusion produce hatred and division[6]–rotten fruit from a rotten seed.[7] Am I prickly, combative, easily provoked[8]–or am I gentle and calm in spirit, sowing peace?[9]

How do I treat other people? Self-centeredness is at the core of all sin. Am I arrogant, unconcerned about others?[10] Do I only think about *numero uno*, or would others say I am kind, considerate, and generous, not only with things, but with the motives of others? Am I merciful as my Father is merciful?[11]

How about impartial and sincere? Am I a player of favorites, loving only those who love me?[12] Am I fake, or am I honest with myself and others?

You can tell a tree by its fruit.[13] Is my life producing fruit that is pure, peaceful, considerate, humble, kind, impartial, and true all the way to the core? This is the kind of wisdom–*sakal*–that gives me true success.

The wisdom of God produces the character of God
in those who are led by His Spirit.

---

[1]Gen. 3:6   [2]*Strongest:* p. 1,493   [3]*Strongest:* p. 1,390   [4]Job 14:4   [5]Hab. 1:13   [6]Hab. 1:3
[7]James 3:15–16   [8]Eccl. 7:9   [9]Ps. 120:7   [10]Ezek. 16:49   [11]Luke 6:36   [12]Matt. 5:46–47
[13]Luke 6:43–44

OCTOBER 6

. . . they ate to the full and were well-nourished;
they reveled in your great goodness.

Nehemiah 9:25

Reveling has such a bad reputation. It conjures up visions of drunkenness and wild orgies, the kind of unrestrained partying that is usually called *debauchery*[1] and *dissipation*.[2] It is a grossly immoral display of unsanctified flesh. How can we connect such an image with the great goodness of God—and not fear a lightning bolt from heaven? Is there such a thing as sanctified reveling?

Why not? *Webster's* says *revel* also means "to take intense satisfaction."[3] How intense? Reveling goes way beyond a mere nod of thanks over a meal. The intensity of our satisfaction fills up our entire being,[4] leaving no room for discontent. After all, complaining is exactly the opposite of satisfaction.[5] It is finding fault with what God has given me, with His blessings.[6] When I think of all He has done for me, my gratitude simply swells up and overflows. It makes me want to dance!

Reveling involves abandon. Let me abandon my inhibitions and celebrate the God who gave Himself for me! Whether I sing, shout, clap my hands, jump, dance, or whatever[7]—let my joy so fill my life that there's plenty to share. Nothing that happens to me in this life can overwhelm or snuff out the goodness of God,[8] the joy of Jesus that turns wrong into right,[9] last into first.[10]

Reveling in the goodness of God calls for me to *choose* to praise and thank Him—no matter what.[11] It's finding the positive—the good—in all things and celebrating *that* instead of focusing on the rain and the pain.

Like David, I need to let go of propriety sometimes. He reveled so enthusiastically for his joy in bringing the ark of his God to Jerusalem, his proud wife was embarrassed.[12] But he loved the Lord so much, he simply couldn't thank Him enough.

Words are insufficient for the astonishing goodness of God to me. I will show the world His great goodness by reveling with a Psalm 150-kind of abandon.

The intensity of our satisfaction fills up our entire being,

leaving no room for discontent.

---

[1]Exod. 32:6, 25 [2]1 Pet. 4:3–4 [3]*Webster's:* "revel" [4]Ps. 63:5 [5]Num. 14:27 [6]Jer. 2:5
[7]Ps. 98:4–9 [8]Ps. 27:13 [9]Prov. 10:12 [10]Matt. 20:16 [11]Hab. 3:17–18 [12]2 Sam. 6:12–22

OCTOBER 7

Who can discern his errors? Forgive my hidden faults.
Psalm 19:12

Shakespeare wrote, "This above all: to thine own self be true."* Wise words. But to be true to myself, I must first know myself. Who am I, really? How accurate is my self-portrait? If you watch any old-time Hollywood movie, you'll see what I mean. The heroine, the leading lady, is always filmed with a rosy, diffused lens that minimizes her flaws and maximizes her beauty. We do the same thing for ourselves whenever we look within.[1] Objectivity is not our strong point.

How then can we ever become like Christ if we are blind to those parts of us that are *not* like Christ? If it were up to us alone, we could never do it. Jeremiah wailed, "The heart is deceitful above all things, and desperately wicked: who can know it?"[2] God agreed: "Neither can you do good who are accustomed to doing evil."[3] The good news is that it is not up to us alone. The Lord reassured Jeremiah: "I the Lord search the heart and examine the mind."[4] He'll be glad to share His findings!

God wants to open the eyes of the blind[5]—and we are blind in many more ways than mere natural sight.[6] Jesus told the Laodicean church that although they thought they were rich and needed nothing, they were actually wretched, pitiful, poor, blind, and naked![7] What a horrible condition! Yet of all the tragic things they were, they were not *hopeless*. Among the remedies Jesus prescribed, He told them to buy from Him salve to put on their eyes so they could see.

We may be blind to our faults, but God isn't.[8] Buying salve from Jesus is admitting, as the psalmist does, that we need His eyes to see ourselves truly. Then we can ask Him to show us our hidden faults. If we are serious about changing, about conforming to the image of Christ, He will. He teaches by the "show, don't tell" method.[9] Rather than a voice from heaven listing our flaws, Jesus will allow situations to arise that will reveal what is truly in our heart. Pay attention! When ugliness surfaces, we need to repent, realign ourselves with His Word—and rejoice for the revelation! God will continue to reveal, as long as we continue to listen.

Buying salve from Jesus is admitting
you need His eyes to see yourself truly.

---

[1]Prov. 16:2   [2]Jer. 17:9 [KJV]   [3]Jer. 13:23   [4]Jer. 17:10   [5]Luke 4:18   [6]Isa. 29:9   [7]Rev. 3:17–18   [8]Job 10:6   [9]Ps. 143:8   *Biblio. p. 386

OCTOBER 8

Your laws endure to this day, for all things serve you.
Psalm 119:91

*O*h, to be as dumb as a rock! They at least know how to take up the slack when we are obstinate and rebellious. They will shout praise if we refuse: "'I tell you,' he replied, 'if they keep quiet, the stones will cry out.'"[1]

Creation actively serves its Creator. The seas obey His voice: to open a path for the Israelites—and to close again upon the Egyptians, to rage in a storm against a rebellious Jonah—and to calm again once he was cast overboard.[2] The trees obey His command: They clap their hands in praise[3]—and devoured the enemies of His anointed King David.[4] The weather serves the Lord: rain comes and goes at His command,[5] and hail pounds His enemies into the dust. Even the sun changes its course in the galaxy to grant more hours in a day for His victory,[6] and to reassure His servant of His promise.[7]

The animal kingdom, too, yields allegiance to the Lord. At His bidding, a donkey spoke to rebuke a prophet,[8] frogs and gnats and flies and lice plagued Egypt; a fish rescued a man,[9] and the ravens fed His prophet.[10]

All things serve the Lord. The heavens above us never hesitate to witness. They speak of the eternal God day after day, night after night. The ants teach us His ways;[11] the animals, birds, fish, and even the earth itself declare the mighty deeds of the Lord.[12]

Man alone lives in rebellion. Because of us, our earth groans under a curse.[13] Yet the Lord uses even our rebellion, our wrath, to praise Him.[14] God is so great, He will use even the attacks of the enemy to accomplish His purpose, like Joseph in Egypt. Man has used his God-given intellect to reason away God—how foolish![15] Like a child refusing to swallow the medicine that will heal him, we have refused to swallow our pride and serve our Maker.

All things serve You, Lord. May I never be out-rejoiced by a tree or out-shouted by a rock. May You never again have to turn to a fish to rescue one of your children. I, too, will serve you gladly!

The heavens above us never hesitate to witness. The speak of the eternal God day after day, night after night.

---

[1]Luke 19:40   [2]Jon. 1:3–4, 15   [3]Isa. 55:12   [4]2 Sam. 18:8   [5]James 5:17–18   [6]Josh. 10:11–14
[7]Isa. 38:7–8   [8]2 Pet. 2:16   [9]Jon. 1:17   [10]1 Kings 17:4   [11]Prov. 6:6   [12]Job 12:7–9   [13]Gen. 3:17
[14]Ps. 76:10 [KJV]   [15]Ps. 53:1

OCTOBER 9

Though I constantly take my life in my hands,
I will not forget your law.
Psalm 119:109

*D*oes anybody really like a backseat driver? How much worse is one who keeps reaching over and grabbing the wheel while you're driving! Not only is it annoying, it is downright dangerous. You are far more likely to end up in the hospital or worse, rather than at your intended destination. Why would anybody be so foolish?[1] People who do this are suffering from an over-inflated estimate of their abilities,[2] a poor opinion of *your* abilities,[3] or a combination of the two.

It is remarkable how many backseat drivers there are among believers. In one breath, we pray, "Into your hands I commit my spirit,"[4] and in the next breath we kick against His commands.[5] We surrender our lives to Him—but snatch back the wheel when we don't like the route He's taking[6] or the speed He's driving.[7] We've over-inflated our opinion of ourselves and what we can do apart from the Lord.[8] Somehow we think we can do a better job! We know how to get there—one of our infamous shortcuts—and we just know we can speed things up a bit.[9] We may not be aware of every blind curve or pothole on the way, but we are convinced we would see them coming in enough time to react. We've got great reflexes, right?

We cast our cares on the Lord[10] and reel them back. Oh, it's not His loving concern we doubt. We know He cares for us. It's really not His abilities we question. What we do not trust are His *intentions*. We tend to picture a bottomless inbox next to His throne where an infinite number of our cares can be stored—those burdens taken off our hands, but with no action actually planned for them. We just don't believe that God will literally *do something* about our problems.

The Lord is not a bureaucrat who takes our tearful prayers and buries them in the bottom of a forgotten file cabinet somewhere. "Will not God bring about justice for his chosen ones? . . . I tell you, He will see that they get justice, and quickly."[11]

Let's stop taking our life in our hands. Let's trust God and let go of the wheel!

Do we believe that God will
literally do something about our problems?

---

[1]Jer. 10:23 [2]Job 40:7–14 [3]Gen. 18:14 [4]Ps. 31:5 [5]Acts 26:14 [6]Isa. 42:16 [7]Ps. 27:14
[8]John 15:5 [9]2 John 1:9 [10]1 Pet. 5:7 [11]Luke 18:7–8

OCTOBER 10

*I will listen to what God the LORD will say; He promises peace to his people,
His saints—but let them not return to folly.*

Psalm 85:8

urn right and go straight: simple directions to get to heaven.[1] God's ways are simple—man likes to complicate them. Simplicity convicts us: if it is that easy, then why are we failing? Complication excuses us: it's too hard, too mysterious, too out of reach. That's a lie from the enemy of our souls! God Himself warned us, "Now what I am commanding you today is not too difficult for you or beyond your reach. It is not up in heaven . . . nor is it beyond the sea . . . No, the word is very near you."[2]

Peace—the peace that is the absolute rest of knowing that all is right between you and God,[3] the peace that every single soul longs for—is a simple matter of listening to what God the Lord will say—and doing it. Anything else is pure folly.[4] Folly is much worse than mere silliness; it is a lack of good sense; it is evil, wickedness, especially lewd behavior, even criminally or tragically foolish actions. It is an excessively costly or unprofitable undertaking.[5] How costly? Like a bird darting into a snare, little knowing it will cost him his life.[6] How unprofitable? Jesus said, "For what shall it profit a man, if he shall gain the whole world and lose his own soul?"[7] That is a cost too steep, too dear, for me!

Any reason why I should not listen? It is God the Lord who speaks, who promises peace. He has the right, for He is God, *El*, The Creator, the One who spoke worlds into existence. If He can speak all of creation out of complete chaos, He can surely speak order out of my mess! He has double dominion to lay down the law, because He is also the Lord, Yahweh—the great I AM, the omniscient, omnipotent, omnipresent Ruler of the universe. When the One with all life's answers speaks, only a fool refuses to listen.[8]

Listening is more than hearing. Listening is paying attention, taking what He tells me to heart, and believing what He says is just, true, and perfect.[9] Listening is *doing*.[10] When I truly listen to what God the Lord says, I close the door on any other option but obedience.[11] Only a fool returns to folly!

---

*When the One with all life's answers speaks,
only a fool refuses to listen.*

---

[1]Deut. 1:33   [2]Deut. 30:11–14   [3]1 John 3:19–21   [4]Prov. 5:23   [5]*Webster's: "folly"*   [6]Prov. 7:23
[7]Mark 8:36 [KJV]   [8]Prov. 18:2   [9]Jer. 25:3   [10]Mark 9:7   [11]John 6:68

OCTOBER 11

Sing to the LORD a new song, for He has done marvelous things . . .
Psalm 98:1

*I*f I am walking with God, my view should be changing. I should not be in the same place I was when I first met Jesus.[1] No one can have a relationship with someone they met only once and have had no further contact with. A relationship means dates, meetings, times spent together, conversations shared, experiences gone through. A relationship is a constant unfolding[2] of thoughts and hopes and dreams and personality quirks—both give and take—until two who once knew nothing at all about each other can now anticipate the other's moods, needs, wants, and thoughts.[3]

If I were to ask a woman about her husband and everything she told me had happened twenty years ago, I would wonder if they were divorced or if her husband were dead. Have they had no recent experiences? Are they not talking?[4] Or has their life become so boring and routine that she has to go back to their early days to recapture that spark?[5] I would be likely to ask, "What happened? Where is he now?"

Singing to the Lord a new song is not about a dissatisfied striving for excitement and thrills; it is not a constant quest for stimulation to stave off boredom. That kind of movement is merely a restless stirring of the flesh—lust. Singing to the Lord a new song is finding a new way *today* of telling Him, "I love You,"—and listening for His response. It is adding a line of harmony to my continuing song, finding a new verse. It is waking up excited every day, thanking Him for yesterday's dance and looking forward to what we will share today as we walk and work side by side.[6]

Singing to the Lord a new song is moving from faith to faith, strength to strength,[7] victory to victory,[8] constantly learning and growing. Kindergartners can be proud of learning their ABCs and how to fit a round peg into a round hole, but there is something wrong if a twelfth-grader's total school experience is about the day they learned their colors.

Where is my husband[9] today? I will sing Him a new song, for He does marvelous things *every* day!

Singing to the Lord a new song is finding a new way
today of telling Him "I love You."

---

[1]Deut. 1:6   [2]Ps. 119:130   [3]Matt. 6:8   [4]Rev. 2:4–5   [5]Matt. 24:12   [6]Song 7:10–13   [7]Ps. 84:7
[8]Ps. 44:4   [9]Isa. 54:5

OCTOBER 12

*. . . Go throughout the city of Jerusalem and put a mark on the foreheads
of those who grieve and lament over
all the detestable things that are done in it.*

Ezekiel 9:4

Although the joy of the Lord is our strength,[1] there are times when sorrow can save our life! On a visit to London, I toured Madam Toussaud's famous wax museum, including the gruesome section of infamous crimes and criminals. What I saw sickened me. The prophet Ezekiel also toured the scenes of Israel's most horrible crimes as God took him in vision from exile in Babylon to the temple in Jerusalem. There the Lord showed him what was in the hearts of priests and people alike: vile idolatry and worship of pagan gods in the holy places where God had put His name.[2] He saw sin—and a casual attitude toward it.

What he saw sickened him, too, because Ezekiel knew that those things were really happening. Anyone with a heart to love the Lord would feel His pain, His sorrow over such rejection[3] of His goodness and His law.[4] Anyone whose spirit was joined to the Spirit of God, the Spirit of holiness and purity and truth, would be touched with the fire of His righteous indignation. Anyone who knew the Lord at all would feel personally the insult to His honor and His name.[5]

Helplessness tortures a righteous soul.[6] I cannot change another, no matter how sternly I rebuke them or how earnestly I plead with them. When I've done all I can do, said all I can say, and the rebellious continue to boldly sin, I may grieve, yet I long for God to defend the honor of His name.[7] It is this grief more than any other that Jesus meant when He said, "Blessed are those who mourn, for they will be comforted."[8]

Blessed, indeed, for God knows those who belong to Him—and who does not.[9] He will command judgment beginning at His sanctuary[10]—but He knows those whose spirits are one with His, who grieve and lament over the sins of His people. He has set His mark upon them to spare them from the fire of His wrath. They are spared because they love God enough to love what He loves[11]—and to hate what He hates.[12]

God knows those who belong to Him.

---

[1]Neh. 8:10   [2]Ezek. 8:1–18   [3]1 Sam. 8:7   [4]Jer. 8:5   [5]Ps. 69:9   [6]2 Pet. 2:7–8   [7]Ps. 74:22   [8]Matt. 5:4
[9]Mal. 3:17   [10]Ezek. 9:6   [11]1 John 5:1   [12]Ps. 97:10

OCTOBER 13

They repay me evil for good and leave my soul forlorn.
Yet when they were ill, I put on sackcloth
and humbled myself with fasting. . . .
Psalm 35:12–13

"What would you be willing to sacrifice for someone you love?" asked a certain preacher. How far would I go to spare my children from suffering?[1] Parents for children; husbands for wives; brothers and sisters; friends. . . . Even we, bad-wired as we are, have an amazing capacity to sacrifice for those our hearts hold dear.[2] People from every place and time understand the drive to give ourselves for those we love.

But is that the kind of love that Jesus calls us to? Or rather, is that *all* He calls us to?[3] "If you love those who love you, what credit is that to you? Even sinners love those who love them."[4] How far does my love go? Where do I draw the line for self-sacrificing?[5] Blood kin? Married kin? Friends? Acquaintances . . . ? What about all those faceless, nameless people I hardly even brush elbows with? What would I be willing to sacrifice for someone who means nothing to me personally?[6] (Why do they mean nothing to me . . . ?[7])

The good Samaritan did this. This is neighbor-love.[8] Sacrificial, yes, but I'd always imagined the rescued man's gratitude was a decent reward. But you know what? Jesus never mentioned the man's response. Odd. Wouldn't that have helped as motivation for us?

Not odd at all—because Jesus is asking us instead, "What would you be willing to sacrifice for someone who hates you? Who repays you evil for good? Insults and abuses you?"[9]

"Love your enemies," He says.[10] "Love them—whether they thank you or curse you. Love, even if they refuse it, reject it, mock it. Love the ones whom you feel don't deserve it, the ones whom you feel don't qualify. Love them, because *I* love them. Serve them, because I love *you*."[11]

What would you be willing to sacrifice
for someone who hates you?

---

[1] Kings 3:23–27   [2] Matt. 7:9–11   [3] John 13:34   [4] Luke 6:32   [5] John 15:13   [6] Luke 16:19–25
[7] Jer. 22:16   [8] Luke 10:30–37   [9] Matt. 5:38–42   [10] Luke 6:27–31   [11] John 13:12–17

OCTOBER 14

. . . I . . . will make the Valley of Achor a door of hope. . . .
Hosea 2:15

*A*chor: *trouble*. The stone of stumbling,[1] the valley of sin. The place of our greatest defeat and failure. The Valley of Achor is not like Egypt; it is not our pagan, sin-soaked past. The Valley of Achor is that place within Canaan, just inside its borders; the place where we have relaxed our guard. We have crossed our Jordan, we have tasted the power of God in sweet victory. The next battle looks so easy, we do not tremble at our own weakness as we did at first, at our Jericho.[2] We feel comfortable, confident. God is with us and will never forsake us . . . even if we compromise.

Oh, we know what God wants and what He hates. We know what God requires.[3] Yet we have justified it in our minds, and we simply do it anyway. We may hide it, bury our sin (and our conviction) under our tent;[4] we think God is like us, that He won't do anything but overlook it.[5] After all, it is just a little thing, isn't it? I can always deal with this issue later—I can only handle so much at a time, and right now I'm dealing with Ai.

For Achan, who ignored God's explicit instructions to destroy everything that was part of Jericho, who tried to hold onto a small bit of plunder, who didn't think that the God Who Sees Me[6] really saw him—the Valley of Achor was his complete undoing, his downfall, his death. He died—not for a few bars of gold and a robe; he died because he did not fear the Lord enough to obey Him. He died because he did not love God with all his heart and soul, and because he did not love God's people enough to care how his actions affected them.[7] He died because he refused to repent.

For us, God is promising to make *our* Valley of Achor a door of hope. Our greatest obstacle to total victory in Christ is not Ai, it is Achor. Our greatest obstacle is the stumbling stone in our life right now—the compromise, the little rebellion that we have buried in our tent. By the grace of God, our greatest obstacle is about to become the vehicle of our victory. Israel defeated Ai only when they overcame Achor—and we will, too.[8] If we repent, the Valley of Achor will not be our defeat, it will be a door of hope.

Your greatest obstacle
is the stumbling stone in your life right now . . .

---

[1] 1 Pet. 2:8 [2] Josh. 7:1–25 [3] Mic. 6:8 [4] Prov. 28:13 [5] Ps. 50:21 [6] Gen. 16:13 [7] Josh. 22:20
[8] Luke 20:18

OCTOBER 15

*The Sovereign Lord has given me an instructed tongue, to know the word
that sustains the weary. He wakens me morning by morning,
wakens my ear to listen like one being taught.*

Isaiah 50:4

iscipline is the bridge between desire and reward. Many have said,
"I wish I knew the Bible like she does," or, "He prays so simply and
powerfully; I wish I could do that." For most, that is all it is—an
idle wish. Their desire has no drive, their wish has no will power behind it.
They are like browsers in a mall, stopping to admire a sharply tailored suit or a
finely wrought necklace—but quickly moving on once they read the price tag.[1]

Knowing the truth doesn't stop them from hoping that perhaps if they put
the Bible under their pillow, the words would seep into their brain while they
slept. It doesn't keep them from praying, "God, give me wisdom"—and expecting Him to download it in a mega-dump while they're out golfing. Many want
a closer relationship with Jesus, but what they imagine is a sudden spate of
dreams and visions, voices and visitations. They want Him to come to them—at
a convenient hour—in between all their regularly scheduled programming.

But God says, "You will seek me and find me when you seek me with all
your heart."[2] Seeking is a process; it is *hunting*.

If I am a hunter, I must go to where my quarry is;[3] search out and sniff out
His tracks and pursue Him[4] through brush, over boulders, around blockages. If
I abandon the pursuit, I will never bag the prize.[5] Many a hunter has returned
bloodied, muddied, ragged, and worn—but grinning from ear to ear as he held
up his trophy. He would say the prize was worth every effort.[6]

If I hunger for more of God, I must discipline myself to His morning-by-
morning training. He will waken my ear, often at uncomfortable hours and in
outrageous ways. It is not glamorous, and takes more time, sweat, and ache
than I might imagine. My determination will be tested at every turn. Many
give up and fall by the wayside.[7]

How much do we really want it? The cowardly[8] and those who shrink back
will not make it.[9] Heaven—the knowledge of God—is not for wimps, but it is
worth everything we will endure!

*Heaven—the knowledge of God—is not for wimps,
but it is worth everything we will endure.*

[1]Job 28:12–19 [2]Jer. 29:13 [3]Exod. 20:21 [4]Ps. 63:8 [KJV] [5]Gen 15:1 [6]2 Pet. 3:14 [7]Luke 14:28
[8]Rev. 21:8 [9]Heb. 10:38–39

OCTOBER 16

. . . Anyone who has seen me has seen the Father. . . .

John 14:9

f you know Jesus, but are uncertain about the Father, take heart. Even Philip begged Jesus for a revelation he'd already had. We have a strong tendency to cast Jesus and the Father into good cop/bad cop roles. Jesus saves us, the Father punishes us; Jesus loves us, the Father is angry with us. We focus so much on the gentleness of Jesus versus the judgment of the Father, we forget that the *two are one.*[1] The same God who spoke tenderly to His bride Israel[2] called the Pharisees hypocrites, snakes, and sons of hell.[3] The same God who told Ezekiel that He Himself would search for His sheep and look after them,[4] told the hard-hearted Jews they would die in their sins.[5] The same God who spoke as a doting Father, "It was I who taught Ephraim to walk . . . and bent down to feed him,"[6] stood in the midst of His temple with a whip in His hands and fire in His eyes, tossing booths and tables like matchsticks.[7]

It is not a Jekyll-and-Hyde situation; the Father is everything Jesus is, and Jesus is everything the Father is. The hand that wrote doom on the wall of Babylon's palace[8] wrote forgiveness in the dust of the temple courts.[9] The still, small voice that whispered hope to Elijah[10] thundered in rage at the cheating money changers. The God who commanded Abraham to sacrifice his son Isaac[11] became the Sacrifice Himself.

When you see Jesus touch a leper, bless a child, or reach for the coffin of a widow's only son, you see the hand of the Father reaching out in compassion. When you hear Jesus say, "Neither do I condemn you,"[12] you are hearing the yearning cry of our merciful Father. When you feel the piercing eyes of Jesus baring your very soul, you are feeling the burning holiness of God the Father commanding, "Go now, and leave your life of sin." In everything Jesus said and did, you hear and see only what the Father told Him to speak and do.[13] He is the invisible God wrapped up in flesh,[14] the exact representation of His being.[15] When you see Jesus, you see the Father.

The Father is everything Jesus is,

and Jesus is everything the Father is.

---

[1]John 10:30   [2]Hos. 2:14   [3]Matt. 23:15, 33   [4]Ezek. 34:11   [5]John 8:24   [6]Hos. 11:3–4
[7]John 2:13–16   [8]Dan. 5:5, 25–28   [9]John 8:6   [10]1 Kings 19:12   [11]Gen. 22:2   [12]John 8:11
[13]John 12:49; 14:31   [14]John 1:14   [15]Heb. 1:3

OCTOBER 17

But Nineveh has more than a hundred and twenty thousand people
who cannot tell their right hand from their left . . .
Should I not be concerned about that great city?

Jonah 4:11

God does not dance on anyone's grave. "I take no pleasure in the death of the wicked, but rather that they turn from their ways and live."[1] The most God-like quality any man can hunger for is love.[2] Compassion is love in action, love with hands and feet. Because God is not like man, He does not lump people into *us versus them* categories. He sees us all as straying sheep. Some have returned to the fold, but most are still wandering in dangerous places—willful, rebellious, and hard-headed. And He has compassion on us all.[3]

Very few of us are happy about this aspect of God. We tend to take more comfort in the thought that God will deal justice and vengeance on our enemies.[4] We conveniently forget that what God avenges are the wrongs done to *Him*, the sins against *His* law. He takes vengeance on *His* enemies—and there, but for His grace, go you and I.

Jonah had a revelation of this compassion of God. He was a rare Israelite who understood that God actually loved *everybody*—even their enemies. And it made him mad! When God sent him to preach destruction against Nineveh, Jonah ran the other way. It wasn't fear that sent him sailing, but hatred. Jonah *wanted* God to rain His fire on that sinful oppressor—and he did *not* want to give the Ninevites any warning, any chance to repent![5]

There is a bit of Jonah in many of us. We have trouble understanding why God often blesses the wicked,[6] why He sends rain on the righteous and the unrighteous.[7] We ignore the fact that God Himself "looks down from heaven . . . to see if there are any who understand, any who seek God. All have turned aside . . . there is no one who does good, not even one."[8] Instead, we want to see *those* people punished.

"Love your enemies," Jesus said, "and pray for them."[9] The most effective way of conquering an enemy is to make him a friend. I don't want to be like Jonah, so I will tell my enemies the truth. I will take the message to them.

They might actually repent!

The most God-like quality any man can hunger for is love.

---

[1]Ezek. 33:11 [2]John 13:34–35 [3]Mal. 3:6 [4]Isa. 66:6 [5]Jon. 4:1–3 [6]Ps. 73:1–12 [7]Matt. 5:45
[8]Ps. 14:2–3 [9]Matt. 5:44

OCTOBER 18

. . . He awoke from his sleep and thought,
"I'll go out as before and shake myself free."
But he did not know that the LORD had left him.
Judges 16:20

*T*he curse of mercy is in the cancellation of consequences.[1] It is a serious mistake to take grace for granted, yet we do every time we persist in that which does not please God. We convince ourselves that His all-sufficient grace will always be available, so we postpone our pain—and our victory—for another day. We buy the enemy's lie that we'll be stronger for the struggle later,[2] and we ignore the truth that each sin, each compromise weakens us, sapping our spirit of even the inclination to break free.[3] God's explicit word on our issues notwithstanding, we wait until He personally and directly convicts us of sin—and even then we do not act. Consider how many times we have heard, "I know—God has been dealing with me about that . . ."

God had been dealing with Samson's rebellious pride, too. Only his stubborn foolishness did not recognize that Delilah did not have his best interests at heart as she tried *three times* to betray him to his enemies.[4] He had used the grace of God each time to break free, and he assumed that grace—his strength—would always be there for him. I think about the times I had my sin find me out,[5] and I cried out for mercy. What did I do with the mercy I received? Did I count it precious and turn away from my sin?[6] Or did I, like Samson, lay my head once more in Delilah's lap and go to sleep, expecting God's grace to still be there when I awoke?[7]

It is possible to procrastinate repentance long enough that we become too comfortable in our sin—and we will be unaware that the Lord has left us. He tells us to seek Him while He may be found,[8] for a day will come when we will be unable to find Him—and we will not even feel the need.[9]

Grace is too precious for me to dally it away with my head in Delilah's lap!

What do you do with the mercy you receive from God?

---

[1]Eccl. 8:11   [2]Eccl. 12:1–5   [3]Eccl. 8:8   [4]Judg. 16:4–14   [5]Num. 32:23   [6]Ps. 85:8   [7]Judg. 16:18–20
[8]Isa. 55:6   [9]Rev. 22:11

OCTOBER 19

. . . Then suddenly the Lord you are seeking will come to his temple . . .
But who can endure the day of his coming?
Who can stand when he appears? . . .

Malachi 3:1–2

*I*t has often been said, "Beware of what you ask for—you just might get it!" My heart has yearned for the manifest presence of God, for the fire of heaven to fall on my sacrifice, for the sight of His glory and the feel of the hem of His garment, yet I find myself trembling every time the congregation prays for the Almighty I AM to show up. Just look at what happened whenever men were visited by *angels*—not even the most dedicated saint among them could remain on his feet. Every one of them fell groveling in abject terror! All felt their sinfulness and guilt so keenly, it sucked the very breath from them—even Daniel, whom all heaven highly esteemed.[1] I can just imagine what would happen if God dared to lift the veil that shields us from the fullness of His glory: Our God is a consuming fire.[2] He is *holy*. God warned the Israelites innumerable times that if they were irreverent toward His holiness, they would *die*.

We stand in His presence by *faith*, not by presumption. Faith glorifies God and greatly reverences His holiness.[3] Faith dares to come boldly to His throne.[4] Not because we think we're deserving, but because we know that only Jesus has made a way with His blood. It is ignorance and arrogance that would ask God to show up, to reveal Himself and His power, while one still has sin clinging to his soul.

It took a minimum of three days of solemn self-examination, repentance, and consecration before the Israelites could stand to hear the voice of God and see glimpses of His glory through the thick darkness shielding him[5]—and even then they were so terrified they begged Moses to ask God to stop speaking to them![6]

God *has* made Himself accessible to us. He longs to come in and sup with us.[7] But never let this intimacy numb the sense of His holiness. Do not let familiarity breed contempt. Learn to be reverent and stand in awe of God.[8]

We stand in God's presence by faith, not by presumption.

[1]Dan. 10:7–9, 15–19   [2]Heb. 12:29   [3]Josh. 24:19   [4]Heb. 4:16   [5]Exod. 19:9–11   [6]Exod. 20:18–19   [7]Rev. 3:20   [8]Eccl. 5:7

OCTOBER 20

*. . . how can anyone enter a strong man's house and carry off his possessions
unless he first ties up the strong man? Then he can rob his house.*

Matthew 12:29

There is a lot of stuff out there about spiritual warfare, some of it good and some of it . . . "out there." The essence of all spiritual warfare is in this statement by Jesus, made after casting out a demon. We *are* engaged in a battle;[1] we fight against the devil and all his forces, influences, and tactics every day.[2] I remind myself of this all the time, because it's easy for me to forget and to think that *people* and *circumstances* are my enemies.

"Know thy enemy," the old saying goes. Good advice, but I can also get so caught up in studying the devil that I forget how much more powerful Jesus is.[3] That's the point He was making here: yes, demonic power is *bad* and the devil is strong—he is not to be ignored. *But*—I'm the one busting in, tying him up, and rescuing those he thinks he owns. So, who is stronger?

In all my daily struggles, I can always remember that my Commander is far stronger than my enemy. Spiritual warfare is real;[4] I am not just defending against the enemy's attacks. I am a soldier in the army of the Lord, fighting to advance His kingdom and to take back, to rescue,[5] those the devil has held captive.[6] Jesus said that the gates of hell would never prevail against us.[7] Gates are not offensive weapons; Jesus is picturing His people, His church, storming the enemy's stronghold! Wow!

To do so effectively, I need to trust my Commander. When I remember how many times Jesus sent the demons packing—begging for mercy all the way—my confidence in Him soars. That helps me to obey His orders—for spiritual warfare is not fought like regular war, and His tactics seem counterintuitive. Spiritual war is not waged by argument, ugliness, or force. We fight spiritually by submission to Jesus[8] and by obedience; by faith, love compassion, truth[9]—and by not compromising our walk. It is easier to do this when I trust His strength and power, when I know that the only truly strong man is Jesus.

---

*In all my daily struggles, I can always remember that my
Commander is far stronger than my enemy.*

---

[1]Ps. 18:34   [2]Jer. 51:20   [3]Exod. 14:31   [4]Rev. 12:17   [5]Jude 1:22–23   [6]James 5:19–20
[7]Matt. 16:18 [KJV]   [8]James 4:7   [9]Acts 10:37–38

OCTOBER 21

What is truth?...
John 18:38

The saddest, most wasted life is the unexamined life.[1] To float through life not thinking, not questioning, never challenging your own or another's assumptions is to be a robot, an automaton programmed by someone else. It is to remain a child, and a child is not his own. A child becomes an adult when he takes responsibility for what he believes—questioning what he has been taught, rejecting the wrong and choosing the right.[2] How can we grow up in our salvation?[3]

It begins with this question—*the* question—that Pilate asked of Jesus: "What is truth?" The simplest, yet the most profound question ever asked—and Pilate did not wait to hear the answer!

What is truth?

But it has always been done this way....

"Thus you nullify the word of God by your tradition."[4]

But that's what I was taught....

"Their worship of me is made up only of rules taught by men."[5]

But I read it in a book somewhere.... But that's just the way I was raised... But I heard... I assumed... I never thought about it...

"But they all alike began to make excuses."[6]

What is truth? God demands that we ask. He holds us accountable not only for what we know, but for what we could have known if we'd sought Him.[7] "Let us examine our ways and test them, and let us return to the LORD."[8] We must no longer be a sponge, absorbing whatever we contact; rather, we must take charge of our thoughts—think about what we are thinking about. We are to be like the noble Bereans, taking what we are told and examining it by all that God has revealed about Himself throughout Scripture, to see if it is truth.[9] We dare not make assumptions. We should be constantly asking, "Is this what Jesus taught? Is it how He walked?"

The Holy Spirit guides us into the truth[10] as we study the Scriptures, ask God, seek, fast, and pray until He gives us understanding. There is no shortcut. Taking someone else's word for it is an open invitation to delusion and deception.

What is truth? God demands that we ask.
He holds us accountable for what we could have known.

---

[1]Prov. 14:8   [2]Isa. 7:16   [3]1 Pet. 2:2   [4]Mark 7:13   [5]Isa. 29:13   [6]Luke 14:18   [7]John 12:35–36
[8]Lam. 3:40   [9]Acts 17:11   [10]John 16:13

OCTOBER 22

Esther had not revealed her nationality and family background,
because Mordecai had forbidden her to do so.
Esther 2:10

Oh, the power of the silent witness! To live for Christ is to speak the truth without using words, to testify to the power of God without argument or debate.[1] Some have condemned the book of Esther because it does not mention God. How foolish! God is mentioned on every page, in words unspoken yet undeniable, at every twist and turn in this wondrous drama.

We in the free world don't get it, but our persecuted brothers and sisters all around the world understand it fully—and Esther was written about a persecuted people in the land of their exile. It is as Francis of Assisi reportedly said: "Preach Christ. And if you must—use words."* Live for Him, live in Him,[2] and we will reveal Him to others.[3] None can deny the power of a changed life; none can silence the witness of love. Holiness and purity adorn us with the divine just as surely as they adorn His house for endless days.[4] All should be convinced we serve a different master.[5]

If our witness for Christ is only our words, we ought to keep them to ourselves. It is true that if someone's body language does not match his words, people will believe what his body is saying and count him a liar.[6] If our witness is, "Do as I say, not as I do," we do more harm to the cause of Christ than if we were outright pagans.[7]

Esther lived her faith in the very hotbed of hell: one step from the throne of a heathen king, *her own husband.* What are my circumstances? She exemplified a life submitted and conformed to a holy, compassionate God. Because her character was her witness, she was chosen. Because her courage did not fail her in the time of need, she was used by God. Ecclesiastes says, "There is a time to be silent and a time to speak."[8] Esther lived godliness even if she did not speak of God—yet when the time for words came, she did not flinch. The persecuted church lives this everyday, working as long as it is day.[9]

We should speak when God calls us to but remember we are held accountable for applying to our own lives what we speak into the lives of others.

Live for Him, live in Him,

and we will reveal Him to others.

---

[1] 1 Pet. 3:15   [2] John 15:5   [3] John 17:20–23   [4] Ps. 93:5   [5] Matt. 23:8   [6] Prov. 30:6   [7] Rev. 3:15
[8] Eccl. 3:7   [9] John 9:4   *Biblio. p. 385

OCTOBER 23

*. . . How much more should we submit
to the Father of our spirits and live!*
Hebrews 12:9

*H*ow far will I go to obey God? At whatever point I draw the line,
that is the point of my death. Life is found only in submission to
Him.[1] If there is ever a place where my proud waves tell Him,
"This far I will come and no farther,"[2] I am no longer submitted to God. I have
deposed Him from the throne of my heart, usurping His authority for myself.

God has promised us many good things in Christ, and all His promises are
true.[3] Every word is faithful;[4] every "Thus saith the Lord" will come to pass
for us—in the fullness of time. In the meantime, we must pass through the *but
first* part of the promise and do His will. God promised to deliver the Israelites
from Egypt, *but first* He would have to humble Pharaoh's hard heart with a
long series of miraculous disasters.[5]

But first for Joseph meant years in prison on a trumped-up charge. *But
first* for Moses meant forty years in the wilderness before he could deliver the
Israelites, and another forty years in that same wilderness afterward—because
they, not he, had sinned. *But first* for David meant years of running for his life
from a jealous, murderous King Saul. *But first* for Jeremiah meant beatings,
imprisonment, and a forced exile to Egypt. *But first* for Mary meant bearing
the false accusation of adultery and the agony of helplessly watching her Son
die. *But first* for every one of the apostles meant exile or martyrdom.

What does *but first* mean for me? It may be rejection,[6] it may be accusation[7]. It may be to bear injustice, hardship,[8] years of weary toil with no obvious
reward.[9] It may be hatred or persecution.[10] It may be blood.[11] Will I shrink
back? Will I flinch, flounder, and fail Him who went all the way to hell and
back for me?[12] How far will I go to obey God, to love the Lord my God with
all my heart and soul and mind and strength?[13] When He calls, will I answer,
"Here am I. Send me!"[14] and take whatever He assigns me and say, "I have
come to do your will, O God"?[15] Submit to the Father of your spirit—and live!

*How far will you go to obey God,
to love the Lord your God . . . ?*

[1]Matt. 10:39 [2]Job 38:11 [3]2 Pet. 1:4 [4]Ps. 145:13 [5]Exod. 3:19–20 [6]Jer. 12:6 [7]Acts 6:11–14
[8]Heb. 12:7 [9]Heb. 11:39 [10]John 15:18 [11]Rev. 2:10 [12]Heb. 10:38–39 [13]Mark 12:30 [14]Isa. 6:8
[15]Heb. 10:9

OCTOBER 24

Then I heard the voice of the Lord saying, "Whom shall I send?
And who will go for us?" And I said, "Here am I. Send me!"
Isaiah 6:8

*I*n the military, experienced soldiers warn recruits, "Never volunteer for anything!" After a tour or two of night guard shack, latrine, or KP duty, most enlistees learn not to raise their hands too quickly.

Do we realize we are in the military? One of the names of God is *Yahweh Sabaoth*–LORD of All the Armies of Heaven.[1] Not only that, but Christ Himself is the Commander of all the armies of the Lord[2]–and we are His soldiers. He has an assignment for each of us. Are we ready,[3] willing,[4] and able?[5] Not every job is glamorous, not every position is on the front lines. God does not promise us an easy task, nor does He guarantee earthly recognition and rewards. We may have to slash our way through a few jungles of opposition and slog through the mud of temptation and trial. We may find ourselves deep in enemy territory–cold, hungry, and with our uniform worn and tattered.[6] He warns us that we will be under attack, and that we must wear our armor and have our shields and weapons ready at all times.

However, we have the ultimate in combat support! There is absolutely nothing that can take out our communications or cut our supply lines. *Yahweh Sabaoth* promises, "Call to me and I will answer you."[7] "I have already given you everything you need."[8] You may feel like you've been abandoned, left to do it all on your own, but He says He will never leave you nor forsake you,[9] and that He will command his angels to guard you in all your ways.[10] If we are wounded, He has promised, "I will bind up the injured and strengthen the weak."[11] He Himself is our shield.[12] That shield He's equipped you with repels every single attack the enemy could ever attempt to use against you. The evil one cannot even touch you![13]

We are at war, and there is work to do. God is our commander *and* our back-up, and heaven is our reward. He's looking for volunteers–will we each say, "Here am I. Send me!"?

We are at war, and there is work to do.

---

[1]Isa. 6:3, 5   [2]Josh. 5:14   [3]Jer. 1:17   [4]Isa. 1:19   [5]John 6:65   [6]Ps. 107:4–5   [7]Jer. 33:3   [8]2 Pet. 1:3
[9]Heb. 13:5   [10]Ps. 91:11   [11]Ezek. 34:16   [12]Ps. 7:10   [13]1 John 5:18 [KJV]

OCTOBER 25

Jesus said to her, "I am the resurrection and the life. . . ."
John 11:25

*M*artha, Martha, what do you really believe? You believe that Jesus is the Christ, the Son of God—but do you realize that He *is* God?[1] He *is* the great I Am.[2] "I Am the resurrection and the life." "In Him was life, and that life was the light of men."[3]

The God who rules makes the rules. Martha believed in the resurrection; she knew Lazarus would live again—someday, eventually, at the end of time. It was the plan, the way things were, the rules. Jesus looked deep into her eyes, straight into her spirit, and reminded her, "I Am the resurrection." The resurrection is not only an event, it is a state of being. It *is* Jesus. He doesn't *have* the resurrection to give us; we are resurrected, because we live in Him, in the resurrection and the life. He is not bound by time nor by the natural order of things. Our God is in heaven; he does whatever pleases him.[4]

In Christ there is no rule, no requirement—no *must be, must have, must do*—that He cannot override, if it so pleases Him, to accomplish His purpose. "Is anything too hard for the Lord?"[5] He asks. There is no law that can stand against His purpose. He will turn the king's heart;[6] He shatters the mighty and sets up others in their place.[7] He will shut the mouths of hungry lions, take the fire out of fire itself, and make water a solid floor. He doesn't need an airplane; He can lift you up and set you down wherever He needs you to be. Whatever the world calls *impossible* is the glory of God to do. "Did I not tell you that if you believed, you would see the glory of God?"[8]

He will cancel a prison sentence if He has a purpose for you elsewhere. Red tape becomes a red carpet for you, because He *is* the resurrection and the life. When He moves, He does not have to explain Himself.[9] When men scratch their heads, saying, "I don't understand it, but . . ." as they hand you your answer—it's God. Just tell them, "He *is* the resurrection and the life!"

The resurrection is not only an event;
it is a state of being.

---

[1]John 1:1   [2]John 8:58   [3]John 1:4   [4]Ps. 115:3   [5]Gen 18:14   [6]Prov. 21:1   [7]Job 34:24
[8]John 11:40   [9]Prov. 25:2

OCTOBER 26

. . . However, when the Son of Man comes, will he find faith on the earth?
Luke 18:8

Can you even imagine Jesus being pessimistic? This one statement comes so close, I can hear the ache and frustration in His voice. He was not even talking about moving mountains, healing the sick, or raising the dead. He wasn't teaching here about performing miracles or casting out demons. Jesus was disappointed many times by the disciples' lack of faith in those areas, yet we tend to sympathize with the twelve. After all, we may admit that we'd be just as terrified in an open boat trying to row through a hurricane[1]—and not many of us have come face to face with a thrashing, foaming-at-the-mouth demon![2] We *don't* automatically think, "5,000 people are coming for dinner—these five loaves of bread and two smoked herring will be just fine!"[3]

But Jesus wasn't talking about *that* kind of faith. He was talking about prayer, about asking God for help. He wasn't even talking about asking for a natural impossibility, for a tree to be uprooted and planted in the sea,[4] or for deadly poison not to hurt us in any way.[5] Jesus was talking about asking God for favor in a simple legal matter—and He was questioning whether anybody would trust God enough to persist in such a prayer.

God is so faithful, loving, and intimately involved in our lives that Jesus *expected* us to have faith enough to trust Him for everything we need *and* desire. He *expects* us to believe that God is good, that He will provide all our needs,[6] that every good and perfect gift comes from Him,[7] and that no good thing will He withhold from us.[8] He *expects* us to trust that no matter how bad things may seem, God will make it all come out good.[9] He *expects* us to trust that God listens to us—and that we can expect Him to answer! Jesus *expects* us to have faith.

When he comes again, He is coming for the faithful. The faith He is looking for is a faith that has trusted Him completely, a faith that did not give up or give in when his timing was not ours, that knew and relied on His love,[10] even when His answers did not look like we expected—but that always expected Him to answer. When He comes, will He find this faith in me?

Jesus expects us to have faith enough to trust the Father
for everything we need and desire.

---

[1]Matt. 8:23–27   [2]Mark 9:17–19   [3]Matt. 14:15–21   [4]Luke 17:6   [5]Mark 16:18   [6]Jer. 5:7
[7]James 1:17   [8]Ps. 84:11   [9]Ps. 71:20–21   [10]1 John 4:16

OCTOBER 27

. . . He asked them, "Do you believe that I am able to do this?"
Matthew 9:28

J ask Jesus for a lot—some of which I actually see happen, and some I
am still waiting to see happen.[1] Is praying merely a habit, or do I really
believe that Jesus is *able* to do what I am asking?[2]

The two blind men had followed Jesus, crying out to Him for mercy. They
called Him the Son of David, one of the Jews' commonly-used titles for the
Messiah. When Jesus spoke with the blind men away from the crowd, He asked
them the above question. Why? The blind men obviously thought He could do
it, or they wouldn't have asked Him. But Jesus wasn't just asking about ability;
He was talking about that Son of David part. "Do you really believe I am the
Messiah? That I can do this, because I am who I claim to be?"[3]

Why do I believe Jesus can do the things I ask? Because He is some kind
of cosmic magician pulling answers out of His hat, or because He is the Son
of God, my Lord?[4] My faith is being put on the line. Do I have faith in what
Jesus can do, or in who He is?[5] If my faith goes beyond my shopping list of
wants and needs, then I acknowledge that *He* is God with divine right[6] to not
only say *yes* to my prayers, but to say *no* or *not now*. I trust Him to do what
He knows is best.[7]

It also means I come to Him, not as a customer, but as His subject. He is
the Messiah, the Lord. I do not pull His strings, I submit to His strength.[8] I
don't know if the two blind men got this. After receiving their sight, Jesus gave
them a direct order—which they promptly disregarded.

Jesus still answers prayers. He rescues, provides, protects, and delivers,
because He is merciful and loving. God sends His blessings on the righteous
and the unrighteous.[9] He feeds the 5,000—but He is looking for those who want
Him more than they want mere bread. He is looking for the true believers.[10]

Do I have faith in what Jesus can do,

or in who He is?

[1]Ps. 33:20–22 [2]Mark 9:22–23 [3]Matt. 22:41–45 [4]John 6:26–27 [5]John 8:23–24 [6]Hos. 6:6
[7]Isa. 48:17 [8]Luke 6:46 [9]Matt. 5:45 [10]John 4:23

OCTOBER 28

They were all trying to frighten us, thinking.
"Their hands will get too weak for the work, and it will not be completed."
But I prayed, "Now strengthen my hands."

Nehemiah 6:9

hen we begin to really live for Christ as His witnesses and ambassadors,[1] it is time for those on the other side to kick into high gear. Doing the work that God has assigned each of us is not going to go unopposed by the enemy. After all, what king would allow his kingdom to be invaded and his territory snatched out from under him without a fight? We should not be surprised by opposition, but should learn to recognize it (and its true source) when it comes. Remember, Jesus gave us authority over the enemy.[2]

Since everything from God—His grace, forgiveness, righteousness, blessings, and power—is received by faith, the enemy of our soul is going to do all in his power to steal our faith. He knows that if he can get us into fear in any of its forms, he has us in his grip.[3] Everybody knows the strength-sapping power of fear. When we are afraid, it paralyzes us. Doubt is fear that God cannot be fully trusted, that His Word will not come to pass for us.[4] Worry is fear that God will fail us and do nothing to help us in our time of need.[5] Fear magnifies the power of the enemy and minimizes the power of God. Fear believes the problem will defeat us, not that God will defeat the problem!

If the enemy fails to steal our faith, he will undermine our relationship with God. He will try to separate us from God through compromise and sin.[6] He knows that God's blessings—and His protection—are conditional upon obedience. Once he gets us out of the will of God, he will also try to keep us there: "How dare you ask for forgiveness *again*! Too many times—He won't forgive you. He doesn't want *you* any more!"[7] Lies!

Throughout history, God's people have fought opposition—obvious and subtle, from without and within—whenever they set out to fulfill their purpose. We should learn from their successes *and* their failures. Build up our faith,[8] guard our righteousness in Him, and walk in love.[9] The enemy will flee from us seven ways every time![10]

The enemy of our soul is going to do
all in his power to steal our faith.

---

[1]John 17:14–19 [2]Luke 10:19 [3]1 John 4:18 [4]James 1:6–7 [5]Matt. 6:25–34 [6]Isa. 59:1–2
[7]1 John 1:9 [8]Jude 1:20 [9]1 John 3:16–18 [10]Deut. 28:7

OCTOBER 29

*Let us rejoice and be glad and give him glory! For the wedding
of the Lamb has come, and his bride has made herself ready.*
Revelation 19:7

*D*o we realize that all of heaven is waiting for *us*? The Lamb has
already gone to the altar; He has done His part and prepared our
places for us![1] The wedding banner is lifted high,[2] the flowers are
fresh and undying–the precious Rose of Sharon and the Lily of the Valley.[3] The
music includes the "Song of Moses" and the "Song of the Lamb" sung by a very
special choir, handpicked by Jesus Himself.[4] The lighting is glorious–we, the
light of the world, marrying Him who is the glory of God and the lamp of the
New Jerusalem![5] The supper is ready, the table is laid–but where is the bride?

Am I lingering, perhaps not aware that the hour draws near? Surely it cannot be that I hesitate, longing for my ex-lover? Surely I can remember how
poorly he treated me, how little he esteemed me, how greatly he abused me!
The few and wretched things he gave me were of little value and did not last,[6]
and what little I managed to hold onto, he snatched back with wicked glee.

Surely I cannot be desiring the struggles of my single life when I was the only
breadwinner and provider? With no heavenly help, it was all up to me. Oh,
the long and exhausting hours of labor for so little return![7] My few recreations
seemed diverting, but came at such cost! Too many times, I returned from my
"fun" empty, cold, and sick in body and at heart.

Have I been away from my Beloved too long? Have His beauty and grace
faded in my memory? Do I have trouble recalling the music of His voice, the
wonder of His smile? Have I forgotten the incredible joy of first love,[8] the unut-
terable peace of pleasing Him,[9] of fulfilling my purpose in Him? Perhaps the
distractions of this world have called me away from my wedding preparations.[10]

But it is not too late. No matter how cold or distant we may feel, He is never
far away. If we turn to Him in sincere repentance, fixing our eyes on Him and
Him alone,[11] His loving arms will gather us close–even now.

The supper is ready, the table is laid,

but where is the bride?

[1]John 14:2   [2]Song 2:4   [3]Song 2:1   [4]Rev. 15:2–3   [5]Rev. 21:23   [6]Matt. 6:19   [7]Hag. 1:5–9
[8]Rev. 2:4   [9]John 8:29   [10]Luke 8:14   [11]Heb. 12:2

OCTOBER 30

No, new wine must be poured into new wineskins.
Luke 5:38

The essential difference between new wineskins and old is expandability, also called resilience or stretch. Old wineskins are tough, dried up, and rigid.[1] They have settled into one shape and hardened into it.[2] To try to reshape them would be to crack, split, and break them. An old wineskin has no capacity for more;[3] its rigidity limits its ability to receive. An old wineskin cannot grow.

Old wineskins never rethink tradition;[4] they like predictable routine, expected methods,[5] assumed moves. Old wineskins will not travel without an itinerary, will not worship without a program, and will not serve without a contract. Old wineskins do things the way they've always been done; they are comfortable with their definition of what God will or will not do.[6]

Old wineskins cannot handle the outpouring of the new wine of the Spirit,[7] because the expandability of it would stretch them beyond their comfort zone. They do not feel their need of the power of the Holy Spirit; they have everything under control.

"Forget the former things; do not dwell on the past. See, I am doing a new thing!"[8] God's new thing requires a new creature—a new wineskin—who will let go of himself enough to admit he doesn't know God like he thought he did[9]—and yet will trust Him all the same. God is looking for new wineskins, for those who are willing to surrender themselves completely, to give up their right to themselves, and to become stretchable vessels for His glory.

New wineskins wake up to a day lived moment by moment: unfamiliar, unscheduled, unpredictable.[10] If they have a routine, they are ready in a moment to cast it aside in order to minister to their interruption. New wineskins trust God's Spirit to lead them by ways they have not known and to guide them along unfamiliar paths.[11] Only a new wineskin can grow big enough to be filled with a God who fills heaven and earth.[12]

Are you a new wineskin for the Lord?

---

*God is looking for new wineskins, for those
who are willing to surrender themselves completely
and become stretchable vessels for His glory.*

---

[1]Deut. 9:13 [2]Jer. 48:11 [3]Ps. 81:10 [4]Mark 7:1–8 [5]John 7:40–52 [6]Lam 4:12–13
[7]Joel 2:23–24, 28–29 [8]Isa. 43:18–19 [9]Job 42:2–6 [10]James 4:13–15 [11]Isa. 42:16 [12]Jer. 23:24

OCTOBER 31

For rebellion is as the sin of witchcraft,
and stubborness is as iniquity and idolatry. . . .
1 Samuel 15:23 [NKJV]

Stubbornness and rebellion conjure up images of conflict: heated words, slamming doors. No matter the specifics, stubbornness and rebellion always mean someone is refusing to submit to authority. I am in prison; I have some serious experience with rebellion. Yet my version was more subtle than merely slamming doors. I have heard it said that the essence of immorality is in making an exception of yourself. The rules apply to everyone else; I'm going to do what *I'm* going to do, regardless. There is nothing as powerful as prison to teach the foolishness of ignoring authority! It is a great training ground for learning that submission brings more peace and freedom than rebellion ever could.[1] Submission is obedience—no buts, no insteads.

I had never realized how serious this kind of disobedience is. But looking at the context for today's verse, we see that King Saul has just returned from a God-commanded mission to destroy the Amalekites.[2] He was hugely successful, too, except for a few details. He knew exactly what God had told him to do, but he only obeyed the parts he liked, the parts that suited him.[3] To justify his actions, he claimed *his* way was necessary in order to do God a service, to offer Him a sacrifice.[4] God told him it wasn't just disobedience, it was rebellion—the same as witchcraft! The *witchcraft* in disobedience is the spell it casts over you, blinding you to your own rebellion.[5]

When I disregard the voice of God in my life,[6] when I do not do what I know He has told me, it's not hard to tell myself it's still okay.[7] I bewitch my own soul to believe the lie—and I easily slide further and further from God.

Obedience breaks the enchantment. The truth is, the only way that Jesus is Lord of my life is if I do what He says.[8] The only way to *truly* love Him is to submit to His authority—to obey Him.[9]

The only way that Jesus is Lord of my life
is if I do what He says.

---

[1]Lam. 1:18–20 [2]1 Sam. 15:1–3 [3]1 Sam. 15:9 [4]1 Sam. 15:15, 20–21 [5]John 12:39–40
[6]Ezek.2:1–7 [7]Jer. 7:9–10 [8]Luke 6:46 [9]John 14:21

NOVEMBER 1

*. . . make every effort to add to your faith goodness; and to goodness,
knowledge; and to knowledge, self-control; and to self-control,
perseverance; and to perseverance, godliness, and to godliness,
brotherly kindness, and to brotherly kindness, love.*

2 Peter 1:5–7

*T*here's another word to describe all those irritating, frustrating, anxious and annoying situations that plague you: *fertilizer.*[1] Those trials and tests are more than just so much manure; they're specifically allowed or designed to nurture you, to make you blossom and produce fruit.[2] The Christian life is a process of growth, of adding to our faith. We start with our seed of faith: we hear, we believe, we receive Christ, and become new creations in Him. We exchange darkness for light, evil for good. By putting off our old ways,[3] we begin to add goodness to our faith.

Goodness doesn't come naturally; we have to learn it.[4] Man's idea of goodness is mixed-up and backwards. As we water our seedling with the Word of God, we grow in knowledge and our lives begin to reflect the true goodness of a sanctified spirit.

As you walk in the knowledge of the truth, chains that bound you break, and strings that controlled you are cut. You are set free—and freedom is maintained by self-control.[5] Scripture teaches us to abstain from sinful desires, which war against our souls.[6] Proverbs says that a wise man keeps himself under control.[7]

Just as you are about to blossom, the enemy tries to steal your growth. "Give up!" he tells you. "It's too much, too hard. Where's the reward for all this work?" Many stumble here, but you need not. Add perseverance; put your roots down deeper and draw up water from the Rock. Though the sun is scorching, you will stay fresh and green![8] Perseverance produces godliness—not one or two acts of goodness, but a character that is consistently Christ-like.[9]

All this growth draws you through kindness more and more fully into the perfection of His love. To walk in the fullness of His love is the highest expression of faith.

Do not let the manure of everyday living sit and rot on you—accept it as fertilizer and grow!

---

*Our life in Christ is a process of growth,
of adding to our faith.*

---

[1]Luke 13:8–9   [2]1 Pet. 1:6–7   [3]Isa. 55:7–8   [4]Jer. 4:22   [5]Prov. 25:28   [6]1 Pet. 2:11   [7]Prov. 29:11
[8]Jer. 17:7–8   [9]Luke 6:40

NOVEMBER 2

Then Simon answered, "Pray to the Lord for me
so that nothing you have said may happen to me."
Acts 8:24

*Y*ou are locked in a burning room. In your hand is a large ring with dozens of keys, only one of which unlocks the door. It is a matter of life and death; you have no time to waste on the wrong key. A desperate situation—but farfetched?

Not at all. We *are* in a locked room with the fires of hell licking at our heels. We do hold the key, and there are many false keys. We do not have time to waste fiddling with the wrong key.

To open the door to salvation, we must repent. It is vital; it is key. It was the Elijah message of John the Baptist: "Repent!"[1] It was the first message Jesus the Messiah preached: "Repent, for the kingdom of heaven is near."[2]

I have to ask myself, "Why do I repent?" Not, "Why must I repent?", or "What is the function of repentance?" I have to ask myself personally, "Why do I repent? What drives me to my knees, pleading for mercy? Why do I cry out, 'Forgive me!'?[3] Why am I sorry?" There are many reasons for repenting, but only one is the key that opens the door to salvation.[4]

Simon chose the wrong key. His choice is a frequently made but deadly mistake. Simon did not repent of his *sin*; he repented of the consequences. He asked for mercy, but only so that "nothing you have said may happen to me." That isn't being sorry for the crime; that's being sorry I got caught, and now I have to suffer.[5] *Motivation* is everything. The wrong motivation means I'd do it again if I could get away with it.[6]

True repentance is being cut to the heart[7] because my sin has grieved God and caused Him pain.[8] It is a change of attitude, that sin is now ugly, evil, and hateful to me.[9] Not because *I* suffer, but because *He* suffers. Love hurts when it has hurt its beloved.

No one gets to heaven because they don't like hell. All-consuming love for God is the only key to true repentance.

True repentance is being cut to the heart
because my sin has grieved God and caused Him pain.

---

[1]Matt. 3:2 [2]Matt. 4:17 [3]Luke 18:13 [4]Isa. 59:20 [5]Exod. 10:16–17 [6]Exod. 9:27–35 [7]Acts 2:37 [8]Gen. 6:6 [9]Job 42:5–6

NOVEMBER 3

. . . their sorrow was turned into joy
and their mourning into a day of celebration.
Esther 9:22

"This, too, shall pass." Wise words from an old saying that can be translated as perspective. The psalmist says it another way: "Weeping may remain for a night, but joy comes in the morning."[1]

It is amazing how many people do not know what to do with joy when it comes. Some, unused to such a wondrously good thing, waste their joy worrying that it will end.[2] They clutch it close and box it up, trying to hold onto it as long as they can. But when they finally carve out a safe and private place to enjoy their joy, they find the box empty and the feeling vanished like a vapor.[3] The bitterness of their loss makes them mistrust joy. It is too fickle for them; they'd rather not risk it. The next time a little joy comes dancing into their life, they scowl it away, their prophecies of doom and gloom self-fulfilling.

Others throw themselves fully into the kiss of joy, convinced that it is theirs by right and ordained to last forever. It becomes the foundation of all their faith: they are forgiven because they feel happy; they are in the favor and will of God because everything is rosy. They mistake external, circumstantial joy as the seal of God's approval, and because they have no root, they quickly wilt and wither away when such transient joy dries up.[4] For this, too, shall pass.[5]

Joy based on circumstances is meant to be celebrated, appreciated as a blessing, a respite from the struggle. It is no more a mark of righteousness than sorrow is a diagnosis of sin.[6] This joy, coming from outside, cannot much be controlled by you and so should not be built upon as though it were permanent.[7] It is not that sustaining, strengthening joy that is the fruit of the indwelling, never-forsaking Spirit.[8]

Does this sound pessimistic? It need not be. It is a reminder that situations are always subject to change. Celebrate and cherish good times when we have them in our hand. Let their warmth keep us from losing faith when sorrow comes—for trouble will surely pass, too.[9] Our anchor is neither joy nor sorrow. Our anchor is Jesus Christ, who is the same yesterday, today, and forever.[10]

Our anchor is not our circumstances.

Our anchor is Jesus Christ.

---

[1]Ps. 30:5 [2]Job 20:5 [3]Job 30:15 [4]Matt. 13:21 [5]Eccl. 3:4 [6]Luke 13:1–2 [7]Matt. 7:26–27
[8]John 17:13 [9]Eccl. 7:14 [10]Heb. 13:8

NOVEMBER 4

. . . And when they heard that the L<small>ORD</small> *was concerned about them and had seen their misery, they bowed down and worshipped.*

Exodus 4:31

*N*eed may be the mother of invention, but it is the emergency room of salvation. In our stubborn density, we persist in thinking we are just fine without God[1]—until disaster strikes. That's why *jailhouse religion* is proverbial—there is nothing like a cold, hard cell to make you reconsider how you got there.[2] Your need screams at you from the cement floor, walls, and ceiling; it mocks you from the other side of the bars.

None can change who feel no need.[3] Yet even a crushing awareness of need requires a door of hope, or the soul will seek refuge in madness and despair. The Israelites knew their need. Abject slavery has a way of doing that, just like the clang of slamming steel bars. But need alone is not the key to freedom. You may be in the emergency room, but you have not yet seen the doctor!

God's love is the doctor in your desperate hour.[4] Four hundred and thirty years of need had not changed the Israelites; not until they knew that the God of their father Abraham had not abandoned them, that He cared about them, and was going to rescue them did their need drive them to Him.[5] It is love that leads to worship.

That is what it takes to draw people to God—desperate need answered by divine love.[6] The cross of Christ is both. The fact of the cross proves our need: we are sinners, and sin must be punished. But it is the love of God that chose who hung upon it. It is the love of God that meets our need.

The Israelites were more needy than they knew; so are we. They thought their problem was the Egyptians, but they were just like them.[7] God didn't come to their rescue because they deserved it; He came because He loved them anyway.[8] It was this amazing love that broke their chains. He showers it on the undeserving, the lost, that perhaps they might not be lost anymore.[9]

Desperate need answered by divine love. That is salvation.

Desperate need answered by divine love
is what it takes to draw people to God.

---

[1]Rev. 3:17 [2]Ps. 142:6–7 [3]Ps. 79:8 [4]Matt. 9:12 [5]Exod. 3:7–8 [6]Matt. 8:2–3 [7]Luke 13:1–5
[8]Deut. 7:8 [9]Luke 19:10

NOVEMBER 5

Ever since I went to Pharaoh to speak in your name,
he has brought trouble upon this people,
and you have not rescued your people at all.
Exodus 5:23

It is a good fight, this fight of faith—but it *is* a fight, not a cakewalk. I don't know what Moses expected, but he was not much different than you and I. God had told him He was going to deliver the Israelites from Pharaoh's hand, but that it would not happen unless a mighty hand compelled him.[1] He told Moses it would take some awesome signs and wonders. He told him Pharaoh would harden his heart and not let them go.[2] He even told him, far ahead of time, that it would take the death of Egypt's firstborn for Pharaoh to change his mind.[3]

Moses (like you and I) heard the first part: "I will deliver you." The promise of God runs sweet to our spirit, and we quickly grab hold. But we shut our ears to the unpleasant aspects,[4] then suffer disappointment and sometimes even stumble in our faith when Pharaoh tells us no.

We need to open our eyes and ears to *all* God has said so we can persevere in our faith and trust when we enter the bricks-without-straw phase of our deliverance. Jesus told us plainly we would be hated, persecuted, cursed, ill-treated, arrested, and even put to death. He said we'd need to take up our cross.[5] He warned us we would be asked to surrender everything: possessions, houses, even family, if need be.

Pharaoh told Moses no *ten times*. As soon as the promise was given, their situation got worse, then disastrous. Yet God's Word did not fail; He did everything He said He would do for them. As He did for them, He will do for us.

We need to persevere.[6] Once God's Word is given, He does not take it back.[7] It will accomplish His purpose.[8] Listen to His *whole* Word. Pay attention to any *if* conditions to be fulfilled,[9] any *but first* circumstances to endure on the way to our deliverance.[10] If Moses had given up after the first, second, or even the ninth *no*, the Israelites might still be making bricks today.

I will keep my heart on the Word and not on my circumstances, for He who promised is faithful![11]

God's Word does not fail.
He will do everything He says He will do.

---

[1]Exod. 3:19–20   [2]Exod. 4:21   [3]Exod. 4:23   [4]Mark 9:31–32   [5]Luke 14:27   [6]Heb. 10:36
[7]Num. 23:19   [8]Isa. 55:11   [9]Deut. 28:1   [10]Luke 17:24–25   [11]Heb. 10:23

NOVEMBER 6

*But I will not drive them out in a single year, because the land would
become desolate and the wild animals too numerous for you.*

Exodus 23:29

Raise your hand if you're perfect. No hands? Good! You and I are in good company. Though perfection is our goal,[1] I'm so glad God does not insist on it instantly. No one expects doctorate-degree knowledge from a kindergartner, and God Himself compassionately remembers we are dust.[2]

Have you ever been like me, frustrated with the pace of your growth, impatient that there is still so much you do not know, with questions for which you are still awaiting an answer, issues with which you still find yourself struggling?[3] You may have said, "I have fought and fought this, and I'm tired of this constant battle![4] I wish God would just take it from me!"

If God did that, we would never learn how to fight and win; we would only know the fight. Victorious armies don't just fight, they fight until they win. Each win makes them stronger for the next battle.

That's the point. We must learn how to fight the enemy *and win*, because each battle strengthens our faith for the next. This is such an important truth that God said He had specifically left some enemies around Israel only to teach warfare to the descendants of the Israelites who had not had previous battle experience.[5]

What is handed to me, done for me, I may not have the strength to keep. The land will become desolate, and I'll be attacked by enemies I do not know how to face. What I have fought for, what I have persisted in all the way through to victory—*that* I possess. God knows this. He is training me, leading me from victory to victory, strength to strength,[6] until I have increased enough to take possession of the land.[7]

So we should not act frustrated. We should patiently grow step by step.[8] Each lesson learned leads us to the next victory. God is driving out our enemies with every forward step we take. Little by little, we will possess the Promised Land.

*We must learn how to fight the enemy and win,
because each battle strengthens our faith for the next.*

---

[1]Matt. 5:48 [2]Ps. 103:14 [3]Ps. 131:1–2 [4]Ps. 51:3 [5]Judg. 3:2 [6]Ps. 84:7 [7]Exod. 23:30
[8]Heb. 6:12

NOVEMBER 7

How will anyone know that you are pleased with me and with your people
unless you go with us? What else will distinguish me and your people
from all the other people on the face of the earth?
Exodus 33:16

*W*hat makes me any different than anyone else? What sets me apart from the world? Throughout the world, there are many differences—physical appearance, culture, language, etc. What makes me different in some places in the world makes me blend into the crowd in others.

Moses was leading a brand-new nation into the midst of other nations. God had already given them a new government, new laws, new traditions, new holidays—even a new calendar![1] They had come out of Egypt, but they were not Egyptian.[2] They were the nation of Israel—no longer just a familial identity, but now a political one as well.

But Moses knew that all of those new things did not make them truly different. The only thing that made them unique, the first in history, was the active, manifest presence of God leading them.[3] Without the presence of God, everything else was just another variety of the same old thing. Every nation on earth had a form of government—some even claimed a god as their king (or their king as a god). They all had laws, holidays, some kind of calendar, ethnic foods. Now, you may say, "Yes, but Israel's God is *real . . .*"

Exactly. That's the difference. The power of a real God, manifested in His presence.[4] That's what set them apart from all the other people on the face of the earth. No matter what a nation claimed, no matter what their religion taught, Israel alone could claim the *power of a present God.*[5]

That is the only thing that truly makes us different from anyone else: The the power of God present in our lives. Anything else is just a shade of "to-may-to/to-mah-to" variety.

Are we different? If there is no power in our lives,[6] we are missing the presence of God. If we are not walking in love, meekness, and mercy (and all the other attitudes Jesus taught),[7] we are missing the presence of God. Salvation is being able to come in and stay in the presence of God.[8]

Are *we* different?

If there is no power in our lives,
we are missing the presence of God.

---

[1]Exod. 12:1 [2]Isa. 52:11 [3]Num. 14:14 [4]Deut. 4:7 [5]Deut. 4:37 [6]Acts 1:8 [7]Matt. 5:3–12
[8]Heb. 4:16

NOVEMBER 8

. . . No one is to appear before me empty-handed.
Exodus 23:15

*I*n the time of bulls, rams and lambs, this command was easy to understand. But now that the one perfect sacrifice has been made, we are left with the question, "With what shall I come before the LORD and bow down before the exalted God?"[1]

Empty hands are a symptom of an empty heart. There is no better illustration of this truth than the incident at Simon the Pharisee's dinner.[2] Jesus was the guest of honor—yet Simon offered Him no honor at all: no kiss of brotherhood; no water to wash His feet; no oil to anoint His head. Simon's dinner was for Simon's benefit, not to honor Jesus, for Simon did not love Jesus.

Not like that woman loved Him—that outcast, that sinner. She wasn't invited to Simon's dinner, but she had heard that Jesus was there, and she wanted to honor Him. She came uninvited, not for her benefit—she could only be exposed by her act. She came to minister to Him. She did not come empty-handed; she brought an offering. The alabaster jar of perfume was only the symbol; her true offering was her tears, her kisses, her worship. She brought Him her love, and she lavished it on Him like the fat of a temple sacrifice.[3]

Our approach to God is much like Simon's dinner. We come because we need Him. We want His power; His answers.[4] For all our needs—and we are needy—He is the owner of the cattle on a thousand hills.[5] He is the King inviting us to the banquet.[6]

Many come for the food, forgetting the purpose of the dinner. They look only to receive, to eat, to be blessed. They come empty-handed, looking to be filled. They seek His hands, not His face.[7]

But we are not the guests of honor at this banquet—Jesus is. It is worship—it is how we minister *to the Lord*. As priests of God, we *do* offer sacrifices: our praise,[8] our gratitude,[9] our willing obedience.[10] (The psalmist said, "Bless the LORD, oh my soul"—not, "Bless my soul, oh LORD!")

I will not come empty-handed.[11] I will bring Him my alabaster box and lavish on Him my love.

Empty hands are a symptom of an empty heart.

[1]Mic. 6:6 [2]Luke 7:36–50 [3]Isa. 43:24 [4]Jer. 33:3 [5]Ps. 50:10 [6]Matt. 22:1–2 [7]Ps. 27:8
[8]Heb. 13:15 [9]Ps. 50:14 [10]John 14:15 [11]Ps. 96:8

NOVEMBER 9

*For we do not have a high priest who is unable to sympathize
with our weaknesses, but we have one who has been tempted in every way,
just as we are—yet was without sin.*
Hebrews 4:15

rugs. Divorce. Prostitution. How can Jesus have been tempted in every way, just as we are? How could He have been tempted to lead-foot it to 100 miles per hour on the interstate? As a single man, how could He have been tempted like married men are? Or married women? He could not possibly have been enticed to do drugs. How can He know the depths of an addict's temptation?

The Scriptures do not say that Jesus faced every temptation we face. It says He was tempted in all the *ways* we are tempted. The devil threw temptation at Jesus from every direction, using every trick and trap in his arsenal. He used the direct, indirect, subtle, sweet, bitter, and brutal approaches. He came at Him face to face,[1] sideways,[2] and backstabbing.[3] He used the religious[4] and the demonic[5] approaches. He tried royal threats,[6] a "concerned friend,"[7] even His own family.[8] The enemy tried flattery,[9] disdain,[10] and betrayal.[11] He used Jesus' physical needs against Him.[12] He tried the soft voice,[13] and he came at Him shouting.[14]

In *all* ways, just as we are. Not in *form*, but in *principle*. The immediate action is the form; the attitude behind it is the principle. Temptations feed off emotions, and Jesus felt all the same emotions we feel. All temptation boils down to the lure to not trust God, to not wait for God's timing, or to not do things God's way.

When I am tempted, I must ask myself, "What am I *really* being tempted with?" The enemy offers nothing new; he is just playing variations on an old theme. And Jesus has already faced them all down, exposed them as lies, and triumphed over them!

He knows what we are being tempted with and how it feels. He's been there—He'll help us win!

---

*Temptations feed off emotions,
and Jesus felt all the same emotions we feel.*

---

[1]Matt. 4:1–11   [2]Luke 7:18–19   [3]Luke 22:60–61   [4]Luke 13:14   [5]Mark 1:34   [6]Luke 13:31–32
[7]Matt. 16:22   [8]John 7:3–5   [9]Matt. 22:15–17   [10]John 8:48   [11]John 13:21   [12]Luke 4:2–3
[13]Luke 4:22   [14]Luke 4:33–34

NOVEMBER 10

Jesus replied, "Love the Lord your God . . .
This is the first and greatest commandment."
Matthew 22:37–38

*I*f we are saved by faith, if everything in the kingdom of heaven is received by faith, if the righteous shall live by faith,[1] then why isn't the greatest commandment to have faith?

There are two kinds of faith—and one of them is dead.[2] You see, faith works through love.[3] Love is the power that animates faith, that makes it alive. Just as God is three in one—the Trinity of Father, Son, and Holy Spirit; just as man is a reflection of that Trinity[4]—spirit, soul, and body; so also salvation is a triplet—faith, hope, and love. Faith is the body, the substance of things hoped for.[5] It is the *way* we are saved.

In man, the soul is the mind, will, and emotions. That is where hope resides. Hope is based on knowledge—we hope for what we have been promised.[6] We cannot hope for what we know nothing about. The hope of the Word of God is a confident expectation, because He who promised is faithful and true.[7] Hope is the soul of salvation; it is the *truth* of His Word in us.

But love! Love is the one way that others will know our faith is genuine.[8] Faith is intangible; it is an idea, a thought, an attitude of the mind. You cannot touch faith, but you can touch love. You can touch the hand of him who reaches out to you in your need;[9] you can feel someone's arms around you when you grieve. Faith is invisible, but love can be seen. You see it in the warm smile of welcome when you're a stranger; you can see it in money, medicine, blankets, and bread. Love is the spirit of our salvation; it is the *life*.

There's no mystery about it—even an outright heathen can point out dead faith. They may not understand all the theology behind it, but they know dead faith like they know a dead body—it is cold and stiff.[10] And they know the real thing when they see it.

All three are needed: faith (the way), hope (the truth) and love (the life).[11] But the greatest of all is love.

Faith is invisible, but love can be seen.

---

[1]Hab. 2:4   [2]James 2:17   [3]Ps. 85:10   [4]Gen. 1:27   [5]Heb. 11:1   [6]1 Pet. 1:13   [7]Heb. 10:23
[8]John 13:35   [9]1 John 3:17–18   [10]James 2:26   [11]John 14:6

NOVEMBER 11

. . . I write this to you so that you will not sin. . . .
1 John 2:1

Change is the only constant in life. Everything changes, everything alters. It is the law of entropy in action: all things tend to disorder. Yet the wise man wrote, "Whatever is has already been, and what will be has been before. . . ."[1] There is nothing new under the sun."[2] We point to great inventions and call it progress—yet underneath it all, man has not changed. Man cannot change;[3] we can only *be* changed.[4]

The *good* in the good news is that change is now possible! In our addiction to sin, we could not even change our minds, let alone our behavior. Through Christ, the chains are broken: "If the son sets you free, you will be free indeed."[5] You can choose!

To choose Christ is to choose change. To confess sin is to repudiate sin—not go on living in it. Every life touched by Christ is a life transformed to the glory of God. Everywhere Jesus went, there was change. The sick were healed, the possessed were made sane, the lost were found. He that cheated, restored what was stolen and stole no more.[6] She that had committed adultery went and sinned no more.[7] Prostitutes entered the kingdom of heaven;[8] sinners were made righteous.[9]

The gospel of Jesus Christ is a search-and-rescue operation. It finds us in our chaos and pain, lifts us out of our degradation, and transforms us into sons and daughters of the Most High God. You cannot meet soul to soul with Jesus Christ and not be changed.

Being changed is not immediate perfection. The second half of our verse for today says. "But if anyone does sin, we have one who speaks to the Father in our defense—Jesus Christ, the righteous one." Yet as Jesus is speaking to the Father, His blood is speaking to us:[10] "Be cleansed."[11]

I have met the Holy One. I have felt His mercy and grace. The person I was before—the things I thought and did before—are not who I am anymore. I *want* to change. The old me had no power to change. I love the new me. Change may be a struggle, but victory is worth the battle!

To choose Christ is to choose change.

---

[1]Eccl. 3:15   [2]Eccl. 1:9   [3]Jer. 13:23   [4]1 Sam. 10:6   [5]John 8:36   [6]Luke 19:8   [7]John 8:1–11
[8]Matt. 21:31   [9]Luke 18:13–14   [10]Heb. 12:24   [11]1 John 1:9

NOVEMBER 12

"Unless you people see miraculous signs and wonders,"
Jesus told him, "you will never believe."
John 4:48

*T*he crucifixion of Christ is a stumbling block to those who seek displays of supernatural power. Those who seek after signs are never satisfied—the Jews who were filled by the loaves and fishes were still brushing off the crumbs of their last miracle and asking for another.[1] How could it be?

No amount of miracles will convince a hardened heart.[2] Jesus had healed the sick, the blind, the deaf, the mute, the crippled. He had multiplied a handful to feed thousands. With a mere word, He had cast out legions of demons. He controlled the weather and walked on water. He had raised the dead. After all this, it wasn't enough. As He hung on the cross, they asked yet again for a sign: "Come down now from the cross and we will believe."[3]

They were blind to the greatest miracle of all, hanging before their eyes: the miracle of humiliation, of utter submission to the will of God.[4] It took a greater miracle to keep Jesus on the cross than it would've been to come down. We preach—not the exaltation of power—but the power of humility.[5]

The crucifixion of Christ is foolishness also to those who seek eloquence and sophistry. The crucifixion is a harsh, brutal statement that closes the door to all debate. It exposes us, bares the ugly truth of our nature: all our eloquence and reasoning have nothing to offer to negotiate with God.

For those who are like the Jews, demanding confirmation of the truth through yet another miraculous sign, Christ crucified *is* the miracle they seek. Those who humble themselves to obedience will know what is and is not of God.[6] For those who are like the Greeks, relying on logic, reason, and eloquent debate?[7] God's wisdom is the wisdom of paradox; it runs counter to all we think we know.

What will it take for you to believe? The proof of the gospel is Christ crucified. The power of the gospel is the crucified raised again.[8] Let's live like that.

All our eloquence and reasoning
have nothing to offer to negotiate with God.

---

[1]John 6:29–30   [2]Luke 16:31   [3]Mark 15:32   [4]Matt. 26:39, 42   [5]James 4:10   [6]John 7:17
[7]Acts 17:21   [8]Rev. 1:18

NOVEMBER 13

*This is what the Sovereign L*ORD *says: Woe to the foolish prophets*
who follow their own spirit and have seen nothing!
Ezekiel 13:3

*W*herever there is truth, there is the lie trying to confuse.[1] Wherever there are the real—the genuine—there are also the counterfeits.[2] We have been strongly warned that there *will* be many false Christs and false prophets,[3] especially as time winds down. There are some who teach that prophecy is no longer given to nor needed by believers, that the Bible contains all the revelation we will ever need. It *is* true that no new revelation will alter the path of salvation. We are redeemed from eternal death by faith in the blood Jesus shed on the cross and will rise to live forever with Him because *He* rose to live forever.[4] There will never be a new truth that makes a different way available.[5]

But that is not all that prophesying includes. God used prophecy to warn the early church about a coming famine: a message for a group of people for a specific time to prepare them to deal with it.[6] He also used prophecy to tell two individuals what was about to happen to their lives.[7] This kind of prophesying is simply speaking God's words, His message, to a specific person or group of people to warn, to prepare,[8] to encourage, or to direct them in their specific situations. Many do this often without realizing the import of their actions. There are very severe consequences for declaring, "Thus says the Lord,"[9] for telling someone what God is supposedly saying to them about their situation without first prayerfully seeking God's will for that person.[10]

Jesus warned us that darkness does not like the light,[11] that people like to hear only what is soft and comfortable.[12] I need to hear the cold truth about myself, but I also have to fight the tendency to want to tell others only soothing messages. Whitewashing sin or deciding by myself what God's intentions are for someone else is, indeed, being a false prophet! I dare not declare, "God says . . ." when I am only following my own spirit and not diligently seeking the Holy Spirit.

Whitewashing sin or deciding by myself
what God's intentions are for someone else is,
indeed, being a false prophet!

---

[1]John 8:43–45 [2]Matt. 7:15–16 [3]Mark 13:21–22 [4]John 14:6 [5]Acts 4:12 [6]Acts 11:27–29
[7]Acts 5:1–11 [8]Ezek. 13:5 [9]Jer. 8:10–12 [10]Ezek. 13:9 [11]John 3:19–20 [12]Isa. 30:9–11

NOVEMBER 14

And though the city will be handed over to the Babylonians,
you, O Sovereign LORD, say to me,
'Buy the field with silver and have the transaction witnessed.'
Jeremiah 32:25

*I*n the place of turmoil, disaster, and destruction, Jesus speaks. Whenever it appears that all is lost, trust in Him. No one takes a limo ride to heaven. We all must endure many troubles before we enter the kingdom of God.[1] Sometimes suffering is to test us,[2] refine us, and purify our faith.[3] Jesus warned us about this kind of suffering—persecution from a world diametrically opposed to God, darkness that hates the light, evil that detests righteousness. "By standing firm you will gain life," He promised.[4]

But the suffering the Jews endured at the hand of Babylon was not a result of their righteousness—not by far. It was punishment for their persistent disobedience.[5] Chastisement from the Lord is hard to bear. Not only do we struggle with a guilty conscience, but we must endure His displeasure.[6] Jeremiah had spent his entire prophetic career pleading with his people to turn from their sins, warning them of judgment to come. His heart broke as his message was repeatedly rejected[7] because he knew that punishment would be as devastating as it was inevitable. They would be invaded, conquered, ruined, and exiled.[8] The northern kingdom of Israel had already been destroyed by the Assyrians, and now the southern kingdom of Judah—stubborn and unrepentant—was to be wiped out, taken in chains, captive to Babylon.

Their sin was so deep, their rebellion so profound, their repentance so unforeseeable, that Jeremiah despaired. God's anger was aroused—thoroughly justified—but would He completely destroy them?[9] Was there no hope?

God's reassurance that He would one day turn again to them in mercy and restore them in spite of themselves almost made him laugh.[10] Even as Babylon laid siege to Jerusalem,[11] God told him to go and buy a field and save the deed—it would one day be valuable again!

Have you, too, sinned greatly? Are you somewhere in exile, despairing that God will not receive you? Take heart. In the midst of His discipline, return to Him, and He will restore you. He will never forsake you.[12]

In the midst of His discipline . . .

return to Him, and He will restore you.

---

[1]John 16:33   [2]Rev. 2:10   [3]1 Pet. 1:6–7   [4]Luke 21:19   [5]Jer. 32:17–24   [6]Heb. 12:5–11   [7]Jer 6:10
[8]Jer. 6:6–8   [9]Jer. 44:11   [10]Jer. 32:15   [11]Jer. 32:1–2   [12]Heb. 13:5

NOVEMBER 15

Do I have any power to help myself . . . ?
Job 6:13

One of the side effects of understanding exactly how little *nothing* is, as in "By myself I can do nothing,"[1] is a profound sense of gratitude. When I realize that without the Spirit He gives me, I would crumble into dust,[2] I learn to look to Him to wake me, to stand me on my feet, to draw breath. "Thank you, Father," comes more readily to my lips for everything, from good news received to the fact that my heart is beating today. When we really get the revelation of this, we start looking to Him for everything. And then, finally, our Holy Spirit schooling can begin.

It's a good thing God has mega-patience, because getting us to this point must be something like watching a five-year old trying to assemble a 5,000-piece jigsaw puzzle and refusing all help: "I can do it myself!" It's not hard to figure out that some pieces will end up missing, others mangled, and if any two are actually connected correctly, it'll be purely accidental.

It is pride that gets in the way of acknowledging our dependency—who wants to admit such helplessness?[3] God has ways of demonstrating our helplessness, however.[4] For Pharaoh, who dared to think himself a god, the Lord showed him how little power he had over his land, his possessions, his health, and his loved ones.[5] For Nebuchadnezzar, who boasted of his great Babylon, God showed him he not only couldn't keep his throne, but he couldn't even keep his sanity on his own.[6] Those who walk in pride, He is able to humble.[7]

The lessons need not be so traumatic, though. God would prefer that we simply listened to His gentle nudges, His quiet reminders of who is on the throne.[8] When we stop making decisions and forging ahead without seeking God,[9] we will avoid a lot of missed turns, wrecks, and dead ends. Our lives will work better, and God will no longer be hindered from blessing us like He wants to.[10]

When you really get revelation,
you start looking to God for everything.

---

[1]John 5:30 [2]Eccl. 12:7 [3]2 Chron. 20:12 [4]2 Chron. 25:8 [5]Exod. 12:31–33 [6]Dan. 4:31–34
[7]Dan. 4:37 [8]Lam. 3:33 [9]James 4:13–16 [10]1 Pet. 5:5–6

NOVEMBER 16

You know the way to the place where I am going.
John 14:4

*J*esus was going home. Not to Nazareth, not to Bethlehem, but *home*. Jesus was on His way to glory. And He said we would follow Him—not now, but later.[1] He said we know the way.

The way to glory, to heaven, is not a smooth and easy road. The streets of heaven may be paved with gold, but the road to glory is paved in blood, sweat and many tears. It is the way of suffering, the way of great sacrifice. Just days earlier, as some Greeks asked to see Jesus, our Lord cried out in the Spirit, "The hour has come for the Son of Man to be glorified."[2] The glory He spoke of was only to be found as He surrendered Himself to His Father's will; as He let His life fall to the ground and die—a seed that would bear much fruit. Jesus was given a vision of great joy, a vision of bringing many sons to glory.[3] The path to that joy led through the cross.[4]

We, too, have been given a vision of great joy: a place in the Father's house prepared especially for us by the hands of Jesus Himself,[5] a hint of its glory laid out in living color, recorded by John.[6] A place of unspeakable joy, to which Jesus will carry us on the clouds, accompanied by all the angels of heaven.[7]

The path to that joy leads only through the cross.

If we want the glory, we must lay down our life.[8] For some, that means death. For others, torture and pain. For all, it means sacrifice.[9] For *you*, it may mean the loss of all your earthly possessions.[10] Your sacrifice may be your comfort, your security, your safety, your reputation. We are called to follow Jesus, who had no place to lay His head.[11] We are called to glorify God and to walk as Jesus did.[12]

Jesus walked through crowds who wanted to throw Him off a cliff, to stone Him, to crucify Him. Jesus walked through this world misunderstood, hated, betrayed. Jesus walked loving those who rejected Him, healing their sick, sharing His bread with the ones who would scream for His blood, washing the feet of the one who had sold Him.

We know the way to where Jesus was going. It is the way of the cross.

We are called to glorify God and walk as Jesus did.

---

[1]John 13:36   [2]John 12:23–26   [3]Heb. 2:10   [4]Heb. 12:2   [5]John 14:4   [6]Rev. 21, 22   [7]Mark 13:26–27   [8]1 John 3:16   [9]Heb. 11:35–38   [10]Luke 14:33   [11]Luke 9:58   [12]1 John 2:6

NOVEMBER 17

You are the light of the world. . . .
Matthew 5:14

Light does not exist so you can look at it. No one turns on a lamp in order to look at the lamp. Light, when taken out from under its bushel and set upon a stand, is not supposed to jump up and down, saying, "Look at me! Look at me!"[1] Light exists so you can see something else.

I am the light of the world. If I let my light shine the way the world's light shines, I attract attention to myself. Those who look at *me* and are attracted to *me*–who admire me, flatter me, and follow me[2]–are like moths fluttering uselessly around a flame that can never feed them and will only end up frying them.

I must realize, of course, that the same Jesus who said, "You are the light of the world," also said, "I am the light of the world."[3] How can it be both? Who is the light? I am the light–only so long as it is Jesus who is shining through me.[4] Moths never try to fly at the sun; only at some dim-bulb imitation. The more moths I have flapping around me, the more my light is just me and not Jesus.[5]

When it stops being about me, then God can use me.[6] Where is a light needed? *In a dark place.* (Stars shine brightest at night.) That's why Jesus said, "My prayer is not that you take them out of the world."[7] He needs us to be separate from the world, but still in and amongst it; not hermits, but helpers. There are lots of lost souls stumbling around in the dark. Am I willing to be put on a shelf in a dark place–in a literal hellhole–to be the exit light for others? Or will I cry, "Why me?" and refuse to be a light bearer? A light bearer sets aside his comfort in order to fulfill his commission. "Go . . ."[8]

If I go, I must shine in such a way that God gets the glory. My light lets people see *Jesus*, not me. Like a flashlight lights up the path in front, I must shine mine forward, on the way.[9] The light shows the way to God, the way of God, and highlights *His* work.[10] I'll know that I'm shining my light right when people praise God for what they see, not me.[11]

When it stops being about me,

then God can use me.

---

[1]Matt. 23:5   [2]Acts 8:9–11   [3]John 8:12   [4]John 14:10, 20   [5]Luke 11:34   [6]John 12:23–24
[7]John 17:15   [8]Mark 16:15   [9]Ps. 119:105   [10]Matt. 5:16   [11]Luke 3:4–6

NOVEMBER 18

. . . this happened so that the work of God might be displayed in his life.
John 9:3

Job had a lot of friends. You can find them everywhere, especially when you are suffering. These are they who do not like an unanswered "Why?" They must find a reason for your pain, no matter how painful their reasoning may be—or how wrong. The disciples, trained by a religious tradition that taught that all suffering was a direct result of personal sin, came up against a knotty problem: a man born blind.[1] If suffering were the sufferer's own fault, could this man have sinned in the womb? Or was the parent's sin being visited upon his unfortunate head? Why was very important; *blame* was the issue.[2]

But Jesus brushed aside the whole question of cause, instead pointing to the *purpose*: "That the work of God may be displayed in his life."

Jesus was concerned about the disciples' response—our response—to the suffering around us.[3] Suffering is not a matter of intellectual or theological debate. Suffering is a matter of compassion.[4] We are to do God's work[5] so the mercy and grace of our Father may be displayed.

But what about those whose suffering *is* because they have sinned? What if they *are* under the judgment of God, experiencing the consequences of disobedience?[6] Won't our help actually be enabling unrepentance?[7] We cannot know the right action on our own. God alone knows why someone suffers, and He knows the perfect response. If we consistently seek His will, He will tell us when and how to help. We will truly be His hands and His heart to those around us.

All suffering, no matter the cause, can serve the purpose of displaying the work of God if we submit to His Word and allow Him to heal us. Jesus first had to do a work in the man,[8] then the man had to cooperate and obey. If he had just sat there complaining of the unfairness of his lot,[9] and demanding to know why it had happened—why God had let it happen—he would have remained blind—and a beggar.

Is there suffering around us? Let us respond with compassion and do the work of God. Are *you* suffering?[10] Listen to Jesus, submit,[11] and let His work be displayed in you.

We are to do God's work so the mercy and grace
of our Father may be displayed.

---

[1]John 9:1–2 [2]Prov. 3:30 [3]Heb. 13:3 [4]Matt. 9:35–36 [5]John 9:4 [6]Job 22:4–5 [7]Prov. 19:19 [8]Lam. 3:39 [9]Job 7:1–11 [10]Job 2:10 [11]Job 42:1–6

NOVEMBER 19

John's baptism—where did it come from?
Was it from heaven, or from men? . . .
Matthew 21:25

*M*iracles, signs, and wonders,[1] messages, and messengers:[2] which are from God, and which are only from men? There is *so much* at stake.[3] I don't want to be fooled and end up following what turns out to have only been a fad or worse.[4] How do I evaluate such things? How do I discern the real hand behind events?

When the religious leaders confronted Jesus with their, "Who do you think you are?" attitude, Jesus confronted them right back with a soul-exposing question. *Not once* in their debate did they ever ask, "What is the truth?" They were not interested in the truth. They were not seeking God. All they considered was how the answer would affect their position of power.[5]

I can clearly see *their* error, but am *I* really any different? When I encounter a teaching, do I truly seek God's heart concerning it, or do I only look at how following it might disrupt my life?[6] Obedience is always costly. Something of this world dies with every step toward God. If I am too attached to this world, obedience looks very much like losing.[7] I would not want to risk the changes that doing things God's way requires. *True* obedience flows from loving God.[8] The religious leaders did not love God, did not want God. Jesus had nothing for them.

But obedience, though costly, is also unimagineably rewarding. Something of heaven comes alive in me with every step I walk with God.[9] A heart at peace with God is *so* precious, nothing in this world is worth risking it.[10] Through all my years of learning to walk with Jesus, I am convinced that *God's ways work. The kingdom of heaven is real.*

How do I discern what is and what is not from God? Jesus said that those who really want to do the will of God will know.[11]

When I encounter a teaching, do I truly seek God's heart concerning it?

---

[1]Matt. 24:24   [2]Matt. 11:9–11   [3]Matt. 12:24–32   [4]Rev. 13:13–17   [5]Matt. 21:25–27   [6]Luke 19:1–9
[7]James 4:4   [8]John 14:15, 21   [9]Luke 17:21   [10]Luke 19:42–44   [11]John 7:17

NOVEMBER 20

*Take my yoke upon you and learn from me, for I am gentle
and humble in heart, and you will find rest for your souls.*
Matthew 11:29

*R*est! Sweet, glorious rest! We know we love it. That snooze button is nearly worn off our alarm clocks. Face it, life is tiring. It takes a lot of work. It may sound like a paradox, but life drains the life out of you! No wonder Jesus' invitation to rest is appealing.[1]

But if Jesus promised us rest, why are so many believers struggling to exhaustion? Why do so many complain that the way of Christ is so hard? Jesus said, "My yoke is easy and my burden is light."[2] It was not just Jesus saying one of those nice-but-impossible things that we've written off a lot of His teachings as. John said it, too: "His commands are not burdensome."[3] Those are the words of someone who flows in supernatural rest, someone who has submitted himself to Jesus' yoke-exchange program.

That's the real reason some have not experienced that deep-down, unshakable soul rest of Jesus: we have not taken His yoke upon us. We have not learned from Him. We insist on carrying our old, familiar yoke—the yoke of *our* strength, *our* thoughts, *our* ways.

You will never find rest without radical change.[4] "Let the wicked forsake his way and the evil man his thoughts. Let him turn to the LORD, and he will have mercy on him, and to our God, for he will freely pardon. For my thoughts are not your thoughts, neither are your ways my ways."[5] I have tried to do things my way. Look where it has gotten me. I tried to think it through, tried to figure out how it's all supposed to work, but I'd been learning on my own understanding.[6] God said the way that seems right to a man leads straight to death.[7] Doing it *my* way, by *my* strength, is foolish, because He is so much stronger than I am. He is the source of all strength.[8]

Stop. Let's put down our old yoke and take *His* yoke. Let us learn from Him: how to think like He thinks and work like He works, with all His powerful presence working in us.[9] We will find rest for our souls.

You will never find rest without radical change.

---

[1]Heb. 4:1   [2]Matt. 11:30   [3]1 John 5:3   [4]Matt. 18:3   [5]Isa. 55:7–8   [6]Prov. 3:5   [7]Prov. 14:12
[8]Isa. 28:6   [9]John 14:10

NOVEMBER 21

Ignoring what they said, Jesus told the synagogue ruler,
"Don't be afraid; just believe."
Mark 5:36

*I*n the military, it is standard procedure to obey the last order given. Until a different order is issued, you are to continue to press on in pursuit of your last command. Circumstances and conditions do not change that.[1]

What an awesome principle for believers in Christ to follow! If God's Word is our marching orders, then who has the authority to countermand it? What God has said must be taken to heart as the last word on the matter,[2] the last command given. Since the order has been given, we are to press on in pursuit of that purpose until it comes to pass in our lives, and nothing—not circumstances, conditions, or obstacles—is to change our minds.[3]

Jesus operated from this principle. A storm on the lake didn't stop Him from reaching the other side;[4] the fickleness of popular opinion didn't change His teachings;[5] the threats of King Herod didn't make Him run and hide. He told the bearers of doom, "Go tell that fox, 'I will drive out demons and heal the sick today and tomorrow, and on the third day I will reach my goal.'"[6]

That's what He was telling Jairus, the synagogue ruler. "I have promised to heal your daughter, and I will. It does not matter *whatever* happens between that promise and its fulfillment—no change in circumstances, no worsening of conditions and no bad reports can stop My promises from coming to pass. Not even death. *But you must believe I will do what I promised I will do."* And Jairus' daughter lived.

That principle has not changed. God's promises have not changed.[7] His Word to you is His last order given. Obey it. Spend yourself to your last breath obeying it, never yielding, never conceding to the enemy's onslaught of propaganda: sudden calamities, adverse conditions, contradictory circumstances. God will not change His order,[8] because He said though heaven and earth pass away, His words would never pass away.[9] Follow your last order given!

God's Word to you is His last order given. Obey it!.

---

[1]John 16:33   [2]Matt. 4:4   [3]John 9:4   [4]Matt. 8:18–26   [5]John 2:23–25   [6]Luke 13:32   [7]Num. 23:19
[8]1 Sam. 15:29   [9]Matt. 24:35

NOVEMBER 22

Do not let your hearts be troubled. Trust in God; trust also in me.
John 14:1

This has been a season of upheaval in my life: many changes, rumors of changes, speculation, and uncertainty.[1] My expectations, routines–especially my comfort zone–have been threatened. Temptation presses down on me to give into fear, dread, and worry.[2] "Panic! Lose sleep over this!" it yells.[3]

How easy it would be to give in, since everyone around me has been indulging in doom and gloom–and asking for my opinions on it all.[4] Basically inviting me to join in the seething pot of discontent and despair. When the first rumor broke, my heart clenched up in dread. "If this is true, I'll lose my job. . . ."[5]

Instantly, Jesus was there. "Do I not rule in your life?" He asked.[6] Did I trust Him? Did I really believe that nothing touches my life that He has not designed or permitted[7]–all for my benefit and His glory?[8]

When Jesus said, "Do not let your hearts be troubled," the disciples' world was about to be turned upside-down far more than merely challenging their comfort zones. But Jesus insisted, "Trust in God; trust also in me." Would I let my heart be troubled, or could I trust Jesus with my life, even in the uncertainty?

Well, why not? If I didn't, why even bother following Him? The instant I chose to trust and not worry, His peace settled on me like a comforter fresh and warm from the dryer.[9] Yes, I want to grow in Jesus, to become more like Him. This *requires* me moving out of my comfort zone. I decided to embrace the changes as challenges to grow my character, to draw closer to my Jesus. And it actually did become a joyful thing![10] I even got to share the source of my peace with others.[11]

Yes, I lost my job. But God gave me another one, better than the first. And the other changes? Not really pretty, but pretty good at helping me to keep my eyes on Jesus and not on this world.

Could I trust Jesus with my life,
even in the uncertainty?

[1]Ps. 112:7–8 [2]Isa. 8:12–13 [3]Ps. 127:2 [4]Prov. 18:2 [5]Matt. 7:25–34 [6]John 13:13 [7]Ps. 55:22 [8]John 17:9–12 [9]John 14:27 [10]James 1:2–4 [11]1 Pet. 3:15

NOVEMBER 23

"But what about you?" he asked. "Who do you say I am?"
Matthew 16:15

An old television game show offered its top prize for whoever could correctly answer "the $64,000 question." It was popular enough that it became a catchphrase for any piercingly pivotal question. To win $64,000 for trivial knowledge is fortunate, but if you missed it, at least you were no worse off than before you started.

To miss *this* question, however, is far more costly than missing a mere $64,000.[1] This is not a matter of trivia. Upon my answer hangs my destiny. Every single soul that has ever lived will be asked this question. I have already been asked it; and I will continue to be asked it for the rest of my life.[2]

The world would have us think it is multiple choice, and it offers only these options: a) a good man, b) a great moral teacher, c) a prophet, d) a sincere but deceived fool, e) a madman, or f) all of the above. Jesus offers none of the above. He never intended for it to be anything but a full-contact essay question.[3]

When we are asked the question, what we say counts for only a fraction of our grade.[4] The full-contact part is more intensely evaluated. My life is my essay. What I really believe about Jesus is written with the days of my existence.[5] Who Jesus is to me is revealed by my actions, my fruit.[6] Words only go so far. Even Peter, who was blessed by divine revelation from the Father in heaven to be able to confess that Jesus is the Christ, the Son of the Living God,[7] later used that same mouth to utterly deny even knowing Him.[8] His life, however, revealed his true answer; he repented, and served his Lord even unto death.

What about you? Who do you say Jesus is? No—don't tell me. I would rather read your answer in your life. Write it carefully, for all of heaven is reading your answer, too. And the prize for answering correctly is worth so much more than $64,000.[9]

---

*What you really believe about Jesus is written
with the days of your existence.*

---

[1]Heb. 12:25   [2]Exod. 5:2   [3]John 8:24   [4]Matt. 7:21   [5]Matt. 23:3   [6]Matt. 3:8   [7]Matt. 16:16
[8]Matt. 26:72   [9]Heb. 11:26

NOVEMBER 24

How can I curse those whom God has not cursed?...
Numbers 23:8

*T*here are supernatural forces involved in our lives every day, and many of them are not benevolent. Jesus warned us of war in heaven and of an enemy as strong as a dragon making war against us![1] All of the subtle powers of darkness are arrayed against us, and the enemy knows well how to demonstrate his power to deceive. He performs miracles, signs, and wonders all the time,[2] feeding the greed and ambition of those who crave power without submission to God. The power of many false religions includes spells to control or curse others.

Should we fear them? Some who have grown up around Voodoo, Santeria, Wicca, and other such religions have seen the power of darkness work. They remember, and they take care to burn or flush away their nail clippings, shed hair, or other such remnants, for fear that the enemy might have access to them through these.

While the enemy's power is real and we should be aware of his strength, we should never forget that the Greater One lives in us,[3] and if we trust in God, what can mortal man do to us?[4] He is our protection, our shield,[5] against all the enemy's devices and his schemes. We bear Jesus' name, and we carry His divinely given authority to trample on snakes and scorpions and to overcome all the power of the enemy.[6]

Our defense is not to hide our vulnerabilities and weakness from the enemy, our defense is to overcome our weakness with God's strength.[7] When we remain in Christ,[8] we are tuned in to the Spirit, who keeps us alert to the plots of the enemy. He can try, but if we pay attention and do as God directs, Satan cannot frustrate God's purpose. Jesus promised that the enemy cannot harm us when we are operating in His authority.[9] That is why the devil prowls around like a roaring lion;[10] he is trying to panic us into disobedience so he can devour us.

No one can curse those whom God has not cursed. If we dwell in the shelter of the Most High and abide in the shadow of the Almighty,[11] we are blessed—and no power of earth or darkness can curse us.

---

*Our defense is to overcome our weakness
with God's strength.*

---

[1]Rev. 12:7–9, 17   [2]Matt. 24:24   [3]1 John 4:4   [4]Ps. 56:4   [5]1 Pet. 1:5   [6]Luke 10:19   [7]Isa. 40:29–31
[8]John 15:4   [9]1 John 5:18   [10]1 Pet. 5:8   [11]Ps. 91:1

NOVEMBER 25

. . . Everything is possible for him who believes.
Mark 9:23

*T*he phrase "I can't" is the greatest enemy of change. Everything else, including knowledge, skill, resources, environment, regulations, and opportunity, can be overcome. The attitude of failure cannot. I used to have a picture on my wall of Dustin Carter, a high school wrestling champion with an awesome record of 41 wins and only 2 losses. His record, though inspiring, was not the reason his picture was on my wall. I don't like sports, but Dustin Carter challenged me every time I saw his photo. You see, Dustin Carter is a quadruple amputee. Due to a blood infection at age 5, his legs were amputated at mid-thigh and his arms just above the elbow. On his picture I had written in bold letters, "No excuses!"

The world has discovered the power in positive thinking. Most millionaires, sports champions, and great artists have used it to achieve fantastic goals. The concept is not new at all, however. In the spiritual realm, it is called *faith*. Faith in Jesus Christ is far more powerful than even the world's most successful version of positive self-talk. Natural "I can do it!" optimism is still limited to what is within man.[1] Faith takes the limited ability of man and floods it with the unlimited power of an omnipotent God.

The *everything* in "everything is possible" is absolutely unlimited. When we believe God, when we have faith in Christ, we can do whatever He calls us to do. Though we face opposition and obstacles, He will fight our battles[2] and make a way through.[3] Even the miraculous is not out of reach.[4] There is no such thing as impossible for the one who looks to the strength of Jesus Christ.[5] The evil one cannot touch us or harm us.[6] Through faith in Jesus, we will survive even death!

Success is guaranteed for the one who does everything through Christ.[7] He'll teach us what we need to know, renew our strength,[9] and provide every single thing we will need to accomplish our task.[10] He is not bound by time or place, nor is He limited in resources. If we believe Him, trust Him, and get out of His way, He'll even step in and do it for us, in us, through us.[11]

There are no excuses. *Everything* is possible for me when I believe in Him.

Success is guaranteed for the one
who does everything through Christ.

---

[1]Job 6:13   [2]Josh. 23:10   [3]Ps. 77:19–20   [4]Matt. 10:8   [5]Luke 1:37   [6]1 John 5:18   [7]Ps. 1:3
[8]1 John 2:27   [9]Ezek. 34:16   [10]Matt. 6:33   [11]John 14:10–12

NOVEMBER 26

Do not withhold good from those who deserve it,
when it is in your power to act.
Proverbs 3:27

*S*ome of the most condemning skeletons in our closets are not the things we did, but the things we did *not* do. Our darkest corners are piled with the bones of good intentions unfulfilled. Many of those were not just nice ideas we came up with on our own; where is it really in man to do good?[1] Those bones are the remains of times God wanted to love someone through us, times His Holy Spirit nudged us to be kind, generous, and faithful. Times we may have even agreed to do what was asked–but never quite got around to it.[2]

Those bones are our secret sins of omission, the good we knew to do and did not do.[3] To be sure, it is harder to hide something I actually did than it is to hide the fact I allowed a good deed to slip by me. Some sins are blatant, obvious to all in their doing. But things that are not done are easier to hide, to keep secret.[4] Most of us are not conscious of how many of these secret sins are shadowing behind us. Many are not even aware that these missed opportunities *are* sins.

Those of us who struggle with procrastination need to beware![5] The dust cloud kicked up by the load we drag can choke the Holy Spirit's voice right out of our life. "Every good and perfect gift is from above."[6] Those "thoughts of good and not of evil"[7] do not come from man, but from the Father of the heavenly lights. It is the Spirit of Christ in us, thinking the thoughts of Christ[8] and speaking those thoughts into our spirit. To think to do good, to be presented with an opportunity to do good, is to hear the voice of God speaking to us.

God tells us there will be a time for every activity, a time for every deed.[9] To put it off is to miss that divinely designed moment of maximum impact. We need to be alert and notice the need around us. I don't want to stand before Jesus Christ one day with nothing to lay at His feet but a reminder of all the opportunities He presented . . . and I missed.

The only cure is prayerful action.[10] Do the good that God has spoken to you *today*.

Our darkest corners are piled with the bones
of good intentions, unfulfilled.

---

[1]Jer. 13:23   [2]Matt. 21:30   [3]James 4:17   [4]Ps. 90:8   [5]Heb. 4:7   [6]James 1:17   [7]Jer. 29:11
[8]John 16:14   [9]Eccl. 3:17   [10]Ps. 119:60

NOVEMBER 27

A prudent man keeps his knowledge to himself,
but the heart of fools blurts out folly.

Proverbs 12:23

*N*obody likes a know-it-all. It's aggravating when he doesn't, but it's unbearable when he does. People discredit the one and brush off the other. In either case, such arrogance is deceptive and divisive,[1] because nobody but God truly knows all. And He does not flaunt or parade the fact that He is omniscient, nor does He rub our faces in the fact that we're not.[2]

Proverbs tells us that love covers over all wrongs.[3] A sensitive heart makes for a silent tongue—because it considers the feelings of others before it speaks.[4] Everybody at one time or another has walked up on an unflattering conversation about himself. We are all well aware of the shock of that pain in our soul.[5] Love thinks about not only the possible effects of its words but its motivation as well. Love asks itself, "Why do I feel the need to say this? What is my purpose?" It also asks, "How would I feel if someone else said this about me?" We would do well to heed a doctor's Hippocratic oath that says, "First, do no harm."

There is other knowledge besides gossip that is not always wise to spill.[6] It is interesting to see how often Jesus did not directly answer questions,[7] preferring instead to help the questioner discover the answer himself or to turn the tables on their motives. Too often, we are eager to tell what we know, because we want to impress people. That is very shaky ground; it's easy to play pride's game of one-upmanship. It is too full of self-interest and therefore cannot be love, because love is considerate of others[8] and constantly seeks to build them up.[9] Love is humble,[10] able to concede that it may be mistaken, that another may have better knowledge. It is able to share the spotlight.

A truly wise person also knows you rarely learn while you're talking. If you are silent and listen,[11] you may add to your knowledge, and you will add a friend.

A truly wise person knows
you rarely learn while you're talking.

---

[1]James 3:15–16   [2]James 1:5   [3]Prov. 10:12   [4]Matt. 7:12   [5]Eccl. 7:21–22   [6]Eccl. 3:7   [7]Luke 20:2–8
[8]James 3:17   [9]Heb. 3:13   [10]1 Pet. 3:8   [11]James 1:19

NOVEMBER 28

It is the glory of God to conceal a matter;
to search out a matter is the glory of kings.

Proverbs 25:2

"*I* want you to want me,"* the lyrics of a classic rock song cry out. Who would have thought that the world could echo so well the heart-cry of our heavenly Father? Yes, we are created by Him and for Him, and with eternity planted deeply in our hearts,[1] ". . . O Lord, . . . our heart is restless until it finds its rest in You,"** as a man named Augustine of Hippo once said. So why is He so elusive? Why is He a God who hides Himself?[2]

Oh, He could dissolve the heavens, roll up the sky like a scroll,[3] and step down from His throne onto the earth amid thunder, lightning, and heart-stopping trumpet blasts, making every eye see him,[4] and all would have to confess that He is real, He is Lord, and bow before Him.[5] And one day, He will do just that. So, why not now?

Because who wants forced acknowledgment? Who wants lip service only and not heartfelt devotion? "I want you to want Me." Therefore, He has concealed the whole matter and has engaged us in a game of hide and seek, a scavenger hunt of cosmic and eternal proportions. We are treasure seekers compelled by an ancient tale,[6] armed with a cryptic map, following clues to a fortune beyond our wildest imaginations.[7]

Our God goes before us, leaving a trail of hints, whispering encouragements, rewarding the diligent pursuers as they draw closer and closer to the truth.[8] The half-hearted don't make it. The hunt is too demanding, the effort required is more than they imagine the reward is worth. But for those who hunger and thirst for God,[9] who really *want* Him, the search becomes a divine dance, a sacred courtship. Each new piece of the puzzle, though found and fitted through blood and tears, is filled with holy joy, the laughter and delight of our God sharing glimpses of His glory.[10] He is not running away from us; He is drawing us into fuller and deeper revelations of Him.

We are His priests and kings, and it is our glory to search Him out. "You will seek me and find me when you seek me with all your heart. I will be found by you."[11]

The half-hearted seekers of God don't make it.
The hunt is too demanding.

---

[1]Eccl. 3:11 [2]Isa. 45:15 [3]Isa. 34:4 [4]Rev. 1:7 [5]Isa. 45:23 [6]Jer. 6:16 [7]Isa. 65:17–25 [8]Heb. 11:6
[9]Matt. 5:6 [10]Exod. 33:18–20 [11]Jer. 29:13–14 */**Biblio. p. 386

NOVEMBER 29

Look to my right and see; no one is concerned for me.
I have no refuge; no one cares for my life.
Psalm 142:4

*N*o wonder they call depression that *down* feeling—you get it from looking down instead of up. Looking down means you're not lifting your eyes to where your help truly comes from. When all your hopes are built on man, prepare to be disappointed. Man will fail you: "Can a mother forget the baby at her breast and have no compassion on the child she has borne? Though she may forget, I will not forget you!"[1]

Our God is a jealous God.[2] "I am the LORD; that is my name! I will not give my glory to another or my praise to idols."[3] If you have been looking to the right or the left for your comfort and strength,[4] you have been looking in the wrong direction.[5] Our Father is the Wonderful Counselor,[6] and He will not allow us to place our confidence in weak, undependable flesh any more than we would allow our child to cross a deep gorge on a paper bridge. It would collapse out from under him when he needs it most.

Man is not our comfort and our strength, our helper, our answer, or our provider. He is not the one to go to when the going gets tough. Man does not open doors for us; he cannot bless us. Man is limited in knowledge; he does not know what is best for us, because he does not know the path chosen for us. Man is limited in ability; he cannot create the answer to our needs, nor can he change anyone's heart to show us favor. Man's love is severely limited; he is too bound up in his self-concern to be concerned about us. When it comes down to "me" or "you," man always chooses "me." With such a shaky foundation, no wonder looking down is depressing!

Look up! "I will not forget you," He said. "I will receive you.[7] Cast your cares on Me, *because I care for you.*[8] The details of your life matter to Me; I even keep count of the hairs on your head.[9] I know your needs; I will provide.[10] I am your refuge and your strength.[11] Call to Me and I will answer you."[12]

"I have loved you," says the Lord,[13] "and My love never fails."

Man is not your comfort and your strength, your helper,
your answer, or your provider.

---

[1]Isa. 49:15 [2]Exod. 34:14 [3]Isa. 42:8 [4]Ps. 69:20 [5]Prov. 4:27 [6]Isa. 9:6 [7]Ps. 27:10 [8]1 Pet. 5:7
[9]Matt. 10:30 [10]Matt. 6:32–33 [11]Ps. 46:1 [12]Jer. 33:3 [13]Mal. 1:2

NOVEMBER 30

I will hasten and not delay to obey your commands.
Psalm 119:60

*W*hat if God held us to the Golden Rule? What if He did to us as we did to Him? If He responded to us as quickly as we respond to Him? Throughout the Psalms, we cry out, "Come quickly to help me, O Lord my God."

We are not known for being quick to obey. Instead, the record shows that man has been quick to turn away,[1] quick to rush into evil,[2] quick to quarrel,[3] quick with our mouths,[4] and quick to flee.[5] All this haste, and we are missing the way.[6]

Speed is not the problem, however. The problem is direction. If we're headed in the right direction, why would we drag our feet? If God is all I say He is—if He is beauty, light, truth, holiness, love and life—why would I hesitate when He calls? If everything He does is good,[7] why would I wait to follow Him? If He truly is omniscient, knowing the end from the beginning (and everything in between),[8] why would I not seek His input on everything nor take His word as the last word on the matter? Why would I argue with God?

Only if I am not fully convinced of these things. Every hesitant *but* I utter or ponder is based on a fragment of doubt. There is a clinging, *what if?* fear that holds me back. What I say is only what I've heard or read or even want to believe, but it has not yet hit my heart as absolute, dependable truth.

The truth that God is good all the time, that He can be completely trusted in everything, with anything, is the truth that sets us free[9]—free from fear, dread, doubt and hesitation. We will run in the path of His commands, for He has set our heart free.[10] Nothing can hold back a heart sold out to all-consuming love. In His hands is the safest place to be; no one can touch us, harm us, snatch us away from His love[11] and from His life.

Delay is doubt. Faith hastens to obey His commands.

The truth that God is good all the time sets us free.

---

[1]Exod. 32:8   [2]Prov. 6:18   [3]Prov. 20:3   [4]Eccl. 5:2   [5]Jon. 4:2   [6]Prov. 19:2   [7]Ps. 119:68   [8]Isa. 46:10   [9]John 8:32   [10]Ps. 119:32   [11]John 10:28–29

DECEMBER 1

. . . but the Lamb will overcome them because He is Lord of lords and King of kings—and with him will be his called, chosen, and faithful followers
Revelation 17:14

"*M*any are called, but few are chosen."[1] Called to what? To acknowledge not only the existence of God, but His sovereignty—His divine right to rule. And we are called to surrender to His rule and follow Him, to let Him lead us out of darkness into light,[2] out of death into life.

Who are the many? Everyone, everywhere—whosoever in the whole world.[3] God does not want anyone to perish, but everyone to come to repentance.[4] No matter how they may deny it, everyone gets the call.[5]

But to be called is not enough. Actors responding to a casting call know that they must also be chosen—and just as actors do not do the choosing, Jesus reminds us, "You did not choose me, but I chose you."[6] What is the criteria? Thank God it is not by our appearance or performance! No, He chooses whoever believes in Him.[7]

But believing is more than just saying, "Yup, that's true," and going about our business as usual. *Believing* means believing in His call—to acknowledge, surrender to, and follow His divine right to rule our lives. This is where the *faithful* part comes in. Those who will be with the Lamb are those who have persevered,[8] who have faithfully sought His face (not just His hands), who have forsaken their ways for His ways and their thoughts for His thoughts.[9] Those who follow the Lord of lords and King of kings have heard (and heeded) His call to love Him with everything in us—all we have and all we are,[10] and to show that love by obeying Him.[11]

I have been called; am I chosen? And if I am chosen, am I faithful?

Believing means . . . to acknowledge, surrender to, and follow His divine right to rule our lives.

---

[1]Matt. 22:14 [KJV]   [2]1 Pet. 2:9   [3]Ps. 19:1–4   [4]2 Pet. 3:9   [5]Isa. 45:23–24   [6]John 15:16
[7]John 3:16, 36   [8]Heb. 10:36   [9]Isa. 55:7   [10]Mark 12:30   [11]John 14:15, 21

DECEMBER 2

How can a man be born when he is old? . . .

John 3:4

"Born again"[1] is a phrase so over-used, its transforming implications have been almost lost. I used to think that Nicodemus' question, "How can a man be born when he is old?" was one of those dumb questions that are not supposed to exist. But it raises a good point. If no one can see the kingdom of God unless he is born again (John 3:3), and no one can enter a second time into his mother's womb to be born, then is Jesus saying that the kingdom of God is only for after we die? Only for the next life?

But we know it is not. Jesus said, "The kingdom of God has come to you,"[2] and "The kingdom of God is within you."[3] He rebuked the religious leaders, saying, "The tax collectors and the prostitutes are entering the kingdom of God ahead of you."[4] What had they done that the Pharisees had not?

They had died. The truth is, you cannot be born when you are old. You have to die first. The word for this is *repent*. Repenting is not just changing your mind. It's more than changing trains when you realize you're going in the wrong direction. Repenting is much more drastic than that. Repenting means realizing that there is no cure for you:[5] "From the sole of your foot to the top of your head there is no soundness—only wounds and welts and open sores . . ."[6] Repenting is dying—dying with Christ, dying to sins and living for righteousness.[7]

Jesus explained to Nicodemus, "Flesh gives birth to flesh." He told the crowds, "The Spirit gives life; the flesh counts for nothing."[8] The trouble is, too many people are trying to be born again without dying, trying to patch up their lives by adding religion. They take "come as you are" to mean "stay as you are." Dying is scary. But Jesus reassures us, "I am the resurrection and the life. He who believes in me will live, even though he dies."[9] The life Jesus gives is born when we die to sin.

Don't be afraid; let go—die—you will not lose.

You cannot be born when you are old.
You have to die first. The word for this is repent.

---

[1]John 3:3–8   [2]Luke 11:20   [3]Luke 17:21   [4]Matt. 21:31   [5]Jer. 30:12–13   [6]Isa. 1:6   [7]1 Pet. 2:24
[8]John 6:63   [9]John 11:25

DECEMBER 3

*. . . you made a fatal mistake when you sent me to the LORD your God
and said, "Pray to the LORD our God for us;
tell us everything He says and we will do it."*

Jeremiah 42:20

The Israelites were guilty of an unfortunately common mistake. They had made their plans after the desires of *their* hearts, *then* asked the Lord to approve them.[1] Beware your strong desires! They can easily interfere with true submission to the will of God.[2] Strong desires can blind us to the leading of the Holy Spirit, and we will miss the revelation of God's plan for us.[3]

Seeking the Lord's will is not the last step. We need to remember that God's ways are higher than ours.[4] His point A to point B might take us through places and experiences we would never have imagined on our own. Often our greatest seasons of growth have come in ways we would never have chosen in our limited understanding,[5] and through people we would never have given a second thought to had we been left to our own devices and choices.[6]

"Didn't God promise to give us the desires of our hearts?"[7] some ask. Absolutely! But we must not skip over the condition on which that promise is based: "Delight yourself in the Lord." A soul that truly and fully delights itself in the Lord has learned that God can be trusted. That soul takes pleasure in letting God have His way, because he knows that God has a strength-to-strength[8] pilgrimage, custom designed to bring him through *every* trial, *every* test, and *every* trouble, *every* time! To such a one, submission is not a dreaded, heel-dragging must, but an amazing partnership and privilege. It is a constant surprise, yes,[9] but never a path we will regret. When we seek His will, remember: He is our Lord, not our consultant. Let's not make the mistake the Israelites made—when we ask, let's ask with a heart to do what He says.

---

*A soul that truly and fully delights itself in the Lord
has learned that God can be trusted.*

---

[1]2 Chron. 18:3–4   [2]James 4:13–15   [3]Ps. 25:12   [4]Isa. 55:6–9   [5]Ps. 66:10–12   [6]Isa. 28:11   [7]Ps. 37:4
[8]Ps. 84:5, 7   [9]Isa. 42:16

DECEMBER 4

*How beautiful on the mountains
are the feet of those who bring good news . . .*
Isaiah 52:7

The Gospel is good news—good news of great joy for all people.[1] It is rain to the drought stricken, sun to the darkness, seed to the sower, and bread to the eater.[2] It is cool healing to fevered brows; it is morning's light to the dark night of the soul. It is good news because it is conviction, not condemnation. Jesus did not come to condemn the world[3]—but He *did* send the Holy Spirit to convict the world of guilt.[4] Conviction of guilt is what makes the good news good—who needs a doctor except the sick?[5] The difference between condemnation and conviction is that one has only hopelessness and despair, and the other has a *solution*.

We are not the pointing finger of God, and we are not His gavel. We are ambassadors of the kingdom of light, messengers of the *unconditional* love of God; we bear *good news*! For those around us ensnared by Satan's schemes, held captive by their own evil choices,[6] we do not stand outside the bars jabbing them with the sword of the Lord—we offer them the key to freedom!

We, too, were the wounded, the sick, the dying.[7] We, too, were in that cage—our days like a shadow, without hope.[8] We know what that feels like, and we know how it feels to be free. We have been commissioned—not into a Holiness Police Patrol, but into the army of the Lord, His Special Forces Rescue Squad.[9] Just as Jesus' mission was to seek and to save the lost,[10] so is ours.

To the lost and dying around me, I will be merciful as my heavenly Father is merciful.[11] I will not delight in condemnation, but offer them hope. I will tell them the good news!

Let's all point to the Savior. Let's lift Him up, and He will draw their wounded souls to Him[12] that they may be saved. We will repay cursing with blessing and evil with good[13]—the good news of the gospel of Jesus Christ.

---

*The difference between condemnation and conviction
is that one has only hopelessness and despair,
and the other has a solution.*

---

[1]Luke 2:10 [2]Isa. 55:10 [3]John 3:17 [4]John 16:8 [5]Matt. 9:12 [6]James 1:13–15 [7]Ps. 14:2–3 [8]1 Chron. 29:15 [9]Jude 1:22–23 [10]Luke 19:10 [11]Luke 6:36 [12]John 12:32 [13]Luke 6:28

DECEMBER 5

Gather to me my consecrated ones,
who made a covenant with me by sacrifice.
Psalm 50:5

"*H*ow much easier it is to die for you, my love/for dying is an end, but living hurts a thousand times."* So reads an old poem, and its truth is hard. Many have wondered what it really means to worship the Lord "in spirit and in truth."[1] Worship from the spirit, in the Spirit, is much more than ecstatic praise, lifting the hands, laughing and crying, song and shout. Coming from the heart, all of these are ways to worship our great and awesome God, yes[2]—but true, complete, spiritual worship is sacrifice.[3]

From the beginning, deep gratitude and reverence always expressed itself in worship that bowed the worshipper to the ground.[4] It is an act of humility and submission, a servant to his Lord. We do not slaughter animals, nor do we lay bulls and goats upon an altar. But that does not mean we do not sacrifice. Our sacrifice today is not a sacrifice of guilt for forgiveness, not of blood, for the Blood of the Lamb is all-sufficient. No, today we offer the sacrifice of ourselves—*we* climb up on His altar and lay ourselves down.[5] It is bowing down to the Lord our Maker, surrendering our right to ourselves, our lives, our future.[6] We give them to Him to do with as He pleases—and it pleases Him to use us to love and serve others.[7]

My body—my strength, ability, even my presence—are no longer mine to do with as I please. I offer myself to Him to use me, send me, command me as He desires.[8] To my Sovereign Lord I kneel and vow, "Your wish is my command—and my highest honor and pleasure." This involves a continual bowing down of my will, because although it is easy to make such a vow, living it out requires great determination and commitment.[9]

That is sacrifice. And if my heart is right, when I have done all God has asked me to do, my attitude toward any hardship will be, "That? That was nothing. It was an honor. I only did my duty."[10]

It is easy to make a vow. Living it out
requires great determination and commitment.

---

[1]John 4:24   [2]Ps. 150:1–6   [3]Ps. 51:17   [4]Gen. 24:26   [5]Matt. 26:39   [6]1 Pet. 4:1–2   [7]Luke 22:26
[8]Isa. 6:8   [9]Eccl. 5:4–6   [10]Luke 17:7–10   *Biblio. p. 386

DECEMBER 6

I, even I, am he who comforts you. . . .
Isaiah 51:12

*H*ow tender and loving is our God,[1] how awesome is His mercy toward us! Although many times He gives us tough love, when we are truly broken and in pain,[2] His compassion is delicate, gentle, and supremely kind.[3] I cannot count the many times He has come and sat with me as I mourned a loss, often doing nothing else but letting me feel His presence.[4]

Man is uncomfortable in the presence of sorrow and suffering. We don't know what to say, and we are helpless to change or fix the situation. We feel impotent. But God is never uncomfortable around brokenness. Over and over again, the Bible tells us that God is close to the brokenhearted.[5] He doesn't rebuke us for our tears—He catches them in a bottle and remembers them.[6] He doesn't yell at us for being weak—He knows how we are formed, he remembers that we are dust.[7] He doesn't command us not to mourn; He only reminds us that those who mourn will be comforted.[8]

The greatest comfort God gives is the gift of His understanding presence. The hope that sustains us in our grief and mourning is the vision of eternal joy,[9] the certainty of that day when God will wipe away all tears from our eyes, and there will be no more sorrow, nor crying, nor pain.[10] We can take comfort and encouragement also in the knowledge that this—even this—God will use in wondrous ways for the triumph of good.[11] With this peace, reassurance, and compassion He gives us, we need never be uncomfortable around another's sorrow again, for He gives us an instructed tongue to know the word that sustains the weary.[12] We can share God's gift of comfort with the suffering.

---

*The greatest comfort God gives
is the gift of His understanding presence.*

---

[1]Hos. 2:14 [2]Ps. 51:17 [3]Isa. 40:11 [4]Lam. 3:55–57 [5]Ps. 34:18 [6]Ps. 56:8 [7]Ps. 103:14 [8]Matt. 5:4
[9]Heb. 12:2 [10]Rev. 21:4 [11]1 Pet. 1:6–7 [12]Isa. 50:4

DECEMBER 7

Do not repay evil with evil or insult with insult, but with blessing . . .
1 Peter 3:9

*H*ave you ever found yourself gritting your teeth at the thought of turning the other cheek? I know the meekness of blessing those who cursed me and praying for my persecutors frustrates me! And I used to argued, "God doesn't really expect me to do nothing at all when some-one wrongs me, does He?"

God is wiser than that at waging war. He loves us too much to leave us unarmed and naked[1] before an enemy as ruthless as the roaring lion we face.[2] He did not tell us to do *nothing*. He gave us specific weapons, specific strategies that are charged with all of God's power: His undefeatable, inside-out power that no evil can stand against.[3] I had resisted His commands, because I had not understood the power His ways unleash.[4] I had not used His weapons, because I had not realized that that is exactly what they are: weapons. I did not recognize them as the demon-destroying, evil-smashing, curse-blasting, sin-overcoming arsenal that they are until I had a chance to experience their true power.

Oh, if you could only see the damage done to the realm of darkness when we bless another! God showed me how much the devil writhes in agony when I forgive instead of hate, how he cries out in pain when I am kind and patient to those who are rude and ugly.[5] One word of peace spoken in love, one deed of selflessness drives back the darkness and advances the kingdom of light.

That's how Jesus fought evil. He actively blessed others[6] and went about doing good and healing all who were oppressed by the devil.[7]

Humility, kindness, mercy, gratitude, generosity, and—above all—love[8] are spiritual smart bombs. They are *incredibly* powerful weapons in the war against wickedness, sin, and evil. Goodness is not a doormat; goodness is a spiritual samurai—a Holy Ghost ninja warrior—demolishing Satan's strongholds. When we arm ourselves with God's weapons, with His ways, we will overcome evil with blessing.

Goodness is not a doormat;
goodness is a spiritual samurai,
demolishing Satan's strongholds.

---

[1]Heb. 13:21   [2]1 Pet. 5:8   [3]Matt. 16:18   [4]Isa. 55:8–11   [5]Luke 6:32–35   [6]Matt. 11:2–6   [7]Acts 10:38
[8]Matt. 7:12

DECEMBER 8

See to it that you do not refuse him who speaks. . . .
Hebrews 12:25

I was not raised to believe that God speaks to ordinary people.[1] Those who did claim to hear God were considered highly suspect: probably insane, certainly deluded. Then I encountered Jesus—and one word from Him changed my life.[2]

Yet I was a bit behind the eight ball. I had a lot of misunderstanding to overcome about how to hear from God beyond that one word. Reading the Bible for myself, I discovered that the Holy Spirit is given to us to teach us, correct us, guide us, remind us of everything Jesus said—*to speak to us*.[3] I watched others more experienced in the things of God, and I was on fire to hear from Jesus, too. The trouble was, I didn't know how to recognize His voice.[4] I wasn't even convinced He would speak to *me*.[5]

Overcoming my naïve expectations of what God's voice would sound like was the easy part. Scratch that thunderous basso voice coming from somewhere outside of myself. "The kingdom of God is within you."[6] God's Spirit speaks to my spirit within me.[7] He sounds like me inside me! And often, a picture is truly worth a thousand words. He speaks mostly in impressions and flashes of insight—not necessarily in English Composition 101 complete sentences.

Much more difficult was "getting it" in my heart. I didn't have to *get Him* to speak to me; He already was—and had been all along![8] Hearing from God requires faith—believing that He does, indeed, speak to me. Now that I understand that, it has become a matter of attention and obedience. Although God had been speaking, I hadn't paid attention.[9] I learned I have to *intentionally* listen. God speaks to a quieted and waiting spirit that seeks Him in prayer.[10]

And not to refuse him who speaks. Disobedience dulls my hearing. After all, *why* do I want to hear from God, except to do what He says?[11] Hearing from God is not about prestige, not a badge of spiritual honor. It is a life-or-death responsibility. This is not a game; this is *God*. I dare not refuse Him who speaks.

God speaks to a quieted and waiting spirit
that seeks Him in prayer.

---

[1]John 9:29 [2]Matt. 9:9 [3]John 14:26 [4]John 10:4–5 [5]2 Sam. 7:18–19 [6]Luke 17:21 [7]John 14:17 [8]Job 33:14 [9]Isa. 42:19–20 [10]Prov. 8:33–34 [11]Luke 6:46

DECEMBER 9

*Land that drinks in the rain often falling on it and that produces a crop
useful to those for whom it is farmed receives the blessing of God.*
Hebrews 6:7

Knowledge is a wonderful thing, but it is easy to get sidetracked pursuing it. Jesus held no theological degrees,[1] but He could stop cold the religious leaders of His day by his penetrating applications of Scripture.[2] The "religion" that Jesus lived was exactly that: lived, not argued. It was intensely practical.[3] He summed up all of the do's and don'ts, all of the rules and rituals of religion, with the simplicity of "love God and love your neighbor."[4] He defined eternal life as *knowing God.*[5]

Everything I strive to learn, to know, to understand about following Jesus, must be driven by these two things: to know God and to love. The more I learn, the deeper these two simple things become. As humans, we think we know so much. Jesus had to come down and show us what it's really all about. He went about doing good:[6] helping, healing, providing, rescuing. No one was unimportant; everyone was worth His time and attention.

Because He loved them in a hands-on kind of way, they listened to His words.[7] The saying is true: people don't care how much you know until they know how much you care. This is the fruit that is produced by one who knows God, who believes in Jesus, the One He has sent.[8] This is the fruit that Jesus has appointed us to bear.[9]

As I drink in knowledge, let me not get sidetracked and forget that the purpose of learning is not to know *things*, but to know *Him*.[10] Let me keep my focus, my eyes on Jesus, always applying what I learn—growing more and more like Jesus every day.

I want to learn in order to do.

Learn in order to do.

---

[1]John 7:14–15   [2]Mark 12:26–27   [3]James 1:27   [4]Mark 12:24–31   [5]John 17:3   [6]Acts 10:38
[7]Luke 5:15   [8]John 6:29   [9]John 15:16   [10]Jer. 22:15–16

DECEMBER 10

*And anyone who does not carry his cross
and follow me cannot be my disciple.*
Luke 14:27

These were not words of encouragement to the weary. They were not meant to strengthen us to bear with frustration, sorrow, pain, or any of the myriad burdens of a sin-sick world. Jesus had other words for that. No, this was not intended to warn us that life would bring troubles. Jesus was saying that following Him would kill us.

"Count the cost," Jesus said.[1] To be a disciple of Jesus Christ, I must die. I cannot encounter the holiness of God and live.

To the Jews—His listeners—the cross meant only one thing: death. To carry the cross meant to pick up the instrument of your death and carry it to the place where you would be killed. There was nothing pretty, nothing noble, nothing honorable in it. Execution by crucifixion was brutal, grisly, and ignominious. The cross was a criminal's death, yet by volunteering to be the criminal, Jesus turned a horrible thing into something gloriously honorable.

Death has always been a terrifying thing,[2] so it isn't surprising that we kick against anything that stinks of it. But what Jesus did with His cross took the sting out of death,[3] robbed it of its finality and defeat,[4] and set us free from fearing it.[5] But in order to let *all* of me go, I had to realize that nothing in me was godly—nothing was good or healthy.[6] Trying to salvage my old self was keeping me from becoming new. The only answer was to die.

Jesus is saying, "I don't want to patch up your life,[7] cutting out just the 'bad' parts—it's *all* bad parts! I want to birth[8] an entirely new being in you.[9] Will you let Me? Will you die so you can live forever?"[10]

We need to stop trying to plea bargain our way into good standing with God. We cannot get right with Him by changing our behavior. We must die—die to sin[11]—before we can be raised to newness of life.[12]

I will take up my cross and follow Jesus. This means denying what my flesh is screaming for. It means accepting and embracing the dark valley. It means choosing to let Christ choose for me. When I do, Jesus turns all the horrible things in *my* life into something gloriously honorable, too.

To be a disciple of Jesus Christ, you must die.

You cannot encounter the holiness of God and live.

---

[1]Luke 14:28 [2]Ps. 55:4 [3]Hos. 13:14 [4]John 11:25–26 [5]Heb. 2:14–15 [6]Isa. 1:5–6 [7]Mark 2:21 [8]John 3:7 [9]Isa. 43:19 [10]Mark 8:35 [11]1 Pet. 2:24 [12]John 5:21

DECEMBER 11

. . . And who knows but that you have come . . . for such a time as this?
Esther 4:14

Living life on purpose means always keeping eternity in view.[1] It means being conscious of God all day, with every step, through every conversation, in every activity. It means an end to aimless, careless, mindless drifting. Living life on purpose makes every moment an opportunity to learn from God, share with God, and become more like God[2]—in order to display God to a watching world.[3]

God does not float along nor drift. Everything He does is done *on* purpose, *for* a purpose. In becoming like Him, we must learn to do the same. It does not matter how we got where we are now, whether it was through obedience or disobedience. It only matters that we are there now, and God can use it for good.[4]

Joseph was in Egypt for a purpose. Moses was in Midian for a purpose. David was in hiding for years for a purpose. Esther was in the palace of Persia for a purpose. Mary and Joseph were in Bethlehem for a purpose. We are where we are for a purpose. If we keep this ever in mind, our lives will never be dull and routine again. We'll break out of our "I/Me/Mine" box, and our hearts will beat a little more passionately for the souls around us. We'll never again simply stand in line, go to the store, sit in school or at work without meaning—without glory—again. We will be actively displaying God: searching out those who weep, to weep with them; for those who laugh, to laugh with them; for those who ache, to share Christ with them.

"I looked for a man among them who would build up the wall and stand before me in the gap . . ."[5] "For I have raised you up for this very purpose . . ."[6] We are living in momentous times, with time itself hurtling toward it climax, and many run to and fro,[7] desperate for what we have. Stand up! We must stop mindlessly meandering through our days as if God didn't mean it when He said, "Behold, I am coming soon!"[8]

Who knows but that you have come to exactly where you are . . . for such a time as this?

Display God to a watching world.

---

[1]Matt. 6:19–21 [2]Luke 6:40 [3]Isa. 61:3 [4]Gen. 50:19–20 [5]Ezek. 22:30 [6]Exod. 9:16
[7]Dan. 12:4 [KJV] [8]Rev. 22:12

DECEMBER 12

Because your love is better than life, my lips will glorify you.
Psalm 63:3

*T*he question has come to me: how much is the everlasting love of
God worth to me? What would I exchange for His unconditional
and complete acceptance? Whatever it is in my life that interferes
with my fellowship with God has become the price tag of His love. That is
what it is worth to me. Not that God will stop loving me because of it,[1] but
because continuing in it prevents me from communing in that love with Him.

Our sins separate us from God,[2] and our sweet fellowship is broken. We cannot speak;[3] He will not hear.[4] What agony that should be! And yet we linger in
our lusts, fake excuses for our failures, and put off prostrating ourselves before
His throne of grace to receive the very mercy[5] He suffered death to provide!

It is not the stumble that breaks His heart, for "He knows how we are
formed, He remembers that we are dust."[6] It is the carelessness and lightness
of conscience with which we regard it. What breaks His heart is that it does
not break ours. That which is lightly esteemed is easily lost.

The good news is, there is a cure! Peter did not continue to deny his Lord.
Every single one of the disciples who deserted Him were later martyred for
Him. God Himself, if we will allow Him, will give us a heart of flesh. He will
give us an undivided heart and put a new spirit within us.[7] A tender heart, a
soft heart that loves so deeply, it cannot conceive of causing the Father any
more pain. This spiritual heart transplant comes as we sit at the foot of the
cross, considering the cost of His love. A new, soft heart grows within us as
we gaze up at the power of pure and perfect love, a love so much better than
life that He was willing to lay life itself down to give us such love. Behold what
manner of man is this . . . ?[8]

Truly, our Abba-God, Your love is better than life itself!

---

*A new, soft heart grows within us as we gaze up at
the power of His pure and perfect love.*

---

[1]Jer. 31:3   [2]Isa. 59:2   [3]Matt. 22:12   [4]Ps. 66:18   [5]Heb. 4:16   [6]Ps. 103:14   [7]Ezek. 11:19
[8]Matt. 8:27 [KJV]

DECEMBER 13

. . . yet not my will, but yours be done.
Luke 22:42

*I*f I am a follower of Christ, it is not a matter of "Can I pray the prayer of Gethsemane?" As a follower, I can do no less. Jesus said, "Whoever serves me must follow me; and where I am, my servant also will be."[1] Where is Jesus? He has sat down at the right hand of the throne of God.[2] But to be able to do that, He first had to endure the cross—and that road must pass through Gethsemane. In its very shadow, He told His disciples, "Where I am going, you cannot follow now, but you will follow later."[3] They did not understand. They would follow Him anywhere! To prison! To death![4] But to Gethsemane?

We are very much like them. We have heard His call; we have left our nets to follow Him.[5] With visions of glory, we follow Him. Through miracles of wine and bread and healing, we follow Him. Down the road to Jerusalem, waving our palm branches and shouting our praises, we follow Him—full of hopes, full of expectations, seeking the desires of our hearts,[6] little heeding that Friday is coming. Friday, when all the cherished plans of man come face to face with the astonishing, shocking purpose of God.

Jesus knew this, and in the deep places of my heart, I know it, too. "You know the way to the place I am going," Jesus said.[7] We know Gethsemane, for we have been there many times. We are following Jesus, and He *always* leads us to Gethsemane. He has designed, overruled, or allowed every twist and turn in our lives in order to bring us to this garden, this place to surrender our will and choose His.

Sometimes we slept, and the opportunity passed. Often we lashed out at our circumstances, cutting off the chance. Other times, in sheer terror, we fled naked from the dreaded choice.[8] These were but detours, not defeats, for the infinite patience of God draws us inexorably back to this place.

We will face Gethsemane over and over again, until every last shred of self-will has died. Yet we can pass through Gethsemane if we will stop limiting our surrender to just this or that part of our life. We cannot die piece by piece. We must give it *all* to Him. Only then will we find the fullness, the total sufficiency of the risen Lord. Only then will we learn that surrender is not loss, and we will be able to prove that God's will is the only path to life.

We cannot die piece by piece. We must give it all to Him!

---

[1]John 12:26 [2]Heb. 12:2 [3]John 13:36 [4]Luke 22:33 [5]Matt. 4:20 [6]Ps. 37:4 [7]John 14:4
[8]Mark 14:32–52

DECEMBER 14

*. . . these men have set up idols in their hearts
and put wicked stumbling blocks before their faces.
Should I let them inquire of me at all?*
Ezekiel 14:3

*W*e have heard of false prophets and false teachers, but there is another falsity that God has warned us against: false *seekers*. False seekers come in various forms, but self-deception is the common ingredient.[1] They fool *themselves*, but they are also a danger to any who follow their lead.

The religious leaders who came to Jesus were *definitely* false seekers. They weren't interested in truth; they were looking for ammunition against the one they saw as a danger to their traditional thinking.[2] These false seekers are confident in their own rightness.[3] They aren't looking to learn or to question their own assumptions. They tend to put a lot of trust in education and titles. They have trouble accepting instruction from upstart, unlearned carpenters. Can God speak to me and challenge my understanding through ordinary people?[4]

There is *another* kind of false seeker that hits close to home: the unsurrendered seeker. These make God a *part* of their lives, but only a part. They are still in charge, leaning on their own understanding,[5] making their own plans,[6] and only afterwards seeking God's input—His stamp of approval on an already-made decision.[7] They don't see that by holding back a part of their lives, they have withheld it *all*.[8] Is Jesus *truly* Lord of my life with the right to run it as *He* desires?

Another version of the *unsurrendered* seeker is the *unfaithful* seeker. These hold onto sin openly or in a hidden way and refuse to hear what God is trying to tell them about repenting and obeying.[9] They want advice on other matters, not correction.[10] God finds this so obnoxious, He forbade His prophets from giving them any messages at all other than "Repent."[11]

Am I truly seeking what God wants to say, or just what I want to hear? What kind of seeker are you?

---

*Am I truly seeking what God wants to say
or just what I want to hear?*

---

[1]Rev. 3:17   [2]Mark 12:13–17   [3]Luke 18:9–14   [4]Acts 4:13   [5]Prov. 3:5   [6]James 4:13–15   [7]Hos. 8:2–4   [8]Luke 14:33   [9]Isa. 58:1–4   [10]Prov. 12:1   [11]Ezek. 14:6

DECEMBER 15

*. . . for the joy of the L*ORD *is your strength.*
Nehemiah 8:10

*I*n war, strong armies are not usually attacked directly, nor are they engaged in battle by a straight, frontal assault. Any general worth his stars knows that to defeat a powerful enemy, you must first wear him down—sap his strength. The devil knows this, too. He knows that the joy of the Lord is our strength. What is he going to try to steal? Our joy.

I need to constantly remind myself that as a believer, I am the beloved child[1] of the All-Powerful, All-Knowing, All-Seeing God of all creation. He is ever-present with me.[2] His own Spirit lives inside me;[3] His warrior-angels surround me to minister to and protect me.[4] Is there anything the devil can take from me that I do not give him? The devil cannot steal my joy unless I hand it over. Why do you think the Scriptures speak of him shooting his arrows from the shadows?[5] *Because arrows are long-distance weapons.* With all that protection around us, he has to shoot at us from afar!

So he lobs in some disappointments and watches my reaction. Can he shake my peace? Is my posture a little slumped, not boldly confident? He'll set up a bombardment of bad news, calamities, trials, and confusion—often one on top of another—until he can insinuate his demonic forces behind my lines. Anger, depression, doubt, fear, worry—*all* of his imps are joy-stealing specialists. They operate on negative power: gossip and slander; spite, malice, and envy; and especially self-pity.[6] Once I've surrendered my joy, that's when temptation steps in—when I am no longer strong, bold, full of faith, and singing God's praise.

The Scriptures tell us that "strength and joy [are] in his dwelling place."[7] To keep my joy, my strength, I have to be where they are—in His dwelling place. Joy is not in circumstances; it is in His presence.[8] If I abide in Him,[9] no one—not all the demons in hell—can steal my joy or sap my strength.

The devil cannot steal your joy
unless you hand it over.

---

[1]Deut. 33:12   [2]Heb. 13:5   [3]John 14:17   [4]Heb. 1:14   [5]Ps. 11:2   [6]Ps. 55:9–11   [7]Ps. 16:27
[8]John 15:9–11

DECEMBER 16

He asked me, "Son of man, can these bones live?"
Ezekiel 37:3

*H*opeless is a word invented by the devil. He is the one who whispers it in our ears. Have you ever faced a situation so desperate or unmovable that you felt it could *never* change? Have you found yourself crying out to God in prayer over it, only to have your shoulders slump, your hands fall limp, and your voice trail off . . . because the word *hopeless* suddenly overwhelmed your spirit? Have you ever prayed about something or someone for so long that the words now seem mechanical, something you could say in your sleep? Sometimes we pray so long for something that when God does actually grant it, we're caught off-guard and shocked—shocked because we suddenly realize that we'd stopped expecting an answer!

God knows about dead situations. But He would also have us remember who holds the keys of death, and it isn't the devil.[1] Jesus invaded Satan's territory,[2] destroyed his power *and* his works,[3] and took back the keys! What he opens, no one can shut.[4] He can breathe life into the deadest situation just as surely as He breathed life into dirt and made man. It doesn't matter if it's been dead so long, the bones themselves are crumbling into dust—*nothing is impossible for God!*

Got a dead situation? Don't give up! God knows the perfect time for everything."[5] *Do you know He's got a plan*? God can split the sea, rain down bread, make the sun stand still, turn our water into wine, pull money out of a fish, and dispossess the devil. Cold, hard reality melts into miracles in His hands. Give your cares to Him, because only He can make five plus two equal 5,000! He can turn a funeral into a parade, turn bitter water sweet—and He can turn a king's heart.[6]

But we cannot give up! Do not turn back in the day of battle.[7] Do not throw away your confidence; it will be richly rewarded.[8] We need to persevere and do the will of God—and we will receive what He has promised. Yes, dead bones *can* live!

Got a dead situation? Don't give up!
Do not turn back in the day of battle.

---

[1]Rev. 1:18 [2]Heb. 2:14 [3]1 John 3:8 [4]Rev. 3:7 [5]Eccl. 3:1 [6]Prov. 21:1 [7]Ps. 78:9 [8]Heb. 10:36

DECEMBER 17

Ask the Lord of the harvest, therefore,
to send out workers into his harvest field.
Matthew 9:38

*H*ave you ever prayed for a lost loved one, asking God to send someone across their path, into their life who will speak words of life to them and point them to Jesus? Or prayed that God would surround them with godly people—people they would listen to?[1] You may even have prayed today's verse specifically. After all, you can be assured that this prayer is God's will, because Jesus Himself told us to pray it.[2]

As I was doing this one day, God began to show me the faces of people around me, and He told me about their mothers and daughters and sisters and brothers who were praying this same prayer for them. "I will answer *your* prayer, if you will help be the answer to *their* prayers. The workers are indeed few."[3]

It took me awhile to realize this was not a tit-for-tat proposition. God is not looking for employees who are willing to only work for the benefits they demand.[4] Jesus said that hired hands care nothing for the sheep, so when trouble comes, they run away.[5] I am not a mercenary, a hired hand; I am family.[6]

Many times I have prayed for God to do something, not realizing that He wants to do it through me. When I pray for His kingdom to come,[7] I am to be the light that brings it.[8] When I pray for His will to be done on earth, whom do I expect will be doing it, if not me? When I pray for God to send workers into His harvest field, am I not willing to go?

The longer I live serving God, the less I bargain with Him for benefits, and the more I trust Him to take care of me one way or another.[9] I am willing to leave the details up to Him.

By pointing out that the workers are few, Jesus searches my heart. It is hard to find those who will serve for love of the Lord, not for pay or reward. What is my motivation?

Your harvest fields are all around me, Lord. I will gladly serve.[10]

It is hard to find those who will serve
for love of the Lord, not for pay or reward.

---

[1]Isa. 28:11 [2]1 John 5:14–15 [3]Matt. 9:35–38 [4]Matt. 6:20–21 [5]John 10:12–13 [6]Matt. 12:50
[7]Matt. 6:10 [8]Matt. 5:16 [9]Matt. 6:33 [10]Matt. 21:28–31

DECEMBER 18

*. . . You give a tenth of your spices . . . But you have neglected
the more important matters of the law—justice, mercy and faithfulness.*

Matthew 23:23

arl Marx was right about one thing—religion *is* the opiate of the masses. Is this shocking? It shouldn't be, once you realize that the only religion Marx saw was like a Fabergé egg: fabulous jewels and gold encrusting an empty shell. Beautiful to the eyes, but its heart was cold nothingness.[1] Like a placebo, it tricks you, but it can't cure you.[2]

Those without a relationship with the God of their religion cannot understand the purpose and place of His commandments.[3] Without the Spirit to guide them, they must guide themselves, defining and measuring and classifying and making endless lists—the *do*'s and *don't*s of Marx's religion.[4] Attendance is recordable. Tithing is easy: ten percent—a quantifiable number. But how do you measure justice, mercy, and faithfulness? How do you quantify love? When can you know you've done enough to check that requirement off your list? Is an afternoon volunteering at a homeless shelter enough to count as loving others? Is a pilgrimage to a holy site or a sizable donation impressive enough to satisfy the requirements for loving God?[5]

Commandment love—true love—is insulted by such an idea. The very life of love is expression.[6] You simply cannot bottle it and put a cap on it to contain it in any way. It is like fire shut up in my bones.[7]

The greatest commandment is to love God with everything in us. The second is to love each other.[8] Everything else we would do is either icing on the cake, or a total waste.

The religious-without-a-relationship, church-going (but not church-*being*) legalist is extremely nervous about that. It sounds unfulfillable. The truly surrendered God lover, however, instantly grasps its truth:[9] it *is* unfulfillable—meaning it is never fulfilled and *therefore, never finished.*[10] The gift of salvation, you see, is the healing of the heart—the restoration of love—not as a deed, but as a lifestyle. That relationship is what Marx never understood. There is only love.

The greatest commandment is to love God

with everything in us.

The second is to love each other.

---

[1]Matt. 23:27   [2]Jer. 30:15   [3]John 5:39–40   [4]Isa. 28:9–10   [5]Mark 7:7   [6]1 John 3:18   [7]Jer. 20:9   [8]Matt. 22:38–39   [9]1 John 4:7   [10]Heb. 13:1

DECEMBER 19

The King will reply, "I tell you the truth, whatever you did
for one of the least of these brothers of mine, you did for me."
Matthew 25:40

*E*ver since I began to walk with Jesus, I have wondered, what *is* my calling? What *is* my purpose? Some people make much of seeking after spiritual gifts and special "anointings," desperately hoping for an earth-shaking purpose, a chance to serve God in some spectacular way. They watch wistfully as others preach to millions, teach through their mega-ministries, or lay healing hands on the multitudes (as if numbers were the measure of God's touch). Longingly they beg (like Esau), "Me, too! Bless me, too, my father!"[1]

Yet they—we—already have within us the greatest spiritual gift of all.[2] The pure, holy, soul-touching, life-changing, unconditional love of God has been breathed into us as we received His Spirit![3]

The highest calling, the greatest purpose, is not to prophesy, or preach, or move mountains by faith[4]—Jesus Himself said many who were very successful in such ministries will be shocked to find themselves cast out of the kingdom: "I never knew you . . . evildoers!"[5]

No, the greatest saint is not necessarily the powerful or the proclaimed, the honored or the recognized. The most faithful servant of God is the one who, day in and day out, in obscurity and ordinariness, strives to love others—not with mere words, but in actions and in truth.[6] The greatest in the kingdom of heaven[7] is the one who, for love of God, looks past the rudeness, abuse, undeservedness, and unloveliness in the faces of those around him and sees instead the face of Jesus—and serves Him. "Is that not what it means to know me?"[8] This is our sacred purpose; our highest calling.

The most faithful servant of God is the one who,
day in and day out, strives to love others
in action and truth.

---

[1]Gen. 27:34   [2]John 7:38–39   [3]John 20:22   [4]Mark 11:22   [5]Matt. 7:21–23   [6]1 John 3:18
[7]Matt. 23:11   [8]Jer. 22:16

DECEMBER 20

. . . Do not my words do good to him whose ways are upright?
Micah 2:7

One of the enemy's greatest lies is that doing things God's way is hard, impractical, and leaves you on the losing end. He makes *surrender* sound like *giving up*—like tremendous loss. The very idea drives many souls to hesitate. Yet even Jesus urged us to count the cost.[1] "Think about it," He said. "You *will* leave some things behind. You must decide if it is worth it, if eternal life is worth it—if *I* am worth it."

Oh, yes—we *will* give up some things. I took a good, hard look at those things: what God calls me to give up was only stealing my peace, killing my joy, and destroying me body and soul.[2] Who really wants to hold onto ways that are nothing but ruin and destruction?[3] I saw the truth: what we gain in Christ is vastly, infinitely better than *anything* He could ever ask us to give up, including our very lives. "Whoever loses his life for me will find it. What good will it be for a man if he gains the whole world, yet forfeits his soul?"[4]

The devil *knows* what heaven is like—he used to live there! But since he lost his place, he is like a jealous, spurned child: "If I can't have it, *nobody* will!"[5] But God is not a sadist. He does not willingly bring affliction or grief to the children of men.[6] His thoughts toward us are of peace, not of evil. His plans are plans to prosper us and not to harm us.[7] It breaks His heart when we disobey—not because His ego can't stand losing worship, but because obedience is to our benefit. His ways give us peace . . . like a river,[8] and in keeping them there is great reward.[9] God knows that disobedience is the cause of all heartache, pain, misery, and death we suffer. If we would just do things His way, we would find fulfillment, satisfaction, and true happiness.

Obedience is no trouble when you are convinced that God's ways actually *work*—when you know that His words do good to him whose ways are upright.

Obedience is no trouble
when you are convinced that God's ways actually work.

---

[1]Luke 14:28   [2]John 10:10   [3]Isa. 59:7–8   [4]Matt. 16:25–26   [5]Song 8:6   [6]Lam. 3:33   [7]Jer. 29:11
[8]Isa. 48:18   [9]Ps. 19:11

DECEMBER 21

Then God said, "Take your son, your only son, Isaac,
whom you love, and go to the region of Moriah. . . ."
Genesis 22:2

*N*ow. God sure didn't make this any easier on Abraham. Like an icicle to the heart, He touched the very center of the *cost* of His command. Before Abraham could stammer a single, *but*, God assured him, "Oh, yes. I *do* know exactly what I'm asking, and how much this will hurt." Obedience is often painful. That's why Jesus warned us to count the cost[1]—even as He assured us that the reward is worth it.[2]

But what struck me as I read this passage again were the words, "your *only* son, Isaac . . ." It confused me, because Isaac was *not* Abraham's only son. He had Ishmael, too . . . a son even God had consented to bless "because he is your offspring."[3] If God had acknowledged Ishmael then, why does He not now?

Because Ishmael was not God's plan. Ishmael was Sarah's idea, and Abraham never sought God's will before agreeing.[4] Oh, his *intentions* were good. Abraham never doubted God's promise of a son.[5] Ishmael was his way of trying, by his own efforts, to fulfill God's promise. But good intentions[6] are no substitute for seeking God's actual intentions, His plan.[7] Ishmael was not God's plan. Only Isaac—conceived in faith and birthed by the power of God alone for His plan and His purpose—only Isaac counted.[8]

No matter what my intentions may be, no matter what I accomplish, if I do it outside of God's plan, it is not His will.[9] If I do it on my own, outside of His strength and grace, it doesn't count.[10] It doesn't matter how much I *want* to honor God; if I am building a cathedral when He wants me to build a stable, I am not fulfilling my purpose. I am not honoring God.

Good intentions cannot change my Ishmaels into God's Isaac.

No matter what I accomplish,
if I do it outside of God's plan, it is not His will.

---

[1]Luke 14:25–33   [2]Matt. 13:44–46   [3]Gen. 21:13   [4]Gen 16:1–3   [5]Heb. 11:11   [6]Prov. 14:12
[7]Prov. 19:2   [8]Heb. 11:17–19   [9]1 Chron. 15:12–13   [10]John 15:4–5

DECEMBER 22

I have come to bring fire on the earth,
and how I wish it were already kindled!
Luke 12:49

*J*esus longed to bring fire to the earth. I have sometimes wanted to do that, too—to see it all go up in smoke, be reduced to ash. But that was just my all-too-human frustration. No, the fire that Jesus longed for was not total destruction, but purification.[1] The fire that comes straight from the altar in heaven—one touch, and our sin is atoned for, our guilt taken away.[2] One touch from the fire of His blood.[3] and we are made whole[4]—and set on fire. Purification and passion.

I sigh as I write that, because I have struggled with passion. I could do it in bursts, now and then, here and there. But a sustained life passionately on fire for Jesus? Is it even possible?

Yes, it is—once I realize that the passion Jesus is looking for is not that heart-thumping, burning emotion that you see in the first flames of new love or in crazed sports fans. They are passionate, yes. But the passion that Jesus is longing to kindle in us is the kind that follows Him in total trust,[5] that does His will for the love of Him,[6] not as part of some twelve-step plan required to get to heaven.[7]

I discovered that this passion *is* in me—especially when I think about what Jesus did for me. The more I ponder the cross[8]—His agony, His love—the more I simply *want* to follow Him. I don't have to sit around and wait for some supernatural experience to set me on fire. Jesus Himself *is* the fire He longed to bring. He is in me. His passion for me is in me. When I take hold of that spark, that coal, and feed the flame continually by turning to Him in Scripture, in prayer, and listening for His voice,[9] I feel the passion grow. Not as a sustained emotion, but as sustained faith and trust—demonstrated through obedience.[10]

Let Your fire be forever burning in me, Lord.[11]

The passion that Jesus is longing to kindle in us
is the kind that follows Him in total trust.

---

[1]Isa. 4:4 [2]Isa. 6:6–7 [3]Rev. 1:5 [4]John 7:23 [5]John 12:26 [6]Ps. 40:7–8 [7]Heb. 10:1–3 [8]Heb. 12:2 [9]Matt. 17:5 [10]John 14:23 [11]Lev. 6:13

DECEMBER 23

"I am the Lord's servant," Mary answered.
"May it be to me as you have said. . . ."
Luke 1:38

$\mathcal{I}$ used to wonder why Mary was troubled when the angel greeted her as one who was highly favored of the Lord.[1] I thought of how much I'd love to have such inarguable proof that I was in His will. But Mary may have had a point. After all, the great favor of God is often coupled with great persecutions. She knew her people's history and well remembered the stories of others God had greatly favored: Noah *in the flood*, Daniel *in the lion's den*, and David—anointed by God, *hunted by Saul*.

Mary did realize that something was afoot, and even her young and inexperienced mind could easily see the complications that could arise because of the honor God was bestowing upon her. Although every pious young woman in Israel dreamed that she would be chosen to be the mother of the Messiah,[2] none ever imagined that the conception would be like this.[3] Mary must've known that no one would believe her, although I can picture her hoping that those who loved her and knew her best would trust her enough to allow the possibility. Surely they would know she was not that kind of a girl; she would never be promiscuous. Surely they would accept that God could make a girl pregnant without a man if He wanted to . . . right?[4]

Did she believe that, or did she know that the villagers (her neighbors and friends) would consider her a sinner and a liar, that her betrothed, Joseph, would think to repudiate her (albeit quietly)?[5] That years later, they would throw it back in her face; "Isn't this Mary's son—?"[6] Not Joseph's. "*We* are not illegitimate children."[7]

The amazing thing is not that she knew all this; the amazing thing is that she knew all this and *still said*, "Yes." Mary loved God, trusted God enough to know that whatever God wanted, she wanted. She did what Jesus told us to do. She counted the cost[8] and considered it worth losing everything to gain Christ[9]—to bear the Christ.

The greatest blessing of God is to be used for His glory. Though a sword may pierce your own soul, too,[10] would you still be willing to be the Lord's servant?

The greatest blessing of God
is to be used for His glory.

---

[1]Luke 1:38   [2]Isa. 9:6   [3]Luke 1:35   [4]Luke 1:34   [5]Matt. 1:19   [6]Mark 6:3   [7]John 8:41   [8]Luke 14:28
[9]Mark 8:35–38   [10]Luke 2:35

DECEMBER 24

*. . . She wrapped him in cloths and placed him in a manger,
because there was no room for them in the inn.*

Luke 2:7

*Y*ou know the saying, "Hindsight is always 20/20"? It is easier to see
how God has worked *through* our circumstances than to trust Him in
the *midst* of our mess. After the chaos, we can look back and see how
God not only brought us through,[1] but that the chaos itself was a blessing in
disguise.[2] If only we would remember this the next time trouble bites!

Keeping a heart open to trust God no matter how bad it looks is what faith
is all about. Like Mary and Joseph. Their situation looked desperate—and as if
it were getting worse. They did not look like chosen vessels, blessed by God to
carry out the greatest task ever given to a child of Adam. They looked more like
they had been abandoned by the God who had put them into this predicament.

Not only was Mary enduring an unbelievable pregnancy, but at the last minute, the emperor decreed a census that forced her and Joseph to travel nearly
70 miles over rough terrain to Bethlehem.[3] The rushing crowds elbowed them
out of every available space. Then Mary went into labor as they wandered the
streets, desperate for a place to stay.[4] The stable, to weary eyes, could've looked
like a slap in the face from a silent God. How much worse could things get?

Yet the stable was one of those disguised blessings, proof that God *did*
care.[5] In a town bursting at the seams with people, there alone could He give
them privacy and peace.[6] Inns back then were little more than one or two
rooms, with one large common room where everybody ate, drank, jostled,
shouted, and sang.[7] People slept on tables, benches, and on the floor. Hardly
a hospitable birthing room![8]

They had not been abandoned—and neither have I.[9] He has promised to
be with me through fire and flood.[10] When I remember what He has done for
me before, I can trust Him to do the same now.

---

*Keeping a heart open to trust God
no matter how bad it looks is what faith is all about.*

---

[1]Ps. 77:7–15   [2]Isa. 38:17   [3]Luke 2:1–3   [4]Job 39:1–3   [5]1 Pet. 5:7   [6]Isa. 32:18   [7]Ps. 64:2   [8]Ps. 84:3
[9]John 14:18   [10]Isa. 43:1–2

DECEMBER 25

. . . Then they opened their treasures
and presented him with gifts of gold and of incense and of myrrh.
Matthew 2:11

God has ways of providing of which the logical mind of man cannot conceive, bound as it is by time and the laws of physics. In His infinite wisdom, God sent His Son to be born not to royalty and wealth, but into the humble and austere circumstances familiar to most of us on earth. By choosing Mary and Joseph, God clearly demonstrated that He is on our side,[1] that none are beneath His love. He also proved that our circumstances will not hinder His plan and His purpose. He truly is *Jehovah-jireh*, our Provider.

Mary and Joseph had no idea that God was about to send them on a long journey that very night.[2] But God knew all about it. He was not caught off-guard by Herod's jealous plot to destroy Jesus; He knew it was coming. He also knew well in advance how to counter it and what His chosen people would need. He knew it long before there ever were a Mary, Joseph, or King Herod.

Consider how long God had been moving all the pieces into place. He'd called Abraham out of his home country to make sure that later, there would be a people of God called Israelites.[3] He created a whole nation and gave them His righteous laws[4] so there would be a young couple someday who knew Him and loved Him enough to be favored by Him; who could be trusted to raise His Son rightly, in holiness.[5] He allowed a stubborn and greedy prophet to try to curse the Israelites so He could place a specific prophecy in the records of a faraway nation—a prophecy that would one day alert the magi that a holy king was born.[6] He put it in them to come all the way to a tiny Jewish town and lay their treasures at His feet—because His chosen vessels were going to need some serious provision to afford the cost of a long sojourn in Egypt. Truly, "before they call, I will answer."[7]

Whatever your calling and purpose may be, rest assured that God has an answer for every detail, every need[8]—even if He has to send someone from half a world away to lay it at your feet. *You can trust God.*

Rest assured God has an answer
for every detail, every need.

---

[1]Luke 1:46–53   [2]Matt. 2:13   [3]Gen. 18:19   [4]Deut. 4:8   [5]Luke 1:26–28   [6]Num. 24:17   [7]Isa. 65:24
[8]Matt. 6:8

DECEMBER 26

For to us a child is born, to us a son is given . . .
Isaiah 9:6

*T*o the disciples staring in shock at the heavens that had received back their beloved Lord, God sent a pair of angels to reassure them: "This same Jesus, who has been taken from you into heaven, will come back in the same way you have seen him go into heaven."[1] Perhaps they were the same angels who had joyously announced to the watching shepherds, "Today in the town of David a Savior has been born to you."[2]

To *you*, to *us*. God did not give us Jesus only to take Him back. "To us a child is born, to us a son is given." God reminded us through Isaiah: "My unfailing love for you will not be shaken nor my covenant of peace removed."[3] What He has given to us, He has given for all time—and beyond. Jesus was made like us—like His brothers—in every way.[4] When He rose from the dead, He rose glorified, with a new body, yet a body still with flesh and bones,[5] as ours will be.[6]

Jesus is ours forever. When He returns, he will return as the Son of Man—Jesus Himself promised us this.[7] Stephen saw Him thus: "I see heaven open and the Son of Man standing at the right hand of God."[8] We will be able to see Him, to touch Him like Thomas did and cry out, "My Lord and my God!"[9] We will sit and eat with Him, laugh with Him, and feel His touch as He gently wipes away our final tears. Although He'll look different than we may have imagined Him, we will know Him, know His voice as Mary Magdalene did,[10] recognize His particular movements and habits as the two on the Emmaus road knew Him when He blessed the bread.[11] We will know each other the same way.

Jesus is the greatest gift ever given. He may have come quietly, His gift wrapping the swaddling clothes a young bride named Mary wound about His newborn body—but He came nonetheless. Had God included a gift tag, it would've read, "To my beloved children, with all My heart and soul and mind and strength. I love you forever and always, Your Abba. PS: Don't wait! Open at once! Today!"

Jesus is the greatest gift ever given.

---

[1]Acts 1:10–11 [2]Luke 2:11 [3]Isa. 54:10 [4]Heb. 2:17 [5]Luke 24:39 [6]1 John 3:2 [7]Matt. 24:30 [8]Acts 7:56 [9]John 20:28 [10]John 20:16 [11]Luke 24:30–31

DECEMBER 27

For where your treasure is, there your heart will be also.
Matthew 6:21

*T*he whole point of investing is to get a return, an abundance. People who understand investing are willing to put in whatever it takes—time, effort, money, etc., because they expect to get something valuable for it. It's worth it to them.

What is valuable to you shows in your actions much more than in your words.[1] Jesus told a pointed parable about just this while at a dinner party one day. He had sat back watching the crowd jockeying for the best places in the house—elbowing each other out of the way, shoving and maneuvering to be first. Once everyone was finally situated, He talked about humility and selflessness and spoke of heavenly rewards for doing things God's way.[2] I can almost picture the uncomfortable, embarrassed silence as everyone looked to someone else to say something! Finally, one man ventured a good-sounding, religiously-correct response: "Blessed is the man who will eat at the feast in the kingdom of God,"[3] he sighed wistfully. I can see everyone else nodding, and maybe a few amens.

But they weren't fooling Jesus. He followed up with another parable, this time exposing how little they actually valued their invitation to that feast. One by one, He showed them how much more they valued earthly possessions, earthly business, and earthly relationships above any heavenly blessing or treasure. As a consequence, they were forfeiting their invitations to others who would value and appreciate it.[4]

Before we condemn those foolish dinner guests, we must consider how our own actions prove what we value more. How eager are we to forgo an earthly reward for a heavenly one?[5] How willing are we to go unhonored by men for our good deeds because we prefer God's reward?[6] Do we become upset when we are not thanked for our efforts?[7] If we understood the true nature of heavenly rewards,[8] we would never be reluctant to bless others for no earthly return whatsoever.[9] Our hearts will be where our treasure is.

What is valuable to you shows in your actions
much more than your words.

---

[1]Luke 16:10–12   [2]Luke 14:7–14   [3]Luke 14:15   [4]Luke 14:16–24   [5]Matt. 6:16–18   [6]Matt. 6:5–6
[7]Matt: 6:1–4   [8]Heb. 12:2   [9]Luke 6:32–35

DECEMBER 28

Simon Peter answered him, "Lord, to whom shall we go?
You have the words of eternal life."

John 6:68

No one gets to heaven by accident; you cannot stumble upon the pearly gates. The destination is deliberate, the journey chosen by an act of will. There are some places you can get to halfheartedly, sooner or later, with a maybe/maybe not attitude–but not heaven.[1] The way is too narrow, the path is too steep.[2] There are hard teachings.[3] There are forsakings to be done,[4] forgivings to be made[5] that cannot be made by one who has left his options open. When Jesus taught about eating His flesh and drinking His blood,[6] many of His followers said, "Whoa! Too much! Count me out." So what did they do, then? Go back to their fishing boats? Back to the family business? Bury themselves in Plan B? Only if they thought there *was* a Plan B, that there was another way.

Not so Simon Peter. He knew the truth: there is no other way. No matter how strong the teaching, no matter how dark the night, how unimaginably hard the requirement,[7] if it took everything he had and asked for more.[8] There were no other options. He had forever settled the question: Jesus is Lord. Whatever He said, Peter would do. Wherever He went, Peter would go[9]–no argument, no hesitation, no longing looks backward. Because backward is death.

Have I truly settled the question? Is Jesus Lord, or do I still greet His commands with a hesitant, frantic search for options? When what He requires seems impossible, something my heart had said I would never do, what then?[10] Is it "so long"–or surrender?

If I could, I would carry with me a small pouch of ashes–to remind myself that the bridge is burned.[11] There is no going back. Jesus is the only way.[12]

Is Jesus Lord, or do I still greet His commands
with a hesitant, frantic search for options?

---

[1]James 1:7–8 [2]Matt.7:13–14 [3]Matt. 16:25–26 [4]Luke 14:33 [5]Matt. 6:14–15 [6]John 6:54 [7]John 15:12–13 [8]Luke 12:48 [9]John 13:33–37 [10]John 6:66 [11]1 Kings 19:21 [12]John 14:6

DECEMBER 29

Sanctify them by the truth; your word is truth.
John 17:17

*W*hen I was very young, I remember my older brother telling me about things like macaroni bushes, spaghetti farms, and side-hill willies (cows with two legs shorter than the others, enabling them to stand sideways on a hill without falling over). My belief in such things went the way of Santa Claus and the Tooth Fairy as I grew older. Fables have a way of not standing up to close examination.

Some beliefs—even long-held traditions—don't fare so well, either. There comes a time in our lives when we become responsible for questioning what we have been taught, what we have always believed. Solomon put it concisely when he said, "A simple man believes anything, but a prudent man gives thought to his steps."[1] We must give thought to what we believe. Don't just be a sponge, indiscriminately soaking up whatever spills out of someone else's mouth. We should ask ourselves, "Why do I believe this? What is it based on? Is it really so? What if it is not true?"

Some issues are not really important.[2] They don't affect our salvation, and they don't merit getting all heated up over.[3] But how do I know what is important and what is not? How can I determine if my eternal destiny is affected by that belief? We can keep ourselves firmly grounded in the truth, not only by pointing ourselves constantly to the Scriptures,[4] but by letting the Holy Spirit teach us their true meaning.[5] We can look to Him who is the way, the truth and the life[6] to see how Jesus lived the truth He spoke.

We must ask questions;[7] God is not afraid of our questions. After all, our guide into all truth[8]—the Holy Spirit—is His gift to us. If I want to distinguish between right and wrong, truth and error—not merely to file the facts away in my mental library, but to please God—I will know.[9] God's Word is truth, and He is the Spirit of Truth.[10]

Give thought to what you believe.
Don't just be a sponge, indiscriminately soaking up
whatever spills out of someone else's mouth.

---

[1]Prov. 14:15 [2]Matt. 17:24–27 [3]Heb. 9:9–10 [4]John 5:39–40 [5]1 John 2:26–27 [6]John 14:6
[7]James 1:5 [8]John 16:13 [9]John 7:17 [10]John 14:16–17

DECEMBER 30

Now this is eternal life: that they may know you,
the only true God, and Jesus Christ, whom you have sent.
John 17:3

*E*ternal life is knowing God, and knowing Jesus the Messiah. It is the answer to the devil's first accusation to Eve—that God was holding out on them, keeping back knowledge for Himself that rightfully belonged to them.[1] They took the bait, and in their hunger for knowing, they lost what knowing they had: they no longer knew God as He really is. Sin immediately twisted their knowledge of God, and they became afraid of Him.[2]

Before their sin, Adam and Eve knew God intimately and innocently. They saw Him face to face; they talked with Him and walked with Him in the cool of the day. But sin drove them from His presence,[3] and that separation brought death.

Every generation since has widened the gap, sinning more and more,[4] letting the lies all but obliterate the truth of God. His character was smeared, His mercy minimized, and His wrath made to look cruel and capricious. His holiness became frightening,[5] His purity unattainable,[6] and His requirements too high for us.[7] The fact that He has provided a way for all to obtain the impossible has been ignored and suppressed by an enemy who knows the truth: God is love.[8] That he has cut himself off from that love, that life, drives him mad with hate and jealousy. What he cannot have, he would keep from us.[9]

Eternal life is not sacrifice,[10] it is not holiness. Eternal life is *knowing* God. Everything in my life flows from what I know in the depth of my heart. "Above all else, guard your heart, for it is the wellspring of life."[11] How well I *know* God is clearly displayed in my actions.

Jesus Christ is the bridge, the door, the gateway to God. We must know the One to get to the other.[12] There is no other way.

In all things, through all things, let our striving be only to know God. This is eternal life.

How well I know God
is clearly displayed in my actions.

[1]Gen. 3:4–5   [2]Gen 3:10   [3]Gen. 3:23–24   [4]Gen. 6:5   [5]Exod. 20:18–19   [6]Job 15:14   [7]Josh. 24:19   [8]1 John 4:8   [9]John 8:44   [10]Heb. 10:4   [11]Prov. 4:23   [12]John 14:6

DECEMBER 31

*Now that you know these things,
you will be blessed if you do them.*

John 13:17

This is not technically a daily devotional. This is a book. The words in a book can *inspire* devotion, but a *true* daily devotional is a day lived according to what you have learned. The blessing of God is not in the knowing, it is in the doing. All the reading, studying the Scriptures, and growing in knowledge will only condemn those who do not do what they know.[1]

Do I want to live a life full of joy and peace, to be blessed by God and mightily used by Him for His glory? I must do what I know.[2]

Am I struggling with issues in my life? Does it seem like everywhere I turn, I am blocked? Am I doing all I already know?[3]

Some are impatient with their level of spirituality. They want to grow closer, stronger, wiser, faster—but they refuse to do all they know.[4]

Others accumulate books upon books, searching for the one secret to unlocking all their problems.[5] They try gimmick after gimmick, formula after formula, praying certain prayers in certain positions at certain times.[6] Some attempt great and arduous pilgrimages to holy sites, hoping to tap into the power that once worked a miracle on that spot—as if a plot of ground can hold the power of God more than can a human heart dedicated to Him. Many desire and seek out an extraordinary task, a labor of Hercules, that, once accomplished, will win them a revelation of God—or at least earn them a place on the hierarchy of heaven.[7] Hungry souls give money to causes promising various blessings of God for different donations, as if God were like us and could be bought.[8]

All this desperation, and the answer is so simple. There is no secret to having God's power flow in your life—it is poured out on all who do what He has said. When you read it, do it. When He speaks it, do it. What you know, do.[9]

Devote this day—and *every* day—to your Lord. Don't just *tell* Him you love Him; *show* Him. We don't need to learn more until we are practicing all we already know.[10]

There is power enough in what we already know to break every chain and turn our world around. "Go and do . . . "[11]

Don't just tell God you love Him; show Him.

---

[1]Luke 12:47 [2]John 9:31 [3]James 4:17 [4]Matt. 7:24–27 [5]Eccl. 12:12 [6]Matt. 6:7 [7]Mark 10:17–22
[8]Acts 8:20 [9]James 1:22 [10]Heb. 2:1 [11]Luke 10:37

ABOUT THE AUTHOR

Cynthia A.Y. Rupel

I am Solitaire. Most people in prison have nicknames. In the depths of my despair, shame, and fear, I gave myself the name Solitaire. I was a high-profile inmate—a prison correctional officer accused of first-degree murder. My case (and my face) had been splattered all over the news. I couldn't let others connect *me* to "that woman on TV." I was horrified and ashamed . . . humiliated. That woman *couldn't* be me!

But she was.

Let them think I was Solitare for love of the card game. They didn't need to know the truth: *I am alone. Abandoned. I am Solitaire.*

My journey from the good girl—from the straight-A student . . . the Air Force enlistee entrusted to work in the White House . . . the wife, the mother of two girls . . . a civilian career in police communications, then corrections, baptized and active in the church in all the usual ways—my journey from all this to betrayal, lies, adultery, and now cold-blooded murder is a story of the astonishing deceptiveness of sin, of a heart unsurrendered to Jesus Christ. I could never have imagined that I—the conflict avoider, the goodie-two-shoes—could ever have ended up in prison for the horrendously violent crime of murder. It boggles my mind to this day.

Yet God warns us all, "The heart is deceitful above all things and desperately wicked (Jer. 17:9). By choosing to live my life on my own terms and not submitting to God, my own heart fooled me and led me down a path I was powerless to resist. Powerless, because I had not submitted my heart and life to Jesus Christ. The holes in my soul had to be filled, and since I wasn't letting God do it, those empty places drove me, blind to the darkness inside.

It may sound strange, but it became a very good thing that God allowed my life to go all the way into that darkness, into prison, before He got my full attention (although He *had* intervened several times before He allowed me to make my choices that brought me face to face with a possible death penalty). I had nowhere else to run, and I couldn't hide from Him any longer. I certainly couldn't fool myself anymore that I was a "good girl." Now I understood how much wickedness owns our hearts apart from His grace. No one can be saved who doesn't truly see the magnitude of their own sinfulness. I was finally in a good position to shut up and listen!

Covered in shame, humiliation, and outright terror, I was still not abandoned by the God who loves us all. He sent people to me—volunteers, staff, even other inmates—all calling me to Him. And yes, like most, I still resisted, until I finally agreed to go to a Bible study group—just to get these people off my back! But after the final prayer, the volunteer asked me if I was saved.

It was then I heard His voice for the first time. He only said one word: *"Today."*

It only takes one word when He is the one speaking it. I gave up the whole fight-or-flight thing and said yes to Jesus Christ. It changed everything. *He* changed everything. He did not cancel the earthly consequences of my crime. I am currently serving a Life Without Parole sentence, justly earned. But He has set me free! Until you experience it yourself, no one can truly describe the joy and power that comes from being at peace with God, from learning to do things His way. Compared to being driven by the need of my self-centered heart, this is true freedom.

Now I have purpose, a reason to get up and smile every day. I get to serve Jesus by serving the women around me. He has given me a great love for His Word, and He has spent years peeling off the layers of religious tradition to help me understand who He is and *how* He is. He has granted me the grace to encourage and teach others. My prayer is that my life will always be a revelation of Jesus Christ as Lord and Savior. As I cried out to Him in a cold, dark cell, "I want to be a walking, talking, skinful of God!"

I *am* Solitaire. But I am no longer alone.

www.words-unbound.blogspot.com

take.it.up@outlook.com

LOST

—by Cynthia A.Y. Rupel*

What will you do
    When the Judge takes the stand,
And you're found with the blood
    Of His Son on your hands?
What will you say?
    How will you explain
Ignoring the mercy
    He was murdered to gain?
Make no mistake —
    There will be no more chances,
No more time, no excuses,
    When the Judge merely glances
At Jesus, and sees Him
    Shaking His head;
Your name was not found
    In His book, signed in red.
The blood that could've saved you
    Has condemned you instead.

To be lost!
    How tremendous the shock and the shame;
To be lost!
    When you could've been cleared of all blame;
To be lost!
    To discover too late you were wrong;
To be lost!
    When you could've been saved all along . . .

You thought that somehow
   God would make it okay—
That you weren't all bad,
   That He's too loving to say,
"Depart. You're condemned.
   You cannot enter in."
You refused to believe
   What He said about sin.
But He is the One
   We all have betrayed;
It's His right to decide
   How a sinner is saved;
No mantra, no karma
   Can clean up your mud.
You can't ride to heaven
   On your own moral flood—
You can't do it your way;
   You must come by the blood.

To be lost!
   How tremendous the shock and the shame;
To be lost!
   When you could've been cleared of all blame;
To be lost!
   To discover too late you were wrong;
To be lost!
   When you could've been saved all along . . .

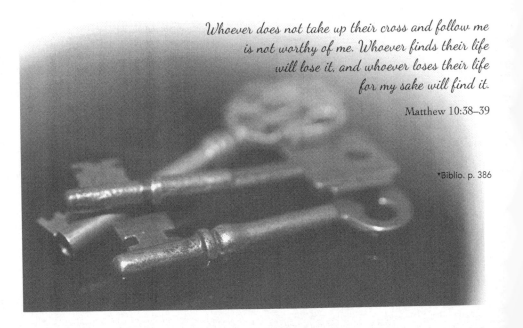

Whoever does not take up their cross and follow me is not worthy of me. Whoever finds their life will lose it, and whoever loses their life for my sake will find it.

Matthew 10:38–39

*Biblio. p. 386

BIBLIOGRAPHY

February 12, p. 57

"The blood of the martyrs is the seed of the church."

Tertullian, (c.155–c.240 AD). In his writing *Apologeticum*, 50. https://en.wikipedia. org/wiki/Tertullian (Dec. 17, 2015).

February 19, p. 64

"True knowledge is knowing that you know nothing."

Socrates, (469–399 BC). http://www.brainyquote.com/quotes/quotes/s/socrates 382301.html (Dec. 10, 2015).

February 25, p. 70

Actual movie quote: *"Stupid is as stupid does"*

Forrest Gump, (1994) Directed by Robert Zemeckis. Film based on a 1986 novel by Winston Groom. Performed by Tom Hanks. Paramount Pictures, Hollywood, CA. https://en.wikipedia.org/wiki/Forrest_Gump (Dec. 10, 2015).

February 26, p. 71

"Is he willing to prevent evil, but not able? Then he is impotent. Is he able but not willing? Then he is malevolent."

Epicurus, (341–270 BC). https://en.wikipedia.org/wiki/Epicurus (Dec. 10, 2015).

March 4, p. 78; October 22, p. 310

"Preach Christ, and—if you must—use words."

Francis of Assisi, (c.1182–1226). https://cn.wikiquote.org/wiki/Francis_of_Assisi (Dec. 10, 2015).

May 7, p. 142

"What God has for me, it is for me"

Cooper, Marc Antonio & Joy, (Marc 1971–; Joy 1969–). "It Is for Me," on the album *It's Praying Time*, Mississippi Mass Choir, Savoy Records, Savoy Music Inc., 1997. http://www.allmusic.com/album/its-praying-time-mw0000026504 (Dec. 10, 2015).

May 23, p. 158

"Life is pain . . . anyone who tells you differently is selling something."

The Princess Bride, (1987). Directed by Rob Reiner. Film based on the 1973 novel of the same name by William Goldman. Performed by Cary Elwes. 20th Century

Fox, Act III Communications, Los Angeles, California. http://www.allmovie.com/movie/the-princess-bride-v39218 (Dec. 11, 2015).

July 4, p. 200

"I am the master of my fate/I am the captain of my soul"

Henley, William Ernest, (1849–1903). "Invictus." Written in 1875, published in 1888 with other poems in *Book of Verses*, in the section *Life and Death (Echoes)*. https://en.wikipedia.org/wiki/Invictus (Nov. 4, 2015).

September 1, p. 259

"Rage, rage against the dying of the light," "go gentle into that good night"

Thomas, Dylan, (1914–1953). "Do Not Go Gentle into That Good Night." Written in 1947. Published in *Botteghe Oscure* in 1951, and in *In Country Sleep, and Other Poems* in 1952. https://en.wikipedia.org/wiki/Do_not_go_gentle_into_that_good_night (Nov. 4, 2015).

October 7, p. 295

"This above all: to thine own self be true."

Shakespeare, William (1564–1616). "Hamlet." Likely written in the early 17th century. First published in the so-called "bad" *First Quarto*, 1603. https://en.wikipedia.org/wiki/Shakespeare_bibliography (Nov. 5, 2015).

November 28, p. 347

"I want you to want me"

Nielsen, Rick, (1946–). "I Want You to Want Me." Written in 1975. Published in *In Color* in 1977 by Cheap Trick, © Sony/ATV Music Publishing LLC. http://www.lyricsoverload.com/lyrics/Cheap-Trick-I-Want-You-to-Want-Me--Early-Version-lyrics/369681 (Nov. 4, 2015).

November 28, p. 347

". . . O Lord, . . . our heart is restless until it finds its rest in You."

Augustine of Hippo, (354–430 AD). Written in an autobiographical work called *Confessions* between 397 and 400 AD. http://www.goodreads.com/quotes/42572 (Dec. 11, 2015).

December 5, p. 354

"How much easier it is to die for you, my love/for dying is an end, but living hurts a thousand times"

Rupel, Cynthia A.Y., (1959–). "Love Sacrifice" Written in 1984. Unpublished. © 1985 Cynthia A.Y. Rupel. (Nov. 6, 2015).

"Lost" Poem, p. 383–4

Rupel, Cynthia A.Y., (1959–). "Lost" Written in 2013. Published *Words Unbound*. © 2013 Cynthia A.Y. Rupel. (Dec. 13, 2015).

57328078R00232

Made in the USA
Charleston, SC
10 June 2016